DIGITAL PARTICIPATION THROUGH SOCIAL LIVING LABS

Chandos
Information Professional Series
Series Editor: Ruth Rikowski
(email: Rikowskigr@aol.com)

Chandos' new series of books is aimed at the busy information professional. They have been specially commissioned to provide the reader with an authoritative view of current thinking. They are designed to provide easy-to-read and (most importantly) practical coverage of topics that are of interest to librarians and other information professionals. If you would like a full listing of current and forthcoming titles, please visit www.chandospublishing.com.

New authors: we are always pleased to receive ideas for new titles; if you would like to write a book for Chandos, please contact Dr Glyn Jones on g.jones.2@elsevier.com or telephone +44 (0) 1865 843000.

DIGITAL PARTICIPATION THROUGH SOCIAL LIVING LABS

Valuing Local Knowledge, Enhancing Engagement

MICHAEL DEZUANNI

MARCUS FOTH

KERRY MALLAN

HILARY HUGHES

Chandos Publishing is an imprint of Elsevier
50 Hampshire Street, 5th Floor, Cambridge, MA 02139, United States
The Boulevard, Langford Lane, Kidlington, OX5 1GB, United Kingdom

British Library Cataloguing-in-Publication Data
A catalogue record for this book is available from the British Library

Library of Congress Cataloging-in-Publication Data
A catalog record for this book is available from the Library of Congress

ISBN: 978-0-08-102059-3 (print)
ISBN: 978-0-08-102060-9 (online)

For information on all Chandos Publishing publications
visit our website at https://www.elsevier.com/books-and-journals

Publisher: Glyn Jones
Acquisition Editor: George Knott
Editorial Project Manager: Lindsay Lawrence
Production Project Manager: Surya Narayanan Jayachandran
Cover Designer: Christian J. Bilbow

Typeset by MPS Limited, Chennai, India

CONTENTS

LIST OF CONTRIBUTORS

Cherie Allan
Queensland University of Technology, Brisbane, QLD, Australia

Philippa J. Collin
Western Sydney University, Penrith, NSW, Australia

Angela Cooke-Jackson
Emerson College, Boston, MA, United States

Hilary Davis
Swinburne University of Technology, Melbourne, VIC, Australia

Michael Dezuanni
Queensland University of Technology, Brisbane, QLD, Australia

Jane Farmer
Swinburne University of Technology, Melbourne, VIC, Australia

J. Ferreira
Cork Institute of Technology, Bishopstown, Cork, Republic of Ireland

Marcus Foth
Queensland University of Technology, Brisbane, QLD, Australia

Youri Havenaar
Delft University of Technology, Delft, The Netherlands

Hilary Hughes
Queensland University of Technology, Brisbane, QLD, Australia

Rachel Jacobs
University of Nottingham, Nottingham, United Kingdom

Margaret Kettle
Queensland University of Technology, Brisbane, QLD, Australia

Ally Lankester
Queensland University of Technology, Brisbane, QLD, Australia

Silvia Leal
Fluminense Federal University, Niterói, Brazil

Kerry Mallan
Queensland University of Technology, Brisbane, QLD, Australia

Beth Massey
University College Cork, Cork, Ireland

Ingrid Mulder
Delft University of Technology, Delft, The Netherlands

Tanya Notley
Western Sydney University, Penrith, NSW, Australia

Rosie O'Shannessy
The Storyelling Project, Toowoomba, QLD, Australia

Roger Osborne
Queensland University of Technology, Brisbane, QLD, Australia

N. Pantidi
University College Cork, Cork, Republic of Ireland

Sarah Peters
Southern Queensland University, Toowoomba, QLD, Australia

Long Pham
University College Cork, Cork, Ireland

Stuart R. Poyntz
Simon Fraser University, Burnaby, BC, Canada

Emilia L. Pucci
Delft University of Technology, Delft, The Netherlands

Ellie Rennie
RMIT University, Melbourne, VIC, Australia

Amanda Third
Western Sydney University, Penrith, NSW, Australia

Christer Windeløv-Lidzélius
Kaospilot Business and Design School, Aarhus, Denmark

FOREWORD

LIVING LABS PIONEER THE SOCIO-ECOLOGICAL TRANSITIONING THAT SOCIETY NEEDS

Movements that are part of the open innovation ecosystem, such as Living Labs, Fab Labs, Maker Labs, Open Innovation 2.0, Knowledge Alliances and Citizen Science, all involve citizens or end-users in participatory innovation. The European Network of Living Labs (ENoLL) was created with the support of the European Union during the Finnish EU Presidency in 2006. Since then, the worldwide network of Living Labs has progressed the design of open participatory research, development and innovation (RDI). Advanced mechanisms, methods and tools for better collaboration have been designed and developed to improve the communication and engagement in multistakeholder and end-user driven innovation. These collaborations also involve citizens, scientists, companies, cities and other public authorities and policymakers, as well as civil society and third-sector organizations contributing to the joint knowledge, innovation and value creation processes.

Innovation designed with, for and by end-users and conducted through real-life experiments democratize innovation and shorten the time from research, innovation and product design to market. Moreover, based on their bottom-up approach and best grassroots level practices, the most active local innovation ecosystems encourage a new entrepreneurial spirit and increase potential for public and private investments.

Open RDI with multiple players rarely happens without support, therefore orchestration, interpretation, facilitation and matchmaking is required to effectively bridge the knowledge, skills, innovation and investment gaps. As orchestrators, matchmakers and sociocultural animators (Foth, 2006), the living labs bring together the local needs and challenges with the scientific rigour and technological know-how of what is possible. Moreover, the living labs have the capacity and required methods to facilitate the cocreation, codesign, coinnovation and experimentation processes, and to assess the impact of proposed solutions and new business models to create value and sustainability.

Successful innovation is a two-way process. It is founded on the values and needs of people and the environment, therefore it has the capacity to change the way we behave, consume and live our lives, and it can create distributed markets. Therefore innovation emerging from living labs often calls for the integration of different types of sociotechnical systems, and a variety of cultural, social, service, technology, design and business innovation. It is often the social innovation, social enterprise and social entrepreneurship that thrive on diversity and enable the fusion of different types of contributions. Together, they make up the dynamism of an open innovation ecosystem that resonates with participants. The ecosystem fostered by living labs is also what propels us forward on Europe's path of socioecological transitioning towards the real structural and systemic change society needs (Aiginger et al., 2016).

Local living labs engage people with their different roles (as users, enablers, designers, entrepreneurs, activists, etc.) in every phase of an open participatory RDI process; from the identification and definition of a challenge, the concept or prototype design and the experimentation, towards the pre- and postlaunch of a novel product, service, social innovation or other solution. Moreover, with their cross-disciplinary teams, it is particularly the types of social living labs discussed in this book that rely not just on technology but engage the social sciences, arts and humanities. This enables them to guide the technological and business design processes towards socially, humanly and ethically sustainable solutions.

The book's coverage broadens the discourse from still significant issues of access and literacy to include questions of digital participation and social inclusion. Often, a combination of both online and offline methods of interaction, such as face-to-face workshops and digital collaboration tools are needed to jointly create value with a diverse group of stakeholders. Creative projects conducted in innovative spaces, using new methods and digital support tools, have proven that it is possible to build on and develop new approaches to digital participation and social inclusion. ENoLL's most successful work in this field stems from the artful integration of artistic, educational, scientific and technological processes. Based on ENoLL's long-standing experience with living labs, we agree with Collin, Notley, and Third (2017), coauthors of a chapter in this book, who argue that 'cultivating digital capacities' can usefully 'shift the focus from individuals to communities and from personal deficits to shared strengths and opportunities'.

In Chapter 5, The School as a Living Lab – The Case of Kaospilot, Windeløv-Lidzélius (2017) indicates a positive relationship between the employability or job-creation capabilities, and the praxis of a school that is devoted to cocreation experimentation and exploration. A practical example from Finland supports his finding. Having applied the living lab approach for nearly 25 years, Laurea University of Applied Science became the most awarded University of Applied Sciences in Finland. It has a 9-year continuous succession of nominations as a National Centre of Excellence (both for excellence in regional impact and educational excellence) by the National Evaluation Council. This success has been due to Laurea's innovative *Learning by Developing* and *Living Labs* strategies integrating university curricula and RDI activities to the need of its stakeholders. Based on cocreation and experimentation these strategies provide Laurea graduates with excellent employability opportunities. Consequently, Laurea is currently one of Finland's most popular higher education institution among all the university applicants.

In order to make the most from the European single market and to speed up the global take up of innovation, ENoLL, as an international network of living labs, makes simultaneous transnational coinnovation and experimentation processes possible for globally oriented municipalities, businesses, communities, researchers and innovators. More research is needed to create standardized protocols, relevant business models and localization services for cross-national pilots and validation. Most importantly, integrating digital technologies in trans-regional and cross-national community initiatives will boost global digital citizenship, digital participation, community engagement and social inclusion. The studies and projects reported in this book provide a magnificently strong signal that we are on track and that it is in fact living labs that are the pioneers of the socioecological transitioning society needs. However, more work is required to develop international legislation, ethical codes of conduct and sustainable value models in order to minimize risks and dysfunctions such as digital divides and social exclusion, and to transition towards a fair, just and sustainable world.

Dr Tuija Hirvikoski
President, European Network of Living Labs (ENoLL), Brussels, Belgium
http://www.openlivinglabs.eu

REFERENCES

Aiginger, K., Schratzenstaller, M., Leoni, T., Schaffartzik, A., Wiedenhofer, D., Fischer-Kowalski, M., ... Behrens, A. (2016). Europe's path towards the socio-ecological transition. *Intereconomics*, *51*(4). 184. http://dx.doi.org/10.1007/s10272-016-0599-6.

Collin, P. J., Notley, T., & Third, A. (2017). Living labs and cultivating digital capacities. In M. Dezuanni, M. Foth, K. Mallan, & H. Hughes (Eds.), *Digital participation through social living labs – Valuing local knowledge, enhancing engagement*. Cambridge: Chandos Publishing.

Foth, M. (2006). Sociocultural animation. In S. Marshall, W. Taylor, & X. Yu (Eds.), *Encyclopedia of developing regional communities with information and communication technology* (pp. 640–645). Hershey: IGI Global. Available from http://dx.doi.org/10.4018/978-1-59140-575-7.ch114.

Windeløv-Lidzélius, C. (2017). The school as a living lab – The case of Kaospilot. In M. Dezuanni, M. Foth, K. Mallan, & H. Hughes (Eds.), *Digital participation through social living labs – Valuing local knowledge, enhancing engagement*. Cambridge: Chandos Publishing.

PREFACE AND ACKNOWLEDGEMENTS

Our social realities and futures are entwined with digital technologies in complex ways that demand new approaches to addressing the challenges of community participation, social mobility, work, leisure, education and entertainment. Adapting to rapidly changing digital environments provides unprecedented opportunities for some to reimagine their futures, to find new solutions to problems and to prosper in various facets of life. Despite the promise of the digital future, though, underparticipation and nonparticipation with digital technologies continue to be a problem for many. Underparticipation may include people who regularly use digital technologies in their daily lives, but who are not knowledgeable and skilled in ways to allow them full and equitable involvement in the community or across the digital economy. Digital nonparticipation in an increasingly networked society may threaten social and familial connection, access to basic services like banking and education, and much reduced prospects for employment.

The wide-ranging, international research represented in this book reflects a deep belief that harnessing potential and finding solutions to problems can come from citizens and communities, through codesign and coinvestigation. To harness the opportunities of digital participation and to address the challenges of digital underparticipation and nonparticipation, researchers are well located when they value local knowledge and work alongside the community to enhance engagement. These beliefs underpin social living labs approaches presented in this book and present a more nonhierarchical approach to community-based research than is available in many traditional social research approaches. At its heart, social living labs approaches aim to bring together resources, knowledgeable mentors (often available within the community) and coordination of community resources to foster a knowledge ecology approach. From this perspective, researchers may act as cofacilitators of social and community change.

The idea for this book coincided with the development of a 2-day seminar that reported on findings from a nationally funded research project in Australia called *Fostering Digital Participation Through Living Labs in Regional and Rural Australian Communities* (digitalparticipation.net.au). Held as a preconference workshop in conjunction with the ACM

Designing Interactive Systems (DIS) conference 2016 in Brisbane, the seminar brought together project participants from Queensland University of Technology as well as researchers from other leading Australian institutions, members of the Australian Living Labs Innovation Network (ALLIN) and researchers and practitioners from other parts of the world. The workshop acted as a Living Lab experience with the goal of identifying innovative and practical solutions to foster sustained digital participation, particularly in regional and rural communities. Day 1 consisted of practitioner and research reports, while day 2 provided an opportunity for participants to imagine and collaboratively design future digital participation strategies. Most of the reports presented during day 1 of the seminar are represented as chapters in this book. The editorial team also invited colleagues using social living lab like practices in other parts of Australia, and internationally, to contribute to the book; and contributions were subsequently peer reviewed and revised accordingly.

The book's chapters cover interconnected aspects of digital participation, connected learning, creative practice and social inclusion. The conceptual interweaving across chapters reflects the productive fluidity of social livings labs. The authors featured in the book come from diverse disciplines and contexts, pointing to the transferability of the social living labs methodology. Tuija Hirvikoski's foreword locates the book and social living labs in the broader international field of living labs research. The opening two chapters then investigate questions of digital inclusion, interest-driven participation, digital skills enhancement, digital capacities and literacy. Chapters 3–7 share a focus on innovative, artistic and entrepreneurial digital activity in community settings. Chapters 8–10 explore examples of community connectedness and situated learning with and about digital technologies. Chapters 11–14 provide examples of specific community interventions to enhance digital engagement through connecting to local knowledge. The final four chapters take up policy questions, providing critical insights into different instances of how regional and national governments attempt to foster digital participation. Together the authors explore latest thinking about the nature and potential of social living labs to foster digital participation in the community. The book enhances understanding of this innovative approach to social capacity building by distilling previous living labs research and practice, the insights offered by this book's authors, and the findings of the *Fostering Digital Participation Project.*

This book would not have been possible without the support of a range of people and organizations. The *Fostering Digital Participation* project originated within Queensland University of Technology's *Children and Youth Research Centre* (CYRC). The CYRC was a transdisciplinary research centre located within QUT's Faculty of Education in partnership with all QUT Faculties. The editors are highly indebted to CYRC staff, Dr Karleen Gwinner who provided significant research assistance during the development of the project and to Jill Nalder who provided financial advice and management. Dr Cherie Allan's highly professional research assistance was crucial to the development and implementation of the project; and Dr Roger Osborne's expert oversight of the development of the project website, the organization of our dissemination seminar and management of project reporting have been vital. Roger's management of this book project has also been essential as he has proficiently liaised with authors and the editorial team at Chandos/Elsevier. We would also like to thank our production manager at Elsevier, Lindsay C. Lawrence, who has provided us with ongoing support during the book's development. Throughout the project, we have had great fortune and pleasure in working with a host of wonderful community-based research assistants, including Dr Ally Lankester, Sabine Carter, Rike Wolf, Dr Sarah Peters, Cassie Kowitz and Andras Csabai. Other QUT research centres have also provided support for this project, including the Urban Informatics Research Lab (www.urbaninformatics.net) – now part of the of the QUT Design Lab (qut.design), and the School of Communication's Digital Media Research Centre (research.qut.edu.au/dmrc).

We would like to acknowledge the financial support we received, without which this project would not have been possible. This includes support from the Australian Research Council (ARC) Linkage Projects scheme and the financial and in-kind support of our partner organizations and investigators; these include Jane Cowell (State Library of Queensland), Warren Cheetham (Townsville City Libraries), Sean Petrie (Toowoomba Regional Library Service) and Jeanette Wedmaier (Empire Theatre, Toowoomba). Of course, the project would not have been possible without the generous and passionate involvement of the many community members from the Toowoomba and Townsville regions who became coinvestigators with us as we sought to address questions of digital participation in regional and rural Australia. The social living labs methodology provides democratic ways to work with community members to identify new opportunities for digital participation. In many respects this is an evolving methodology that will continue to develop in new and exciting ways as it is used by scholars who see the value in recognizing locally based knowledge. We hope this book is taken up by researchers in Australia and internationally as part of an ongoing project to foster digital participation to promote enhanced social futures for all.

CHAPTER 1

Social Living Labs for Digital Participation and Connected Learning

Michael Dezuanni, Marcus Foth, Kerry Mallan, Hilary Hughes and Roger Osborne
Queensland University of Technology, Brisbane, QLD, Australia

Digital and new media technologies are profoundly reshaping how people communicate, seek entertainment and education, conduct commercial activity and access community-based services (Erdiaw-Kwasie & Alam, 2016). Digital technologies are almost ubiquitous in postindustrial societies (EY Sweeney, 2016), and considerable research illustrates that those at risk of social and economic marginalization are especially vulnerable to digital nonparticipation or underparticipation, which potentially compounds disadvantage and lack of opportunity (Alam & Imran, 2015; Clayton & Macdonald, 2013; Notley & Foth, 2008; Townsend, Sathiaseelan, Fairhurst, & Wallace, 2013). People rely on digital media and technology as part of their everyday lives in order to: stay informed; remain connected to family, friends and community; purchase goods and services; gain an education; participate as digital citizens; seek employment or remain employed in contemporary work settings; access government services (see Chapter 2: Cultivating (Digital) Capacities: A Role for Social Living Labs?, Chapter 4: Going Digital: Integrating Digital Technologies in Local Community Initiatives and Chapter 10: Pittsworth Stories: Developing a Social Living Lab for Digital Participation in a Rural Australian Community).

Digital literacies are no longer optional. Rather, they are rapidly becoming as essential as the traditional literacies associated with print, audio and visual texts. Importantly, digital literacies are necessary for social and economic inclusion. There is also increasing recognition that being 'tech-savvy', or 'digitally-connected' in specific aspects of life, does not necessarily translate or convert to ways that lead to expanded social or economic mobility. The young person who frequently uses social media is not necessarily able to apply social media skills to an entrepreneurial

Digital Participation through Social Living Labs. DOI: http://dx.doi.org/10.1016/B978-0-08-102059-3.00001-0

activity. The business operator who relies on computers every day does not necessarily know how to use technology to innovate and operate their business in more sustainable ways. The grandparent who proficiently uses a tablet computer to stay connected with distant family does not necessarily know how to use the device to access government information. Despite the somewhat obvious nature of these statements, we contend that public policy promoting digital literacy often elides the complexity of promoting successful digital participation. Furthermore, Gurstein (2003) argues participation needs to be understood in terms of 'effective use', i.e., 'how and by whom and under what circumstances, and for what purposes ICTs can and should be used to benefit individuals, communities, and societies as whole' (Introduction, para. 6).

Our goal in bringing this volume together has been to stimulate a forum to promote dialogue about community-based work involving participants from urban, rural and remote contexts who were at different stages of digital participation, who had little to no digital participation and who had varying levels of digital literacy. In the context of uneven provision and take-up of fast Internet, digital nonparticipation and underparticipation are at greater levels of risk in regional, rural and remote communities than in urban areas (Alam & Shahiduzzaman, 2013; Dobson, Jackson, Gengatharen, 2013; Rennie, Ewing, & Thomas, 2015; Thomas et al., 2016). This issue is fast becoming the focus of regional and national policy in Australia, as well as overseas, and several of the chapters (see Chapters 15–18) discuss the policy implications in Australian, Irish and Canadian contexts. The remaining chapters give accounts of timely urban digital inclusion/participation stories.

A range of approaches, initiatives and interventions to foster digital participation through the development of digital literacies has been employed in the past with varying degrees of success (Alam & Imran, 2015; Carew et al., 2015), with one of the key challenges being sustained digital participation. As Armenta, Serrano, Cabrera, and Conte (2012) have shown, community-based digital inclusion interventions often fail, because 'the majority of projects only [take] into account telecommunications infrastructure and hardware, leaving social and human factors unattended' (p. 347). With its foregrounding of *social living labs*, this book engages with the 'social and human factors' of digital participation.

The impetus for this volume comes from an Australian research project entitled 'Fostering Digital Participation Through Living Labs in Regional and Rural Australia', conducted from 2014 to 2016 (Australian

Research Council Funded Linkage Grant LP130100469), in partnership with the State Library of Queensland, Townsville CityLibraries, The Toowoomba Regional Library Service and Toowoomba's Empire Theatre. The project-specific chapters (6, 8, 9, 10, 13, 14, 18) are complemented by accounts of related research conducted by other contributors from across Australia and internationally. Several of the chapters discuss how participatory methodologies, especially those originally developed within the European 'living labs' movement, have been redeployed to promote systems of socially connected learning for digital participation, which leverage people's capacity to use digital technologies to enhance their lives. Not all the chapters explicitly use the term 'living lab' or 'social living lab', but they nevertheless provide examples of researchers working directly with participants to enhance digital participation by harnessing community resources and people's capacities, interests and desire to participate through digital technologies.

As detailed below, a living lab approach promotes collaboration between researchers, industry and participants and seeks to identify user-centred solutions to digital opportunities and challenges. A social living labs approach shifts the focus away from industry towards sociospatial and material questions that relate to people's successful digital participation within their communities. The book provides examples of how local organizations such as libraries, schools, community centres and arts organizations are well placed to foster socially oriented living labs to provide opportunities for interest-driven and connected learning for digital participation and enhancing digital inclusion.

DIGITAL INCLUSION AND SOCIAL MOBILITY

Since the early 2000s, digital inclusion has been linked to social inclusion and civic participation, particularly in relation to the rapid development of Internet technologies and services, and governments' expectations of participation by citizens (Alam & Imran, 2015). Much government policy has concentrated on increasing access to technology, although the need for strategic responses to increase digital participation and inclusion remains.

Over the past decade or more, there has been growing international consensus that the focus of digital inclusion initiatives must move beyond mere access to digital technologies to address the development of social capacity (Dutta-Bergman, 2005; Rice, 2002). Cautioning against technological innovation without social innovation in formal education contexts, Warschauer (2003) states: 'research has shown that beyond just having the hardware, what is important is the "social envelope" it comes in' (para 4). In their study of the town of Sunderland in the United Kingdom, Clayton and Macdonald (2013) corroborate Warschauer's assertion, arguing that: 'While technology may often be interesting, exciting and useful, it is not a "magic bullet"' (p. 962). These are not isolated cases. Investigating the influence of mobile technologies on social exclusion in two urban areas in the United Kingdom, Mervyn, Simon, and Allen (2014) found:

> *A range of pre-existing information needs and barriers were revealed, but in some cases the technology itself presented a barrier. Issues with literacy, technology skills and in some cases the socioemotional condition of some of the socially excluded combined with the complexity of their information needs fundamentally undermines the direct access model for this section of the community (p. 1086).*

The above studies direct attention to local communities and the complex mixture of their inhabitants (see also Chapters 9–12, 15). Ultimately, this complex mix of people with diverse levels of skill, education and socioeconomic status and cultural backgrounds makes it difficult to offer simple solutions to digital inclusion through access alone (Fernback, 2005; Hick, 2006). Drawing attention to the so-called 'social envelope' to foster digital participation, the Tinder Foundation's (2011) study of 12,000 'excluded' people in the United Kingdom demonstrated that digital literacy initiatives have impact, but it is difficult to predict longer term influence on social cohesion, civic participation, and life chances over time (p. 5). Assumptions about the advantages that access and participation provide require more attention; particularly, there is a need to ensure that highly complex social scenarios are included in assessments of digital and social inclusion within specific communities.

Examining the impact of digital technologies on various groups of people in the city of Sunderland (UK), Clayton and Macdonald (2013, p. 962) direct attention to the key role that class and occupational status play in levels of digital engagement and the subsequent benefits accrued from technology, stressing that unemployment remains a significant barrier to digital participation. Such barriers also have an impact on digital sustainability in the lives of the unemployed and those living in poverty (Hick, 2006). Gonzales (2016) argues that for low-income citizens in the United States, the focus of addressing the 'digital divide' should shift from issues of ownership in relation to digital technology and towards issues of sustainability: 'low-income users must work to maintain access, often experiencing cycles of dependable instability' (p. 234). The dual problem of stability and sustainability has particular implications in remote regions of Australia. As Rennie et al. (2016, p. 24) have found in their study of remote Indigenous communities, 'Internet adoption is not a fixed event or a linear trajectory from non-use to advanced use' (see also Chapter 17: Effective Digital Participation: Differences in Rural and Urban Areas and Ways Forward). Rather, adoption is increasingly affected by individual choice within a 'particular sociality of place' (p. 26).

The experience of digital participation faces further challenges in regional and rural areas because of the volatility of public services hinted above. Additionally, there are the complexities of the 'social envelope' that need to be taken into account in order to foster constructive digital participation and to promote digital and social inclusion that should follow. After examining the needs of several rural areas in the United States, Armenta et al. (2012) conclude:

> *it is necessary to implement a strategy focused not only on technology to achieve full use of broadband infrastructure. It is necessary to develop comprehensive and more in-depth research studies to better understand all the factors involved in the process of adoption of broadband technologies in rural and underserved populations (p. 352).*

In the United Kingdom, Townsend et al. (2013) identify distinct disadvantages for rural economy and culture that can follow from low levels of digital participation, leading to significant social variation within the country: 'Rural communities that are well connected may be more attractive places to live and work than those that are not – this has clear implications for social and environmental sustainability' (p. 592).

While there is limited research literature on digital inclusion initiatives in Australian regional and rural communities, existing studies reinforce the findings of international literature. For instance, in their study of seven rural local governments in New South Wales, Park et al. (2015) found that 'rural digital exclusion results from a multi-layered divide where elements of infrastructure, connectivity and digital engagement are intertwined' (p. 3631). Warburton and colleagues (2014) considered whether improved access to ICTs has the potential to build social inclusion among rural older people. Their study concluded that there exist major barriers due to poor ICT usage by many rural agencies, and poor

ICT usage among rural older people, brought on by a lack of skills as well as lack of access and resources.

The impact of limited digital participation can have ramifications across an entire community. For instance, low-income migrants living in regional areas are particularly at risk of nonparticipation, according to a study of the adoption of digital technology among migrants in the regional Queensland city of Toowoomba (see Chapter 9: Connecting Digital Participation and Informal Language Education: Home Tutors and Migrants in an Australian Regional Community). Alam and Imran (2015) conclude: 'There is a digital divide among refugee migrant groups and it is based on inequalities in physical access to and use of digital technology, the skills necessary to use the different technologies effectively and the ability to pay for the services' (p. 344). Indicators of social well-being clearly show the impact that digital exclusion can have on migrants and particularly young people. Daly, Dugdale, Honge Gong, and Abello (2014) analysis of census data found areas of Australia, particularly in regional Australia, that have relatively low proportions of children who have access to the Internet at home. Positive correlations with the Child Social Exclusion index indicate that these children are at risk of social exclusion and poor educational outcomes. The ramifications of poor educational, health, and social outcomes within regional and rural communities cross all sectors of society, and have implications that can potentially impact the well-being of an entire town or region (see Chapter 11: Urban Communities as Locations for Health, Media Literacy and Civic Voice and Chapter 12: Including the Rural Excluded: Digital Technology and Diverse Community Participation).

The urgency to deal with the problems of low levels of digital participation is particularly acute in Queensland, where, in this regard, it ranks sixth out of Australia's eight states and territories. The Australian Digital Inclusion Index (Thomas et al., 2016) indicates more regional and local initiatives will be necessary in order to combat the widening gap in a 'geographical digital divide' (p. 5) that positions rural and regional citizens at a distinct disadvantage against people who live in urban areas. For instance, Queensland's most digitally included subregion is the highly urbanized Brisbane West, and the least digitally included subregion is North-West Queensland (approximately 1800 km to the northwest), demonstrating a clear geographical divide (Thomas et al., 2016, p. 18). The Digital Inclusion Index reveals that, despite more than a decade of federal and state initiatives designed to improve digital participation, many Australians with low levels of income, education and employment are still significantly less digitally included; and gaps continue to widen. In Queensland, the 'capital – country' divide has widened slightly in recent years, in line with conditions faced by other disadvantaged groups, such as people with less than a secondary education, people older than 65, Indigenous Queenslanders, and those people with an annual income between $10,000 and $25,000 (Thomas et al., 2016, pp. 18–19).

DIGITAL INCLUSION, PUBLIC LIBRARIES, AND POLICY DISCREPANCIES

A key aspect of digital inclusion is the civic infrastructure such as broadband. However, as McShane (2013) notes: 'Australian local authorities have taken few initiatives to provide it [broadband] as a local public good, similar to physical facilities and community services' (p. 109). Furthermore, McShane argues that in other parts of the world, municipal authorities play a key role in providing broadband within their jurisdictions, but in Australia 'the idea that digital inclusion might also include provision of local public broadband has barely registered in national broadband debates' (p. 109). The public and political debates in Australia have focused on the rollout of the Australian Government's broadband Internet access strategy, the National Broadband Network (NBN), which has meant that little attention has been given to whether the role that municipal public libraries play in 'hosting the nation's public Internet system' should be extended (McShane, 2013, p. 110).

In the United States, Thompson and colleagues contend that federal policies 'rely on public libraries to promote digital literacy and digital inclusion', but the same public libraries are expected to do so with reduced budgets and little say in 'decision-making processes' (Thompson, Jaeger, Taylor, Subramaniam, & Bertot, 2014, p. 36). To alleviate this situation, researchers have encouraged public libraries to develop stronger advocacy campaigns and to recognize the importance of partnerships with local governments and nonprofit entities. It is hoped that such activities will lead to more convincing arguments addressed to policymakers and aimed at attracting increased funding and stronger political support.

Recent Australian reports have attempted to provide libraries and cultural institutions with advocacy materials and a vocabulary to communicate the value of their activities to policymakers (SGS Economics & Planning, 2012), but funding restrictions continue to hamper the ability of many local libraries to effectively contribute to the improvement of digital literacy and, therefore, digital inclusion. However, there are signs that local libraries are playing an important part in bridging the digital and physical city (see Houghton, Foth, & Miller, 2014; see also Chapter 8: Mapping a Connected Learning Ecology to Foster Digital Participation in Regional Communities and Chapter 10: Pittsworth Stories: Developing a Social Living Lab for Digital Participation in a Rural Australian Community). For Thompson et al. (2014), the health of a local public library provides an indicator of 'policy discrepancies' that will inevitably affect the individuals and groups within any community they are chartered to serve.

Not only has it been difficult for libraries to be included in these debates about digital inclusion and broadband infrastructure, but also people living in remote areas continue to miss out on the benefits of the NBN vision, as Rennie et al. (2016) argue:

> *Commonly held aspirations for broadband relating to better service delivery, overcoming remoteness and hardship, and cost savings, reflect a set of external priorities. The agendas of government and NGOs are not necessarily aligned with those of people living in remote communities (p. 22).*

The difference between government digital inclusion rhetoric and reality is not unique to Australia (see Chapters 16–18, and Chapter 15 for a Canadian example). Research undertaken in the United States has revealed 'policy discrepancies' between the rhetoric of federal and local government regarding issues of digital inclusion, and the practical measures that governments support with funding streams (Jaeger, Bertot, Thompson, Katz, & DeCoster, 2012). In addition to the impact on public libraries, such policy discrepancies can impact a variety of local initiatives driven by external motivations. For instance, Smith et al. (2016) discovered that after their installation of Internet kiosks in remote Australian communities, community members recognized the benefits of access, but they called for a broader range of locally relevant information that is responsive to community needs. This desire to participate and have more input in the creation of information indicates the need for a shift in policy and provision, transforming the kiosks from passive information nodes to active 'community hubs' (pp. 4–5). These findings stress the need to pay closer attention to local knowledge 'ecologies' and to incorporate these systems into any initiative or research project from the beginning. As Notley and Foth (2008) argue:

> *A prerequisite for inclusion is access, but the use and exploitation of networks also requires specific skills, literacies, information and knowledge. These need to*

be accompanied by structural policies and programs that enable and support inclusive networks and thus create an inclusive networked society (p. 102).

With various gaps in Australia's digital divide slowly widening, there is a need for new methodological approaches that will address community needs on a local level. In addition to participatory design (Schuler & Namioka, 1993) and participatory action research (Foth, et al., 2016), variations of living labs as a methodological model and practice, as well as combinations of these approaches, have emerged and are being used to fill this gap (see Chapters 2, 4–6, 13).

FROM LIVING LABS TO SOCIAL LIVING LABS

If effective digital inclusion relies on a collaborative environment that draws on the local knowledge of community members, then the living labs methodology offers significant potential for promoting digital inclusion, particularly for projects that are more socially oriented than product oriented. Living labs have been described in many ways, but most meanings in the literature fall under five main categories, according to Schuurman, De Marez, and Ballon (2015):

i. An innovation system consisting of organised and structured multidisciplinary networks fostering interaction and collaboration.
ii. Real-life or 'in vivo' monitoring of a social setting generally involving experimentation of a technology.
iii. An approach involving users in the product development process.
iv. Organisations facilitating the network, maintaining and developing its technological infrastructure and offering relevant services.
v. Or even the European movement itself (p. 16–17).

Ståhlbröst and Holst (2012) acknowledge the varied types of living labs in Europe and internationally, and provide a strong definition of what a living lab can accomplish:

In a Living Lab, the aim is to accomplish quattro helix by harmonizing the innovation process among four main stakeholders: companies, users, public organisations and researchers. These stakeholders can benefit from the Living Lab approach in many different ways, for instance companies can get new and innovative ideas, users can get the innovation they want, researchers can get study cases and public organisations can get increased return on investment on innovation research (p. 6).

While the European living labs movement has been established for some time, no unified approach or methodology has emerged. In a systematic review of the literature, Schuurman, De Marez, and Ballon (2015) examine the use of theoretical frameworks such as 'open innovation', 'user innovation', 'user-centred design' and 'participatory design', all of which have loosely informed living labs practice during the last decade. However, they conclude 'the current literature stream is still inconsistent and sometimes contradictory' and that 'there is no general methodology towards user involvement in Living Labs. [...] The most clear definition sees Living Lab projects as a quasi-experimental approach with a "pre" and a "post" assessment of users with an intervention stage' (p. 24).

This lack of an established/generally accepted definition has proved beneficial in extending the scope of living labs towards social innovation and beyond 'technology and efficiency-centred approaches' that dominate more industrial living labs research (Franz, 2015). This shift has challenged the accepted terminology within associated literature, and influenced the adoption of terminology more fitting to social science methods. For instance, in the emerging adaptation of accepted terminology within recent social living labs research, 'space of encounter' may replace 'real-life environment'; 'open concept' may replace 'experimental environment'; 'public sector' may replace 'producer'; 'private individual' may replace 'user' and 'collaboration and cocreation' may replace 'cocreation and coproduction' (Franz, 2015, p. 59). The selected or constructed 'space of encounter' where 'phases of interaction' with citizens can occur provides a real and conceptual space 'for mutual knowledge exchange and cooperative learning processes' (Franz, 2015, p. 63).

With this evolution of terminology within social living labs research, new catchwords have emerged in the living labs literature, such as 'empowerment', 'participation' and 'cocreation', creating what Franz sees as 'an open, participatory and do-it-yourself environment that includes citizens (users) and local actors (producers) as agents in processes of co-creation and improved living spaces' (2015, p. 56). Furthermore, Franz sees mobilization, participation and cocreation on the part of local actors and citizens (i.e., all stakeholders) as leading to cocreated and improved living spaces – outcomes frequently sought in initiatives designed to foster digital participation.

CREATIVE SPACES, CONNECTED LEARNING, AND INNOVATION ECOLOGIES

The social change in direction for living labs research has parallels in the 'participatory turn' experienced in the gallery, library, archive and museum sector (Mansfield, Winter, Griffith, Dockerty, & Brown, 2014; Nguyen, Partridge, & Edwards, 2012). Economic, technological and social change has encouraged a convergence of these institutions and a reevaluation of the spaces they provide, influencing many to develop creative spaces that better serve the needs of the community (Bilandzic & Foth, 2013; see also Chapters 3, 6–8, 10). Libraries often have been frontrunners in the movement to develop creative spaces for the communities they serve.

In terms of digital inclusion, initiatives such as Tech Savvy Seniors in Queensland public libraries and Indigenous knowledge centre spaces have brought older residents (Indigenous and non-Indigenous) together to learn new digital skills (State Library of Queensland, 2017a). The Australian Federal Government's National Broadband Network 'Digital Hubs' initiative also saw the conversion of libraries and other public spaces into digital resource centres to support the implementation of high-speed Internet (Libraries of South Australia, 2017). At the cutting edge of these initiatives are sites that support collaborative activities using various technologies like 'makerspaces' and 'fablabs', for instance, at 'The Edge' at the State Library of Queensland (SLQ) and the Adelaide FabLab (Bilandzic & Foth, 2017). SLQ encourages such innovations through its future vision for public libraries (State Library of Queensland, 2017b), working towards institutions that serve communities informed by four common themes:

Creative community spaces
Connectors – physical and virtual
Technology trendsetters
Incubators of ideas, learning and innovation.

These initiatives point to the vital role libraries and other public institutions may play in communities as part of the overall social and institutional structures that support meaningful digital participation and informal, connected learning. Central to digital participation initiatives promoted by connected learning is interest-driven learning, or learning connected to people's existing and emerging interests and passions (Dezuanni & O'Mara, 2017). Interest-driven learning often contrasts with the educational opportunities provided by formal education institutions like schools and universities. It also contrasts with prescribed or directed programs of learning implemented by institutions like libraries, where there is often little effort to connect to participant's individual interests.

As sites for digital literacy and informal learning, libraries offer supportive, digitally rich environments for people to connect and learn according to shared needs and interests. This trend aligns with the emerging 'Connected Learning' approach (Ito et al., 2013) and its potential to span the whole community beyond formal educational institutions. Ito and colleagues use the metaphor of an 'ecology' to stress these broader contexts and their interconnection, particularly when new media is a part of the equation. Ito et al. suggest:

> *The notion of ecology refers to the complex character of spaces in which young people develop. It also positions the young person in meanings, practices, structures and institutions contextualized by family, neighborhood, culture, and global contexts (p. 40).*

The notion of ecology can be applied to situations beyond young people's learning (see Hearn & Foth, 2007). Benton, Mullins, Shelly, and Dempsey (2013) argue that a makerspace in a public library is an appropriate initiative to further the 'innovation ecosystem' of any community. Sebring et al. (2013) employ the 'connected learning' methodology in the design and evaluation of the YOUMedia project at Chicago Public Library. Established in 2009, YOUMedia is a space where high school students are welcome to hang out, socialize and experiment with traditional and digital media. Drawing on the research by Ito et al. (2009), the program was built on the premise that young people would learn more with new and old technologies if they were allowed to 'hang out', 'mess around' and 'geek out'. This premise fed into the development of the 'connected learning' model that promotes 'learning that is socially embedded, interest-driven, and oriented towards educational, economic or political opportunity' (Ito et al., 2013, p. 4). The success of the program is the result of an effective balance between structured and unstructured activity that is facilitated by an agenda driven by both teens and adults, a choice of activities determined primarily by teens, organized and unorganized activities, a prominent mentoring presence, limited staff-parent communication and the freedom to drop in at any time.

In Australia, Bilandzic and Foth (2017) report on the use of various social spaces by coworking groups, hackerspaces and meetup groups to learn in 'connected' ways. Connected learning is described in this work as 'an aggregation of individual experiences made through intrinsically motivated, active participation in and across various socio-cultural, everyday life environments' (p. 8). In the Bilandzic and Foth study, a number of interventions were introduced in small and large spaces to facilitate social learning, including the employment of a 'a full-time person to catalyse connections between members' (social facilitation), social media platforms to stay connected with other members when away from the social space, and spatial facilitation 'designed with collaboration and social interaction in mind' (p. 202). For instance, different zones in the commercial coworking space Hub Melbourne supported social learning in a variety of situations. A shared kitchen became an area 'where conversations between random individuals are easily initiated, as there is a mutual understanding that the other person is not being interrupted at work'; '"half-social, half-information meeting type situations"' (p. 202), as one participant put it.

By way of further illustration, Chapter 8, Mapping a Connected Learning Ecology to Foster Digital Participation in Regional Communities, presents findings of a study that mapped a connected learning ecology of digital learning and participation in Townsville, Australia. This ecology connects adult learners from three different peer groups who are connected through a shared interest in digital technologies.

CONCLUSION: SOCIAL LIVING LABS AS DIGITAL LEARNING ECOLOGIES

As digital learning ecologies, social living labs encourage the development of networks through which participants can simultaneously widen their worldview and share local knowledge. They achieve this by enabling people with shared purposes to interact locally and at a distance, e.g., through digital history telling. Through digital initiatives, such as creation of a shared makerspace, social living labs become catalysts for community engagement.

Digitally rich social living labs are essentially flexible and open-ended, allowing people to participate in differing ways depending on their needs. They can be characterized as: interest-led and productive; active and experimental; socially oriented and culturally inclusive; cross-community and intergenerational; open-minded and peer-supported. These principles support the design and implementation of social living labs for various informal learning contexts.

The findings of the Fostering Digital Participation project, and the complementary insights of this book's authors, extend understanding about the nature of social living labs, by highlighting their potential to foster digital participation and learning in the community. As illustrated in the following chapters, social living labs are enlivened by digital technologies and foster connected learning that is interest-driven, peer-supported and inclusive (Ito et al., 2013). This new emphasis reflects the evolving nature of living labs from commercially driven product testing vehicles to community-based learning ecologies that support digital capacity building for social well-being.

This chapter has raised many of the key issues that impact digital participation, connected learning, and support for enhancing digital literacies at individual and community levels. In locating the issues we have canvassed a wide range of research to illustrate the scope and impact of digital participation and associated methodologies, as well as highlight points at which the contributions in this book complement and expand upon current work in the area.

A key challenge that remains for fostering digital participation is finding ways to connect to the existing interests of people in a range of complex situations. In regional, rural and remote areas, for instance, there are potentially fewer public institutions, resources and available mentors to foster digital participation and learning across a range of contexts to meet a diversity of needs. As Chapter 12, Including the Rural Excluded: Digital Technology and Diverse Community Participation, and Chapter 15, Vancouver Youthspaces: A Political Economy of Digital Learning Communities, illustrate young and older residents alike often complain that digital learning initiatives and 'computer classes' are less successful when they do not connect to something of interest that will compel them to want to keep practicing new knowledge and skills. Codesigning solutions with local residents through social living labs approach is particularly important in these contexts. Consequently, this book proposes the potential of social living labs, in various forms, to foster digital participation within and across communities.

REFERENCES

Alam, K., & Imran, S. (2015). The digital divide and social inclusion among refugee migrants: A case in regional Australia. *Information, Technology and People, 28*(2), 344–365.

Alam, K., & Shahiduzzaman, M. (2013). *Community preferences for digital futures: Regional perspectives.* Australian Centre for Sustainable Business and Development, Toowoomba, University of Southern Queensland. Retrieved from <https://eprints.usq.edu.au/23617/1/SDRC_Report.pdf>.

Armenta, A., Serrano, A., Cabrera, M., & Conte, R. (2012). The new digital divide: The confluence of broadband penetration, sustainable development, technology adoption and community participation. *Information Technology for Development, 18*(4), 345–353.

Benton, C., Mullins, L., Shelly, K., & Dempsey, T. (2013). *Makerspaces: Supporting an entrepreneurial system.* City of East Lansing Library. Retrieved from <https://reicenter.org/upload/documents/colearning/benton2013_report.pdf>.

Bilandzic, M., & Foth, M. (2013). Libraries as co-working spaces: Understanding user motivations and perceived barriers to social learning. *Library Hi Tech*, *31*(2), 254–273.

Bilandzic, M., & Foth, M. (2017). Designing hubs for connected learning – Social, spatial and technological insights from coworking, hackerpaces and meetup groups. In L. Carvalho, P. Goodyear, & M. De Laat (Eds.), *Place-based spaces for networked learning* (pp. 191–206). Oxford: Routledge.

Clayton, J., & Macdonald, S. J. (2013). Social class, occupation and digital inclusion in the city of Sunderland, England. *Information, Communication and Society, 16*(6), 945–966.

Daly, A., Dugdale, A., Honge Gong, C., & Abello, A. (2014). Social inclusion of Australian children in the digital age. In S. Baum (Ed.), *E-Governance and social inclusion: Concepts and cases* (pp. 164–181). Hershey: IGI Global.

Dezuanni, M. L., & O'Mara, J. (2017). Impassioned learning and minecraft. In C. Beavis, M. L. Dezuanni, & J. O'Mara (Eds.), *Serious play: Literacy, learning, and digital games*. New York: Routledge.

Dobson, P., Jackson, P., & Gengatharen, D. (2013). Explaining broadband adoption in rural Australia: Modes of reflexivity and the morphogenetic approach. *MIS Quarterly, 37*(3), 965–992.

Dutta-Bergman, M. J. (2005). Access to the internet in the context of community participation and community satisfaction. *New Media & Society*, 7(1), 89–109.

Erdiaw-Kwasie, M., & Alam, K. (2016). Towards understanding digital divide in rural partnerships and development: A framework and evidence from rural Australia. *Journal of Rural Studies, 43*, 214–224.

EY Sweeney. (2016). *Digital Australia: State of the nation*. Retrieved from <https://digitalaustralia.ey.com/>.

Fernback, J. (2005). Information technology, networks and community voices: Social inclusion for urban regeneration. *Information, Communication & Society, 8*(4), 482–502.

Foth, M., & Brynskov, M. (2016). Participatory action research for civic engagement. In E. Gordon, & P. Milhailidis (Eds.), *Handbook of civic technologies*. Cambridge: MIT Press.

Franz, Y. (2015). Designing social living labs in urban research. *Info, 17*(4), 53–66.

Gonzales, A. (2016). The contemporary US digital divide: From initial access to technology maintenance. *Information, Communication and Society, 19*(2), 234–248.

Gurstein, M. (2003). Effective use: A community informatics strategy beyond the digital divide. *First Monday, 8*(12). December. Retrieved from <http://journals.uic.edu/ojs/index.php/fm/article/view/1107/1027>.

Hearn, G., & Foth, M. (Eds.), (2007). Communicative ecologies: Editorial preface. *The Electronic Journal of Communication, 17*(1–2).

Hick, S. (2006). Technology, social inclusion and poverty: An exploratory investigation of a community technology center. *Journal of Technology in Human Services, 24*(1), 53–67.

Houghton, K., Foth, M., & Miller, E. (2014). The local library bridging the digital and physical city: Opportunities for economic development. *Commonwealth Journal of Local Governance, 15*, 39–60.

Ito, M., Baumer, S., Bittanti, M., Boyd, D., Cody, R., Herr-Stephenson, B., ... Tripp, L. (2009). *Hanging out, messing around, and geeking out: Kids living and leaning with new media*. Cambridge: MIT Press. Retrieved from <http://ebookcentral.proquest.com.ezp01.library.qut.edu.au/lib/qut/reader.action?docID=3339094>.

Ito, M., Gutiérrez, K., Livingstone, S., Penuel, B., Rhodes, J., Salen, K., ... Watkins, S. C. (2013). *Connected learning: An agenda for research and design*. Irvine: Digital Media and Learning Research Hub. Retrieved from <http://dmihub.net/wp-content/uploads/files/Connected_Learning_report.pdf>.

Jaeger, P. T., Bertot, J. C., Thompson, K. M., Katz, S. M., & DeCoster, E. J. (2012). The intersection of public policy and public access: Digital divides, digital literacy, digital inclusion, and public libraries. *Public Library Quarterly, 31*(1), 1–20.

Libraries of South Australia. (2017). *Digital hubs*. Retrieved from <http://www.libraries.sa.gov.au/page.aspx?u=558> Accessed 06.01.17.

Mansfield, T., Winter, C., Griffith, C., Dockerty, A., & Brown, T. (August 2014). *Innovation study: Challenges and opportunities for Australia's galleries, libraries, archives and museums*. Australian Centre for Broadband Innovation, CSIRO and Smart Services Co-operative Research Centre, [so-called GLAM report].

McShane, I. (2013). Local public broadband—the missing link in Australia's broadband debate. In *Proceedings of the 3rd national local government researchers' forum, 5–6 June 2013, Adelaide, South Australia*.

Mervyn, K., Simon, A., & Allen, D. K. (2014). Digital inclusion and social inclusion: A tale of two cities. *Information, Communication and Society, 17*(9), 1086–1104.

Nguyen, L. C., Partridge, H. L., & Edwards, S. L. (2012). Towards an understanding of the participatory library. *Library Hi Tech, 30*(2), 335–346.

Notley, T., & Foth, M. (2008). Extending Australia's digital divide policy: An examination of the value of social inclusion and social capital policy frameworks. *Australian Social Policy*, 7, 87–110.

Park, S., Freeman, J., Middleton, C., Allen, M., Eckermann, R., & Everson, R. (2015). The multi-layers of digital exclusion in rural Australia. In *48th Hawaii conference on system sciences* (pp. 3621–3640). doi:10.1109/HICSS.2015.436.

Rennie, E., Ewing, S., & Thomas, J. (2015). Broadband policy and rural and cultural divides in Australia. In K. Andreasson (Ed.), *Digital divides: The new challenges and opportunities of e-inclusion* (pp. 109–125). Boca Raton: CRC Press.

Rennie, E., Hogan, E., Gregory, R., Crouch, A., Wright, A., & Thomas, J. (2016). *Internet on the outstation: The digital divide and remote aboriginal communities*. Amsterdam: Institute of Network Cultures. Retrieved from <https://issuu.com/instituteofnetworkcultures/docs/tod19-issuu>.

Rice, R. E. (2002). Primary issues in internet use: Access, civic and community involvement, and social interaction and expression. In L. A. Lievrouw, & S. M. Livingstone (Eds.), *Handbook of new media: Social shaping and consequences of ICTs* (pp. 105–129). London: Sage.

Schuler, D., & Namioka, A. (Eds.). (1993). *Participatory design: Principles and practices* Hillsdale: Lawrence Erlbaum.

Schuurman, D., De Marez, L., & Ballon, P. (2015). Living labs: A systematic literature review. In *Research day conference proceedings 2015. Open living labs day* (pp. 16–28). <https://www.scribd.com/doc/276089123/ENoLL-Research-Day-Conference-Proceedings-2015#download>.

Sebring, P. B., Brown, E. R., Julian, K. M., Ehrlich, S. B., Sporte, S. E., Bradley, E., & Meyer, L. (2013). *Teens, digital media and the Chicago public library. Research report*. Chicago: University of Chicago Consortium on Chicago School Research. Retrieved from <http://files.eric.ed.gov.ezp01.library.qut.edu.au/fulltext/ED553156.pdf>.

SGS Economics and Planning Pty Ltd (2012). *The library dividend technical report*. State Library of Queensland. Retrieved from <http://www.slq.qld.gov.au/__data/assets/pdf_file/0009/225864/the-library-dividend-technical-report.pdf>.

Smith, K., et al. (2016) Digital Futures in Indigenous Communities, Melbourne Networked Society Institute Research Paper, No 3, University of Melbourne, Parkville.

Ståhlbröst, A., & Holst, M. (2012). *The living lab methodology handbook*. Retrieved from <https://www.ltu.se/cms_fs/1.101555!/file/LivingLabsMethodologyBook_web.pdf>.

State Library of Queensland. (2017a). *Tech Savvy Seniors*. Retrieved from <http://plconnect.slq.qld.gov.au/resources/seniors/tech-savvy-seniors-queensland> Accessed 06.01.17.

State Library of Queensland. (2017b). *Vision 2016: The next horizon for Queensland public libraries*. Retrieved from <http://plconnect.slq.qld.gov.au/manage/21st-century-public-libraries/vision2017> Accessed 06.01.17.

Thomas, J., Barraket, J., Ewing, S., MacDonald, T., Mundell, M., & Tucker, J. (2016). *Measuring Australia's digital divide: The Australian digital inclusion index 2016, Swinburne University of Technology, Melbourne, for Telstra*. Retrieved from <https://digitalinclusionindex.org.au/wp-content/uploads/2016/08/Australian-Digital-Inclusion-Index-2016.pdf>.

Thompson, K. M., Jaeger, P. T., Taylor, N. G., Subramaniam, M., & Bertot, J. C. (2014). The policy gap. *Library Journal*, *139*(14), 36.

Tinder Foundation. (2011). *Digital inclusion, social impact: A research study*. Retrieved from <http://www.tinderfoundation.org/our-thinking/research-publications/digital-inclusion-social-impact>.

Townsend, L., Sathiaseelan, A., Fairhurst, G., & Wallace, C. (2013). Enhanced broadband access as a solution to the social and economic problems of the rural digital divide. *Local Economy*, *28*(6), 580–595.

Warburton, J., Cowan, S., Winterton, R., & Hodgkins, S. (2014). Building social inclusion for rural older people using information and communication technologies: Perspectives of rural practitioners. *Australian Social Work*, *67*(4), 479–494.

Warschauer, M. (2003). *Technology and social inclusion*. Cambridge: MIT Press.

FURTHER READING

Dell'Era, C., & Landoni, P. (2014). Living lab: A methodology between user-centred design and participatory design. *Creativity and Innovation Management*, *23*(2), 137–154.

Edwards-Schacter, M. E., Matti, C. E., & Alcantara, E. (2012). Fostering quality of life through social innovation: A living lab methodology study case. *Review of Policy Research*, *29*(6), 672–692.

Følstad, A. (2008). Living labs for innovation and development of information and communication technology: A literature review. *eJOV: The Electronic Journal for Virtual Organization & Networks*, *10*, 99–131.

Franz, Y. (2014). *Chances and challenges for social urban living labs in urban research*. ENOLL OpenLivingLab Days 2014, Amsterdam. Retrieved from <https://www.academia.edu/8253590/Chances_and_Challenges_for_Social_Urban_Living_Labs_in_Urban_Research>.

Jaeger, P. T., Bertot, J. C., & Gorham, U. (2013). Wake up the nation: Public libraries, policy making, and political discourse. *Library Quarterly: Information, Community, Policy*, *81*(1), 61–72.

Light, B., Houghton, K., Burgess, J., Klaebe, H., Osborne, R., Cunningham, S., & Hearn, G. (2016). *The impact of libraries as creative spaces*. QUT Digital Media Research Centre. Retrieved from <http://www.plconnect.slq.qld.gov.au/__data/assets/pdf_file/0003/339717/SLQ-Creative-Spaces-Low-Res.pdf>.

CHAPTER 2

Cultivating (Digital) Capacities: A Role for Social Living Labs?

Philippa J. Collin, Tanya Notley and Amanda Third
Western Sydney University, Penrith, NSW, Australia

INTRODUCTION

Digital technologies continue to rapidly transform the ways we communicate, learn, work and live. Highly developed countries such as Australia have significant levels of both Internet and mobile use as well as access quality (ITU, 2016). For example, in 2015 Internet access in countries ranged from 1% (Eritrea) to 98% (Falkland Islands and Bermuda). Australia had 85% Internet access and 133 mobile subscriptions for every 100 people (ITU, 2015a, 2015b). However, disparities in the quality, practices, meanings and social arrangements afforded by standard Information Communication Technologies (ICTs) persist and opportunities are not evenly distributed across national or global populations (Livingstone & Helsper, 2007). When compared to their peers, those from disadvantaged backgrounds often experience more limited or poorer quality digital access and digital literacy (Blanchard et al., 2008; Helsper, 2011; Third, Forrest-Lawrence, & Collier, 2014). This can exacerbate existing digital and educational disadvantages and compromise education, employment, health and social outcomes, as well as produce disproportionate associated long-term costs to families, communities and governments (Helsper, 2011). Investigating how and why both individuals and groups use and imagine ICTs is more important than ever. Yet, researching and responding to these issues is not easy, not least because conventional research and policy practices are not always appropriate. In this chapter, we critique key concepts and methods used to research the access, use and implications of ICT for social life and consider how we might augment our investigation and response toolbox.

Reflecting on 20 years of digital technology research, policy and practice highlights that how we conceive of and name sociotechnological change really matters. Access to and use of ICTs has, at different times,

Digital Participation through Social Living Labs. DOI: http://dx.doi.org/10.1016/B978-0-08-102059-3.00002-2

been constructed as an opportunity, a risk, a deficit, a need and a right, and each of these framings produces different consequences for users and their environments. Key concepts to define and understand access and use have included the digital divide, digital inclusion and digital participation. Focusing in particular on the Australian context, this chapter firstly unpacks and critiques how these concepts have developed and framed the way the digital is signified, experienced and mobilized in everyday life. Drawing upon insights from a current project that aims to rethink the conceptual frameworks, tools and environments for examining the role of the digital in contemporary societies, we introduce the concept of Digital Capacities as a holistic, relational and strength-based complement to the suite of existing concepts and approaches (We acknowledge the contributions of the other members of the *Cultivating Digital Capacities* project team: Liam Magee, Emma Kearney, Sam Yorke, Delphine Bellerose, Paul James, Justine Humphrey and Louise Crabtree. For more information see https://www.westernsydney.edu.au/ics/research/projects/digital_capacity_index). Finally, we consider how digital capacities might be operationalized in the context of social living labs in ways that bring diverse stakeholders together to research, design and implement strategies to enhance the benefits that technology can offer.

CONCEPTUALIZING DIGITAL TECHNOLOGY ACCESS AND USE: A BRIEF HISTORY

As ICTs have evolved, scholars, policymakers and popular commentators have proposed concepts for explaining the drivers and consequences of connectivity. Among these concepts, those of the digital divide, digital inclusion and digital participation have had particular purchase in policymaking and practice. It is to the history of their implementation that we turn first.

The idea of the digital divide was first adopted in the mid-1990s by academics and policymakers. It emerged in response to predictions that information-based, technology-focused industries and global information flows would drive and determine future economic growth. This vision positioned a technologically adept citizenry as critical to future national prosperity, prompting countries to measure disparities in access to computers and the Internet in order to inform the development and implementation of policy responses. Wealthy countries – including Australia, the United Kingdom and the United States – were all faced with evidence that a so-called digital divide had emerged between those with and without access to the Internet. Moreover, data showed that this divide was largely determined by socioeconomic and geographic factors as well as by age and ethnicity, with those in lower sociodemographic and more marginalized communities less likely to have access to the Internet and associated technologies (Bauer, Berne, & Maitland, 2002; Mossberger, 2003; Mossberger, Tolbert, & McNeal, 2007). National datasets pertaining to the digital divide soon permitted cross-country comparisons and, as a consequence, the global digital divide – defined and measured primarily as individual access to an Internet connection – occupied the agendas of international forums and agencies including the United Nations, the World Bank and the G8. Underpinned by a development discourse, by the turn of the new millennium concerns regarding the digital divide had extended well beyond the implications for economic participation and growth to incorporate social, political and cultural participation. The 2000 G8 Digital Opportunity Task Force (DOT Force) and the 2003 and 2005 World Summits on the Information Society (WSIS) focused government, private sector and civil society participants on a common vision to build a 'people-centred, inclusive and development oriented information society' (Okinawa G8 Summit, 2000; WSIS, 2003).

However, while global initiatives raised the prominence of the digital divide debate they also directed the attention of government policies towards issues of Internet access rather than the more complex issue of use. In Australia the digital divide was tackled by piecemeal government policies that were designed and implemented at local, state and national levels (Notley, 2008a, 2008b; Notley & Foth, 2008). Australia's haphazard approach to addressing the digital divide was amplified by nongovernment organizations working ad hoc in partnership with major corporations, such as Microsoft, Cisco and Westpac, to deliver hardware, Internet connections, software and basic technology skills to disadvantaged communities. Critics highlighted that while skills development was often an aim of these programs (e.g., Blanchard et al., 2008), digital divide initiatives continued to focus on technology access rather than the questions of how ICTs change people's lives (Gurstein, 2003; Mansell, 2002; Murdock & Golding, 2004; Norris, 2001; Solomon, Allen, & Resta, 2003; Warschauer, 2003).

In an attempt to broaden the discussion to address issues of access *and* use, the concept of 'digital inclusion' emerged. For Warschauer (2003), the need to shift from a focus on access (digital divide) to that of use (digital inclusion) was a direct response to the fact that, across the globe, many digital initiatives designed to provide access to poor communities had failed to have any long-term impact. He proposed that, just as the concept of 'social exclusion' had been used in EU and UK policy to consider barriers to participation in society, 'digital inclusion' could enrich digital divide policies by focusing on the role of ICTs for overcoming inhibitors to social participation (Warschauer, 2003). Taking a slightly different approach, Wilhelm (2004) argued that since technology use is not predetermined or homogenous and can be used to empower or control, unite or divide, what was needed was the integration of ideas of social justice and fairness in developing ICT policies. For example, he made the case that governments and social institutions should only implement online services if they had considered how such a shift might deepen inequalities and had developed strategies for addressing such challenges.

While the concept of digital inclusion usefully moved the debate on, it also met with considerable critique. For example, Notley (2008a, p. 63) argued that it may become too easy for governments to adopt digital inclusion as a catch-all concept to support preexisting policy. Drawing upon Sen's definition of human development as the capacity for individuals to live a life of freedom (1999, 2000), she proposed that 'digital inclusion can be understood as *the ICT capabilities people require to participate in society in ways that they have most reason to value*' (Notley, 2009, p. 1212 emphasis in original) and that digital inclusion initiatives be used 'to respond to people's own needs, rather than to fixed, value-laden and time-specific goals set by governments' (Notley, 2008a, p. 63). However, in countries including Australia, digital inclusion continued to be used in a limited way by governments, resting on an access binary of 'inclusion/exclusion' and focusing on the role of ICTs for addressing a limited number of predefined socioeconomic benefits, particularly those relating to health, education and employment. In doing so, digital inclusion strategies failed to encompass the more playful, popular, niche and everyday uses of the Internet. Moreover, in Australia, because digital inclusion was tightly wedded to the concept of social inclusion – an idea only embraced by progressive political parties – it never received bipartisan support, which hampered its adoption into policy and practice.

In the mid to late 2000s, with the rise of mobile devices and social network services, the concept of 'digital participation' gained currency. The term signalled a more comprehensive understanding of the role of ICTs in developing and mediating social, cultural, civic and political participation (Bennett, 2003; boyd, 2014; Dahlgren, 2009; Jenkins, Purushotma, Clinton, Weigel, & Robison, 2006; Vromen, 2007). Digital participation acknowledged the diversity of technology practices, finding that differences could not be accounted for merely by people's technology access or by their age, ethnicity, socioeconomic or geographic status. For example, Livingstone and Helsper (2007) argued that children's Internet use develops according to a 'ladder of opportunity' whereby users' ability to access opportunities online increases through 'exposure to and confidence in using digital media for an increasingly broader range of activities as they grow older. Children appear to follow a remarkably consistent "staged" process of "going online", which – ideally – sees them progressively develop new skills and increase the scope of their engagement over time' (Third, 2016b, p. 9). Yet while children's online entertainment and communication activities create pathways to a broad range of opportunities, 'many of the creative, informative, interactive and participatory features of the digital environment remain substantially underused even by well-resourced children' (Livingstone & Bulger, 2013, p. 4). Nevertheless, digital participation's central tenet of promoting the benefits of producing, sharing and consuming digital content was influential in policy and practice, particularly in relation to teaching approaches that were seen to enable children and young people to benefit from the informal learning that occurs in participatory media environments such as online gaming, the remixing of content within fan cultures and social network sites (see Hague & Williamson, 2009; Hartley, 2009; Jenkins et al., 2006; Notley, 2008a, 2008b). Significantly, at the same time, a powerful discourse of cybersafety emerged, centring on heightened concerns about the perceived risks and harms associated with 'being online', particularly for 'vulnerable users' (Notley, 2008a; Third et al., 2014).

Like every new concept, 'digital participation' opened up and closed off possibilities. For example, Buckingham (2009) suggested that the 'participation imperative' and associated promotion of digital literacies reproduced a technological euphoria that failed to acknowledge that participation in commercial environments could also lead to surveillance and exploitation, and that serious critique of the political economy of technology producers and providers was required. Third and colleagues have argued that digital participation emerged to counter the effects of the 'risk paradigm' that dominates the policy and associated services and programs in many countries, including Australia (Third et al., 2014). Others argue that much policy and research has been underpinned by normative assumptions of what constitutes 'good' digital participation and has largely failed to consider the meanings and motivations of users themselves or the influence and diversity of the contexts in which they live and go online (Collin, 2008; Vromen, 2007).

This brief discussion highlights that these three concepts have both utility and limitations, even in the present context. Furthermore, they have also informed one another over time: the digital divide now incorporates issues of use; digital inclusion has been broadened in some contexts to value social uses of the Internet and digital literacies have become a central concern within each of these concepts. However, when considered together, they reveal three persistent challenges for the study of digital life. Firstly, they underscore the need to move conceptual debates and discussions away from an instrumental focus on the technology and what happens 'online' and towards increasingly nuanced consideration of the ways technology mediates social life. Secondly, they highlight how a concern for individual, community or population access and use can overshadow how the value and meaning of technology is produced *through* our relationships to one another, the places we live and sometimes because of sociostructural disadvantage. Thirdly, if the conceptual starting point for action is to address perceived and predefined deficits, opportunities to support and build upon shared strengths will be missed.

These issues suggest we also need to critique our methods: while small-scale, in-depth qualitative studies on particular communities can illuminate the very local, and large-scale quantitative surveys can reveal regional or national patterns of technology access and use, both approaches have benefits and limitations. We argue that researchers, policymakers and practitioners should be looking at opportunities, existing affordances and experiences *in context*, as a starting point for action and that relevant groups, networks and communities should be involved in this process. In Section 2.3 we propose a concept of digital capacities to address the limitations outlined above.

TOWARDS A CONCEPT OF CAPACITIES FOR DIGITAL SOCIETY

Researchers working critically with the concepts discussed earlier have produced valuable methods and measures, often focusing on the skills and literacies required to navigate online spaces, and on identifying potential barriers to participation. These include measures of access and use (see Livingstone & Haddon, 2009), digital literacy (see Van Deursen,

Helsper, & Eynon, 2014) and digital inclusion (see Thomas et al., 2016). Whilst these measures have been important for advancing the field and generating valuable empirical data, we argue that they are insufficient to account for the increasingly complex social, spatial and temporal contexts, practices and interrelations constituted through ICTs. This is partly because they privilege the technology, thus downplaying the social and cultural contexts in which the digital is meaningfully mobilized at the level of the everyday. As argued earlier, this has limited the potential for explaining *and* measuring the diverse forms and significance of ICTs for contemporary experience and designing effective policies that support all users to mobilize the opportunities of ICTs. Moreover, segmenting out specific components of digital life – such as protecting users from specific online risks or supporting the development of preestablished 'digital skills' – can result in piecemeal and sometimes contradictory approaches that do not adequately prepare users to move up the 'ladder of opportunities' (Livingstone & Helsper, 2007). Consequently, there is a need for a holistic approach that can integrate and push beyond current modes of thinking – and to minimize the likelihood that even well-intended policies and programs produce adverse or limited consequences.

Another complication associated with measuring fixed uses of ICTs – particularly through survey-based studies – is that we reproduce the distinctions between phenomena, rather than illuminating the relationships between them. As argued earlier, while each of the terms discussed more or less seeks to promote the role of ICT in social life, they have had the effect of reinforcing the view that the technology, individual practices and problematic deficits in access and skills matter most to the prospects of people and communities in digital society. By contrast, we argue that a more holistic approach that takes account of the sociocultural and structural forces that shape the digital mediation of social life might help us to see *new relationships and devise ways to support users to maximize opportunities online*. In this regard, we are particularly motivated to address the lack of research in key areas including: the benefits of digital media practices and how to promote online opportunities, particularly for children and other marginalized groups (Collin, Rahilly, Richardson, & Third, 2011; Humphrey, 2014; Livingstone and Bulger, 2013; Rennie et al., 2016; Swist, Collin, McCormack, & Third, 2015); the motivations, aspirations and meanings that underpin people's digital practices (boyd, 2014; Notley, 2009; Swist et al., 2015; Third et al., 2014); and, the kinds of approaches and methods that can more effectively analyse people's experiences and aspirations in digital life (Collin, 2015; Third, 2016a).

Our research draws on the concept of capabilities (Sen, 1999) to foreground the role of context for shaping how people value technologies and practices (Notley, 2009). We use the term *capacities* to emphasize that human flourishing is not simply embodied in the individual but is produced relationally through interaction with social arrangements and material objects. While we acknowledge the key role of the digital in contemporary social life it is nonetheless important that policy and practice move from privileging the technology to cultivating the necessary skills, attitudes and modes of relating to thrive in digitally mediated societies. We define these (digital) capacities – as *users' abilities to mobilize material and symbolic resources in order to maximize benefits, opportunities and aspirations afforded by the digital.* We bracket the 'digital' here to "gesture towards the deep interdependencies between 'the digital' and other dimensions of everyday life; and to open up towards new approaches to thinking about the integral place of the digital in contemporary social, cultural, political, economic and environmental life" (Third, Collin, Wlsh, & Black, 2018). Such a conception is important since capacities are never fixed. Our individual and societal-level needs and interests constantly change, as do technologies. As such, (digital) capacities are socially framed and generated in a process of constant interaction in relation to other beings and material objects.

In 2015 researchers at the Institute for Culture and Society at Western Sydney University, in partnership with the Young and Well Cooperative Research Centre and Google Australia, initiated a project to investigate how to maximize the benefits of connectivity (Third et al., 2016b). The *Cultivating (Digital) Capacities* project aimed to address the limitations of existing concepts and approaches that are operationalized in ICT policy and practice. Rather than replacing available concepts, however, we instead examined the relationship between the concepts of digital inclusion, digital citizenship, digital resilience, digital participation and online safety. We also adopted an expansive notion of ICT which includes socio-technical 'infrastructures' (the devices, practices and social relations (Lievrouw & Livingstone, 2006), but also the role of policies and institutions, physical environments, broader social contexts, motivations and meaning-making *that constitute a process of infrastructuring.* We understand 'Infrastructuring' to be the 'ongoing alignment and transformation of contexts, practices, technologies and social relation through which publics form and act' (Collin & Swist, 2016, pp. 309–310).

The concept of (digital) capacities is intended to shift the focus of discussions of the role of the digital in social life in three critical ways. Firstly, key to the (digital) capacities approach is the idea that the digital is evermore entangled with processes of social transformation. Digital practices never play out solely 'online'; they are deeply grounded in the social, cultural, political and economic contexts that shape everyday life and social experience. Whilst much popular and policy discourse constructs 'the social' and 'the digital' as separate realms, the digital in fact comprises shifting patterns of sociotechnical relations. (Digital) capacities, then, are produced through the relationships between individuals, families, communities, devices, software, platforms, institutions, businesses and systems. They cannot, therefore, be reduced to individual or population level metrics as they are produced *through* our interrelationships with other people and social structures. Implicit in this understanding is the idea that people have agency in determining the purposes to which their digital practices are put – what inclusion and participation through technology might *mean* for them, their families, businesses and communities.

Secondly, the (digital) capacities concept promotes a shift in focus from individuals to communities, from fixed to dynamic needs and contexts and from personal deficits to shared strengths and opportunities. While (digital) capacities may manifest in material or structural ways, they also have an imaginative or discursive dimension; users' (digital) capacities are deeply structured by the ways they *perceive* the affordances of digital media for enhancing their everyday lives and those of the people around them. The concept of (digital) capacities seeks to promote users' mobilization of the digital in ways that are already meaningful to them but it also acknowledges that we are yet to imagine the full range of possibilities afforded by the digital for the positive transformation of social life. Thirdly, then, the concept of (digital) capacities seeks to capture the aspirational potential of the digital for reimagining social life. In foregrounding this potential of the digital, we draw on the idea of 'resilience thinking' (Chandler, 2014) that argues that resilience is not only about surviving or adapting to adversity but also about transforming the very conditions of social life that produce adversity in the first place.

To meet the methodological challenges of researching a 'moving target' (Magee et al., forthcoming) while seeking ways to effectively document and analyse (digital) capacities, we have taken an explicitly process-focused, iterative approach, which builds on our previous work in participatory research and design (Hagen et al., 2012), digital practice (Third et al., 2014), youth engagement (Collin & Swist 2016) and sustainability (James, Magee, Scerri, & Steger, 2015). This work collectively emphasizes the crucial role of diversity, subjectivity, dialogue and agonistic engagement for pluralistic forms of knowing that can respond to complex social phenomena. Whilst some aspects of digital life – such as access – are often tangible and quantifiable, capacities are more abstract and therefore can be more challenging to research. To define, measure and explain changes in (digital) capacities over time requires flexible tools and approaches that can capture the digital practices, skills and literacies of users through attention to their lived experiences of technology. As such, the aim of *Cultivating (Digital) Capacities* is both to work with existing indicators and to develop new, complementary and bespoke indicators capable of generating flexible and holistic measures of the capacities of people and communities in different contexts. We briefly describe here the process used in the *Cultivating (Digital) Capacities* project before looking to its application in a social living lab setting.

A ROLE FOR SOCIAL LIVING LABS?

The first step in the process was for diverse stakeholders to identify critical issues to develop a set of concerns against four domains of social life: ecological, political, cultural and economic (James et al., 2015). These domains acknowledge the complex factors – and interplay between them – that produce digitally mediated social life. For example, affordable Internet, supportive relationships, the topography where one lives, and laws around gender equity in the workplace may all shape the role of the digital for an individual, their family or community and, indeed, larger sections of the population. Our list of critical issues informed a set of indicators against which quantitative and qualitative data were considered. This included a scan of existing datasets, five household visits comprising sixteen in-depth interviews and technology walk-throughs, and a nationally representative survey ($n = 2073$) administered via an online panel provider. This process indicated four key (digital) capacities: *competencies (skills and abilities), interests (motivations), resilience (strategies for navigating risks in order to pursue opportunities) and connectedness (depth and breadths of social interactions)* (Third et al., 2016b). This data enables the analysis of issues and the identification of priorities. It can also directly inform the concept and design phase of potential 'interventions'. This method of identifying suitable indicators also supports community actors to collect data themselves, at scales that may be hyperlocal or nongeographically focused. The key aim of this approach is to use the collective process of identifying indicators to develop a measure that is sensitive to context, but sufficiently consistent so as to allow for replication and comparisons over time and at local, regional and national scales.

While government policies remain critical to action that supports the cultivation of diverse and equally distributed (digital) capacities, other kinds of organizations, groups and networks are playing a pivotal role in enabling innovative and locally responsive forms of research and collective action on the role of the digital in society. These actors have developed or adopted approaches such as local and online programs and workshops in digital storytelling and filmmaking, technology and code camps as well as hackathons. Increasingly, Living Labs and other 'open innovation' methodologies are mobilized to bring together a range of stakeholders with diverse interests, abilities and skills in order to generate new ways of knowing and responding to complex problems, from employment and social enterprise to improved, collaborative and creative urban planning (Eskelinen, Robles, Lindy, Marsh, & Muente-Kunigami, 2015). Central to these approaches is a commitment to involve diverse participants including technologists, researchers, policymakers, citizens and change-makers.

What defines the 'community' in Living Labs varies widely around the world, though most commonly participants are researchers, industry partners, policymakers and potential 'end users' of products and services. One key characteristic of Australian Living Labs is that they support a community-driven process that *integrates research with design* (see Australian Living Labs Innovation Network, n.d.). Moreover, as coresearch and codesign environments that aim to 'address the social dynamics of everyday life' (Mulder, 2012), Social Living Labs, in particular, hold unique promise for expanding the definitions of community, participants and 'end users': from more expert, technical, industry and adult-centric definitions to encompass community members whose 'expertise' is often unrecognized, or seen as marginal, such as children, carers and culturally and linguistically diverse groups. In order to realize this potential in which Social Living Labs might support the research and promotion of digital capacities we suggest the following are required:

- A framing of research that acknowledges that research does not 'objectively' document the 'out there' but is instrumental in creating 'out there's' (Michael, 2012). This is research framed by a different kind of

temporality – one that is implicated in processual knowledges that defy finality and the certainty of 'findings' (Third, 2016a).
- Highly reflexive researchers who acknowledge the power dynamics in which they are embedded (Third, 2016a; Collin & Swist, 2016).
- Particular kinds of tools that can work flexibly with Living Lab processes and harness complexity, not only as a site for analysis, but also for action or 'cultural making' (Swist, Hodge, & Collin, 2016).

Such an approach necessarily foregrounds the relationships between people, place, technologies, practices and the processes through which they are produced. Therefore while activities (e.g., in research and design projects) are important, it is *how* these activities are actualized that matters. Social Living Labs are in a unique position to offer enhanced reflexivity by asking at least two key foundational questions. Firstly, are the concerns of the lab based on the meanings and values of those who stand to benefit from any resulting innovation? Secondly, are the activities and aims of the initiatives designed with the concerns and valued futures of the participants in mind? This orientation is complementary to a capabilities approach (Sen, 2000) and responds to Notley's call for researchers, policymakers, service providers and designers to focus on '. . .the capabilities people require to participate in society in ways they have most reason to value' and also on 'the barriers that impede people from developing their own capabilities' (2009, p. 1211).

To move beyond the limitations of existing concepts and practices, we argue that Social Living Labs must aim to cultivate more than just digital inclusion or participation via promoting the access and skills to use (devices), perform (practices) or relate to others (social arrangements) in relation to the digital. Rather, they should critique, explore, build on and catalyse the ways people choose – or are directed – to navigate digital life as a process. To do so requires new conceptual and practical tools and a commitment to the role that Social Living Lab processes can play in generating, sustaining and transforming publics (Collin & Swist, 2016).

CONCLUSION: THINKING THE DIGITAL DIFFERENTLY IN SOCIAL LIVING LABS

As we have suggested, key concepts for understanding, assessing and responding to the role of ICTs have profoundly shaped policy and practice relating to the digital since the 1990s. An analysis of these concepts reveals much about the assumptions that shape digital policy and practice at the moment they gain currency. Though ideas about the 'digital divide' may have been built on a limited view of technology as 'computers and Internet' and had an overdependence on population-level quantitative methods, the term has served to highlight the importance of basic – and public – infrastructures, and the way that social and economic inequality is often exacerbated by the proliferation of ICTs in everyday life. This concern was further extended by the introduction of the concept of digital inclusion. However, this term failed to recognize the value in social, cultural and playful uses of the Internet. Similarly, though digital participation may have drawn attention to the social and creative dimensions of diverse, citizen-driven and networked digital media practices, it has tended to overemphasize the individual and their particular practices as the units of analysis and the drivers for action, while often neglecting to consider the problems associated with increasing public dependency on the corporations who own the platforms and design the devices that mediate our lives. In this chapter we have argued that these concepts and their affiliated modes of research need reorientation.

We have argued that the concept of (digital) capacities offers a productive conceptual lens through which to investigate how ICTs are implicated and activated in social life; how they are mobilized through social relations and according to the diverse meanings and motivations of people, groups and networks across multiple contexts. Investigating (digital) capacities requires a research approach that adopts reflexive and flexible research methods. Social Living Labs are research and design environments where capacities can be considered, understood, made use of and cultivated from the perspective of the people who stand to benefit the most from the products and publics they generate. They also offer the possibility of adopting collective processes that consider the kinds of environments, practices and resources required to take forward such an approach, identifying and adapting to changing needs.

However, to do so requires that the directors, participants and sponsors of Social Living Labs approach their work *as intervention* (Third, 2016a) – not just as novel, objective exercises in documentation, diagnosis, experimentation or recommendation. Activities to define the critical issues for (digital) capacities in a particular place can include: dialogues to establish the research agenda; identification or cocreation of indicators and datasets; exploration, analysis and visualization of data and development of digital projects. Moreover, these processes themselves can bring about change and increase awareness of the assumptions, commonalities, productive differences and potentialities of technology use, motivations and meanings among participants, as well as support codesign processes that utilize research data and findings (Third & Collin, 2016). Such an approach must necessarily move beyond an instrumentalist view of digital technology – as merely a research tool, or final product of a lab process – to one that is holistic and understands 'the digital' as comprising engagement with technology in dynamic and situated social processes.

The potential of such an approach for addressing inequality, marginalization and harm is significant; it offers opportunities for new forms of dialogue, collaboration and contestation that can powerfully inform policy, products and community action. Such an approach should include concepts and process tools for surfacing tensions, power differentials, diverse experiences, needs, opportunities and ideas among participants – a productive process that can move research beyond description and diagnosis and towards 'interventions' that can cultivate capacities for a digital age.

REFERENCES

Australian Living Labs Innovation Network. (n.d.). <https://openlivinglabs.net.au>.

Bauer, J. M., Berne, M., & Maitland, C. F. (2002). Internet access in the European Union and in the United States. *Telematics and Informatics*, *19*(2), 117–137.

Bennett, L. W. (2003). Communicating global activism. *Information, Communication and Society*, *6*, 143–168.

Blanchard et al. (2008). *Bridging the Digital Divide: Utilising technology to promote social connectedness*. Retrieved from <https://www.cbaa.org.au/article/bridging-digital-divide-utilising-technology-promote-social-connectedness-and-civic>.

Boyd, D. (2014). *It's complicated: The social lives of networked teens*. New Haven: Yale University Press.

Buckingham, D. (2009). The future of media literacy in the digital age: Some challenges for policy and practice. *Medienimpulse*, *2*, 13–24.

Chandler, D. (2014). *Resilience: the governance of complexity*. Oxon: Routledge.

Collin, P. (2008). The Internet, youth participation policies and the development of young people's political identities in Australia. *Journal of Youth Studies*, *11*(5), 527–542.

Collin, P. (2015). *Young citizens and political participation in a digital society: Addressing the democratic Disconnect*. Hampshire: Palgrave Macmillan.

Collin, P., Rahilly, K., Richardson, I., & Third, A. (2011). *The benefits of social networking service: A literature review*. Melbourne: Cooperative Research Centre for Young People, Technology and Wellbeing.

Collin, P., & Swist, T. (2016). From products to publics? The potential of participatory design for research on youth, safety and well-being. *Journal of Youth Studies*, *19*(3), 305–318.

Dahlgren, P. (2009). *Media and political engagement: Citizens, communication and democracy*. Cambridge: Cambridge University Press.

Eskelinen, J., Robles, A. G., Lindy, I., Marsh, J., & Muente-Kunigami, A. (Eds.). (2015). *Citizen-driven innovation—A guidebook for city mayors and public administrators* World Bank and ENoLL. Retrieved from <http://openlivinglabs.eu/sites/enoll.org/files/Citizen_Driven_Innovation_Full%284%29.pdf>.

Gurstein, M. (2003). Effective use: A community informatics strategy beyond the digital divide. *First Monday, 8*(12).

Hagen, P., Collin, P., Metcalf, A., Nicholas, M., Rahilly, K., & Swainston, N. (2012). *Participatory Design of Evidence-Based Online Youth Mental Health Promotion, Prevention and Early Intervention and Treatment*. Abbotsford: Young and Well CRC.

Hague, C., & Williamson, B. (2009). *Digital participation, digital literacy, and school subjects: A review of the policies, literature and evidence*. Futurelab.

Hartley, J. (2009). *The uses of digital literacy*. Creative Economy + Innovation Culture.

Helsper, E. (2011). *Digital disconnect: Issues of social exclusion, vulnerability and digital (dis) engagement*. Retrieved from <http://www.bpb.de/system/files/pdf/IQPRQA.pdf>.

Humphrey, J. (2014). The importance of circumstance: Digital access and affordability for people experiencing homelessness. *Australian Journal of Telecommunications and the Digital Economy, 2*(3), 55.

ITU (2015a). *Percentage of individuals using the Internet 2000–2015*. International Telecommunications Union. Retrieved from <http://www.itu.int/en/ITU-D/Statistics/Documents/statistics/2016/Individuals_Internet_2000-2015.xls>.

ITU (2015b). *Mobile cellular subscriptions 2000–2015*. International Telecommunications Union. Retrieved from <http://www.itu.int/en/ITU-D/Statistics/Documents/statistics/2016/Mobile_cellular_2000-2015.xls>.

ITU (2016). *ICT facts and figures 2016*. International Telecommunications Union. Retrieved from <http://www.itu.int/en/ITU-D/Statistics/Pages/facts/default.aspx>.

James, P., Magee, L., Scerri, A., & Steger, M. (2015). *Urban sustainability in theory and practice: Circles of sustainability*. Oxford: Routledge.

Jenkins, H., Purushotma, R., Clinton, K., Weigel, M., & Robison, A. J. (2006). *Confronting the challenges of participatory culture: Media education for the 21st century*. Chicago: John D. and Catherine T. MacArthur Foundation.

Lievrouw, Leah A., & Livingstone, Sonia (2006). Introduction to the updated student edition. In Leah A. Lievrouw, & Sonia Livingstone (Eds.), *Handbook of New Media: Social Shaping and Social Consequences of Icts* (pp. 1–14). London, UK: Sage.

Livingstone, S., & Bulger, M. (2013). *A global agenda for children's rights in the digital age*. Florence: UNICEF Office of Research. Retrieved from <https://www.unicef-irc.org/publications/pdf/lse%20olol%20final3.pdf>.

Livingstone, S., & Haddon, L. (2009). *EU Kids Online: Final report*. LSE, London: EU Kids Online. (EC Safer Internet Plus Programme Deliverable D6.5).

Livingstone, S., & Helsper, E. (2007). Gradations in digital inclusion: Children, young people and the digital divide. *New Media & Society, 9*, 671–696.

Magee, L., Kearney, E., Bellerose, D., Collin, P., Crabtree, L., Humphry, J., et al. (forthcoming). Measuring a Volatile Subject: Digital Capacities in Australian Households.

Mansell, R. (2002). From digital divides to digital entitlements in knowledge societies. *Current Sociology, 50*(3), 407–426.

Michael, M. (2012). Anecdote. In C. Lury, & N. Wakeford (Eds.), *Inventive methods: The happening of the social* (pp. 25–35). London & New York: Routledge.

Mossberger, K. (2003). *Virtual inequality: Beyond the digital divide*. Washington: Georgetown University Press.

Mossberger, K., Tolbert, C. J., & McNeal, R. S. (2007). *Digital citizenship: The internet, society and participation*. Cambridge: MIT Press.

Mulder, I. (2012). Living labbing in the Rotterdam way: Co-creation as an enabler for urban innovation. *Technology Innovation Management Review, 2*(9), 39.

Murdock, G., & Golding, P. (2004). *Dismantling the digital divide: Rethinking the dynamics of participation and exclusion. Toward a political economy of culture: Capitalism and communication in the twenty-first century* (pp. 244–260). Lanham: Rowman & Littlefield.

Norris, P. (2001). *Digital divide: Civic engagement, information poverty, and the Internet worldwide*. Cambridge: Cambridge University Press.

Notley, T. (2008a). *The role of online networks in supporting young people's digital inclusion and the implications for Australian government policies* (Ph.D. thesis). Brisbane: Queensland University of Technology.

Notley, T. (2008b). Online network use in schools: Social and educational opportunities. *The Journal of Youth Studies Australia, 27*(3), 20–27.

Notley, T. (2009). Young people, online networks, and social inclusion. *Journal of Computer-Mediated Communication, 14*(4), 1208–1227.

Notley, T., & Foth, M. (2008). Extending Australia's digital divide policy: An examination of the value of social inclusion and social capital policy frameworks. *Australian Social Policy*, 7, 87–110.

Okinawa G. Summit (July 23, 2000). *Preamble: G8 Communique Okinawa 2000*. Retrieved from <http://www.g8.utoronto.ca/summit/2000okinawa/finalcom.htm>.

Rennie, E., Hogan, E., Gregory, R., Crouch, A., Wright, A., & Thomas, J. (2016). *Internet on the outstation: The digital divide and remote aboriginal communities*. Amsterdam: Institute of Network Cultures.

Sen, A. (1999). *Development as freedom*. Oxford: Oxford University Press.

Sen, A. (2000). *Social exclusion: Concept, application, and scrutiny*. Asian Development Bank.

Solomon, G., Nancy, J. A., & Resta, P. E. (Eds.). (2003). *Toward digital equity: Bridging the divide in education* Saddle River: Prentice Hall.

Swist, T., Collin, P., McCormack, J., & Third, A. (2015). *Social media and the wellbeing of children and young people: A literature review*. Perth: West Australian Commission for Children and Young People.

Swist, T., Hodge, B., & Collin, P. (2016). 'Cultural making': How complexity and power relations are modulated in transdisciplinary research. *Continuum: Journal of Media and Cultural Studies, 30*(4), 489–501.

Third, A. (2016a). The tactical researcher: Cultural studies research as pedagogy. In A. T. Hickey (Ed.), *The pedagogies of cultural studies* (pp. 93–115). UK: Taylor and Francis.

Third, A. (2016b). *Researching the benefits and opportunities of children online*. London: Global Kids Online. Retrieved from <http://blogs.lse.ac.uk/gko/tools/guides/opportunities/>.

Third, A., & Collin, P. (2016). Rethinking (children's and young people's) citizenship through dialogues on digital practice. In A. McCosker, S. Vivienne, & A. Johns (Eds.), *Negotiating digital citizenship: Control, contest and culture* (pp. 41–59). London: Rowman & Littlefield International.

Third, A., Collin, P., Magee, L., Kearney, E., Liam, M., Yorke, S., ... Crabtree, L. (2016). *Cultivating digital capacities*. Institute for Culture and Society, Western Sydney University. Retrieved from <https://www.westernsydney.edu.au/ics/research/projects/digital_capacity_index>.

Third, A., Collin, P., Walsh, L., & Black, R. (2018). *Young people in (digital) society: Control shift*. London and New York: Palgrave MacMillan.

Third, A., Forrest-Lawrence, P., & Collier, A. (2014). *Addressing the cybersafety challenge: From risk to resilience*. For Telstra Corporation. Retrieved from <http://telstra.com.au/uberprod/groups/webcontent/@corporate/@aboutus/documents/document/uberstaging_279130.pdf>.

Thomas, J., Barraket, J., Ewing, S., MacDonald, T., Mundell, M., & Tucker, J. (2016). *Measuring Australia's digital divide: The Australian digital inclusion index 2016*. Swinburne University of Technology, Melbourne, for Telstra.

Van Deursen, A.J.A.M., Helsper, E.J., & Eynon, R. (2014). *Measuring digital skills. From digital skills to tangible outcomes project report.* Retrieved from <www.oii.ox.ac.uk/research/projects/?id=112>.

Vromen, A. (2007). Young people's participatory practices and internet use. *Information, Communication & Society, 10*, 48–68.

Warschauer, M. (2003). *Technology and social inclusion: Rethinking the digital divide.* Cambridge: MIT Press.

Wilhelm, A. G. (2004). *Digital nation: Toward an inclusive information society.* Cambridge: MIT Press.

WSIS (2003). *Declaration of principles: Building the information society: A global challenge in the new millennium. Published 12th December 2003. World Summit for the Information Society.* Information Telecommunications Union. Retrieved from <http://www.itu.int/net/wsis/docs/geneva/official/dop.html>.

FURTHER READING

Boeck, T., & Collin, P. (2012). Youth and adult researcher reflections on participatory research in Australia and the United Kingdom. In J. Fleming, & T. Boeck (Eds.), *Involving children and young people in health and social care research* (pp. 197–208). Oxford: Routledge.

Burns, et al. (2013). *Game on: Exploring the impact of technologies on young men's mental health and wellbeing. Findings from the first Young and Well National Survey.* Melbourne: Young and Well Cooperative Research Centre.

Couldry, N., & Rodriguez, C. (2016). *Chapter 13–Media and communications in International Panel on Social Progress Report, Draft for commenting.* Accessed 01.12.16.

Hargittai, E., & Walejko, G. (2008). The participation divide: Content creation and sharing in the digital age 1. *Information, Community and Society, 11*(2), 239–256.

Jenkins, H. (2006). Convergence culture: Where old and new media collide. New York: New York University Press.

Magee, L., & Scerri, A. (2012). From issues to indicators: Developing robust community sustainability measures. *Local Environment, 17*(8), 915–933.

Nussbaum, M. (2011). *Creating capabilities: The human development approach.* Cambridge: Harvard University Press.

CHAPTER 3

Digital Participation Through Artistic Interventions

Rachel Jacobs[1] and Silvia Leal[2]
[1]University of Nottingham, Nottingham, United Kingdom
[2]Fluminense Federal University, Niterói, Brazil

INTRODUCTION

This chapter describes a series of interactive artistic interventions that brought together artists, computer science researchers, climate scientists, botanists, educators, school children and the public, working in forests and communities in both the United Kingdom and Brazil. We propose an approach to digital participation that encourages a human focus, combining artistic strategies and local knowledge with technological and scientific processes.

We describe this open and welcoming approach to collaboration in respect of four artistic interventions that were each interlinked, each evolving from the other, creating a journey that reaches across the Atlantic Ocean to forests and mountains, cities, villages and towns, weaving a story of a world that is undergoing complex environmental and technological changes. By introducing mobile sensing and Internet-enabled technologies the participants in these interventions were able to record and respond to the changes in the place where they live, and share these experiences with people on the other side of the world.

We investigate both the digital and analogue tools used for tracking, recording and experimentation – including mobile phones, Internet-enabled and sensor technologies. We ask how these technologies can enable us to engage physically and viscerally within our own geographical context (Burke et al., 2006; Rodaway, 2002; Tuan, 1977), and how we can begin to measure our responses (McCarthy & Wright, 2004; Pink, 2015).

Each of these artistic interventions raises questions around how artists might contribute to a reimagining of the relationships between technology, people and culture. The work promotes approaches to digital participation that encourage a combination of logical, emotional and

Digital Participation through Social Living Labs. DOI: http://dx.doi.org/10.1016/B978-0-08-102059-3.00003-4

material responses to scientific and technological process, through dialogue, artistic intervention and collaboration. Following Michel de Certeau, we describe these approaches as 'tactics' instead of strategy or method (De Certeau & Mayol, 1998), in response to the artistic and cultural conditions of working in Rio de Janeiro, Brazil, where the reality experienced in the field demands a careful and situated response to relationships being forged and the creative tools brought to the proposed work.

The authors propose that the artistic process outlined in this chapter resulted in a wealth of art, science and technology processes, carefully composed to meet a range of audience needs, specific to the location where each of the projects took place, designed and realized through school exchanges, artists residencies and exhibitions.

During this process the artists encountered many digital and knowledge divides that are deeply embedded in both British and Brazilian society, albeit in different and complex ways. This context highlights the importance of negotiating spaces for such experiments to happen, characterized by a fluid approach to collaboration and participation. What becomes apparent is that the adopted practices across each of the described projects has the potential to connect different layers within and across the participant's engagements (Latour, 2005): people, locations, tools, timing, evolving processes, communication, artistic experience, each of which is informed by Brazil's free-software movement (Ferran & Fonseca, 2009), Brazilian contemporary art traditions of concrete poetry and neoconcretism (Amirsadeghi & Petitgas, 2012), performance art and theatre practices (Stiles & Selz, 2012) and the social sculpture practice of Beuys (Beuys & Harlan, 2004) and Sacks (Giannachi & Stewart, 2005, p. 199).

The following projects therefore describe an improvised series of overlapping live moments, whilst maintaining continuity from one project to the other by specific meeting points on both sides of the Atlantic. At these points the artists conducted activities where participants and organizations could meet (physically and virtually) to spend time together where a focus was given to the ethical value of hospitality (Ferran & Márcia de, 2008) by way of schools exchanges, artist residencies, touring exhibitions and Hacklabs. In contrast to the more common idea that a project has a clearly defined beginning and end this approach evolved from and was made possible through the distance between the physical participatory spaces, where intervals between activities were often necessary due to the remote nature of the virtual interactions.

SUMMARY OF PROJECTS

The first project, *The Dark Forest*, began as a conversation during *Mobilefest* in Sao Paulo where the artist collective Active Ingredient presented a location-based mobile game 'Ere be Dragons' (Davis et al., 2005). We talked with *Mobilefest* about developing new tools for visualizing and interpreting data in order to 'reveal the invisible' nature of forests. *The Dark Forest* emerged from these talks, as an investigation into the forests on our own doorsteps, in order to connect forests on either side of the Atlantic Ocean. The resulting project took place in Sherwood Forest, England's most iconic forest and home to the legend of Robin Hood, close to Active Ingredient's base in Nottingham in the United Kingdom; and the Mata Atlântica, the forest that once stretched from Uruguay and Argentina up along the coastal regions of Brazil.

We were later invited to attend an inspiring international workshop event, Paralelo (Rimmer et al., 2009), which brought together a collective of curators, artists, designers and other cultural organizations from Brazil, Holland and the United Kingdom. This event not only opened up new perspectives on digital and environmental practices, but also introduced the authors to each other. We subsequently embarked on our first collaboration as artist-facilitators of *The Dark Forest* schools exchange in Rio de Janeiro and Nottingham.

A Conversation Between Trees evolved from this project. In this work the focus was on a touring exhibition with parallel participatory workshops that connected forests in the United Kingdom and Brazil, using mobile sensor technologies installed in trees in both forests. This tour took place primarily in the United Kingdom, alongside an exhibition at the Museum of Image and Sound in Sao Paulo (MIS), a residency and schools' workshop as part of the Experimental Mobile Studio (Funarte, 2010) in Rio de Janeiro.

These projects resulted in the development of *Timestreams*, a sensing technology platform designed for artists and communities, as part of *Relate* – an academic led research project by researchers from Horizon Digital Economy Institute (at the University of Nottingham), a climate scientist from the Hadley Centre, UK MET Office and a professor in Virtual Theatre and Mixed Reality Performance at the University of

Exeter (Giannachi & Kaye, 2011). *Timestreams* combined the use of technologies such as mobile sensors and a bespoke mobile phone application to allow the artists, educators, school children and hackers to explore the relationship between energy and climate change. This took place through an often difficult and complex process of action, reflection and dialogue between artists and researchers, including a programmer who built the platform 'in the wild' as the team travelled from Nottingham to the Mata Atlântica and Rio de Janeiro, extending the methodological framework of Performance-led Research in the Wild (Benford et al., 2013) developed at the University of Nottingham. It also brought together interdisciplinary research across the disciplines of Climate Science, Human Computer Interaction and Contemporary Art and Theatre as a method for encouraging alternative approaches to engaging the public with scientific data pertaining to energy and climate change (Blum et al., 2012).

Schools Participation Across the Dark Forest and a Conversation Between Trees

It is still a fairly recent practice, particularly in Brazil, to consider how schools engage with the ever-growing use of digital technologies in classrooms. An integral element of *The Dark Forest* and *A Conversation Between Trees* was to explore how digital participation could be integrated into a series of school exchanges and public workshops across the United Kingdom and Brazil, acting as a doorway to learning about science, technology and the environment on both a local and global scale.

The first of these projects – *The Dark Forest* – involved a series of explorations into Sherwood Forest and the Mata Atlântica, to investigate how environmental data might be visualized and understood by groups of school children from secondary schools in Nottingham, United Kingdom and Rio de Janeiro, Brazil. This process allowed the artists and the school children to learn about the forests on their doorsteps, by capturing the scientific data (temperature, humidity, decibels, atmospheric pressure, light and carbon dioxide levels) alongside their own 'felt' experiences of being in the forests (McCarthy & Wright, 2005). They then used Internet technologies (an educational social media website and blogs) to exchange this information with each other, in order to learn about another forest on the other side of the world.

This first schools exchange took place between Djanogly City Academy, a state secondary school based in Nottingham (UK) with a specialism in technology. The school is situated in a modern purpose built building on the edge of a community recreation ground, once the border between the city of Nottingham and Sherwood Forest. The school intake covers an area of the city that is multicultural and relatively economically deprived. At the time, every classroom had an interactive whiteboard, each student had access to laptops and secure Internet access was available throughout the building. Yet, in contrast to the amazing technology resources at their disposal, many of the students had never visited their local forest before, rarely took part in activities on the recreation ground across the road, and the school playground had very little plant life.

In contrast to the high-tech, hugely invested structure provided by the secondary education system in Nottingham, an equivalent state funded school in Rio de Janeiro was found to have resistance towards the use of technologies to improve education. At that point in 2009, it was clear there was no established idea of how to make use of a resource that we actually found was already available. A classroom with computers existed in the school behind a locked door, which was rarely if ever used. The Environment Education Nucleus (NEA) based at the Botanical Gardens of Rio de Janeiro elected the school to work with us because of their already close relationship to the school and its proximity to the Mata Atlântica Forest, which forms a large part of the local Jardim Botânico neighbourhood and the school playground, where the children would often encounter monkeys and other forest animals.

The Dark Forest schools exchange relied on an innovative long-distance series of workshops, realized with children at a fundamental point in their education, aged between 12 and 15 years old, with the aim of fostering a combination of digital and environmental participation that represented both the abundance and lack of access across both schools. The aim of this exchange was to combine thinking about our human and natural experiences of our school and forest environments – whilst developing the digital skills to share and communicate these experiences.

The schools exchange took place over six workshops, syncing events and content so that these activities worked in parallel. We took as our starting point a live link-up over a conference call on 7 April 2010, which led to shared activities encompassing observational drawings, collage, stop-frame animation, photography and performance, relating to the data collected and the individual experiences and reflections of the children as they explored the forests. The activities concluded with a series of live performance experiments in the forest, recorded through photographs and animation, shared through the project website and then discussed back in the classrooms. This process in Brazil was led by the artists along-side a digital culture practitioner and a botanist from the Botanical

Gardens who shared from the outset his passion for the Mata Atlântica biosphere, his deep understanding and appreciation of the rich diversity of plants in Brazil and a practice that spans far beyond his highly skilled work as a scientist (an artist and sculptor in his own right). In the United Kingdom, this process was also supported by the forest managers at Sherwood Forest, sharing their knowledge of the ancient oak and birch trees and the biodiversity that thrives off them.

Interpreting Data as Digital Participation

The ongoing challenges for these forms of digital participation lay firstly in how we could communicate the results between Rio de Janeiro and Nottingham over time, space and a language barrier, and secondly how we might make connections between the data and the children's individual and emotional experiences of being in the forest.

The environmental data collected by both the children and artists was stored on a server hub at the University of Nottingham, which then allowed Active Ingredient to develop a wonderfully ludic and abstract interface, that visualized this data from the two distinct forest locations, viewed simultaneously on a screen as shown in Fig. 3.1.

In response to this interface the children were then encouraged to visualize the data themselves, poetically and through a series of physical experiments. One example of how we facilitated this process with the school children in Brazil involved dividing the class into five subgroups,

Figure 3.1 Presenting the artists' data visualizations to school children in the forest in Brazil.

each dedicated to investigating different environmental measurements: light, humidity, temperature, atmospheric pressure and decibels. We then asked the children to design a simple paper origami fortune-teller, as shown in Fig. 3.2, to represent each measurement and consider how to represent these measurements as they changed. The group was then asked to design and play with objects that represented the data. The 'Light' group made a Camera Obscura from a cardboard box and some black card and a ruler. The 'Decibels' group made three rattles filled with different ingredients: beans, rice, salt and a measuring tape. The 'Humidity' group had a bowl with water, a natural sponge and a bracket. 'Atmospheric Pressure' had a bowl with iced water and a thermometer and finally, "Temperature" had a metal bowl with iced water and a thermometer.

The next phase was to introduce important contemporary art references: Dada (Stiles & Selz, 2012), concrete poetry and the neoconcrete movement (Gullar, 1984). We showed the class visual examples of these artistic forms and discussed how they might help us think of interesting ways to visualize scientific data using words, images and our bodies, to explore the other challenge of communicating and sharing our research and artworks with a group of young people who speak a different language.

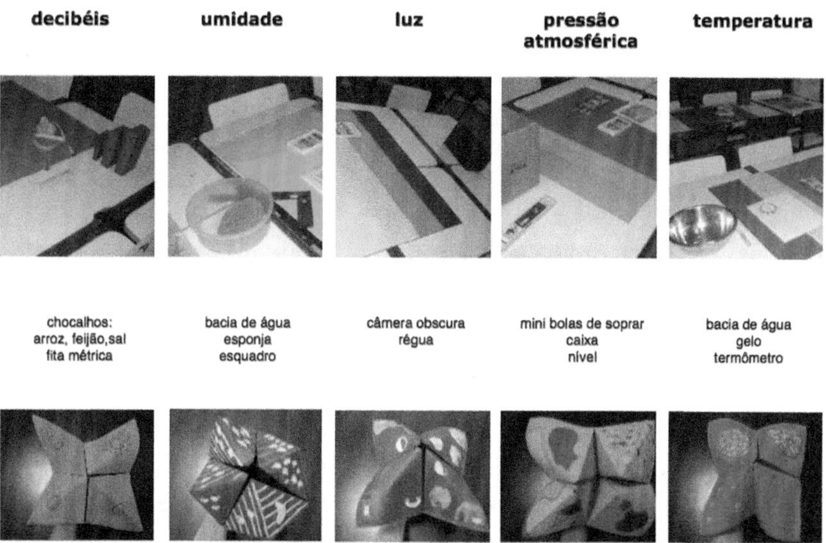

Figure 3.2 Representing environmental measurements using origami fortune-tellers. 'Decibels'=rattles with beans, rice, salt. measuring tape. 'Humidity'=plastic bowl with water, a natural sponge, bracket. 'Light'= camera obscura, ruler. 'Atmospheric Pressure'=mini balloons, cardboard box, level. "Temperature"=bowl, iced water, thermometer.

Finally, borrowed from contributions by the children in Nottingham, the group in Rio de Janeiro were introduced to the process of producing stop-frame animations, to represent the measurements they had captured in the forest with mobile sensors provided by the artists. Using the school's computer lab also allowed our activities to delve into the potential for open-source tools and to encourage the student's learning of computer systems. This enabled us to introduce some of the aesthetic and ethical concerns pertinent to the free-software movement in Brazil. The school's laboratory had been originally installed as a result of the internationally renowned Brazilian public policies implemented between 2003 and 2006, which supported the installation of computer labs in state-run schools around the country. One of the main objectives of this project was to highlight the importance of maintaining a sense of human experience (sensory, visceral and emotional) as the determining ingredient of all our technology interactions (Simondon, 2017).

A Conversation Between Trees followed on from this work. Schools' workshops were conducted with children aged between 4 and 16 in the United Kingdom and Rio de Janeiro. Using similar approaches this project focused on the experience of walking in the forest, and gave participants the opportunity to use the scientific sensor kits to capture temperature, humidity, decibels, light and CO_2 data as they stood underneath trees at various stopping points. The key thread throughout these workshops was an activity that the artists called the 'Human Sensor', a process of opening up the technology and scientific processes through our own physical, emotional and sensory experience of being in a forest.

The 'Human Sensor' involves asking participants to enact being a scientific sensor, recording nonscientific analogue data using their bodies and subjective perceptions of the forest environment. We used this data to compare these individual experiences to the data collected digitally with the scientific sensor kits.

The activity involved:

1. Blinking slowly to capture the light and colour between the branches of the tree canopy, measuring how bright or dark the image captured with your eyes appears from 1 to 10, with 1 being the brightest and 10 the darkest.
2. Measuring the temperature between 1 and 10, with 1 being the coldest and 10 the hottest.

3. Measuring the humidity between 1 and 10, with 1 being dry and 10 being wet/humid; thinking about the effect on your body (sweaty, dry lips, static, wet ground, etc.).
4. Measuring the sound levels between 1 and 10, with 1 being the quietest and 10 the loudest.
5. Measuring the atmospheric pressure between 1 and 10, with 1 being the lowest pressure and 10 the highest. Giving examples of how low pressure can make you feel dizzy (often experienced in high altitudes), high pressure can give people headaches before a storm, sometimes described as the weather being 'close'.

Once the participants had recorded their 'human sensor data' they were invited to visualize their results as 'data maps', creating their own analogue representations – using felt material provided by the artists. Firstly they worked out the percentage for each dataset (e.g., 30% hot), and then worked in groups to decide how to visualize this data using colour, symbols, shape and form. This resulted in each group representing one of the datasets they had captured with colourful, tactile and symbolic visualizations, as shown in Fig. 3.3.

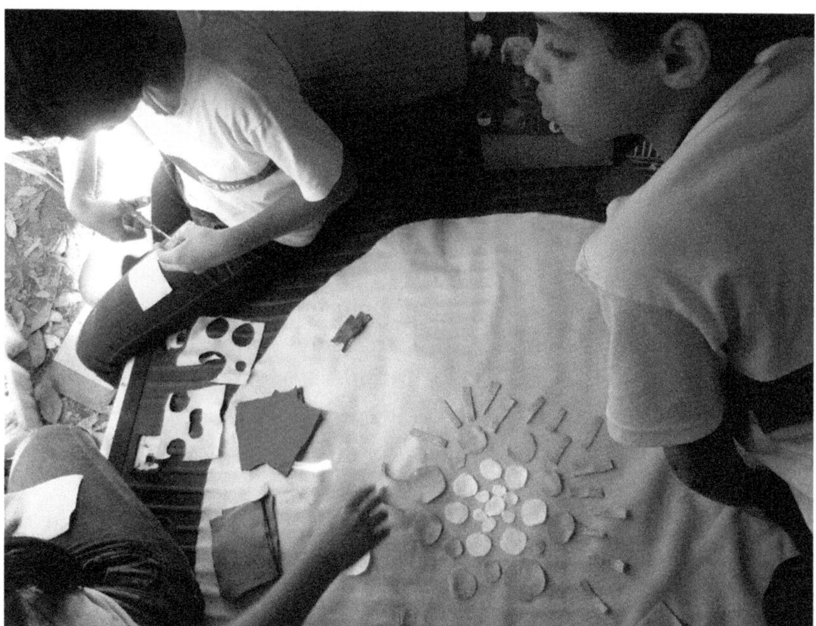

Figure 3.3 School children making data visualizations from felt.

One of the teachers who took part in these workshops described how this process was a rare opportunity to support interdisciplinary thinking and learning amongst the children:

We could have spent a week on that visit alone, with all the links through the maths and the data, the science, the geography. The children were amazed how a piece of technology makes something come alive.

By bringing together analogue and digital processes as a physical and embodied sense of scientific data, we enabled the children to engage directly and emotionally with the technology, developing 'human scale' experiences of how the technology worked, that opened up a process of interdisciplinary learning.

Visitor Participation in the Exhibition of A Conversation Between Trees

The 'human sensor' workshops took place alongside the public exhibition of *A Conversation Between Trees*, touring to forest venues across England. These involved three distinct elements, that each invited visitors into a conversation about the forest where the exhibition took place and the forest on the other side of the Atlantic (the Mata Atlântica) by following clues that pieced together a story of the changes happening across both forests.

Firstly temperature, humidity, CO_2 and decibel data were captured and streamed live from sensors placed in trees in both forests. This data was visualized as abstracted and dynamic images on two large projections that faced each other across the gallery, changing in response to the live data that was being uploaded from the sensors. Juxtaposed between these visualizations sat the *climate machine*, that visualizes recorded and predicted global CO_2 levels by slowly burning circular graphs onto large circular disks of recycled paper, reminiscent of tree rings, with each circular graph representing a year of CO_2 in the atmosphere, as shown in Fig. 3.4. The artists 'performed' the burning of the data on the paper, by working the machine and hanging up each of the disks, that appeared as ever increasing circles, in the gallery space.

An ethnographic study took place to investigate how visitors to the exhibitions engaged and participated with the scientific, technological and artistic processes, using methods of thematic analysis to interpret the 'lived' and 'felt' experiences of the visitors (Jacobs et al., 2013). The study revealed that visitors were able to make connections between themselves

Figure 3.4 The exhibition of *A Conversation Between Trees.*

and the forest environments represented in the work. One of the visitors described how the experience went 'beyond language and cultural references' and somehow tapped into another type of sensory, visual or emotional language, beyond simply processing information, allowing her to imagine being in both forests at the same time. The study also revealed that many of the visitors experienced a strong emotional reaction to the work, through the specific ways technology was used to mediate their experience:

> *... in this instance it wasn't kind of feedback, so you weren't showing people back their emotions, you were kinda maybe showing them something about the trees... what kind of emotional or feeling response you generate from that, that's probably closer to art, but it's art that is using technology, and I think that, that the ambitions for it were artistic but the technology was the medium that you used for that.*
>
> ***Visitor to the exhibition***

One of the key findings was how the scientific data was firstly mediated by the technology and then 'performed' over time, by revealing the slowness of the data through the slow changes in the visualizations of data from each forest and the slow rotation of the scorching mechanism on the climate machine. The 'liveness' of the data being uploaded from both the UK and Brazilian forests (once a minute) also enabled visitors to enjoy going to the tree in the forest outside the gallery, shouting and making noise to change the way the decibel levels were revealed in the visualization. This turned the visitors into artist-participants by allowing them to interact with the sensors in the trees, directly experiencing how their interactions in the forest changed the visualization in the gallery.

Finally visitors could borrow mobile phones from the artists and take part in a digitally mediated walk in the forest, as shown in Fig. 3.5. A mobile phone captured and visualized images of the forest as they walked and displayed the data from the sensors in the trees, the app asked them questions about their sensations of being in the forest – informed by the Human Sensor activity developed during the schools' workshops. Some of the visitors described how this walk in particular pushed them into a new form of sensory engagement with the forest, by placing the technology and data that controlled the exhibition literally in their hands. Through this experience they were able to 'tune in' and focus on details that they might otherwise have missed without the mediation of the technology:

I could hear the sounds more and I could see some of the forest like really clearly, and really it was almost like I'd walked into the forest a bit shut off

Figure 3.5 A digitally mediated forest walk. *From Jacobs, R., Benford, S., Selby, M., Golembewski, M., Price, D., & Giannachi, G. (April 2013). A conversation between trees: what data feels like in the forest. In* Proceedings of the SIGCHI conference on human factors in computing systems *(pp. 129–138). ACM.*

> *really, and in 2D, and when I walked back I was in 3D, like an Avatar. I was walking back, it was quite bonkers, I could see some of the leaves, I just really noticed how amazing the forest was... I had shamefully been tuned out.*
>
> ***Participant in the forest walk in the UK***

Participants who took part in a parallel forest walk in the forest in Brazil appeared to have similar experiences:

> *I thought it was really lovely the moment in which the narrator says that the rules here are different, this raised my expectations. It is interesting to think how little we pay attention to what is around us. I'm more attentive to people than to the natural environment, or even to the city. The environment, which I'd entered through, with the guidance of the narrator, did not differ much from where I was, but I felt a very strong separation. It was more mental than physical.*
>
> ***Participant in the forest walk in Brazil***

In this case, visitors to an exhibition were able to participate in a digitally mediated experience of the forest environment, whilst providing them with the tools and opportunities to emotionally connect to a remote forest on the other side of the world and participate in a dialogue about how our forests (and our world) are changing as CO_2 increases in the atmosphere and temperatures rise.

Technology Research as a Lived Experience

The conditions of the *Relate* project were very different from these previous projects, which had both been artist-led, in contrast *Relate* was research-led. An interdisciplinary team was given the task of exploring how the development of a sensing platform might inform their artistic and participatory practices, in response to the themes of energy and climate change. The researchers then built the platform in response to the artists' needs, considering how it might be presented to other artists, hackers, communities and schools. This project occurred across four phases: (1) through dialogues between members of an artists' collective, a climate scientist and a team of researchers in residence in Nottingham and on a farm in Miguel Perreira in the Mata Atlântica; (2) presenting a showcase and creating collaborations and exhibition at an artist-led studio in the centre of Rio de Janeiro; (3) facilitating a hackday event at Nottingham Hackspace and an exhibition at an artist-led studio in Nottingham and (4) and facilitating a schools exchange that took place in Nottinghamshire and Rio de Janeiro, in this case children aged between 6 and 8 years. The following description focuses on the experience of the artists' residencies in Brazil and how the process of digital participation and artistic responses informed the technical development of the platform.

Upon arrival in Rio de Janeiro's international airport, the group of six researchers were driven directly to Miguel Pereira, a small town 2 hours away from the capital. After a night with our host organization, the group were dropped off at the bus station where they would carry on their journey by foot. The process of monitoring and capturing data began from the moment they began their trek through the forest and fields to reach an isolated farmhouse where they would stay for a week together. A van followed after with everyone's baggage and food supplies, however, the farmhouse was a working farm and had ample produce available to collect and consume. The new element in our research was energy, and how it could be related to an ongoing debate about climate change. Therefore the residency was designed to heighten the group's awareness of their own energy use and consumption throughout their time in the farm. We were all free to investigate the surrounding landscape, use the technologies and more importantly share time together, which resulted in a number of artworks being developed during this relatively short period.

Amongst the possibilities of thinking about energy production and consumption, we installed small mobile solar panels to supply power to the electronic sensors; experimented with different plastic materials placed around the landscape to see how it would change with the weather conditions; documented in photographs, videos and stories the half-farmed, half forested Mata Atlântica environment; and a performance that used the lights in the house to represent the CO_2 data captured by sensors. These were all produced as a result of this short time living intensively together and witnessing each other's independent practices for producing art. On our arrival at the artists' studio back in Rio de Janeiro, we had the opportunity to work with a further six artists and relate what we had produced in Miguel Pereira to the *Timestreams* platform, extending the possibilities that the platform might provoke interest in working with environmental data for the artists. Active Ingredient and the researcher had arrived with *Timestreams* linked up to sensor kits and ready to connect with the practice of these six artists in the artist-led space in Rio de Janeiro, many of whom worked with more traditional visual art practices such as drawing, sculpture and painting. The resulting exhibition in

Rio de Janeiro was open to the public for 7 days, beginning with an opening event with approximately 150 people in attendance. The studios had a shop front looking out to a very busy road in Lapa, which was opened up for the duration of the exhibition. The exhibition showcased sculptures created by two of the artists from the studio in collaboration with the team that involved three colourful inflatable sculptures with fans inside, two of which inflated in reaction to low and medium range decibel levels. The larger sculpture appeared to breathe in response to CO_2 levels captured from the busy street outside, as shown in Fig. 3.6. Other artistic experiments devised by the team at the farmhouse and in collaboration with the artists in Rio de Janeiro were placed around the building.

As with the previous projects an artist-facilitated school exchange took place that built on the human sensor activities from *A Conversation Between Trees*, using scientific sensors and blogs to capture data in both schools. These were shared between the children as part of a process of thinking firstly in an embodied and subjective way about energy and climate, secondly in response to their locality – in terms of their school, their village or area of the city. Finally the school children were encouraged to think globally in terms of the distance between them.

Figure 3.6 The inflatable sculptures at the artist-led studio in Brazil.

The inflatable sculptures, created in Brazil, were presented to the school children in their classroom in the United Kingdom and the children were invited to create their own 'weather machines' in response – designing lightning capture machines, wind machines and one child even designed a planet saving machine. The teacher then used these activities to develop her own parallel work with the children, observing that this process changed the dynamic in the classroom, suggesting that this form of pedagogy which combine sensory, performative and physical approaches was more meaningful to the students that normally struggled with maths, science and technology:

> *There are children who are on our special needs register, a lot of them have remembered a lot of the activities better than some of the other ones.*
>
> ***Teacher participating in the Relate Project***

The Relate project revealed a new set of tensions and opportunities that arose from these forms of digital participation. The process was set up to investigate how a set of research objectives based on developing a new technology system might take place alongside real-world experimentations, revealing a common tension around how the development of technology can intervene with public participation and in turn how artistic processes can hinder the technology development (described by one of the researchers as a 'chicken and egg scenario').

CONCLUSION

The artistic interventions described in this chapter outline an innovative approach to digital participation, that places emphasis on the human side of the human–computer relationship, advocating a practice that focuses on people, places, social relations and the environments we share locally and globally, considered through the lens of a new technical culture.

Traditionally human–computer interaction and digital participation has focused on the relationship of the users to closed technical objects and interfaces, whilst developing methods and frameworks to develop the skills required to access their functionality. In contrast, the practices outlined here involve returning to the body, our senses and the natural environment, using technology to help us navigate our emotional and sensory experience of the world, by placing these experiences at the centre of the development of the technology.

By focusing on schools, through comparative and situated approaches to digital participation, our aim has been to suggest ways in which technology can be appropriated to enable skills development for both students and teachers, through an interdisciplinary approach. We conclude that each of the artistic interventions placed the situated experience first, then introduced the digital, which in turn brought opportunities for mediating our experience of local and global environments. This approach can often have a profound impact on an assembly of unforeseen situations, such as the opportunities to engage children in sensory and visceral learning as opposed to the more traditional approach in schools and particularly technology classes, and the ways in which these processes support both the school children and artists on either side of the world to inform each other's experiences of forest environments.

Poetry and imagination have emerged as a key practice for engaging diverse communities, in this case artists, scientists, researchers, hackers, school children, educators and other members of the public – be they dog walkers in forests or visitors to galleries seeking new artistic visions of the world.

We hope that these approaches contribute to artistic practices being considered in a new light, with artists providing a role that engages people of all ages and different cultural contexts with digitally mediated experiences. The digital participation at the core of this work connects scientific process, artistic practice and lived experience. Yet, at times the technology became a barrier, bringing with it a language and constraints that defied our emotional lived experience, that could only be touched through returning to the forest, sensing the temperature of our skin and the air against our cheeks, listening to the wind in the trees and breathing the air into our lungs.

REFERENCES

Amirsadeghi, H., & Petitgas, C. (Eds.). (2012). *Contemporary art Brazil* London: Thames and Hudson.

Beuys, J., & Harlan, V. (2004). *What is art?: Conversation with Joseph Beuys*. Forest Row: Clairview Books.

Benford, S., Greenhalgh, C., Crabtree, A., Flintham, M., Walker, B., Marshall, J., & Tandavanitj, N. (2013). Performance-led research in the wild. *ACM Transactions on Computer-Human Interaction (TOCHI)*, *20*(3), 14.

Blum, J., Flintham, M., McAuley, D., Jacobs, R., Watkins, M., Lee, R., & Giannachi, G. (2012). *Timestreams: Supporting community engagement in the climate change debate.*

Burke, J. A., Estrin, D., Hansen, M., Parker, A., Ramanathan, N., Reddy, S., & Srivastava, M. B. (2006). *Participatory sensing. Center for Embedded Network Sensing.*

Davis, S. B., Magnus, M., Jacobs, R. W., Riddoch, C., & Cooke, K. (2006). Ere be dragons: heartfelt gaming. *Digital Creativity, 17*(3), 157–162.

De Certeau, M., & Mayol, P. (1998). *The practice of everyday life: Living and cooking* (Vol. 2), University of Minnesota Press.

Ferran, B., & Fonseca, F. (2009). *E-Culture.* <www.sica.nl>. Retrieved from <http://www.sica.nl/sites/default/files/3R_E-Culture.pdf> Accessed 29.03.17.

Ferran, B., & Márcia de N.S., (2008). *O abismo da hospitalidade contemporânea: cidades e migrações.* Observatório Itaú Cultural/OIC – n. 5, (abr/jun), São Paulo (pp. 58–67).

Funarte (2010). *Conexão Artes Visuais* (pp. 78–83). Rio de Janeiro: Ministério da Cultura do Brasil.

Giannachi, G., & Kaye, N. (2011). *Performing presence: Between the live and the simulated.* Manchester: Manchester University Press.

Giannachi, G., & Stewart, N. (2005). *Performing nature: explorations in ecology and the arts.* Bern: Peter Lang.

Gullar, F. (1984). *Vanguarda e subdesenvolvimento: ensaios sobre arte.* Rio de Janeiro: Editora Civilização Brasileira.

Jacobs, R., Benford, S., Selby, M., Golembewski, M., Price, D., & Giannachi, G. (April 2013). A conversation between trees: What data feels like in the forest. In *Proceedings of the SIGCHI conference on human factors in computing systems* (pp. 129–138). ACM.

Latour, B. (2005). *Reassembling the social: An introduction to actor-network-theory.* Oxford: Oxford University Press.

Laurel, B. (2003). *Design research: Methods and perspectives.* Cambridge: MIT Press.

McCarthy, J., & Wright, P. (2004). Technology as experience. *Interactions, 11*(5), 42–43.

McCarthy, J., & Wright, P. (2005). Putting 'felt-life' at the centre of human–computer interaction (HCI). *Cognition, Technology & Work*, 7(4), 262–271.

Pink, S. (2015). *Doing sensory ethnography.* London: Sage.

Rimmer, S., et al. (2009). *Paralelo-unfolding narratives: In art, technology and Environment.* Sao Paulo: MIS.

Rodaway, P. (2002). *Sensuous geographies: Body, sense and place.* Routledge.

Simondon, G. (2017). *On the mode of existence of technical objects.* University of Minnesota Press.

Stiles, K., & Selz, P., Theories and documents of contemporary art: A sourcebook of artists writings (revised and expanded by Kristine Stiles), 2012, University of California Press; Berkeley.

Tuan, Y. F. (1977). *Space and place: The perspective of experience.* Minneapolis: University of Minnesota Press.

FURTHER READING

Chatzichristodoulou, M., & Giannachi, N. (2012). Performing presence: Between the live and the simulated. *New Theatre Quarterly, 28*(2), 207.

Haraway, D. (1988). Situated knowledges: The science question in feminism and the privilege of partial perspective. *Feminist Studies, 14*(3), 575–599.

Haraway, D., & Manifesto, A. C. (2000). *Science, technology, and socialist-feminism in the late twentieth century. The cybercultures reader* (p. 291). New York: Routledge.

CHAPTER 4

Going Digital: Integrating Digital Technologies in Local Community Initiatives

J. Ferreira[1] and N. Pantidi[2]
[1]Cork Institute of Technology, Bishopstown, Cork, Republic of Ireland
[2]University College Cork, Cork, Republic of Ireland

INTRODUCTION

In the current economic climate, social inequality and exclusion have become even more prominent and as a result promoting community resilience is emerging as a key priority at a local and national level (Chandra et al., 2011). Community resilience, as defined by Chenoweth and Stehlik (2001), is 'the ability to respond to crises in ways that strengthen community bonds, resources and the community's capacity to cope'. Adapting and responding to change in our surroundings is therefore an important aspect of resilience; this means that concepts of community resilience go beyond survival to finding new paths of adaptation and growth. In this context, local and national communities across Europe and globally have begun self-organizing in order to cope with deteriorating living conditions and equally have started building their lives around more sustainable ways of being that involve consideration of their local natural environment, small-scale production and consumption (Kent, 2009). There are several examples of such local community initiatives (LCIs) and grassroots movements (e.g., freecycle.org, LETS and Men's Shed). While each of these initiatives may have specific objectives (e.g., decrease 'food miles', unemployment, enable provision of service and goods, and strengthen the local economy), all aim equally to empower the local communities, enable people to reconnect with each other and their surroundings as a means of adapting to and coping with the ongoing adverse conditions triggered by the economic crisis. The emerging communities that grow out of these initiatives with their collective commitments, interests and actions aim to enact political, economic and societal change, develop community resilience, social regeneration and transformation (Kera, Rod, & Peterova, 2013; Shuman, 2013).

Digital Participation through Social Living Labs. DOI: http://dx.doi.org/10.1016/B978-0-08-102059-3.00004-6

As digital technologies are now ubiquitous and readily available in our everyday lives, digital participation is becoming more central for community engagement. Several of these LCIs and grassroots movements start to consider ways to innovate their current practices by harnessing the potential of digital technologies to achieve their aims of community engagement, resilience, social transformation and regeneration. While LCIs use digital media more and more (e.g., the use of online community portals reported by Bell, Budka, & Fiser, 2007), we know very little about the process of decision making that informs the adoption of these technologies, and of the role digital media plays in supporting resilience building and engagement in these communities. As Salemink, Strijker, and Bosworth (2015) put it 'providing the connectivity and technology is just one aspect of keeping up with developments; adoption and actual usage are the next steps that need to be taken in order for digital connectivity to have an impact'. Understanding who these communities are, how they work and what they value can provide insights into the role technology can play in supporting and extending their practices (Pantidi et al., 2015).

This work aims to build on this understanding by drawing on our studies with two such initiatives: the *Bristol Pound*, which seeks social change through changing the money system in a local area, and *iGirls*, addressing intergenerational poverty through educating and empowering teenagers. This chapter sets out the strategies employed and the challenges faced by the members of these two initiatives as digital participation for community engagement was considered, debated and materialized. Our findings show that communities oriented to considerations of how technologies fit with community values, cooperative partnerships inside and outside the community, and maintaining credibility and trust. Based on these findings, we frame technology adoption for LCIs as collective identity work and within this framework we examine the relationship between technology and community engagement and resilience. We suggest areas for future work to improve our understanding of the process of adopting and integrating digital technologies within such settings.

BACKGROUND

Local Community Initiatives and Community Resilience

The ongoing economic turmoil following the global financial crisis has given rise to significant societal shifts in our world and as a response to that, the emergence and visibility of local communities and grassroots movements that aim to mediate adversity and respond to societal needs (by building resilience) across Europe and globally is growing. Examples range from alternative and local currency initiatives (such as the Bristol Pound in the United Kingdom and the TEM in Greece), time-banking (e.g., Talente Taauschkreis Voralberg in Austria) and exchange networks (e.g., freecycle.org and Local Exchange Trading Schemes (LETS)) to initiatives such as food banks, urban farming and men's sheds. What distinguishes these initiatives and communities is their collective, nonprofit, bottom-up response to societal needs. There is a growing interest in the role of LCIs in building community resilience (Cretney, 2013; Seyfang & Haxeltine, 2012). Community resilience encompasses notions of well-being, adaptability and resourcefulness in the face of adverse conditions (Cheshire, Esparcia, & Shucksmith, 2015; Norris, Stevens, Pfefferbaum, Wyche, & Pfefferbaum, 2008). Further, community resilience is fostered when people self-organize, make best use of the existing resources, feel useful and creative, and regain an active role in society by connecting with and helping each other (Chenoweth & Stehlik, 2001; Mark, Al-Ani, & Semaan, 2009).

Until recently, resilience was considered primarily with respect to internal individual characteristics rather than the interactions with others and the environment (e.g., Masten, 1994), however, the emphasis is shifting to how people overcome stress, trauma and other life challenges by drawing on the social and cultural networks and practices that constitute communities (Pfefferbaum, Reissman, Pfefferbaum, Klomp, & Gurwitch, 2005; Rose, 2004). Norris et al. (2008) in their seminal work, which has informed subsequent research regarding factors contributing to community resilience, suggest that communities who demonstrate resilience participate in collective action and experience trust, a sense of belonging, mutual values and solidarity with other members of the community (social identity), and strong voluntary communication networks within and across other similar communities. Several frameworks and metrics have been developed to identify and measure community resilience, e.g., Index of Perceived Community Resiliency (IPCR) (Kulig, Edge, Townshend, Lightfoot, & Reimer, 2013), the Resilience and Well-Being of Small Inland Communities Model (Maybery, Pope, Hodgins, Hichenor, & Shepherd, 2009), the Community and Regional Resilience Initiative (CARRI) model; while these can provide useful insights, they do not address the role of digital technologies within community resilience. This is a significant paucity, especially considering the extent to which technology nowadays has infiltrated our daily lives and more specifically the practices of LCIs.

Digital Technologies for Collective Action

Collective action in LCIs depends to a great extent on building and maintaining social networks that connect individuals with their communities and others who share similar aims and commitments (Pantidi & Ferreira, 2014). Connections are maintained by leveraging various, in some cases mundane, digital technologies (e.g., email, Google Docs, mobile devices, social platforms and open source hardware) for communication and sharing resources (e.g., Canterbury & Hedlund, 2013). Several LCIs have begun to consider and implement technologies that are more tailored to their use by leveraging the smart phone app market (e.g., http://www.nationallandleague.org/). There is great variability in the form of digital technologies that are being used and difference in the levels of technological adoption among these communities. Unpacking the nuances of this variability can help us understand which technologies are better suited to which kinds of communities and their activities, and can in turn inform wider research on the role of digital participation in community engagement and resilience.

Currently the processes around adoption of digital technologies in LCIs are not well documented. The focus has so far been on leveraging digital technologies for collective action and resilience in adverse events such as natural disasters and warfare. Studies show that during and immediately after disaster events people use various combinations of technologies such as blogs, forums and wikis, text messaging, social media and networking sites, mailing lists for informational and coordination purposes (Majchrzak, Jarvenpaa, & Hollingshead, 2007; Palen & Liu, 2007; Procopio & Procopio, 2007; Sutton, Palen, & Shklovski, 2008; Zook, Graham, Shelton, & Gorman, 2010). While such studies show the potential of harnessing digital technologies in adverse one-off events, it is important to start building an empirical understanding of how digital resources and participation can shape the engagement and resilience of a community – not just after one-off shocks, but also under longer term adverse conditions. In particular, there is a paucity of research that investigates the decision-making process of LCIs as they work to innovate their current practices by integrating digital technologies to achieve their goals of social transformation and community resilience. This is in contrast with the large body of literature investigating technology adoption and innovation processes in other contexts such as firms (e.g., Oliviera & Martins, 2011), small-medium enterprises (e.g., Nguyen, 2009), rural enterprises (e.g., Valchovska et al., Unpublished), households (e.g., Turk, Cornacchia, Livi, Papa, & Sapio, 2015), cooperative organizations (e.g., Bruque & Moyano, 2007) and schools (e.g., Billig, Gibson, Sherry, & Tavalin, 2000).

Two studies of LCIs related to our work are that of Erete (2013) and Bell et al. (2007). Erete (2013) developed a framework to support the design of community technologies, however, the framework was based on sociological and urban studies literature and not on in-situ studies of practice as we attempt in this paper. Bell et al. (2007) conducted an ethnographic study of a LCI implementing a locally developed and locally controlled online community portal called MyKnet.org. Bell et al. (2007) describe the emergence and use of MyKnet.org as a social networking technology within in the community despite not being designed as such. This work aims to contribute to a body of knowledge that could grow to inform policymaking. In 'Settings and Research Methods' section, we present the two LCIs (their overall aims, values and context of operation, the digital technologies under consideration) and describe our research methods.

SETTINGS AND RESEARCH METHODS

In this work, we examine two LCIs as they worked to innovate their current practices by integrating digital technologies to achieve their goals of social transformation. The first one is the Bristol Pound, which seeks social change through changing the money system in a local area, and the second one is iGirls, which aims to address intergenerational poverty through educating and empowering teenage girls. Both LCIs were chosen for this inquiry because they provide two examples of LCIs that share agendas of developing resilience, social regeneration and transformation in their respective communities. We present the two initiatives by detailing their overall aims, values and context of operation, the digital technologies in use and under consideration. We follow with a description of our research methods.

iGirls

iGirls is a 12-week programme designed and run by Springboard in Ireland aiming to educate and empower teenage girls who live in areas deeply affected by economic and social adversities over several generations. Such areas experience higher than average social welfare dependency, a higher number of children living in poverty and there are significant number of children at risk of coming into care or facing welfare concerns compared to the overall population.

Springboard

Springboard is a Family and Community Agency that provides family and community support services in two disadvantaged neighbourhoods in the city of Cork. Compared to traditional state services, Springboard is a relatively small agency consisting of five to six people ranging in skills and backgrounds (e.g., clinical and counselling psychologists, social workers). Their services set out to reinforce positive informal social networks and are generally provided to people within their own homes and communities. The primary focus of Springboard and their services is on:

1. integrated care (a holistic approach to care);
2. a *strengths perspective* (Saleebey, 2006b) which emphasizes respect for individual and communities' capacities and recognizes the potential to develop and build on the individual and the communities' resiliency;
3. early intervention aiming to promote and protect the health, well-being and rights of the community with a specific focus on children, young people and their families. As part of their integrative approach to care and their early intervention focus, Springboard has (and continues to) established networks and active collaborations with other agencies in the area.

The iGirls Programme

The specific focus of the programme is on supporting young girls and their mothers towards building their self-esteem — as the official title of the programme suggests: *iGirls — Building a Better Relationship with Myself.*

The programme runs over 12 weeks, with some of those weeks being dedicated to the mothers only (4 weeks), some to the girls only (4 weeks) and some joint (4 weeks). Each session is facilitated by members of Springboard and activities are structured around a specific goal and a set of learning outcomes. For example, for one session the specific aim was that of self-care; the learning outcomes involved that girls and mothers improve on their knowledge around self-care and learn techniques such as meditation and mindfulness that they can use in their everyday lives. The activities of that session included watching videos and engaging in discussion around self-care, participating in group meditation exercises and in drawing and crafts.

In the context of the core values detailed earlier, a key objective of the programme is creating an open, nonjudgemental safe space between the mothers, the girls and the facilitators:

> *Each week there will be no pressure on any mother to talk and participate in anyway. We will make it a comfortable space for a chat, tea, coffee a few munchies. We will use videos and other activities to explore areas that might arise. This will be a cosy, confidential space to meet with other mothers and to discuss the many issues that families have to deal with in these difficult times.*
>
> ***Excerpt from Information letter to mothers***

At the time of the study, the programme was in its very initial stages of conceptualization and planning. A pilot of the programme was implemented with five girls and their mothers without any digital technology being incorporated. Integrating digital technologies and more specifically social media or online blogs was prominent throughout the planning discussions of the pilot phase, but as conversations and concerns continued it was agreed that the technology would be implemented at the second implementation of the programme in 2017.

The Bristol Pound

The Bristol Pound (£B) is a local complementary currency in use in Bristol, England. It was launched by the Bristol Pound CIC (Community Interest Company) in September 2012 and as of September 2016, there were approximately £B1.2 million in circulation and approximately 800 participating businesses. The currency has both paper-based and digital forms. Transactions in £B can be conducted with printed notes, SMS or online via an electronic £B account. While there is no restriction on who can access the printed notes, payments by SMS and online differ from this access model in that they require an electronic £B account. Eligibility to open an electronic account is granted by the Bristol Pound CIC, subject to membership rules which for individuals entail residing or working in Bristol, and for businesses that they are locally owned and operated. Transactions conducted via SMS is called Txt2Pay and supports the exchange of electronic £B. When a member pays another member by sending an SMS text message, the payer requests that the amount in electronic £B be transferred from their account to the payee's £B account.

Aims, Features and Rules of Use

The Bristol Pound's website states the aims of the currency: 'Bristol Pounds stick to Bristol, build community connections and work for people not banks to create fairer, stronger, happier local economy'. For the Bristol Pound members, social change is enacted through implementing and using a different kind of 'money system' outside of the mainstream 'money system', with its own characteristics and rules around its use:

Maintaining circulation: Certain design features of the £B help to keep the currency in circulation and encourage its use. For example, exchanging sterling for £B is free of charge, but £B notes cannot be exchanged back into sterling, there are fees associated with converting electronic £B back into sterling and expiration dates are printed on the notes to encourage spending and guard against hoarding the currency.

Supporting localization: By requiring members to live and work in locations with certain post codes and grant membership based on members producing evidence of that ensures that those who transact in £B do so within a specified geographical area. The slogan 'Love Bristol. Go Local' appears on the Bristol Pound website and other printed material. By implication, those who love Bristol are called on to support the local businesses in the city.

Building cooperative relationships: The Bristol Pound CIC engages in significant efforts to build relationships with entities in Bristol who provide city infrastructure, in order to effectually build more opportunities for spending £B and expanding the £B ecosystem. The most fundamental relationship is the cooperation between the CIC and the Bristol Credit Union (BCU), who maintain the digital infrastructure that enables SMS transactions and provides £B accounts to members. That council tax, utility bills and bus and train fares can now be paid with £B is further evidence of the work the CIC has engaged in with other entities to accept the currency, which the CIC accomplished without the help of institutional or policy requirements.

Accessibility: The Bristol Pound CIC has made deliberate choices to ensure that the currency is usable by as many people as possible within the local bounds. For example, members do not require a particular type of phone or association with a particular mobile phone company to pay by SMS, and anyone who can access the cash points in the city can exchange sterling for £B notes. The most recently added feature of the scheme is BP members' ability to withdraw £B notes from their £B accounts at a cash point – thereby mirroring the cash withdrawal features of the traditional Automatic Teller Machine (ATM).

Research Methods

The methodological approach was ethnographic, involving a combination of participant-observation, individual and group interviews and design workshops. The use of ethnography in this work focused on producing detailed accounts of the situated everyday activities' practices that took place in each setting, detailing how those activities were socially organized, understood and communicated. The ethnographic approach required that the researchers were immersed in the settings and provided access to taken-for-granted behaviours and knowledge about and within the community that could not be gained by simply asking people or studying the literature. The interviews and design workshops were opportunities where the researchers could probe the LCI members about their assumptions and opinions about the use and integration of various technologies, their characteristics and how those technologies might fit with and affect their everyday practices. We were interested in how the members conceived of and articulated what they 'needed' technologically to support them in achieving their aims of social change, in their particular circumstances and how this process of decision making unfolded. Although data was collected independently by the authors, the common themes presented in this work were generated collaboratively between the authors. Through a joint analytic process the ethnographic field notes and transcriptions were iteratively scrutinized for patterns and grouped into themes, as described by Aronson (1995) and Braun and Clarke (2006). The following sections describe the specifics of data collection in each setting:

iGirls

The ethnography with the Springboard team spanned a period of 6 months. During this time the iGirls programme was conceptualized and implemented. In addition to observing the daily activities of the Springboard members, the researcher had access to coordination and planning artefacts, such as documents that were produced by the facilitators and emails exchanged between the researcher and the facilitators. The researcher was not employed as a member of the Springboard team, yet had an active role consulting and contributing to decisions around the content and the delivery of the programme. This provided the researcher with a unique opportunity to gain insight into the facilitators' ideas, feelings, aspirations and concerns about the use of the technology for the purposes of the iGirls programme and their broader aims.

Bristol Pound

The ethnographic investigation of the Bristol Pound spanned a period of 6 months. The currency, along with the Txt2Pay system, had been in use for 1 year at the time the study began. Participant observations and ethnographic interviews were conducted at the offices of the administrative team (the Bristol Pound CIC) and various locations around Bristol where the currency was used. The details of the interviews have been published elsewhere (Ferreira, Perry, & Subramanian, 2015). Two design workshops supplemented the observations and interviews. During both workshops, prototyped payment systems were explored by the participants, who reflected their experiences back to the research team and in so doing enriched our understanding of the issues and considerations around adopting novel technologies. Details of the prototypes have been published elsewhere (Ferreira & Perry, 2014).

FINDINGS

This section sets out the strategies employed and the challenges faced by the members of these two initiatives as they worked to innovate their current practices by integrating digital technologies to achieve their goals of social transformation. The focus of the analysis was on the decision making that ensued in the early stages of the process of technology adoption. The considerations that follow emerged from our analysis and are grounded in the data. Deciding how technology can be integrated in their current practices involved the LCIs considering (1) the appropriateness of technology with respect to their values, (2) ways to ensure that technology underpinned internal cohesion, (3) constraints and possibilities arising from embeddedness and (4) how trust can be sustained.

Considerations of Fit and Compatibility With Values

The LCIs in this study were established, active, value-driven communities. Their organization and actions were defined and motivated according to the sense of their communities' values and during our studies, it became clear how the LCIs navigated decisions of which technologies would be suitable for them by drawing on the values that they believed their communities to uphold. As part of this process, several concerns emerged which made apparent that digital adoption and participation was a contested notion. The usefulness of digital technologies was acknowledged, but at the same time they were equally seen as potentially distracting or clashing with the aims and values of the LCIs.

In the case of the iGirls, facilitators saw significant benefits in using some form of digital technology as part of the programme, given that they were addressing teenagers who they knew were already using smart phones and social media quite heavily. The allure and familiarity of bringing a digital technology into the programme was thought of as a potential way to improve how the girls receive the overall programme. However, facilitators expressed significant concern over how digital technologies, and in particular social media, were in conflict with Springboard's and the programme's core values. The iGirls programme aimed to build on inner strengths and self-appreciation, and digital technologies, especially social media, were thought by the facilitators to be very disparate to the above values and aims, as they encourage self-value based on external approval. Equally, facilitators were aware of social media as a locus of privacy violations and traumatizing experiences for young adolescents (e.g., bullying) which is in sharp contrast with Springboard's core value of providing and sustaining a safe space for its members. As a result, the iGirls facilitators together with the researcher discussed technology options whose features allowed for self-reflection, development of skills and personal growth, while at the same time provided a safe, private space. Given that criteria, a digital blog was considered the most fitting type of technology.

Similar tensions arose during the Bristol Pound design workshops. The researchers suggested to the Bristol Pound team a novel technology which would build a public profile of each member's £B transactions, such that members could track their own and others' local spending. While the Bristol Pound team appreciated that this was a means for members to display their support of the scheme and local businesses, they became concerned over whether making spending visible in this way would inspire a sense of competition among £B users as they compare themselves with others, and encourage a kind of showing off. The Bristol Pound team made clear they would not be supportive of technology that promotes this type of competitive behaviour among members (Ferreira & Perry, 2014).

As the LCIs reflected on their future technology use, it became evident how this could bring potential tensions between technology choices and values into focus. This is clearly illustrated in the case of the Bristol Pound and its Txt2Pay system. While Txt2Pay afforded a certain level of accessibility and ease of use to its members, a participant in the design workshops expressed concern over the ethical implications of using a mobile phone as a payment device. The argument concerned the current drive for consumers to keep up with the latest version of mobile phone and how this contributes to the increasing levels of electronic waste. This was seen as a clash with the environmental sustainability aims of the Bristol Pound initiative. Such tensions highlight the challenges involved for the Bristol Pound in innovating their practices: new payment technologies must compare favourably with existing payment technology, such as credit cards and increasingly popular mobile phone payment systems, but these will be judged by members according to criteria that are shaped by the values of the community.

Building and Sustaining Community Cohesion

Apart from aligning with core values, technology was also considered with respect to community cohesion within the LCIs. The adoption of technologies in both LCIs was considered with regards to their potential in building connections between the members and equally as a means of establishing and mediating membership. In the case of the Bristol Pound, the Txt2Pay system served, apart from its transactional role, as a means of establishing a practical definition of 'local' and hence mediated membership. Previous research of Bristol Pound users found that the Txt2Pay system promoted a strong sense of membership within the community and enabled building community relationships *through the digital transactions themselves* (Ferreira et al., 2015). Given the value placed on social relationships within the community and learning how Txt2Pay was enabling social connectivity, the Bristol Pound team became more aware of and sensitive to preserving the face-to-face interactions of Bristol Pound members during transactions. There was a consensus among the Bristol Pound team that new technologies adopted should not impede face-to-face interaction.

Similarly in the iGirls programme the digital blog was seen to offer an additional interaction and communication space between the three parties (facilitators, mothers and daughters), outside their face-to-face meetings, where conversations that began face-to-face could be continued, and as a result it was hoped that the relationships between them would grow stronger.

In both LCIs membership of the community signalled certain characteristics. Whereas membership of the Bristol Pound community signalled a supportive local, membership of the iGirls signified a situation of risk and, in both cases, this shaped the requirements placed on the future technology and its use. Safeguarding the girls' and mothers' membership in the programme was paramount and the facilitators understood that there would be implications for ownership of and access to the content of the blog that would need to be managed carefully. One aspect considered in this respect was whether viewing access should be provided to others outside the programme (e.g., friends and family of the members). The facilitators could identify both benefits (e.g., sharing and opening) and risks (e.g., bullying and inability to control/limit viewing access to specific nonmembers) by opening up the blog to a wider audience. Another consideration was in regard to the blog involvement and contribution levels between girls and mothers. It was important that the blog was used as a shared space where both girls and mothers felt that they owned the content and could contribute to it, but at the same time the facilitators felt that the girls had to be the primary owners and contributors of the blog due to the educational benefits anticipated. Creating and curating digital content, considering privacy settings and other requirements was regarded as a great learning experience for the girls and an asset to their future personal and professional development and as a result facilitators felt the blog had to be targeted more towards the girls than the mothers.

Maintaining Trust

Both LCIs' work involved confidential information, so maintaining their members' sense of trust was vital and any technological adoption had to be considered in light of that. Both in the case of the Bristol Pound and in the iGirls programme, offline face-to-face practices guided and mediated notions of trust in the technology.

In the iGirls programme, building and maintaining trust with all participants was vital for creating a safe space where everyone would feel comfortable sharing and expressing themselves. If the blog was to be a valuable component of the programme, it should equally ensure and maintain trust and be a safe space where all members could contribute content freely without feeling afraid or judged. The iGirls facilitators were very aware that use of the blog could generate information that, if not handled carefully, could impede trust formation among members.

While the facilitators drew confidence from their extensive clinical and social work experience in creating and maintaining trust in the offline safe space, they were uncertain as to how they could apply this experience to achieve and maintain this online. Their main challenge, as they saw it, was balancing potentially confidential content contributions by the girls against the mothers' viewing of that content. Several ways to address this were discussed, such as providing separate access privileges or separate online spaces for mothers and daughters, but both of these options strayed from or opposed the programme's central values of inclusiveness and communicating openly with one another. The facilitators concluded that the most appropriate way to deal with online confidentiality involved what they referred to as *mirroring offline practices*. This translated to having an open discussion with both mothers and their daughters about the content creation of the blog, where any issues and concerns would be communicated and a joint agreement would be made about how confidential information might be posted and shared (e.g., it could be that some posts remain private initially and shared between mothers and girls at a later stage).

In the case of the Bristol Pound, building and maintaining trust with members was important as financial transactions generate confidential banking data. The Bristol Pound administrators faced a dilemma over whether using members' phone numbers (these were made available to them indirectly through the Txt2Pay system) and contacting them through text messaging would be appropriate. During an interview with a Bristol Pound administrator it was clear that they were unsure how much contact with the members through SMS would be acceptable before members would feel that the contact is inappropriate and potentially breach trust: 'Because the SMS system for payments is a possibility for communicating with the members through SMS. It's difficult to know how much you should be doing. You don't want to be spamming people'.

Technology reliability was another consideration. Bringing in thought-out technologies into the initiative that deal unreliably with confidential data could harm the credibility of the Bristol Pound and people could eventually stop using the currency altogether. Evidence from previous studies indicated that even though the Txt2Pay system had some reliability issues (e.g., transaction confirmations were slow to arrive), the system was reliable enough in other ways to warrant continued use (e.g., balances were updated correctly, confirmation texts did eventually arrive)

(Ferreira et al., 2015). The same study showed how issues of reliability and trust in the Txt2Pay system were moderated through the notion of localness and face-to-face interactions - similar to how reliability and trust were moderated in the iGirls programme by way of offline social protocols.

Negotiating Constraints and Possibilities Arising From Embeddedness

LCI interventions were not taking place in a vacuum and LCIs and their members were very aware of how they were situated within dynamic networks with whom they interact, collaborate or coordinate. Their own understanding of their interdependencies within these networks shaped their considerations of adopting digital technologies and involved negotiating constraints and possibilities in the context of their existing social relations and alliances. This sense of *embeddedness* determined the types of resources the LCIs had access to and introduced possibilities and constraints for the integration of novel digital technologies.

The Bristol Pound team actively worked to establish links between itself and other groups and institutions to create cooperative networks that help it to function as a currency. Since the launch of the currency, the team has worked to build strategic partnerships with the local council, local credit union, transport authorities and utility providers to create more opportunities for spending £B. This association with other entities, with their associated technological infrastructures, simultaneously enables and constrains the options for technological adoption for the Bristol Pound, as new systems will either have to fit with what partners in the network already have, or the adoption process will require a joint negotiation between parties to agree on what the new system will be. The Bristol Pound's cooperation with the BCU illustrates the possibilities and constraints arising from the cooperation; the partnership with the BCU enables the provisioning of online £B accounts and the technology for Txt2Pay. However, due to Txt2Pay being a banking technology, data on account activity is kept private and the BCU only shares this data with the Bristol Pound in an aggregated way, e.g., the outgoing amounts for a month. The Bristol Pound administrators do not know the detailed account data of their members. While this imposes a limitation on the Bristol Pound and how it administers the currency, this situation can also be seen as an opportunity for the Bristol Pound to design alternative ways of accessing Bristol Pound user data, as has been explored in the design workshops with the Bristol Pound team (Ferreira & Perry, 2014).

Similarly, Springboard has established long-term relationships and collaborations with other agencies in the area – schools, voluntary groups and even key individuals in the community – which allow for identifying issues and delivering holistic and timely support to the community members at risk. In the specific context of the iGirls, the programme relied on the facilitators reaching out to other social and mental health services for recruiting appropriate candidates for the programme and for identifying and supporting particular challenges the participants may be facing. This reaching out work was carried out by the facilitators meeting with representatives from the other services face to face or speaking over the phone. This in-person interaction was highly valued by all parties for the interpersonal relationships that was building between individuals and was seen as key to ensuring the successful delivery of the iGirls programme. Therefore a digital component to their outreach work, beyond their existing use of email or phone communications, was not considered desirable at the time but remained an option to be considered in the near future.

DISCUSSION

Based on the findings earlier, we discuss the relationship between identity work and technology adoption in LCIs. In particular, we show that the LCI members engaged in this identity work collectively as they navigated technology adoption considerations. We further discuss the importance of aligning not only socially, but also infrastructurally, with entities outside the communities and the emerging role of digital infrastructure and participation in understanding community resilience. We also propose avenues for future research.

Collective Identity Work and Technology Adoption

Our analysis suggests that the process of considering the adoption of digital technologies by LCIs involved nontrivial collective identity work. By 'collective identity', we mean the attributions of the LCI members to their communities that *place or situate them as social objects* (Snow & Anderson, 1987). In both LCIs studied, members demonstrated that they were able, within a group, to articulate and agree who they were and what values and practices their communities promoted. For example, the iGirls facilitators articulated their concern over adopting social media in their programme by referring to social media's promotion of external approval being in conflict with the values of the iGirls programme that promote self-acceptance. Similarly the Bristol Pound team made clear they would not adopt technologies that promote competitive behaviour among its members. Identity work at the community level shaped the strategies that the LCI members used to collectively assess whether (and which) digital technologies were appropriate.

The ways in which local initiatives and their communities conduct identity work may differ between them. In the discussions regarding whether to adopt digital technologies the notions of 'community values', 'embeddedness', 'cohesion' and 'trust' emerged as the principal sources on which the communities drew to assess the appropriateness of technologies for their communities. Lingel, Naaman, and boyd (2014) reported a similar finding among transnational migrants where identity work 'becomes a means of gauging the efficacy of various technologies in ways that account for the social (as well as purely functional) objectives'. In the present study, LCI members expressed a keen sense that technologies need to fit with and reproduce the values of the community, enhance community cohesion, maintain trust in the initiative and support the ways that members reach out to connect with entities outside the community.

Consistent with studies in organizational settings, such as that by Tripsas (2009), Utesheva, Simpson, and Cecez-Kecmanovic (2016) and Boudreau et al. (2014), the present study found that shared understandings of identity are inextricably part of considerations around technology adoption for LCIs. These studies of organizations have shown how problematic, and potentially disruptive, misalignment between identity and technologies can be for the internal cohesiveness and practices of an organization compromising innovation (Obwegeser & Bauer, 2016) and even long-term survival (Tripsas, 2009). Misalignments between identity and technology could potentially impact on the LCIs in a similar way. In other words, technology adopted to integrate with practices that are aimed at building community resilience, could potentially threaten those very practices, and hence, threaten the community's ability to build resilience. The present study examines LCIs at the point of considering adopting novel technologies – not at the point of implementation or beyond – so it is not possible to say whether novel technologies implemented in these LCIs proved to be disruptive or identity challenging in the way the literature above suggests. However, this could be a useful exploration for future research: how do LCIs address contested notions of digital participation and adapt to disruption introduced by the integration of technologies into their practices?

Extra-Community Infrastructure and Community Resilience

Studies of communities and digital technologies traditionally emphasize social networking through the use of social media. Some examples include how technologies enable/hinder the community's ability for social networking (e.g., Han, Shih, Rosson, & Carroll, 2016), how to better design technologies for social networking (e.g., Foth, Gonzalez, & Kraemer, 2008) or how service delivery to a community can be improved through social media (e.g., Sharif, Troshani, & Davidson, 2014). Our findings show that the LCIs who were in the process of considering adopting digital technology for their communities think beyond the notion of social networking 'within' the community. The activities of the Bristol Pound and Springboard fit with and were shaped by interacting with their wider context, outside of their immediate community networks, as establishing social relations outside of the community was vital for the functioning of the LCIs. In the case of the Bristol Pound these 'extra-community' links with the local council, utility and transport providers, enabled members to use the currency as part of their everyday lives. Even with the best payment technology at the members' disposal, unless they have places to spend their £B, the currency system would not function. Similarly, Springboard relied on their relationships with outside entities to identify those who could most benefit from their programme. These 'extra-community' linkages are a recognized part of building social capital (Widén-Wulff et al., 2008) and building on the community's ability to access and share information and other resources as required.

Our findings have further shown that extra-community links are not limited to social relations – relations were also infrastructural in that the LCIs' considerations around what technologies to adopt required simultaneous considerations about how to connect with infrastructures outside the community, both physically and digitally. Vertesi (2014) highlights how individuals artfully align overlapping and sometimes colliding infrastructures to carry out their work, by drawing on ethnographic studies of planetary scientists. In the same way, LCIs are required to carry out a similar alignment work at the community level, as they deliberate over the desirability of connecting digitally at all and as they explore ways to augment and supplement existing connections. Technological infrastructure and its mediating role in resilience building and community engagement is gaining interest through the notion of 'digital capital', which refers to 'the resources and benefits that can be utilized by communities, from Internet infrastructure to online information, modes of communication and tools, to digital literacy and skills' (Roberts & Townsend, 2015). Further research will be required into the ways communities conduct alignment work of technological infrastructures and how this impacts on their efforts in building community engagement and resilience through digital participation.

CONCLUSION

We described two LCIs – *Bristol Pound* and *iGirls* – that aim to develop community resilience, social regeneration and transformation, and their considerations around digital participation and technology adoption. This early stage in their technology adoption process proved to be an opportunity for careful deliberations over the perceived characteristics of the digital technologies, and over the trade-offs and impacts of its use and nonuse. LCI members expressed a keen sense that technologies need to fit with and reproduce the values of the community, enhance community cohesion, maintain trust in the initiative and support the ways that members reach out to connect with entities outside the community. We consequently framed this process of considering the adoption of digital technologies by LCIs as collective identity work. We proposed that gaining a better understanding of technology adoption in LCIs will require further research into the ongoing identity work in which LCI members collectively renegotiate their conceptions of 'community values', 'embeddedness', 'cohesion', and 'trust' in relation to technology.

Further we highlighted how the LCIs connect with their wider context and that these extra-community connections are not limited to social relations – they also hold implications for how to connect with digital infrastructures outside the community. Further research will be required into the ways communities conduct alignment work of technological infrastructures in order to build digital capital, and how this impacts on their efforts in building community resilience.

REFERENCES

Aronson, J. (1995). A pragmatic view of thematic analysis. *The Qualitative Report*, *2*(1), 1–3. Retrieved from <http://nsuworks.nova.edu/tqr/vol2/iss1/3>.

Bell, B.L., Budka, P., & Fiser, A. (June 2007). We were on the outside looking in. MyKnet.org: A First Nations online social network in Northern Ontario. In *5th CRACIN workshop, Concordia University, Montréal.*

Billig, S. H., Gibson, D., Sherry, L., & Tavalin, F. (2000). New insights on technology adoption in schools. *The Journal*, *27*(7), 42–46.

Boudreau, M. C., Serrano, C., & Larson, K. (2014). IT-driven identity work: Creating a group identity in a digital environment. *Information and Organization*, *24* (1), 1–24.

Braun, V., & Clarke, V. (2006). Using thematic analysis in psychology. *Qualitative Research in Psychology*, *3*(2), 77–101.

Bruque, S., & Moyano, J. (2007). Organisational determinants of information technology adoption and implementation in SMEs: The case of family and cooperative firms. *Technovation*, *27*(5), 241–253.

Canterbury, M., & Hedlund, S. (2013). The potential of community-wide initiatives in the prevention of childhood obesity. *Diabetes Spectrum*, *26*(3), 165–170.

Chandra, A., Acosta, J., Howard, S., Uscher-Pines, L., Williams, M., Yeung, D., ... Meredith, L. S. (2011). *Building community resilience to disasters: A way forward to enhance national health security.* Santa Monica: RAND Corporation.

Chenoweth, L. I., & Stehlik (2001). Building resilient communities: Social work practice and rural Queensland. *Australian Social Work*, *54*(2), 47–54.

Cheshire, L., Esparcia, J., & Shucksmith, M. (2015). Community resilience, social capital and territorial governance. *Ager*, *18*, 7.

Cretney, R. M. (2013). *Ongoing community resilience from the ground up: A relational place based approach to grassroots community resilience (Masters thesis).* Victoria University of Wellington.

Erete, S. L. (2013). Community, group and individual: A framework for designing community technologies. *The Journal of Community Informatics*, *10*(1).

Ferreira, J., & Perry, M. (December 2014). *Building an alternative social currency: Dematerialising and rematerialising digital money across media. Proceedings of HCI Korea* (pp. 122–131). Hanbit Media, Inc.

Ferreira, J., Perry, M., & Subramanian, S. (February 2015). *Spending time with money: From shared values to social connectivity. Proceedings of the 18th ACM conference on computer supported cooperative work & social computing* (pp. 1222–1234). ACM.

Foth, M., Gonzalez, V. M., & Kraemer, K. L. (December 2008). *Design considerations for community portals in master-planned developments in Australia and Mexico. Proceedings of the 20th Australasian conference on computer-human interaction: Designing for habitus and habitat* (pp. 33–40). ACM.

Han, K., Shih, P. C., Rosson, M. B., & Carroll, J. M. (2016). Understanding local community attachment, engagement and social support networks mediated by mobile technology. *Interacting with Computers*, *28*(3), 220–237.

Kent, F. (May 2009). *The upside of a down economy: Going local.* Urban Land.

Kera, D., Rod, J., & Peterova, R. (2013). *Post-apocalyptic citizenship and humanitarian hardware. Nuclear disaster at Fukushima Daiichi: Social, political and environmental issues* (pp. 97–115). New York: Routledge.

Kulig, J., Edge, D., Townshend, I., Lightfoot, N., & Reimer, W. (2013). Community resiliency: Emerging theoretical insights. *Journal of Community Psychology*, *31*(6), 758–775.

Lingel, J., Naaman, M., & boyd, D. M. (2014). *City, self, network: Transnational migrants and online identity work. Proceedings of the 17th ACM conference on computer supported cooperative work & social computing (CSCW '14)* (pp. 1502–1510). New York: ACM.

Majchrzak, A., Jarvenpaa, S., & Hollingshead, A. (2007). Coordinating expertise among emergent groups responding to Disasters.Org. *Science, 18*(1), 147–161.

Mark, G., Al-Ani, B., & Semaan, B. (2009). *Resilience through technology adoption: Merging the old and the new in Iraq. Proceedings of the 27th International Conference on Human Factors in Computing Systems* (pp. 689–698). Boston: ACM.

Masten, A. S. (1994). Resilience in individual development: Successful adaptation despite risk and adversity. In M. Wang, & E. Gordon (Eds.), *Risk and resilience in inner city America: Challenges and prospects* (pp. 3–25). Hillsdale: Erlbaum.

Maybery, D., Pope, R., Hodgins, G., Hichenor, Y., & Shepherd, A. (2009). Resilience and well-being of small inland communities: Community assets as key determinants. *Rural Society, 19*(4), 326–339.

Nguyen, T. H. (2009). Information technology adoption in SMEs: An integrated framework. *International Journal of Entrepreneurial Behavior & Research, 15*(2), 162–186.

Norris, F. H., Stevens, S. P., Pfefferbaum, B., Wyche, K. F., & Pfefferbaum, R. L. (2008). Community resilience as a metaphor, theory, set of capacities, and strategy for disaster readiness. *American Journal of Community Psychology, 41*(1–2), 127–150.

Obwegeser, N., & Bauer, S. (2016). Digital innovation and HCI. In *Lecture Notes in Computer Science (LNCS).*

Oliveira, T., & Martins, M. F. (2011). Literature review of information technology adoption models at firm level. *The Electronic Journal Information Systems Evaluation, 14*(1), 110–121.

Palen, L., & Liu, S. B. (2007). *Citizen communications in crisis: Anticipating a future of ICT-supported public participation. Proceedings of the SIGCHI conference on human factors in computing systems.* New York: ACM Press.

Pantidi, N., & Ferreira, J. (2014). What can HCI do for local currencies? In *Workshop paper presented at #CHImoney: Financial interactions, digital cash, capital exchange and mobile money as part of CHI '14, Toronto, Canada.*

Pantidi, N., Ferreira, J., Balestrini, M., Perry, M., Marshall, P., & McCarthy, J. (2015). *Connected sustainability: Connecting sustainability-driven, grass-roots communities through technology. Proceedings of the 7th international conference on communities and technologies* (pp. 161–163). ACM.

Pfefferbaum, B., Reissman, D., Pfefferbaum, R., Klomp, R., & Gurwitch, R. (2005). Building resilience to mass trauma events. In L. Doll, S. Bonzo, J. Mercy, & D. Sleet (Eds.), *Handbook on injury and violence prevention interventions.* New York: Kluwer, Academic Publishers.

Procopio, C. H., & Procopio, S. T. (2007). Do you know what it means to Miss New Orleans? Internet communication, geographic community, and social capital in crisis. *Journal of Applied Communication Research, 35*(1), 67–87.

Roberts, E., & Townsend, L. (2015). The contribution of the creative economy to the resilience of rural communities: Exploring cultural and digital capital. *Sociologia Ruralis, 56*(2), 197–219.

Rose, A. (2004). Defining and measuring economic resilience to disasters. *Disaster Prevention and Management, 13*, 307–314.

Saleebey, D. (2006b). The strengths approach to practice. In D. Saleebey (Ed.), *The strengths perspective in social work practice* (pp. 77–92). Boston: Pearson Education, Inc.

Salemink, K., Strijker, D., & Bosworth, G. (2015). Rural development in the digital age: A systematic literature review on unequal ICT availability, adoption, and use in rural areas. *Journal of Rural Studies*, In press.

Seyfang, G., & Haxeltine, A. (2012). Growing grassroots innovations: Exploring the role of community-based initiatives in governing sustainable energy transitions. *Environment and Planning C: Government and Policy, 30*(3), 381–400.

Sharif, M.H.M., Troshani, I., & Davidson, R. (2014). Adoption of social media services: The case of local government. In *Handbook of research on demand-driven web services: Theory, technologies, and applications* Information Science Reference (An imprint of IGI Global), Hershey, PA, United States of America (pp. 287–303).

Shuman, M. (2013). *Going local: Creating self-reliant communities in a global age*. New York: Routledge.

Snow, D. A., & Anderson, L. (1987). Identity work among the homeless: The verbal construction and avowal of personal identities. *American Journal of Sociology, 92*, 1336–1371.

Sutton, J., Palen, L., & Shklovski, I. (2008). Backchannels on the front lines: Emergent use of social media in the 2007 Southern California fire. In *Proceedings of information systems for crisis response and management conference (ISCRAM), Washington DC*.

Turk, T., Cornacchia, M., Livi, S., Papa, F., & Sapio, B. (2015). Households technology adoption and use patterns: The case of digital terrestrial television in six Italian regions. *Technology Analysis & Strategic Management*. Available from http://dx.doi.org/10.1080/09537325.2015.1071788.

Tripsas, M. (2009). Technology, identity, and inertia through the lens of "The Digital Photography Company". *Organization Science, 20*(2), 441–460.

Utesheva, A., Simpson, J., & Cecez-Kecmanovic, D. (2016). Identity metamorphoses in digital disruption: A relational theory of identity. *European Journal of Information Systems, 25*, 344. Available from http://dx.doi.org/10.1057/ejis.2015.19.

Valchovska, S., Chamberlain, A., Crabtree, A., Greenhalgh, C., Davies, M., Glover, K., & Rodden, T. (Unpublished). Rural enterprise as an agent for technology development and facilitation in the digital economy. In DE 2013: Open Digital, 4–6 Nov 2013, Salford, UK.

Vertesi, J. (2014). Seamful spaces: Heterogeneous infrastructures in interaction. *Science, Technology & Human Values*, 0162243913516012.

Widén-Wulff, G., Ek, S., Ginman, M., Perttilä, R., Södergård, P., & Tötterman, A. K. (2008). Information behaviour meets social capital: A conceptual model. *Journal of Information Science, 34*(3), 346–355.

Zook, M., Graham, M., Shelton, T., & Gorman, S. (2010). Volunteered geographic information and crowdsourcing disaster relief: A case study of the Haitian earthquake. *World Medical & Health Policy, 2*(2), 7–33.

CHAPTER 5

The School as a Living Lab – The Case of Kaospilot

Christer Windeløv-Lidzélius
Kaospilot Business and Design School, Aarhus, Denmark

INTRODUCTION

Entrepreneurship is a central theme in many countries wishing to secure growth and prosperity. No parties in Denmark, for instance, are against it as a priority, even though the policymaking for improving entrepreneurial conditions differs. As such entrepreneurship and entrepreneurship education have been central themes for policymakers, schools and educators on all levels.

Entrepreneurial education policies and practices rest upon one fundamental assumption that entrepreneurship can be taught and learnt. It is implicit that if students are taught entrepreneurship, they will automatically become entrepreneurial (Kirketerp, 2010). Yet what is to be learnt varies. For instance, Kirby (2004) suggests that:

> *The successful entrepreneur has a set of personal skills that goes beyond the purely commercial. It is these attributes, this way of thinking and behaving, which needs to be developed in students if their entrepreneurial capabilities are to be enhanced and they are to be equipped to meet the challenges of the entrepreneurial climate of the twenty-first century (p. 514).*

Douglas and Shepherd (2002) suggest that business educators (indeed nations in general) will add more value to their graduates by incorporating into their curricula components that augment the development of entrepreneurial attitudes, since these are advantageous to self-employment as well as employment.

Many thought leaders and researchers have pointed out that traditional ways of educating in universities are ill-suited for entrepreneurship education. For instance, Chia (1996) says that:

> *Business Schools, because of their focus on a discipline-based educational curriculum that mirrors the research interests and aspirations of academics themselves, and because this in turn reinforces the intellectual priorities of academia, unwillingly propagate a thought style and a mental attitude that*

Digital Participation through Social Living Labs. DOI: http://dx.doi.org/10.1016/B978-0-08-102059-3.00005-8

> *pays far too much regard to conventional academic priorities of analytical rigor at the expense of a loss of imagination and resourcefulness in dealing with practical concerns (p. 410).*

Cantor (1997) sees experiential learning as a necessary component of formal instruction in colleges and universities, and Mueller (2012) asks the question: 'If learning is based on knowledge from lived experiences, how can university students, who do not possess entrepreneurship experience, learn to be entrepreneurial?' (p. 4).

After researching Kaospilot, Krull and Broberg (2010) suggest that 'action learning and a design approach to learning, combined with an appreciative feedback culture, can create a generative learning space that supports the development of leadership competencies needed to build and lead businesses which seize the opportunity to become corporate citizens'.

This chapter is structured as follows. The concept of the 'living lab' is explored first, to provide a lens within which to understand the Kaospilot case. Here a few key elements are identified that are later used to discuss the findings. The following sections concern Kaospilot, starting with a brief history of the school followed by a description of the scope and range of the school today. Hereafter a deeper dive into the educational philosophy and pedagogy is presented together with a profile of the programme and its aspirations. The challenges facing the school are discussed before the paper ends with a reflection on the school's particularism and universality in relation to inspiring higher education's pursuit of social entrepreneurship and leadership training.

LIVING LAB

There have been numerous attempts to define what a living lab is (Franz, Tausz, & Thiel, 2015; Nielsen & Nielsen, 2011). However, the literature does not agree on any one definition (Følstad, 2008). Some see living labs as innovation platforms where the partners involved develop and exchange ideas in a community. Others consider living labs as test beds, special physical environments where companies and R&D partners are invited to test prototypes with users in a close-to-real-world setting.

According to Dutilleul, Birrer, and Mensink (2010), living labs are quite a new construct, their origin often attributed to MIT Professor William J. Mitchell and his observation of new possibilities in moving innovation research from 'in vitro' to 'in vivo', as a consequence of improvements in computing power and IT development. Følstad (2008) says, 'Living Labs are environments for involving users in innovation and development, and are regarded as a way of meeting the innovation challenges faced by information and communication technology (ICT) service providers' (p. 99). He goes on to say that living labs are also used in fields other than ICT. Leminen, Westerlund, and Nyström (2012) state that living labs take experimentation out of companies' R&D departments to real-life environments.

A living lab usually involves the cocreation and adoption of innovations by users, often in a hybrid online and offline community setting, and also involving business stakeholders (Ballon & Schuuman, 2015). One emerging trend is to see living labs as a way of tapping into the creative potential of users where users and user communities engage in cocreation activities (Følstad & Karahasanović, 2012). Another trend is to regard living labs as environments that enable context research and cocreation activities (Følstad, 2009).

As such it can be argued that living labs are a research concept where one can observe innovation (meaning how users utilize, take advantage of and 'innovate' on given technologies). On the other hand one can move away from the notion of a living lab as a 'test bed' and consider it to be more of a platform for innovation where partners (i.e., members of a community) develop and exchange ideas.

Two key aspects that are often implied are: user-driven innovation (Von Hippel, 1986, 2006) and open innovation (Chesbrough, 2003a, 2003b; Chesbrough, Vanhaverbeke, & West, 2008). One questionable claim is to what extent living labs are 'user-driven'. Does it mean that the user is in 'charge' or just the key for 'progress'? A single user cannot possess all the skills, knowledge and power required to coordinate the resources, processes and stakeholders required for an effective innovation process (Dutilleul et al., 2010). Expanding on Winthereik, Malmborg, and Andersen (2009), participants' uniqueness should not be forgotten, since they have different needs and life situations, as well as individual conceptions of context. As such, a living lab is also an alternative reality negotiated by the participants and interpreted by the researchers.

When looking at schools (i.e., higher education) as living labs, it is useful to understand what characterizes this type of living lab. Leminen et al. (2012) suggest four different types of living labs with respect to the actor driving the network's operation and innovation activities and where the purpose, value-creation logic, and outcomes differ between the four

Figure 5.1 Admission workshop. *Kaospilot.*

types. A school seems to be best suited as a provider-driven living lab. Here the open-innovation network organizes itself around the provider(s). The aim is to promote research and theory development, augmenting knowledge creation and finding solutions to specific problems. The authors state that much of the innovation is about creating value for everyone in the network in the form of information and knowledge.

In this chapter, the school as a living lab is proposed and the potential of using the living lab methodology as an approach to understanding schools as open platforms and how to improve their effectiveness (i.e., using the least amount of resources to obtain the desired outcome) is discussed, using Kaospilot as a case study. Two key notions from the living lab methodology – cocreation and context (Følstad, 2008) – serve as the central concepts for analysing participation for realizing one's own and others' potential and getting the most out of what the school has to offer (Fig. 5.1).

METHODOLOGY

Given the particular role and tenure of the author at the Kaospilot institution, it is important to discuss this in order to understand his bias and preconceptions. Christer Windeløv-Lidzélius (CWL) was introduced to

Kaospilot as a student (1995–98). The school at that time was still young, and much has changed since then. After graduation CWL was connected to the school in terms of lecturing and assessing exam work. In 2001 he was hired to develop a new curriculum together with the then head of studies. In 2005 CWL joined the staff as head of its internationalization activities. In 2006 he became the CEO, and in 2007 he also became the principal of the school. He has maintained the dual role of CEO and principal ever since.

As such CWL has for many years not only been intimately connected to the school, he has also been instrumental in shaping it – on both a strategic level as well as on an operational level. This means that the author is hardly neutral in his observations and analyses. On the other hand his indepth knowledge of the case provides a fairly unique position from which to offer perspectives and reflections on Kaospilot.

This study is framed as a case study of the Kaospilot school, explored through the lens of living labs. The notion of living labs constitutes very much a qualitative approach and as such it is well situated to use data that are chiefly qualitative. The data is based on the author's own experiences and observations and take a sideways approach to reflective practice (Schön, 1995). The data also includes other materials, such as publications, reports, surveys, reports, statistics, internal reports and the Kaospilot website.

KAOSPILOT

Despite its small size, Kaospilot is a nationally and internationally well-known institution. It has been regarded as a front-runner of alternative education – 'alternative' in the sense of not being an accredited programme and not being part of a larger academic institution as well as its unorthodox approaches to education. Surprisingly, though, not much has been published yet by the school and its staff in academic papers. In many ways the main sources for learning about Kaospilot are interviews in public media, as well as different presentations and curricula available online – and of course the projects done by staff, student and alumni.

Nonetheless, there are some publications worth mentioning. Some official evaluations have taken place over the years, for instance, Langager (1994), who evaluated the programme very much in the context of an experiment as it was seen at the time; Deichman-Sørensen (1997) on qualities in the education in terms of its novel orientation and those by the Danish Evaluation Centre (1998, 2000, 2002). The Danish Evaluation

Centre conducted an additional evaluation in 2004 to assess Kaospilot from the standard criteria of accredited professional bachelor programmes within business. Three PhDs used Kaospilot as a distinctive case, if not their only case study: Kirketerp (2010) on pedagogy and didactics in entrepreneurship education; Mueller (2012) on entrepreneurial learning and Krull (2013) on the value of design thinking to social enterprises. A few academic articles have been published as well: Christensen and Kirketerp (2006) on how Kaospilot form their pedagogical concepts of teaching entrepreneurship and enterprise behaviour; Kirketerp (2011) on enterprising didactics; Krull and Windeløv-Lidzélius (2009) on social entrepreneurs challenges and potentials and Krull and Brobjerg (2010) on how action learning and a design approach combined with an appreciative feedback culture can create a generative learning space that supports the development of leadership competencies needed to build and lead businesses that seize opportunities to become corporate citizens.

In addition, there have been a few books written on Kaospilot, two by founder and first principal Elbæk (1998, 2003) and one by second principal Windeløv-Lidzélius & Bauning (2011). Elbæk also wrote a book about his life (2010), which offers perspectives on the school and his thinking around it.

A Brief History

Kaospilot (or Kaospiloterne as it is often called in Denmark) was initiated by two autodidacts (Uffe Elbæk and Thomas Heide) with no prior training or educational background relating to established institutions (Christensen & Kirketerp, 2006). Elbæk founded the school in 1991 and became its first principal. Kaospilot did not come out of nowhere. It grew out of the *Frontrunners* (http://www.frontloberne.dk) environment, which was (and to some extent still is) a municipality-supported initiative with the twofold aim of providing youth with something meaningful to do, and combating youth unemployment. In the 1980s, the Frontrunners mostly engaged in cultural and social projects, but towards the end of the 1980s and the beginning of the 1990s ideas around enterprising initiatives started to emerge. This resulted in numerous smaller companies and initiatives being established, for instance, the magazine *Agenda*, the multimedia company *Mousehouse*, the cycle courier company *Cykelbudene*, a club called *Klub Kronstad* and the event/entertainment company *Café Kølbert*. When the idea of the Kaospilot was conceptualized, it was with the intention of doing something new. Elbæk and Heide wanted to educate 'action-oriented people who can seek out and utilize new knowledge, understand changing needs from users and shift the public/private system to the changing cultural, social and economical realities which are becoming dominant in the massive conversion process taking place in Denmark and Europe' (Heide & Elbæk, 1990).

Based on their experiences from the Frontrunners, an education programme in project management with a focus on – but not necessarily limited to – the cultural sector was launched. On 5 August 1991 the school opened its doors to its first cohort of students (Elbæk, 1998). The goal was to offer a programme that the founders themselves would like to have gone through or 'I would have attended in order to be professionally equipped to meet the challenges I face today' (Elbæk, 1998).

The school quickly gained attention from the public, media and organizations – primarily in Denmark but also throughout Scandinavia and in some places in Europe. The school was very Danish in its first years, with students and staff from Denmark, but quickly it gained students from other Scandinavian countries.

The school was seen as the 'ugly duckling' among established institutions founded on traditional academic traditions (Christensen & Kirketerp, 2006), but became popular within the business and public communities. This could be explained not only by the quality of the graduates and their projects (Deichmann-Sørensen, 1997; Langager, 1994; Windeløv-Lidzélius & Bauning, 2011), but also by the school's surprising creativity, its ability to provide challenging reality checks and the action-oriented learning environment (Christensen & Kirketerp, 2006).

Today, Kaospilot has evolved into an internationally well-known and highly respected institution (Christensen & Kirketerp, 2006). It has been recognized by BusinessWeek (2007) as one of the best design schools in the world, and Fast Company (Kamenentz, 2011) has named it in its Startup Leagues Big 10 – 'preparing you for the fast moving startup economy'. It has been featured in *Ode Magazine* (Visscher, 2005), *Monocle* (Fredriksson, Gocheva, & Hall, 2013), *El Pais* (Menárgues, 2016) and many other publications.

A Brief Status Report

Today, the school has graduated around 800 students from its 3-year programme. More than a third define themselves and pursue careers as entrepreneurs (and out of these around 40% are female); around 50% hold a leadership position, and they work primarily in the private sector (Windeløv-Lidzélius & Bauning, 2011; Danish Evaluation Centre, 2014).

However, the school is more than its 3-year programme. In addition, it offers shorter programmes in the fields of leadership development, educational transformation, cocreation and related fields. The school runs a coworking space for the creative industries of Aarhus, which serves several objectives: to give students access to the industry within the walls of the school and give them a chance to earn money on other projects and find mentors and collaborators. In addition, it is also the school's way of supporting the creative sector in the city and the region. The school also offers consultancy services to essentially all types of organizations in need of the Kaospilot's expertise.

Finally, Kaospilot serves as a cultural and social vehicle in the city of Aarhus by providing space for different types of events (for instance, open lectures), by supporting different types of activities (like festivals), and last but not least by hosting social events such as parties. More than anything, these types of activities are part of building community and engagement – but they also offer ample opportunities for students to train competencies and build networks.

Programme

Kaospilot offers more than one programme, but is mostly recognized for the 3-year programme 'Enterprising Leadership'. Even though the other programmes and offerings are cut from the same cloth, they are not discussed here.

In the school's curriculum (cf. kaospilot.dk), the mission of the programme is:

> *to develop motivated and talented leaders who are committed to realizing their visions and values, while developing abilities, attitudes and knowledge to make a positive difference in the world. The program is committed to and radically in service of the students cultivating a sense of personal agency and possibility to make a meaningful contribution in the 21st century. (From 2016/17 a new curriculum will be implemented. In 2019 it will have fully replaced the old one.)*

Kaospilot is an interdisciplinary approach to creating entrepreneurs, leaders, ideas and growth. It combines elements, traditions and methodologies from business school (b-school) and design school (d-school) thinking (Windeløv-Lidzélius & Bauning, 2011). From here it draws mainly upon the fields of project management, organizational development, entrepreneurship, experience design and design thinking. It is based on the notion of humanism (for instance, Von Wright, 1989), situational leadership (for instance, Hersey & Blanchard, 1977) and positive psychology (for instance, Seligman & Csikszentmihalyi, 2000). The training aspect of the programme focuses on self-efficacy (Bandura, 1997), resilience and mental toughness.

Throughout the programme, the students work only on real projects. This means that the projects have a client (or that the students develop their own idea into a project and find clients and/or stakeholders) with an expressed interest in the execution and the outcome of the project. It also implies that there is not a predefined outcome or a given road map to use per se. Theory is mixed with practice and reflection. There is also a mix of project types (i.e., social, cultural or more business oriented), and there is a mix of individual and group projects.

The goal is very much that when students graduate, they do not only have knowledge about specific things, but they can also accomplish things, i.e., they have certain know-how and a portfolio to show for it. They have developed a network that they can tap into when venturing into their future (Fig. 5.2).

Figure 5.2 Students from Team 20. *Kaospilot.*

Philosophy

Kaospilot as an alternative business and design school has its roots in activism, Bauhaus, the cooperative movement, beatnik culture and folk tradition (Elbæk, 1998, 2003; Monocle, 2014). In addition, the school is also created on the shoulders of a rich school tradition in Denmark, influenced by Christian humanists like Kierkegaard (for an introduction, see https://en.wikipedia.org/wiki/Soren_Kierkegaard) and Grundtvig (for an introduction, see https://en.wikipedia.org/wiki/N._F._S._Grundtvig). Grundtvig also inspired the cultural policy of 'folkeoplysning' (or popular enlightenment) and the folk high school (for an introduction, see https://en.wikipedia.org/wiki/Folk_high_school) movement that was a consequence and a companion of societal changes towards a more democratic society. Here education was seen as the basic tool for development. The Kaospilot school thus has an ethos around growth – professional and personal – generating positive societal change (Elbæk, 2003; Windeløv-Lidzélius & Bauning, 2011) that follows the ideas of Danish school traditions. As stated on the school's website:

> *The mission is to be the best school for the benefit of the world. We want to grow an extraordinary school in which people love to learn and love to create. We want to make a place and a space in which creative people become creative leaders, and where ideas, dreams and values become reality.*

One example of how this approach unfolds can be found in the principle of the 'win-win-win'. This means that when students engage in projects, they need to get something out of it – primarily learning. However, their client or stakeholders also need to obtain something, not merely to be in the service of students' learning. Finally, society at large needs to benefit as well. Of course, the societal 'win' may be difficult to prove, but it is important that the student actively relate to it.

The school has some fundamental beliefs that guide the work that takes place (Elbæk, 2004; Windeløv-Lidzélius & Bauning, 2011):

- *Playful*: We strive to make it motivating, creative and constructive to be at the Kaospilot.
- *Reality-based*: We strive to work with real problems, real people and real needs – because the real world needs real learning, and real learning needs the real world.
- *Streetwise*: We strive to keep in touch with what is happening at street level in society, and to possess the wisdom and know-how to manoeuvre in the worlds of both culture and business.

- *Risk-taking*: We strive to be brave, to step forward, to experiment and to challenge our own fears.
- *Balanced*: We strive for cohesion, coherence, and dynamic interplay between content and form, the individual and the community, the local and the global, praxis and theory.
- *Compassionate*: We strive to alleviate the suffering of other people.

The educational approach takes its root in this philosophy, and the values and aspiration are well integrated into the school's everyday operations (Christensen & Kirketerp, 2006).

Pedagogy

Just as the 3-year programme outlines an orientation of projects, process, business and leadership as knowledge and know-how domains, the pedagogical approach is a combination of different methods and ideas to achieve the stated learning objectives. The specific pedagogical and didactical approach may vary given the specifics of what is to be learnt, but there are some overarching ideas and methodologies rooted in the traditions of praxis and reflection: action learning as rooted in Revans (1983), reflective practice (Schön, 1995) and its notion of 'reflection-in-action' and 'reflection-on-action'; Kolb (1984) around experimental learning and the transformation of information into knowledge and Argyris and Schön (1978) around double-loop learning. Looking specifically at entrepreneurial training, there is a clear leaning towards what Sarasvathy (2001, 2008) would label effectuation logic as opposed to causation logic. The latter is a classic component of many MBA programmes where one starts with the goal and develops plans accordingly, while the former starts with three questions: 'Who am I?', 'What can I do?' and 'Who do I know?' As such, the goal is to a larger extent decided by the means at hand.

By combining the two orientations, learning – within an educational system like Kaospilot – emerges as a combination of sense*making* (Weick, Sutcliffe, & Obstfeld, 2005), 'where the on-going retrospective development of plausible futures images that rationalize what people are doing', and sense*giving* (Gioia & Chittipeddi, 1991, p. 442):

> *... 'sensemaking' has to do with meaning construction and reconstruction by the involved parties as they attempted to develop a meaningful framework for understanding the nature of the intended strategic change. 'Sensegiving' is concerned with the process of attempting to influence the sense making and meaning construction of others toward a preferred definition of organizational reality.*

So while sensegiving can be seen as the explicit as well as nonexplicit motives and ways in which learning can be influenced, in the complex process of sensemaking the actual learning is difficult to foresee and guarantee. It is often more valuable to have a reflective approach where the expressed and recognized learning emerges as a 'negotiated reality' (Gergen, 2009).

The school states four pillars for its pedagogical approach (kaospilot.dk):

1. *Experimental*: In conjunction with the choice of projects and methods, most of the teaching is intended to be experimental, like a research-oriented laboratory. The aim is not only to acquire and transfer existing knowledge, but also to develop new knowledge and new perspectives.
2. *Explorative*: Our approach is goal-directed and rooted in reality. All of our programmes explore current and potential trends within their fields of study. At the same time, students and participants are encouraged and supported to find their own fields of interest, imagine their own desired futures and values, and test theories and methods to achieve that change.
3. *Experiential*: Learning primarily comes from first-hand experience, and the active participation of students is central. Learning is supported and enhanced by reflection on these experiences. Practice within real-time environments encourages not only an increasing level of aptitude, but also a new understanding of the world.
4. *Enterprising*: An enterprising approach empowers students and participants by taking the individual as a starting point and developing a learning environment in which they can move themselves towards new learning, rather than be directed as such. Our programmes and culture are strong on imagination and initiative, and encourage our students and participants to show the same qualities.

An example illuminating the pedagogical approach is a graduation project from a few years ago. Two students (Andreas Lemche and Jesper Krogh Kjeldsen) had made a decision to do their graduation project together. They did not know exactly what they wanted to do, but they knew they wanted it to have social impact. They went through several ideas and iterations around a social phone company, a company to utilize publicly owned cars for advertisement to generate money for social good, a new street coffee company and so on. All of them were discarded for several reasons. Eventually they settled upon creating a tab-water company (Postevand, http://postevand.com) whose products were to be sold in cartons. Given their particular choice of water and packaging, they placed themselves in a more socially and environmentally position than their competitors. With their particular branding and marketing, they have essentially taken on a cause with the end game of limiting the usage of bottled water in general and also making themselves redundant since they promote themselves as only the second best option, only to be purchased if one has to buy water. Here we can see where the school's stated pedagogical pillars come alive and are accentuated by the work of the students. Lemche and Kjeldsen tested out several ideas around social value creation (experimentation), they explored what would make sense to them and where they could find a win-win-win, their work was experiential since they were part of it (they learnt from first-hand participation and creation), and it was enterprising since they created new means based on previous experiences and in an imaginative way they created new value.

Even if social entrepreneurship is not a prerequisite for all projects at Kaospilot, it is very much an aspiration for the participants. The pedagogical platform is an approach to helping people combine their 'inner' drive with external opportunities to do social (and financial) good (as defined partly by themselves). The pedagogical platform can also be seen as part of an 'operating system' for a school as a living lab. The information and knowledge created is shared either directly between the participants or through the school as an intermediate. Here one can argue that the quality of the sharing and what is shared determines the experienced value of a particular living lab (Fig. 5.3).

Figure 5.3 Admission workshop. *Kaospilot.*

DISCUSSION

The school has been assessed several times by neutral parties (Danish Evaluation Centre, 1998, 2000, 2002, 2014; Deichman-Sørensen, 1997; Langager, 1994), and has also conducted its own reviews and evaluations (for instance, Windeløv-Lidzélius & Bauning, 2011). Even though these assessments have differed in scope and range, they collectively provide a consistent message on the employability and job creational capabilities of the school's graduates. Deichman-Sørensen (1997) showed that the number of people who have started a business is more than 50%. Windeløv-Lidzélius and Bauning (2011) concluded that more than 33% saw themselves as entrepreneurs or were running a business, and more than 50% of the school's alumni hold some sort of leadership position, meaning they have personal responsibility for at least one other person. As such the school can be considered highly successful in terms of the number of graduates starting their own business and the number of graduates taking key positions in established organizations as change agents or creative staff members (Rind Christensen & Kirketerp, 2006).

Asking how the school obtains its results yields many answers. It is not easy to claim that it simply selects people who are enterprising. This is certainly one factor, but it is hardly the whole truth. The school's value-system, culture and pedagogical approach are also important factors. However, these also need to be matched in daily life by clear practices. Examples of these from the school are: that it only works with real clients and real assignments (i.e., no case studies); and that one is assessed not on what has been learnt but on what has been achieved through what the students have created (i.e., for the client or in their own developed project where they then have obtained stakeholders). The school also clearly has the ambition that it is team-based – meaning that students together make up a group of people who work together on projects and who are jointly committed to helping each other to learn and develop.

Følstad (2008) suggested two important notions: context and cocreation. Cocreation can be understood in different ways. Franz et al. (2015) state that it is not possible to foresee whether a phase of cocreation can be achieved, because it is based on an explorative environment. However, one can also adopt a less 'result-driven' approach and merely look at it as participation (Følstad, 2009) either through the collection of user feedback in response to given ideas or design suggestions or as participatory ideation and design activities.

According to the Merriam-Webster Dictionary (http://www.merriam-webster.com/dictionary/context), context can be understood as 'the words that are used with a certain word or phrase and that help to explain its meaning' or 'the situation in which something happens: the group of conditions that exist where and when something happens'. Taking a social constructionist approach where meaning is created in between people (Gergen, 2009), context and cocreation become social-relational. Following the findings of Leminen et al. (2012), it is clear that the network around Kaospilot organizes around the school. What unites the network is the pursuit of delivering an education that helps its students achieve its learning objectives. It should be noted though that there are outcomes that are not part of the school's core business per se, but that could be argued to be motivational for the participants and seen as beneficial by the school. For instance, that the participants get a chance to improve their practice and theory and that they develop relationships with other participants. As such value-creation takes place for the different participants on a joint level as well as on an individual level. This balance is crucial for obtaining commitment and flexibility from the different providers at Kaospilot – particularly since the faculty is small (and is more oriented towards designing and facilitating learning than teaching per se) and relies upon others to provide teaching.

At Kaospilot, generating 'research and theory developing' (Leminen et al., 2012) is not exactly how one would describe the explicit aim of the network's operation (see above), but it is true that it can be argued to be the outcome of the network's joint work. Reflective action is the key research methodology used by the staff when learning from operations in order to improve their work. A direct outcome of this is that participants are exchanged for different reasons and/or often change what their contribution is to the school. This is done based on feedback on their previous delivery and by adapting to the expressed situation of where the students are at this time around. This is crucial for providing the best opportunity for learning. In the words of Dutilleul et al. (2010), 'The innovative potential of Living Labs is based on new social configurations for organising innovation'.

According to Vanhaverbeke, Cloodt, and Van de Vrande (2007), it is their absorptive capacity that explains why some organizations are better than others to create and capture value from in-sourcing externally developed technology and technological collaboration with partners. Absorptive capacity can be understood as the ability to assimilate and replicate new knowledge (Vanhaverbeke, Cloodt, & Van de Vrande, 2007), which again can be seen as key to generating new ideas and motivation. On the one hand the value system, where the new and the pursuit of the new is considered good and important, there is a natural orientation towards trying things out. On the other hand, the shadow side of this is that sometimes one runs the risk of not going indepth or really utilizing the potential of a given technology, person and so on. The pedagogical approach also supports this kind of behaviour, but it has an additional effect: assimilation and replication does not present the desired endpoint at Kaospilot. Typically, replication is less desired than innovation in the sense that the individual and system do something new and valuable with what is being taken in. Similarly with the notion of assimilation: given the idea that people should grow and change during their education, there is a strong emphasis on expressing the learning and change, and doing something with what is being offered.

Kaospilot does not offer an accredited programme, which allows its structure, content and means of delivery to be less fixed. That does not mean that it is not rigorous and ambitious, but that it is just more flexible and adaptable. Since the students choose their projects, it becomes a highly student-centred and student-driven education. This also makes it more difficult to replicate, since most other education programmes are restricted. Probably the biggest challenge, however, lies in its orientation towards how one educates someone for something. Schools often teach and emphasize learning *about* entrepreneurship (for instance); the Kaospilot way is to offer experiences and opportunities to *act entrepreneurially*. Even if others do this, it is often not as encompassing or as explicitly demanded.

On a macrolevel, this study shows that it is certainly possible to utilize the concept of the living lab in schools. As a framework it can help us understand what schools also could be and how they could evolve their methodology in terms of making them more user-centred (i.e., student-centred). This would actually be a way to counter some of the more dominant complaints one hears consistently when it comes to higher education: lack of engagement (students), perceived value for money (students) and curricula that are out of touch with market needs. Of course this is largely a generalization, but it is based on what one hears over and over again. By shifting focus to more student-centred and student-driven education, where faculty becomes more like colearners and facilitators, it should be possible to do so.

On a local level, the notion of the living lab can be helpful for Kaospilot to bridge some of the persisting challenges the school faces, to fully communicate what it is and how it differs from other schools. Not just in terms of what is being taught and learnt, but also in terms of how it is done. A school that in its educational philosophy and pedagogy, as well as in its structure and culture, is a learning experience can be difficult to deconstruct and analyse in individualized parts. Here the concept of the living lab can offer a 'condensed' understanding, a terminology that offers an immediate, rudimentary understanding of 'what it is'.

CONCLUSION

In terms of higher education one can argue that on the one hand schools already do operate as living labs – at least to some extent in the sense that they operate with the world outside the school and that they conduct research on their students (although more often evaluations in terms of performance and sometimes of climate and well-being in the school). As students progress into master level and more so PhD level, faculty and students from time to time conduct research together.

It can be argued that Kaospilot is a unique school. Using Kaospilot as a representation on schools as living labs is too limited. There is a multitude of educational setups that may appear similar on an overall level, but on a more practical level are quite different. A suggested area for future research would be to develop a typology of different educational setups and distinguish some key parameters: for instance, the number of participants, nature of engagement and so on. It could be helpful for schools in general to understand how to better include, for instance, stakeholders wanting to test out technology, as well as how to actually go about being an innovation platform for its participants.

A distinctive feature of the concept of the living lab is to include users and communities of users – not just as something to be observed and researched, but also as actors cocreating the value of the living lab. Applied to higher education this notion challenges some stereotypes, as well as offers an opportunity to reconsider and reframe higher education. Students also become comakers of their education. To what extent this orientation would enable education to better meet its challenges is also a question that it would be valuable to obtain perspectives on.

REFERENCES

Argyris, C., & Schön, D.A. (1996) [1978]. *Organizational learning: A theory of action perspective.* Addison-Wesley OD series. 1. Reading, MA: Addison-Wesley.

Ballon, P., & Schuuman, D. (2015). Living labs: Concepts, tools and cases. *info, 17*(4).

Bandura, A. (1997). *Self-efficacy: The exercise of control.* New York: Freeman.

BusinessWeek. Second Annual BusinessWeek Survey, October 4, 2007. Copyright 2000–2008, The McGraw-Hill Companies. All rights reserved. Retrieved October 30, 2016 Retrieved from <http://www.collegexpress.com/lists/list/the-top-design-colleges/147/>.

Cantor, J. A. (1997). *Experiential learning in higher education: Linking classroom and community.* ERIC Digest. ED404948, ERIC Clearinghouse on Higher Education Washington DC.

Chesbrough, H. W. (2003a). *Open innovation: The new imperative for creating and profiting from technology.* Boston: Harvard Business School Press.

Chesbrough, H. W. (2003b). The era of open innovation. *MIT Sloan Management Review, 44*(3), 35–41.

Chesbrough, H., Vanhaverbeke, W., & West, J. (Eds.), (2008). *Open innovation: Researching a new paradigm* Oxford: Oxford University Press.

Chia, R. (1996). Teaching paradigm shifting in management education: University business schools and the entrepreneurial imagination. *Journal of Management Studies, 33*, 409–428.

Christensen, P.R., & Kirketerp, A. (2006). *Entrepreneurial action in shaping education for entrepreneurship: The case of the KaosPilots International.* NCGE Working Paper. 052/2006.

Danish Evaluation Centre (1998). *Kaospilotuddannelsen.* EVA. Retrieved from <http://www.evc.dk>.

Danish Evaluation Centre (2000). *En foreløbig evaluering af Kaospilotuddannelsen.* EVA. Retrieved from <http://www.evc.dk>.

Danish Evaluation Centre (2002). *EVA's vurdering af uddannelses opfølgning.* EVA. Retrieved from <http://www.evc.dk>.

Danish Evaluation Centre (2014). *Ækvivalensvurdering af Kaospiloterne.* EVA. Retrieved from <http://www.evc.dk>.

Deichmann-Sørensen, T. (1997). KaosPiloterne i Tidens Tendenser, Arbeidsforskningsinstituttet Oslo, can be bought at AKADEMINA, Møllergt. 17, 0179 Oslo, Norway.

Douglas, E. J., & Shepherd, D. A. (2002). Self-employment as a career choice: Attitudes, entrepreneurial intentions, and utility maximization. *Entrepreneurial Theory and Practice, 26*(3), 81–90.

Dutilleul, B., Birrer, F. A. J., & Mensink, W. (2010). Unpacking European living labs: Analysing innovation's social dimensions. *Central European Journal of Public Policy, 4*(1), 60–85.

Elbæk, U. (1998). Kaospilot. EN personlig beretning om en skole, en uddannelse og et miljø. Forlaget Klim.

Elbæk, U. (Ed.), (2003). KaosPilot A-Z. KaosCommunication.

Elbæk, U. (2004). *The KaosPilots. Where creativity & innovation go to school.* KaosCommunication.

Elbæk, U. (2010). *Ledelse på kanten.* Gyldendahl.

Følstad, A. (2008). Living labs for innovation and development of information and communication technology: A literature review. *Electronic Journal of Organizational Virtualness, 10*, 99–131.

Følstad, A., (2009). Co-creation through user feedback in an online living lab: A case example. In S. Budweg, S. Draxler, S. Lohmann, A. Rashid, & G. Stevens (Eds.), *International Reports on Socio-Informatics (IRSI), open design spaces supporting user innovation proceedings of the international workshop on Open Design Spaces (ODS'09)*, 6(2) (pp. 43–55).

Følstad, A., & Karahasanovic, A. (2012). *Online applications for user involvement in living lab innovation processes. Proceedings of e-Society 2012* (pp. 257–264). IADIS Press.

Franz, Y., Tausz, K., & Thiel, S.-K. (December 2015). *Contextuality and co-creation matter: A qualitative case study comparison of living lab concepts in urban research.* Technology Innovation Management Review.

Fredriksson, A., Gocheva, N., & Hall, K. (2013). Changing times. *Monocle*, 7(66), 119–121.

Gergen, K. J. (2009). *An invitation to social construction* (2nd ed.). Thousand Oaks: Sage Publications.

Gioia, D. A., & Chittipeddi, K. (1991). Sensemaking and sensegiving in strategic change initiation. *Strategic Management Journal*, *12*(6), 433–448.

Heide, T., & Elbæk, U. (1990). *Kaospiloterne—et udddannelsesforsøg.* Presented by the Frontrunners. Internal document at Kaospilot.

Hersey, P., & Blanchard, K. H. (1977). *Management of organizational behavior . Utilizing human resources* (3rd ed.). New Jersey: Prentice Hall.

Kamenentz, A. (2011). *General assembly provides entrepreneurial skills to a chosen few.* Fast Company. October 30, 2016, Retrieved from <https://www.fastcompany.com/1793488/general-assembly-provides-entrepreneurial-skills-chosen-few>.

Kirby, D. A. (2004). Entrepreneurship education: Can business schools meet the challenge? *Education + Training*, *46*(8/9), 510–519.

Kirketerp, A. L. (2010). *Pedagogy and didactics in entrepreneurship education in higher education from an enterprising perspective (Ph.D. thesis at IDEA).* Syddansk Universitets forlag, (in Danish).

Kirketerp, A. L. (2011). Enterprising didactics—Skub metoden. In A. L. Kirketerp, & L. Greve (Eds.), *Entreprenørskabsundervisning.* Aarhus: Aarhus universitetsforlag.

Kolb, D. A. (1984). *Experiential learning.* Englewood Cliffs: Prentice Hall.

Krull, P. (2013). *The contribution of design thinking to the value creation of social enterprises.* Aarhus: Aarhus University, (in Danish).

Krull, P., & Broberg, T. (2010). Where creativity and innovation go to school: A case study of the KaosPilot school of leadership and social entrepreneurship. *Journal of Corporate Citizenship (JCC), autumn*, 57–86.

Krull, P., & Windeløv-Lidzélius, C. (2009). *Kaospiloterne—deres potentialer og udfordringer.* GEM-antologien, September 2009 (in Danish).

Langager, S. (1994). Evaluering af KaosPiloterne — (parts 1 + 2). Can be bought at the Institute for Psychology and Special Pedagogy at "Danmarks Lærerhøjskole" (in Danish).

Leminen, S., Westerlund, M., & Nyström, A.-G. (September 2012). *Living labs as open-innovation networks.* Technology Innovation Management Review.

Menárgues, A.T. (April 18, 2016). Universidades disruptivas, así se enseña fuera de lo convencional. El País. October 30, 2016, Retrieved from <http://economia.elpais.com/economia/2016/04/15/actualidad/1460734714_976766.html>.

Monocle (2014). *The Monocle guide to good business.* Berlin: Die Gestalten Verlag.

Mueller, S. (2012). *The mature learner: Understanding entrepreneurial learning processes of university students from a social constructivist perspective (Ph.D. thesis).* Robert Gordon University.

Nielsen, J. S., & Nielsen, P. (2011). *Living labs: A user-oriented approach to public—private innovation networks, organisational learning, knowledge and capabilities* (pp. 12–14). UK: Hull.

Revans, R. (1983). Action learning: Its terms and character. *Management Decision Journal*, *21*(1), 39–50.

Rind Christensen, P. & Kirketerp, A. (2006). Entrepreneurial Action in Shaping Education for Entrepreneurship: The Case of the KaosPilots International. National Council for Graduate Entrepreneurship. Working Paper 052/2006. Can be accessed from: http://www.ncge.org.uk/communities/index.php.

Sarasvathy, S. D. (2001). Causation and effectuation: Toward a theoretical shift from economic inevitability to entrepreneurial contingency. *Academy of Management Review*, *26*(2), 243–263.

Sarasvathy, S. D. (2008). *Effectuation: Elements of entrepreneurial expertise*. Cheltenham: Edward Elgar.

Schön, D. A. (1995). *Reflective practitioner: How professionals think in action* (2nd ed.). Arena: Aldershot.

Seligman, M. E. P., & Csikszentmihalyi, M. (2000). Positive psychology: An introduction. *American Psychologist, 55*(1), 5–14.

Vanhaverbeke, W., Cloodt, M., Van de Vrande, V., (2007). "Connecting absorptive capacity and open innovation", 28th October 2007. Can be found at: https://pdfs.semanticscholar.org/c7cb/6e95ee4a5a9ad853f1dbca549ed2bdfb5534.pdf.

Visscher, M. (2005). Most unusual college in the world. *Ode Magazine, October 2005*. 30th October 2016, Retrieved from <https://web.archive.org/web/20071019211033/http://www.odemagazine.com/doc/27/most_unusual_college_in_the_world>.

Von Hippel, E. (1986). Lead users: A source of novel product concepts. *Management Science, 32*(7), 791–805.

Von Hippel, E. (2006). *Democratizing innovation*. Cambridge: MIT Press.

Von Wright, G. H. (1989). *Philosophy of Georg Henrik von Wright*. US: Open Court Publishing Co.

Weick, K. E., Sutcliffe, K. M., & Obstfeld, D. (2005). Organizing and the process of sensemaking. *Organization Science, 16*(4), 409–421.

Windeløv-Lidzélius, C., & Bauning, K. (2011). *20/20*. Aarhus: Turbine forlag.

Winthereik, J. C. T., Malmborg, L., & Andersen, T. B. (2009). Living labs as a methodological approach to universal access in senior design. In C. Stephanidis (Ed.), *Universal access in HCI, Part I, HCII 2009, LNCS 5614* (pp. 174–183). Berlin and Heidelberg: Springer-Verlag.

FURTHER READING

American Psychological Association. (2014). *10 Ways to build resilience. From "The road to resilience"*. American Psychological Association. Retrieved from <http://www.apa.org/helpcenter/road-resilience.aspx>.

Danish Evaluation Centre (2004). *Vurdering af fagligt indhold og niveau*. EVA. Retrieved from <http://www.evc.dk>.

Leonard, H. S., & Marquardt, M. J. (2010). The evidence for the effectiveness of action learning. *Action learning: Research and Practice*, 7(2), 121–136.

Weick, K. E. (1987). *Sensemaking in organizations*. Thousand Oaks: Sage.

CHAPTER 6

Mixhaus: Dissolving Boundaries With a Community Makerspace

Marcus Foth, Ally Lankester and Hilary Hughes
Queensland University of Technology, Brisbane, QLD, Australia

INTRODUCTION

Access to information and communication technology (ICT), the Internet and digital devices may be necessary, but access on its own is not sufficient to tackle digital divide issues and engender social inclusion in society (Notley & Foth, 2008). Gurstein (2003) suggests that 'effective use' of ICT is a more encompassing goal to aspire to, and it requires two further challenges to be tackled: digital literacy and digital participation. The former has long been embraced as part of the new remit of libraries and librarians who have quickly recognized the need to shift their professional rationale towards knowledge brokers and digital literacy educators. As a result, a significant portion of digital literacy skills training is being offered by libraries. However, the next question around digital participation is less about technical skills and more about the way community members can make effective use of ICT for themselves as well as in connection with others.

In this chapter, we present a study that is part of a larger program of research focussed specifically on fostering digital participation through social living labs in regional and rural communities of Queensland in Australia (Dezuanni, Foth, Mallan, & Hughes, 2016). The geographic focus on regional communities stems from both the Australian Government and the Queensland Government's expectation that their sizeable investment in the provision of a National Broadband Network will contribute towards economic development for regional prosperity. Our study sought to untangle some of the relationships between the availability of high-speed broadband Internet access, digital participation through living labs, the current local and national focus on economic renewal through innovation, startups and entrepreneurship, and the impact – potential or real – on regional communities.

Digital Participation through Social Living Labs. DOI: http://dx.doi.org/10.1016/B978-0-08-102059-3.00006-X

Another element that has prominently entered the discussions relating to digital participation is the maker movement (Gauntlett, 2011). With the rise of ubiquitous technology, physical computing and tangible/wearable devices as well as the declining cost for 3D printers and computer numerical control (CNC) laser cutters, the ability to manipulate not just digital bits but physical atoms has started to be within reach of lay people. This domain previously mostly limited to the use by engineers and architects is now seeing an entire movement follow in the pursuit of making objects, digital fabrication, DIY/DIWO (Do It Yourself/Do It With Others) projects and new business and manufacturing models (Anderson, 2012; Caldwell & Foth, 2014). These hybrid activities that combine both physical and digital fabrication tools and techniques happen in so-called makerspaces and FabLabs (www.fabfoundation.org).

In a local pilot project, the research team accompanied and provided financial and research support for a community-led initiative to set up the 'Mixhaus' – a mobile makerspace in Townsville, North Queensland (Fig. 6.1). A disused shipping container was purchased from the local port, renovated and transformed into a makerspace fitted with equipment to allow for fabrication, electronics and physical computing workshops and 'hacking' activities. Guided by a participatory action research (PAR)

Figure 6.1 Mixhaus open for activity in the centre of Townsville.

approach (Hearn, Tacchi, Foth, & Lennie, 2009), we sought to produce a twofold outcome:

1. For the local and regional community: Establish the technical and human resources as well as a governance framework for operating and maintaining the Mixhaus.
2. For the researchers: Collect data that documents the living lab setup process and allows us to evaluate the impact of the Mixhaus on digital participation in the local community and the learning processes and outcomes for fostering future community-led and digital participation initiatives.

In the following, we review related literature to introduce key concepts that are applied to the analysis for this chapter. We then present our participatory action research (PAR) methodology and describe the case study site. The discussion section is informed by a key observation we made in the analysis of our data, i.e., the ability of the Mixhaus as a local community makerspace to act both as a social living lab and as a 'boundary object' (Star & Griesemer, 1989). Beyond the qualities of the physical artefact itself, the Mixhaus contributed to dissolving and mixing boundaries across four dimensions: organizational, social, disciplinary, and spatial.

COMMUNITY SPACES AND PARTNERSHIPS

In this section, we will recap key scholarly contributions around two main concepts that this chapter is concerned with: (1) the changing notion of community space in light of both technology innovation and new technological user practices over time, and (2) different forms of community partnerships that bring about local action and change, specifically with regards to our main interest in fostering digital participation.

First, let us look at community spaces. When the Internet first saw widespread adoption beyond the original military and educational usages, the focus was predominantly on telework, distance education and e-commerce. These extended usages led Cairncross to radically proclaim the 'Death of Distance' (1997). However, there were some scholars interested in the impact these new possibilities would afford local communities. This line of inquiry and thought was first referred to as 'virtual communities' or 'online communities', but later the interest in local- or place-based communities grew, too. Some of the pioneers and thought leaders of this scholarship were Rheingold (1994, 2002), Schuler (1996), Preece (2000),

Gurstein (2000). Walmsley (2000) argued that 'cyberspace might have annihilated distance but not place' (p. 17). Wellman (2001) introduced the term 'networked individualism' to describe the emerging social phenomenon enabled by the Internet, i.e., shifting from door-to-door and place-to-place relationships to person-to-person and role-to-role relationships. Hampton and Wellman (2002) drew on the longitudinal *Netville* study to analyse the relationship between the Internet's global communication affordances and the local neighbourhood community. Around the same time, similar studies were carried out that further corroborated their findings (Arnold, Gibbs, & Wright, 2003; Foth & Hearn, 2007).

Fast forward to today, and the notion of a hybrid space is well established, replacing the old online/offline dichotomy that separated the digital world of cyberspace from the physical, 'real' world (Gordon, de Souza, & Silva, 2011). The significance of place never disappeared, but it changed. From the early accounts of telecentres (Amariles, Paz, Russell, & Johnson, 2007), we now see an array of community spaces and living labs unfold for meeting up, hacking, making and coworking; libraries have played a vital part in championing these activities (Bilandzic & Foth, 2013, 2017; Houghton, Miller, & Foth, 2014). This was also the case in our study with the local libraries playing a key support role in this project. It is in this context that we are interested in the Mixhaus as a community-led, mobile makerspace that provides a physical conduit through which digital participation initiatives are being led and run.

Second, we acknowledge that the term 'community' requires unpacking. On the one hand, it is often used as a convenient umbrella term, and in respect to the Mixhaus initiative it could be assumed to be inclusive of the local community as a whole. On the other hand, we concede that this 'community-led' initiative is in fact not led by the entire community on equal terms, but by specific people, groups and organizations from within the wider community on different terms. This in turn begs the question of the types and nature of community partnerships and governance models at play in the Mixhaus initiative.

Action research lends itself to engendering a balance between research interests and community interests, and with that comes various reasons for employing a participatory approach (Reason, 1998). Borrowing from Gurstein's notion of 'effective use' (2003), the goal is to also build effective partnerships between community stakeholders and organizations (Foth & Adkins, 2006). For win/win outcomes to be achieved, the goals and desires of each participant have to be taken into consideration. In the case of a digital participation initiative such as the Mixhaus, the breadth of aims and concerns is wide including artistic and creative needs, educational outcomes, commercial interests, sociocultural differences and interpersonal difficulties. Mar and Anderson's (2010) report of a partnership between arts institutions, businesses and communities in regional Sydney is relevant to our case, as the complexity of stakeholder interests appears similar. They adopted what they refer to as a '3C' partnership model led by arts partnership broker Jock McQueenie bringing together Community, Culture and Commerce (cf. jockmcqueenie.squarespace.com).

In our analysis of the way that the Mixhaus was initiated, we draw on 'boundary objects' as a conceptual framework (Star & Griesemer, 1989). In both sociology and design research, this notion has proven useful to explore interactions across different community and stakeholder groups.

> *Boundary objects are objects which are both plastic enough to adapt to local needs and constraints of the several parties employing them, yet robust enough to maintain a common identity across sites. They are weakly structured in common use, and become strongly structured in individual-site use. They may be abstract or concrete. They have different meanings in different social worlds but their structure is common enough to more than one world to make them recognizable, a means of translation. The creation and management of boundary objects is key in developing and maintaining coherence across intersecting social worlds.*
>
> ***Star and Griesemer (1989, p. 393)***

Considering the diverse and sometimes even diverging interests at stake across the relevant partnerships, we were curious to find a key quality and ability in the Mixhaus initiative to cross, mix and dissolve boundaries that we will discuss further. The original translational quality between amateurs and professionals as described by Star and Griesemer has been appropriated to the context of communities of practice by Wenger (1998) – amongst others – who recognized the ability of boundary objects to bring communities together and in doing so, enabling different community members and groups to collaborate on a shared venture.

Yet, while the object itself may be a conduit or catalyst for the community to come together, it does not automatically dissipate any potential inequities or dissonance with regards to voice, agency, agendas and power relationships inherent in the diversity of the local community (Foth, 2006a). Studies that employed the notion of boundary object without considering the underlying social repercussions have received negative reviews (Huvila, 2011; Kimble, Grenier, & Goglio-Primard, 2010). In response to this, we complemented our study's data analysis by mapping the communicative ecology of the local community (Foth & Hearn, 2007; Hearn & Foth, 2007) – see Chapter 8, Mapping a Connected Learning Ecology to Foster Digital Participation in Regional Communities.

RESEARCH APPROACH

The Mixhaus initiative is part of a program exploring and fostering digital participation in regional and rural Australian communities through social living labs (Dezuanni, Foth, Mallan, Hughes, & Allan, 2014). As discussed in Chapter 1, Social Living Labs for Digital Participation and Connected Learning, the research team views social living labs as community-led spaces that provide the contextual environment for researchers to work collaboratively with community members to identify particular digital participation needs, and then implement initiatives to build digital capabilities and community efficacy (Carroll & Reese, 2003). Mixhaus is a social living lab initiative seen as both context and participatory process that engenders connected, experiential and 'ideally' transformative learning.

We adopted a PAR approach with a view to stimulating community engagement in the initiative and gain multiple perspectives (Foth & Brynskov, 2016). In keeping with the spirit of social living labs, we felt that PAR was a useful choice for our project, because:

> *Action research is a democratic and participative orientation to knowledge creation. It brings together action and reflection, theory and practice, in the pursuit of practical solutions to issues of pressing concern. Action research is a pragmatic co-creation of knowing with, not on, people.*
>
> **Bradbury (2015, p. 1)**

PAR is commonly used to create knowledge that seeks to address complex problems by producing positive social impact through practical and emancipatory outcomes. It is used in education (Atweh, Kemmis, & Weeks, 2002) to explore transformative outcomes of the kind intended through participation in Mixhaus. Context bound, PAR addresses real life problems, and treats diverse experiences within a community as an opportunity to enrich the research process (Kindon, Pain, & Kesby, 2007).

Action research, that involved different data collection methods at different stages, was used to generate knowledge and collaborative actions through participants and researchers collaborating and learning together in cycles (Carr & Kemmis, 2003; Kindon et al., 2007). Action research was integrated into the project in order to maximize the learning and outcomes of the project while it was carried out, rather than as an evaluation at the end. PAR typically involves a series of iterative cycles, with four main elements: plan – act – observe – reflect (Carr & Kemmis, 2003) or a more flexible action – reflection continuum (Kindon et al., 2007). The researchers took varying roles as: participants in the initiative; members of the organizing Mixhaus collective; observers of the process and outcomes and sociocultural animators (Foth, 2006b).

The following sections describe the main stages of the Mixhaus initiative, including the different PAR elements and research methods.

Initial Concept Design

In response to a call by the larger program of research on digital participation to provide seed funding for a creative entrepreneurship and social change initiative, a visual arts youth worker and local video producer took the idea to develop a community makerspace to the 2015 Townsville Startup Weekend (communities.techstars.com/australia/townsville). At the weekend, a team was formed to develop a business model, gather community interest and aspirations for the space, and pitch the idea to the forum of attendees as well as to a jury at the end. The team named the space 'Mixhaus'.

Shipping Container Fit-Out

Following the Startup Weekend, a collaboration to develop the Mixhaus makerspace was developed between two universities, the library branch of a local government, a youth arts theatre company, an electronics retailer, as well as various other community stakeholders with their own private and professional affiliations. An informal steering committee was formed to facilitate community engagement and make decisions for the space. This committee comprised local community members including representatives of the youth arts theatre company, the local library, the local university and the local government. Members of the research team who provided the seed funding purposefully did not join this committee, because we sought to increasingly make ourselves redundant and transfer the project to the local community (Foth, 2006b; Gilchrist, 2004). A decision was made by this committee to purchase a second hand shipping container to create a transportable 'pop-up' makerspace and organize facilitated STEAM (Science, Technology, Engineering, the Arts, and Mathematics) public workshops to launch the space.

The steering committee organized a community planning workshop with 22 participants to help with identifying what activities (and equipment for these activities) community members desired for the space and what skills they could share (Fig. 6.2). Workshop participants were not only from the participating organizations, but also from the local robotics club, students and staff of the local university, members of the startup scene, and also included individuals from the Townsville community with an interest in physical computing, electronics, hacking and creating. A participatory rapid appraisal method (Theis & Grady, 1991) was used to gather input from community members. This method involved generating lists of ideas for activities and equipment. A mapping of available skills and learning outcomes was also conducted following on from initial suggestions that had been made at the Startup Weekend. Entries were written on posters on the walls of the workshop. First, people added items and then they ticked items they most favoured, which were then given priority by the informal steering committee for designing the space.

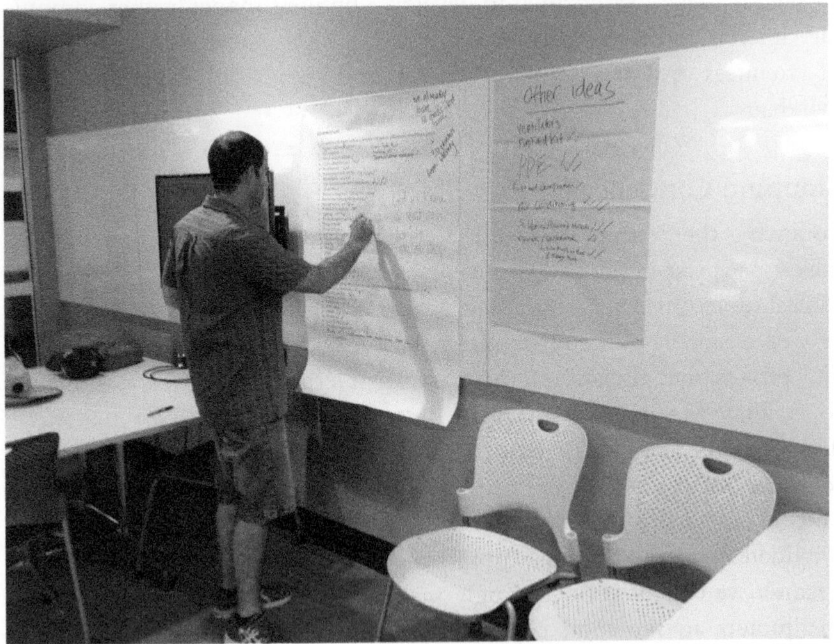

Figure 6.2 Mixhaus participant selecting the activities that he desires most for the space.

The most desired activities and outcomes included: photography, new digital technology, interactive new media art, graphic design, performance installations/participatory art, 3D printing, art, virtual reality, computer developed programming, app and web development, software development, digital privacy, open source data mining and programming, home automation, data aggregations and prototypes (Arduino and sensors), robotic applications, cross-generational engagement, exciting social situations, building a creative community, collaboration with people across sectors/disciplines, an idea factory, jobs (from ideas), self-help workshops (e.g., fix and reuse items) and having a regular informal 'open container' workshop.

The main skills participants said that they could share with others in the space involved photoshop, electronics, software development, web creation and programming, mobile application, ICT, and business and management skills, such as event promotion and marketing.

Although not all of these items on the community wish list have been addressed yet at the time of writing, the process of doing so is well underway. When the Mixhaus became operational, community participants joined the first electronics workshop to make brushbots, mini solar cars and to learn how to solder an LED badge. In the second Mixhaus workshop, people got together to learn and teach each other how to sew conductive thread and LED lights into fabric. In the third workshop, Mixhaus was used to demonstrate and teach environmental sensor building and 3D printing.

Planning for Mixhaus Engagement

The collaborating organizations met to decide on the design and equipment for the container and facilitation of workshops to initiate the space. Five workshops were held with volunteers to design and fit the shipping container out as a maker workspace (Figs. 6.3 and 6.4). These workshops included people with different interests coming together to learn and share DIY building and construction skills. Three community workshops were held to launch the maker/hacker space that occurred at different locations and events with a focus on creative arts and digital technologies/engineering (STEAM). The portability of the Mixhaus afforded the subsequent relocation of the makerspace to local community events, such as Ecofest, Luxlumin and the Townsville Festival of Ideas. It is also planned to collaborate with local secondary schools subject to workplace health and safety issues being addressed.

Our data collection included eight semistructured qualitative interviews carried out with key participants of the Mixhaus initiative – both

Figure 6.3 Fitting out the inside of the container.

members of the Mixhaus collective who created and continue to organize events, and community members who participated in particular Mixhaus activities. Participants self-selected to participate in the initiative and were purposively selected for interviewing using maximum variation sampling (Patton, 2001). The sample of participants were from diverse backgrounds:

P1: A young video producer

P2: An electrical engineer and self-described 'inventor'

P3: An IT developer

P4: A knowledge base technical communication specialist

P5: A university academic

P6: A public servant

P7: A librarian from the local library branch

P8: An artist with a focus on youth engagement

P9: The initial Mixhaus initiative coordinator

In the following data analysis section, we review and discuss the process and outcomes to date of the Mixhaus initiative and consider future opportunities.

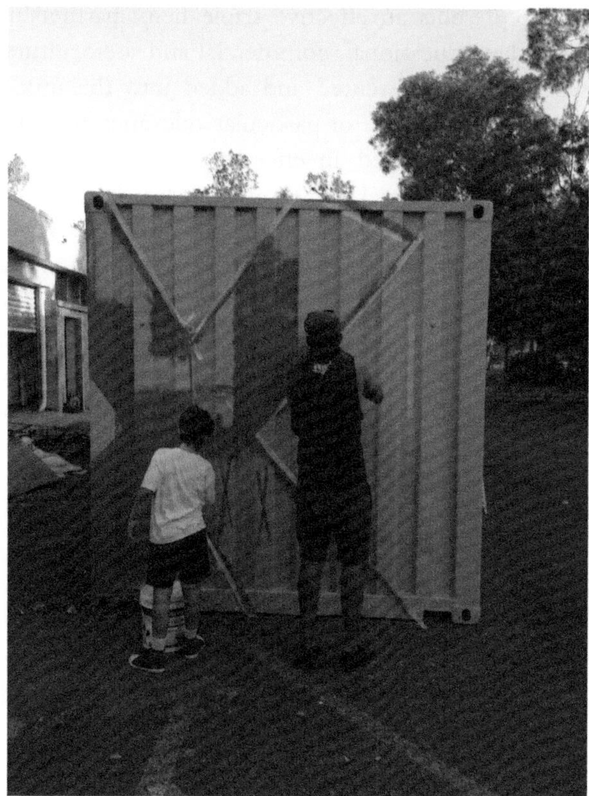

Figure 6.4 Painting the container with the Mixhaus branding.

CROSSING BOUNDARIES

In this section, we present and discuss the data we gathered from interviews, participant observations and community workshops. Our thematic analysis was guided by the aforementioned conceptual framework of boundary objects (Star & Griesemer, 1989). We found that the Mixhaus makerspace presents itself as a tangible artefact or object crossing boundaries along four different dimensions: an organizational mix, a social mix, a disciplinary mix, and a spatial mix. We discuss these four dimensions in turn.

Organizational

As outlined earlier, the Mixhaus is a community-led makerspace that has attracted attention and interest from different organizations that would normally not easily come together, gel or work together. This consortium of organizations represents an effective triple helix partnership (Foth & Adkins, 2006) in that educational, commercial and sociocultural/community interests are being represented and added into the mix. There are two aspects that appeared to be of particular relevance in supporting our analysis that Mixhaus generated an effective organizational mix: (1) the collaborative governance model that evolved from the grassroots process of the initiative, and (2) the significance of key roles that emerged from our chronological genealogy of how people's relationships unfolded.

First, the Mixhaus has been led by an informal steering committee comprising the key organizations lending support and assistance both financial and in-kind. Membership is open and transparent. This collaborative governance has been complemented by a dual approach to online and offline community engagement through a Facebook group (www.facebook.com/groups/mixhaus/) as well as a regular series of in-situ 'working bees'. What is remarkable is the capacity of the early Mixhaus vision during the StartUp Weekend – even before a tangible artefact had been available – to bridge organizational boundaries. As such, the Mixhaus corroborates some of the strategies of strategic essentialism (Dourish, 2010) in that it forges a group identity to realize the overarching Mixhaus vision. That is part of the definition of a boundary object according to Star and Griesemer (1989) who argue that 'boundary objects are both adaptable to different viewpoints and robust enough to maintain identity across them'. Participant P2 exemplifies this further:

> *As you develop relationships it changes where things go and the way you see others' perspectives ... and it also affects the practicalities of trying to achieve those goals or objectives ... it doesn't muddy the water ... just means you are more informed and more to take into account ... there's different institutional or organisational dogma versus what individuals want to achieve versus what we as a group want to achieve ... the articulation of that shared vision and making that clear and bringing that together ... bringing together all those individual goals so that everyone can understand how they can achieve what they want to do and what they want to do as part of that aggregate achievement.*

Second, as part of our data analysis we conducted a chronological genealogy of how personal and organizational relationships formed and evolved over time. This analysis revealed that the genesis moment as part of the local StartUp Weekend brought together university academics with staff from both the local government and the youth arts theatre company over an intense weekend-long engagement process. Each entity then reached out and connected with further prospective partners and community members in a fashion similar to the snowball technique well established in qualitative research methods (Patton, 2001).

Social

In addition to the way that the Mixhaus bridges organizational boundaries, it also brings people together from different sociocultural and professional backgrounds. We found in our data analysis that this social mixing goes beyond the mere temporary collocation of people in the same space for the purpose of a meeting, a working bee or a maker workshop. We will explicate two aspects of the social mix in more detail: (1) different personas involved in the process, and (2) the cross-generational exchange.

First, our data analysis uncovered a number of user archetypes, or personas (Cooper, 1999), that contributed to the organizational mix. In keeping with the idea of design personas, we present them here in a distinct way; however, study participants usually showed characteristics of more than one of these personas.

1. The *community animator* is an instigator and leader – the 'keeper of the vision' – building the momentum by organizing workshops and setting milestones (Foth, 2006b);
2. The *catalyst* is a connector and matchmaker who may not be seen in person often, but they are present digitally and introduce new organizations and community groups, and
3. The *silent stakeholder* may not offer much in terms of physical labour at working bees, however, their in-kind contributions are essential and generous, such as facilitating introductions to new people, donations of equipment and resources, and the provision of space and facilities.

Additionally, we came across personas similar to those that Bilandzic and Foth (2013) found in their study of a library coworking space: 'I-wanna-share-it Garrett' attends working bees with the motivation to contribute their specific skillset to the Mixhaus, e.g., carpentry or electrical wiring. 'What-can-I-do-here Sophia' is sporadically seen at early working bees and meetings, attracted by invites from catalysts, trying to figure out what the Mixhaus is all about and how it may contribute to their personal plans and goals. However, they may not be seen regularly or at subsequent events at all. Examples include creative arts and film/TV students who found that the early setup phase of the Mixhaus did not yet give them enough of an idea of what they will be able to use this new space for in the future.

Second, although in the early phases of development, even the setup of the Mixhaus space brought to the fore examples of cross-generational exchanges between younger and older community participants that are worthwhile discussing. In contrast to the often exclusive focus on young people that many innovation policy frameworks entail these days, we found not only nascent examples of 'senior-preneurship' (Sahut, Gharbi, & Mili, 2015), but also cross-generational exchanges. Community members also aspired for Mixhaus to be a space that generates cross-generational learning, as this participant dialogue illustrates:

> *[Mixhaus is] an opportunity for younger people getting involved and opportunities for less advantaged youth and people. (P1)*
>
> *In so many ways that Mixhaus is a really powerful little statement and needs to be taken full advantage of to try and connect people and it does in little ways and you can see it creates lots of little connections and ideas. (P2)*

Disciplinary

The third dimension along which the Mixhaus can be considered a boundary object is with regards to its inter- and transdisciplinary linkages. Here, we discuss how the boundaries of three typical dichotomies become blurred and intermixed: professionals versus amateurs; digital literacy versus physical skills, and knowledge versus craft.

First, as a makerspace, Mixhaus has attracted both professionals and amateurs. Our data shows how the Mixhaus contributes to forms of connected learning (Bilandzic & Foth, 2017) that complement formal institutionalized education provided by schools and universities. For example, community members interested in learning how to sew with conductive thread were able to participate in a workshop where they learn how to add a glowing LED light to their favourite t-shirt. The workshop facilitator brought her visual arts and sewing skills to bear, supplemented by DIY learning of physical computing components, such as the LilyPad Arduino. This example further corroborates studies outlining the rise of the trend towards DIY and DIWO (Mota, 2011; Paulos, Kim, & Kuznetsov, 2011; Ratto & Boler, 2014). P5 illustrates this aspect by saying:

> *I expect to learn new and different aspects of electronics and building from a hobby point of view, fantastic to make connections with people in local community for solving problems ... So far I am picking up DIY skills in around the container / space, which is really useful going forward ... that I previously didn't have ... once you have a physical space and person ... easier to*

bounce ideas off, compared to online ... someone who is physically there is more likely to trust they will share and the attitude is transparent.

Second, the Mixhaus is equipped to allow for maker projects in a mixed realm that bridges both physical and digital fabrication. The aforementioned example combines physical components such as the fabric of the t-shirt, the conductive thread, the LED light, with digital components such as Arduino software to program different light patterns.

Third, related to the resolution of the digital versus physical dichotomy, the Mixhaus also connects what Francisco (2007) calls specification (knowledge) versus craft culture. The disciplines that are driven by a specification culture largely subscribe to the Greek term 'epistēmē' referring to knowledge-based disciplines and approaches, largely leading to 'white collar', service-oriented jobs. In contrast, 'blue collar' community members with trade qualifications and experience contribute their architectural, design, arts and craft skills (Greek: technē). Rather than reflecting society's two-class system that all too often considers knowledge-based skills superior to craft-based skills, Mixhaus introduces a levelling factor that puts them on a par and makes clear how each skillset makes unique contributions that the other one is not able to fulfil on its own.

In lay terms, this dichotomy is often referred to as the creative-right versus the analytical-left brain. However, it has deeper implications with regards to a society that has increasingly been optimized for a one-sided orientation towards the analytical world of epistēmē. Community members of the crafts/technē persuasion often struggle to establish a sense of belonging. Mixhaus responds to these struggles by offering a supportive and inclusive space to stimulate both the creative/artistic and the analytical/empirical senses of people. In the words of a commentator, Mixhaus resolves the 'conundrum of creating a club for people who hate to belong to a club that has them as a member'.

Spatial

Finally, the Mixhaus as a type of living lab situated inside a portable shipping container offers qualities of a nomadic place for fabrication and making. By moving the Mixhaus from one location to another, it acts as a hyperlocal 'urban acupuncture' device that contributes towards local placemaking efforts (Houghton, Foth, & Miller, 2015). The Mixhaus as an innovation 'skunkworks' (Foth, 2015) in turn has implications for Australia's innovation agenda and regional economic development policies in that it challenges assumptions behind notions of what counts as entrepreneurial and how incubation spaces should function. P3 describes the Mixhaus' spatial dimension by saying:

> *In many ways I think that's where Mixhaus fits in well because it's mobile … and it's not just that identification with one particular group or one particular location.*

Moreover, there are possibilities and opportunities related to the aforementioned disciplinary mix at the intersection of epistēmē and technē. They have led community participants to also question the spatial quality of the Mixhaus. They have started to refer to the Mixhaus not only as a space but a mobile, portable, nomadic platform. This notion illustrates the way that it creates a foundation in the community on top of which other opportunities can be envisaged and initiatives can be built, which in turn can connect with other areas of interest, such as civic activism (Gordon & Mihailidis, 2016). This aspect is further exemplified by the following participant quotes:

> *A platform to get people involved and a new way to create revenue … building things for other things to build on … facebook for game developers and business to market themselves … creating opportunities. (P1)*
>
> *I see Mixhaus as a moulding together of all of them [interests] on a higher level project wise. (P1)*
>
> *Somewhere [Mixhaus] where people can get hands on experience, which is very important with the laws and regulations of the Australian Government. I have worked with university students who don't know what a fuse is so hands on stuff – basic knowledge lost / not being learnt, because [regulations] barred from getting practical experience. Yet, here [with Mixhaus] people are able to step outside the box and have a place to and access to tools to do this. (P4)*
>
> *If something has to be done try to avoid bureaucracy – better to ask for forgiveness than permission – easier to write code and see what happens than ask what someone thinks first, same as physical stuff … could sit around and plan but better to try something from scratch and start again. (P3)*

In summary, the Mixhaus – albeit at an early stage of its ongoing development and uptake by the local community – has demonstrated a twofold benefit. As a physical and moveable object it provides utility and applied learning outcomes fostering digital participation of the local community by way of its mix of technical and human resources. As a social living lab with hybrid – digital and physical – aspects the Mixhaus offers an impartial vehicle for the advancement of a variety of goals, such as youth engagement, urban planning, sustainability and civic activism.

CONCLUSIONS

This chapter presented our critical account of accompanying the development of the Mixhaus from the initial ideation and conceptualization to the actual deployment and first evaluation of its impact. As with many action research studies, the tendency to remain idiographic is inherent in a single case study and its qualitative approach. As a way to allow the community to take shared ownership, the research team sought to increasingly make itself redundant and hand over responsibility and leadership requirements to local community stakeholders (Foth, 2006b). Considering that the academic funding for this project has come to an end, it has been our aspiration right from the start to ensure the Mixhaus makerspace is community-led and continues to have a life of its own. It appears we have partly achieved this goal, yet it is too early to tell to what extent the Mixhaus will have an impact on levels of digital participation in the community, and if the Mixhaus will weather the dynamics of the local community's communicative ecology.

As a boundary object, the Mixhaus has demonstrated its ability to be tailored to the circumstances and limitations of the local community. At the same time, it remained stable enough to continue to work towards a shared vision that hopes to connect different stakeholders and further dissolves boundaries. However, the planning and engagement activities associated with the Mixhaus initiative also brought to the fore challenging social, personal and organizational discrepancies amongst community members. Challenges of forging new partnerships remind us of critiques that the notion of boundary objects has received, which we concur with, and the importance of developing operational processes for communications, collaboration and ensuring continuity and sustainability. We agree that as an inanimate artefact, the Mixhaus does not possess mediating or diplomatic qualities per se; in fact, sensitivity, diplomacy and humility are required as additional skillsets in order to bring community-led initiatives such as social living labs, to fruition.

ACKNOWLEDGMENTS

Complementing similar case study research work in Toowoomba, Queensland, this research project, 'Fostering digital participation through living labs in regional and rural Australian communities' was supported under Australian Research Council's Linkage Projects funding scheme (project number LP130100469). Ethical clearance was approved by Queensland University of Technology (#1400000017). We thank our local partner organization, Townsville City Libraries, and our supporting partners, James Cook University, La Luna Youth Arts Theatre, Jaycar, as well as our community members and study participants.

REFERENCES

Amariles, F., Paz, O. P., Russell, N., & Johnson, N. (2007). The impacts of community telecenters in Rural Colombia. *The Journal of Community Informatics*, *2*(3). Retrieved from <http://ci-journal.net/index.php/ciej/article/viewArticle/256>.

Anderson, C. (2012). *Makers: The new industrial revolution*. New York, USA: Random House.

Arnold, M., Gibbs, M. R., & Wright, P. (2003). Intranets and local community: "Yes, an intranet is all very well, but do we still get free beer and a barbeque?". In M. Huysman, E. Wenger, & V. Wulf (Eds.), *Proceedings of the first international conference on communities and technologies* (pp. 185–204). Amsterdam: Kluwer Academic Publishers.

Atweh, B., Kemmis, S., & Weeks, P. (2002). *Action research in practice: Partnership for social justice in education*. Abingdon, United Kingdom: Taylor & Francis.

Bilandzic, M., & Foth, M. (2013). Libraries as coworking spaces: Understanding user motivations and perceived barriers to social learning. *Library Hi Tech*, *31*(2), 254–273.

Bilandzic, M., & Foth, M. (2017). Designing hubs for connected learning: Social, spatial and technological insights from Coworking, Hackerspaces and Meetup groups. In L. Carvalho, P. Goodyear, & M. de Laat (Eds.), *Place-based spaces for networked learning* (pp. 191–206). Oxon: Routledge.

Bradbury, H. (2015). *The SAGE handbook of action research*. London: SAGE.

Cairncross, F. (1997). *The death of distance*. Cambridge: Harvard Business School Press.

Caldwell, G. A., & Foth, M. (2014). *DIY media architecture: Open and participatory approaches to community engagement. Proceedings of the 2nd media architecture biennale conference: World cities* (pp. 1–10). ACM, 2682893.

Carr, W., & Kemmis, S. (2003). *Becoming critical: Education knowledge and action research*. Abingdon, United Kingdom: Taylor & Francis.

Carroll, J.M., & Reese, D.D. (2003). Community collective efficacy: Structure and consequences of perceived capacities in the Blacksburg electronic village. In *Presented at the 36th Hawaii International Conference on System Sciences (HICSS), Big Island*. Hawaii: IEEE.

Cooper, A. (1999). *The inmates are running the asylum: Why high tech products drive us crazy and how to restore the sanity*. Indianapolis: Sams Publishing.

Dezuanni, M., Foth, M., Mallan, K., & Hughes, H. (2016). *Social living labs for digital participation: Designing with regional and rural communities. Proceedings of the 2016 ACM conference companion publication on designing interactive systems* (pp. 49–52). ACM.

Dezuanni, M., Foth, M., Mallan, K., Hughes, H., & Allan, C. (2014). Fostering digital participation in regional and rural Australia. In K. Alam (Ed.), *Presented at the symposium on broadband enabled communities and regional economic development, University of Southern Queensland, Toowoomba, Australia*. Retrieved from <http://eprints.qut.edu.au/78865/>.

Dourish, P. (2010). *HCI and environmental sustainability: The politics of design and the design of politics. Proceedings of the 8th ACM conference on designing interactive systems* (pp. 1–10). Aarhus: ACM.

Foth, M. (2006a). Network action research. *Action Research*, *4*(2), 205–226.

Foth, M. (2006b). Sociocultural animation. In S. Marshall, W. Taylor, & X. Yu (Eds.), *Encyclopedia of developing regional communities with information and communication technology* (pp. 640–645). Hershey: Idea Group Reference, (IGI Global).

Foth, M. (2015). Australia needs an innovation "skunkworks." *The Conversation, December* (2). Retrieved from <https://eprints.qut.edu.au/90977/>.

Foth, M., & Adkins, B. (2006). A research design to build effective partnerships between city planners, developers, government and urban neighbourhood communities. *The Journal of Community Informatics, 2*(2). Retrieved from <http://ci-journal.net/index.php/ciej/article/viewArticle/292>.

Foth, M., & Brynskov, M. (2016). Participatory action research for civic engagement. In E. Gordon, & P. Mihailidis (Eds.), *Civic media: Technology, design, practice* (pp. 563–580). Cambridge: MIT Press.

Foth, M., & Hearn, G. (2007). Networked individualism of urban residents: Discovering the communicative ecology in inner-city apartment buildings. *Information, Communication and Society, 10*(5), 749–772.

Francisco, S. (2007). The way we do things around here: Specification versus craft culture in the history of building. *The American Behavioral Scientist, 50*(7), 970–988.

Gauntlett, D. (2011). *Making is connecting*. Hoboken, NJ, USA: Wiley.

Gilchrist, A. (2004). *The well-connected community: A networking approach to community development*. Bristol: The Policy Press.

Gordon, E., de Souza, E., & Silva, A. (2011). *Net locality: Why location matters in a networked world*. Chichester: John Wiley & Sons.

Gordon, E., & Mihailidis, P. (2016). *Civic media: Technology, design, practice*. Cambridge: MIT Press.

Gurstein, M. (2000). *Community informatics: Enabling communities with information and communication technologies*. Hershey: Idea Group.

Gurstein, M. (2003). Effective use: A community informatics strategy beyond the digital divide. *First Monday, 8*(12). Retrieved from <http://www.ccnr.net/prato2003/>.

Hampton, K. N., & Wellman, B. (2002). The not so global village of Netville. In B. Wellman, & C. A. Haythornthwaite (Eds.), *The Internet in everyday life* (pp. 345–371). Oxford: Blackwell.

Hearn, G., & Foth, M. (2007). Communicative ecologies: Editorial preface. *Electronic Journal of Communication, 17*(1–2). Retrieved from <http://eprints.qut.edu.au/8171/>.

Hearn, G., Tacchi, J., Foth, M., & Lennie, J. (2009). *Action research and new media: Concepts, methods and cases*. Cresskill: Hampton Press.

Houghton, K., Foth, M., & Miller, E. (2015). Urban acupuncture: Hybrid social and technological practices for hyperlocal placemaking. *Journal of Urban Technology, 22*(3), 3–19.

Houghton, K., Miller, E., & Foth, M. (2014). The local library across the digital and physical city: Opportunities for economic development. *Commonwealth Journal of Local Governance, 15*, 39–60.

Huvila, I. (2011). The politics of boundary objects: Hegemonic interventions and the making of a document. *Journal of the American Society for Information Science. American Society for Information Science, 62*(12), 2528–2539.

Kimble, C., Grenier, C., & Goglio-Primard, K. (2010). Innovation and knowledge sharing across professional boundaries: Political interplay between boundary objects and brokers. *International Journal of Information Management, 30*(5), 437–444.

Kindon, S., Pain, R., & Kesby, M. (2007). *). Participatory action research approaches and methods: Connecting people, participation and place*. New York: Taylor & Francis.

Mar, P., & Anderson, K. (2010). The creative assemblage: Theorizing contemporary forms of arts-based collaboration. *Journal of Cultural Economy, 3*(1), 35–51.

Mota, C. (2011). *The rise of personal fabrication. Proceedings of the 8th ACM conference on creativity and cognition* (pp. 279–288). New York: ACM.

Notley, T., & Foth, M. (2008). Extending Australia's digital divide policy: An examination of the value of social inclusion and social capital policy frameworks. *Australian Social Policy*, 7, 87–110.

Patton, M. Q. (2001). *Qualitative research and evaluation methods* (3rd ed.). Thousand Oaks: Sage.

Paulos, E., Kim, S., & Kuznetsov, S. (2011). The rise of the expert Amateur: Citizen science and micro-volunteerism. In M. Foth, L. Forlano, C. Satchell, & M. Gibbs (Eds.), *From social butterfly to engaged citizen: Urban informatics, social media, ubiquitous computing, and mobile technology to support citizen engagement*. Cambridge: MIT Press.

Preece, J. (2000). *Online communities: Designing usability, supporting sociability*. Chichester: John Wiley.

Ratto, M., & Boler, M. (2014). *DIY citizenship: Critical making and social media*. Cambridge: MIT Press.

Reason, P. (1998). Political, epistemological, ecological and spiritual dimensions of participation. *Studies in Cultures, Organizations and Societies*, *4*(2), 147–167.

Rheingold, H. (1994). *The virtual community: Homesteading on the electronic frontier*. New York: Harper Perennial.

Rheingold, H. (2002). *Smart mobs: The next social revolution*. Cambridge: Perseus Publishing.

Sahut, J.-M., Gharbi, S., & Mili, M. (2015). Identifying factors key to encouraging entrepreneurial intentions among seniors: Entrepreneurial intentions among seniors. *Canadian Journal of Administrative Sciences/Revue Canadienne Des Sciences de l'Administration*, *32*(4), 252–264.

Schuler, D. (1996). New community networks: Wired for change. New York: ACM Press.

Star, S. L., & Griesemer, J. R. (1989). Institutional ecology, translations' and boundary objects: Amateurs and professionals in Berkeley's Museum of Vertebrate Zoology, 1907–39. *Social Studies of Science*, *19*(3), 387–420.

Theis, J., & Grady, H. M. (1991). *Participatory rapid appraisal for community development: A training manual based on experiences in the Middle East and North Africa*. London: International Institute for Environment and Development. Retrieved from <http://pubs.iied.org/pdfs/8282IIED.pdf>.

Walmsley, D. J. (2000). Community, place and cyberspace. *The Australian Geographer*, *31* (1), 5–19.

Wellman, B. (2001). Physical place and cyberplace: The rise of personalized networking. *International Journal of Urban and Regional Research*, *25*(2), 227–252.

Wenger, E. (1998). *Communities of practice: Learning, meaning, and identity*. New York: Cambridge University Press.

CHAPTER 7

Empowerment Through Making: Lessons for Sustaining and Scaling Community Practices

Ingrid Mulder, Emilia L. Pucci and Youri Havenaar
Delft University of Technology, Delft, The Netherlands

INTRODUCTION

The maker movement is providing all kinds of people around the world with the tools and infrastructures to unleash their intrinsic ability to create, make and innovate. This spreading trend of learning-by-doing has the potential to empower people in doing things previously unthinkable, through the potential of 3D printing, laser cutting, Internet of Things, electronics and so on. The unleashing of creative processes can be coined as 21st century skills, which refer to – among others – digital literacy, creativity, critical thinking, problem solving, as well as collaboration and communication skills. It is commonly accepted that these higher order skills are essential for successful participation in society. As the OECD concluded in its report 'Towards an OECD Skills Strategy': 'Numerous efforts have been made to identify "key competencies" and "employability skills" over the past decades. However, apart from the universally acknowledged importance of basic literacy and numerical skills, there is little hard evidence of what other skills are required for workers to obtain better labour outcomes and cope with a more fluid labour market" (OECD, 2011).

In keeping with recent trends in STEM (Science, Technology, Engineering, Mathematics) and STEAM (including Arts and Design) education, we elaborate upon the capabilities that technology labs such as FabLabs (https://www.fablabs.io) and similar concepts called as makerspaces and hackerspaces, bring to a broader audience, and focus on social entrepreneurship and inclusiveness, in particular. FabLabs offer capabilities to everybody, which have until recently been reserved to a few professionals (De Roeck et al., 2012). In keeping with Honey and Kanter (2013), we embrace the value of making and prototyping as a way to

Digital Participation through Social Living Labs. DOI: http://dx.doi.org/10.1016/B978-0-08-102059-3.00007-1

provide deeper, richer learning experiences. Without doubt, the maker movement has impacted the design profession in terms of skills required as well as design methodologies and practices, by making tools and infrastructures easily accessible to a wider spectrum of people. In fact, the FabLab itself provides an excellent framework to facilitate the ignition of practice-based education. This has been demonstrated by the Fab@School project (Blikstein, 2013), among others.

In previous work, we have explored what type of transformational role FabLabs can play in design education as a form of digital participation. Driven by the educational need to prepare students in the field of Communication and Media Design, Media Technology, and Computer Science in the digital revolution in making and prototyping, a technological lab was designed accordingly and established inside the Rotterdam School of Communication, Media, and Information Technology. Its goal is to function as a technical workshop, where students learn how to use, and critically reflect on, the latest digital technologies that are challenging traditional academic curricula. Citylab Rotterdam is a lab for applied creativity, an official FabLab extended with a strong emphasis on electronics and sensor devices, the Internet of Things, and Open Data; the lab bridges the gap between production design, and the integration of microelectronics and programming (Mostert-van der Sar, Mulder, Remijn, & Troxler, 2013; Mulder, 2015). Citylab Rotterdam is also a creative hotspot open to citizens enabling making and prototyping, a space for participation and cocreation. The interdisciplinary setup in combination with a solidly integrated peer-learning and DIY (do-it-yourself) approach empowers its users to 'make almost anything'.

We, therefore, use the term *technological lab* to distinguish the equipment and physical space in a FabLab (or makerspace), from a *living lab*. The latter term we use to include the space for participation and cocreation, and the community of 'makers'. A *social living lab* however, includes both the technological lab and the community, while studying the local community context as well.

In this chapter, we elaborate on two participatory cocreated social living labs where digital fabrication technologies were made accessible to a broader audience of children and young adults living in low socioeconomic communities, aiming to provide them with a broader skillset enhancing their digital literacy, and consequently enhance their social participation in society. In 'Context' section, we introduce the context of these two social living labs.

CONTEXT

The social living labs reported in this chapter have been carried out in two highly multicultural cities in the Netherlands, Rotterdam and The Hague. Both social living labs are established in underdeveloped neighbourhoods, where a lack of infrastructures and support systems for the local youth has been identified as a key issue hindering their development as well as the sociocultural well-being of the neighbourhood itself.

Afrikaanderwijk, Rotterdam

Afrikaanderwijk is a highly multicultural neighbourhood in Rotterdam South, the Netherlands, traditionally inhabited by blue-collar workers employed in the local port industry: here, the generally low level of education of the inhabitants and their ethnic background relegate them to a lower level of society. In our earlier work, young adults from Afrikaanderwijk were interviewed to gain insights on their lifestyle, needs and passions (Pucci, 2013a, 2013b). The interviewees were for the most part of non-European descent and second-generation immigrants. They all displayed a few common traits. They attended low-level schools, struggled to find a job and are frequently stigmatized as problematic by other members of the neighbourhood and by governmental institutions more widely. When asked about their dreams, answers tended to be vague: some young adults wanted to become star soccer players like Lionel Messi, others idolized older siblings and family members as their role models, but the most common answer was that they did not have any specific skill they were compelled to improve their ability in. From their answers and behaviours, it seemed as though they did not feel allowed to have any dreams and ambitions nor to be able to cultivate their interests and develop their talents to become empowered role models themselves. Interestingly though, all of them showed to be tech savvy, digitally social and full of passions, yet with no engagement in their neighbourhood and little means to pursue their dreams for the future. As we identified a strong unexpressed, inherent potential in the young adults, who actually belong to the first generation of digital natives (Prensky, 2001), we decided to trigger the natural fluency in their relationship with new technologies to unlock their hidden talents while cocreating with them a workshop on 3D printing and digital fabrication in a participatory bottom-up living lab setting.

Schilderswijk, The Hague

The Schilderswijk in The Hague is a quarter where ethnic diversity and illiteracy rates are high, and the number of youngsters with education and/or a job generally low. Teenagers and young adults oftentimes lack a connection to their neighbourhood and the other inhabitants. Consequently, they often feel misunderstood and, by lack of ambition, they reside mostly on the streets, hanging around or worse – engage in petty crime. Both local and national government bodies are investing a lot of time, money and effort in trying to tackle these problems nationwide, but a real connection to the youth is still missing. In the city of The Hague, an initiative with the Central City Library aimed to bring the youngsters of the quarter together through building an enhanced sense of belonging to their neighbourhood by leveraging key qualities of the uprising maker movement. A first bridging step was the setup of a technological laboratory within the library located in Schilderswijk, which was on the verge of reopening, after being closed for several years. Elaborating upon the experiences in Afrikaanderwijk, the corresponding social living lab was inviting the local youth to join forces in the collaborative setup of the technological lab, and at the same time establishing the maker-community making the lab living.

APPROACH

The social living labs undertaken in both cities used a Research-through-Design approach (Frayling, 1993), with multiple iterations carried out in a participatory, bottom-up fashion with the local communities, in order to ensure the recipients of the work were at the same time active cocreators. Research in these social living labs was done through collaborative design activities informing a final design. The research focus is on the intrinsic ability to create and make, and its effect on empowerment. Empowerment, a crucial construct in connecting individual well-being with a larger environment, links individual capabilities, competences and proactive behaviours to social policy and social change (Rappaport, 1987). We elaborate on the research findings and refer to the respective social living labs (including their design activities and final designs) as the design (in Research through Design) for exploring how empowerment could be stimulated through making. As our research has an exploratory nature, we use the Self-Determination Theory as a guiding principle

(Ryan & Deci, 2000) to gain insights on empowerment and related constructs.

In 'Star(t) to Shine: A Platform for Empowerment' and 'New Dutch Makers' sections, we introduce the codesigned platforms *Star(t) to Shine* and *New Dutch Makers*, which aim to empower the local community in both Afrikaanderwijk and Schilderswijk through hands-on participation and making, respectively. Subsequently, we discuss the findings which helped us gaining a better view on empowerment, the opportunities and challenges in promoting it, and conclude with key lessons relevant for sustaining and scaling community practices.

STAR(T) TO SHINE: A PLATFORM FOR EMPOWERMENT

> *A constellation of stars. Each star shines of its own light, yet together they create a beautiful image. Invisible connections allow the creation of the pattern in the blue sky.*

The above interaction vision has been used to guide a series of codesign (Sanders & Stappers, 2008) activities with the 'hidden stars', the often 'neglected' young adults in the age group of 16–24 years. In keeping with Ryan and Deci's Self-Determination Theory (2000), the present project aims at strengthening the young adults' awareness of their individual passions and talents, motivating them to share these with their peers in order to develop their talents together, empowering them both as individuals and as a cohesive community, in order to obtain respect and recognition in a process of mutual benefit towards and from the social ecology of Afrikaanderwijk.

Searching for the Right Cocreative Partnerships

The first engagement strategy attempted with the youth of Afrikaanderwijk was to involve the founder of an independent youth association in the project, who was also involved in the previous study, and proved to be a crucial connection to the young adults at that stage of the project. After multiple encounters with the youth association founder as well as an informal interview with his mentees, initial interest was shown towards the organization of a workshop on 3D printing. As a trigger to spark the young adults' interest in 3D printing, personalized key chains of their local football team were 3D printed and given to them. The outcome of this strategy was not positive: the founder of the association, after initially displaying interest in collaborating to empower his young adults, dropped out of the project without any explanation. Our linking pin and ambassador had turned into a gatekeeper. This unpleasant experience showed that an unexpressed mismatch in agendas between designer and stakeholders can undermine the design process, when not uncovered and taken care of. It also showed that designing 'for' someone is not the most fortunate route to take. Although key chains were designed (and did function well) as a sensitizing prototype to spark their interest and the choice of the design was selected after analysing the adolescents' answers to the interviews, the design was made 'for' them and not 'with' them. The element of active involvement and personal empowerment of the adolescents needed more careful consideration.

The second engagement strategy, therefore, stressed partnering with a local school to cocreate a project of youth self-empowerment through 3D printing. In our search for local high schools in the neighbourhood, we were more sensitive towards engaging with a committed partner with a compatible agenda in achieving the goal of empowering their students. Two schools were regarded as potential partners: one regular high school and a 'Wijkschool', which is a local initiative offering alternative education to students who dropped out of the national education system. The Wijkschool students can get a basic certificate equivalent to the lowest level of regular education, which enables them to enter the Dutch labour market. In the residents' view, the Wijkschool is 'the last chance school to participate in society'. The director of the regular high school expressed his doubts about his students' capability to carry out a workshop on 3D printing due to their low educational level, and was unwilling to explore a collaboration. Nevertheless, a first meeting with a coach and her students at the Wijkschool immediately opened up opportunities to collaborate. The Wijkschool coach showed a proactive and open attitude towards the proposal, and displayed no doubt about her students' ability to learn how to 3D print. Interestingly, the two educators displayed opposite views of their students' abilities: while the former seemed to underestimate their potential, the latter educator was actively involved in promoting their talents and ability to develop their skills.

Cocreating a Plan for Empowerment

Obviously, the Wijkschool became our partner in codesigning a workshop series on talent empowerment. A tight collaboration with Sophie, the coach of the Wijkschool, enabled an effective codesign strategy to activate young adults' talents through 3D printing; the resulting workshop proposal consisted of six iterative steps. The division in steps was meant to empower the students gradually and intrinsically from within their own interests and qualities. The following steps were carried out once a week during the students' workshop hours:

Step 1. *Share your passions*: students were introduced to the FabLab concept and then invited to share their passions and interests using a questionnaire;

Step 2. *Share your ideas*: the students sketched an initial product idea through group brainstorming;

Step 3. *Share your designs*: at the FabLab, the students transformed their design into a 3D model with Tinkercad (tinkercad.com) and 3D printed it;

Step 4. *Share your knowledge*: students made an *Instructable* (tutorials to make almost anything at instructables.com) to share their knowledge with the global maker community;

Step 5. *Share your opinion*: students were invited to evaluate the workshop, learning how to provide feedback;

Step 6. *Share your experience*: the students presented their work to their own local community, becoming an inspiring force to their peers.

In the remainder of this section we elaborate on how we carried out the workshop steps through learning-by-doing and evaluated its influence on self-empowerment with the students of the Wijkschool. The experiences of the workshop series clearly stressed the synthesis of the most valuable interactions for a peer-to-peer workshop platform aimed at activating the students of the Wijkschool to self-empowerment. Differently put, the outcomes informed the design of a workshop platform for empowerment through making, which employs online social media, FabLabs, and ubiquitous technologies to foster community participation and peer-to-peer learning. The platform aims at allowing a community of students to share and develop their portfolio of skills through a series of hands-on workshops within their school or youth centre, where they can become active cocreators according to their level of participation. Fig. 7.1 shows how the 'ladder of student participation', inspired by Arnstein's model (1969), assigns different roles to the students, according to their engagement in the workshop activities. The hierarchical structure depicted in the model is not static; on the contrary, social mobility is encouraged, allowing the students to move up and down the ladder throughout different workshop cycles. As will be described later, the

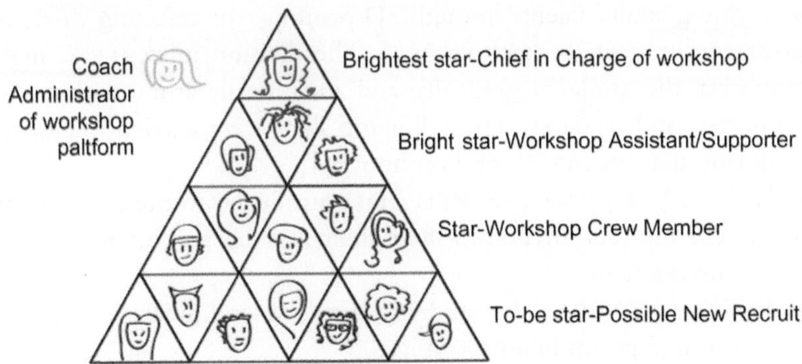

Figure 7.1 Ladder of student participation.

'Brightest Stars' are the ones who take ownership of leading the workshop organization and enactment in one cycle as 'Chief in Charge', while the 'Bright Stars' are the students who assist the 'Chief in Charge' during get the execution of the workshop. The 'Stars' are the students participating in the workshop without extra responsibilities, while the 'To-be-stars' are the students who might join the next workshop cycle. Of course, aiming to become eventually a Chief in Charge.

Usually, the teacher (or another professional coach) is the Chief in Charge when the platform is introduced within a school or youth centre. The first step is *Join the Group*, where the coach introduces the new workshop platform to the students and invites them to join the dedicated Facebook group. The second step is *Design your Badge*: here students personalize their membership badge. Each badge has a unique RFID tag connected to a personal Facebook profile. After the launch, the workshop runs in cycles, which are sustained by the student community. In the third step the coach launches a *Call for Themes* for the next workshop. Students propose their ideas and vote for the best one. In the fourth step the *Winner* is announced: the idea with the most votes wins. The winner receives a 'relay stick' with an active RFID, and is entrusted with authority and central communication functions to become the Chief in Charge. In the fifth step, *Invite*, the Chief in Charge has a week to organize a workshop, and invites peers by connecting with the relay stick (see Fig. 7.2). The sixth step consists of the *Workshop and Instructable*, at the FabLab, where students make their own real 3D printed or laser cut product. Then they create an Instructable to share their knowledge. After the workshop the students *Rate the workshop*: by tilting the relay stick, the students give their rating, which appears on the Facebook group.

Figure 7.2 RFID badge creation and active RFID relay stick.

A week later, during the Be Inspired Day, the Chief in Charge and the Crew Members inspire their peers by sharing their workshop experience. The platform as illustrated in Fig. 7.3 has been evaluated with the participation of students from two different Wijkschools during two workshops on laser cutting. The outcomes confirmed the results on students' empowerment and far exceeded expectations (Pucci, 2013a, 2013b; Pucci & Mulder, 2015).

NEW DUTCH MAKERS

The technological laboratory built in Schilderswijk, The Hague, was realized by installing machinery and equipment, and by initiating workshops to provide a pioneer group of youngsters with a basic skillset to operate the available machinery. Through participation in these initial workshops, the participating youngsters became interested in the initiative, before the official launch of the laboratory, scheduled during the reopening of the library. After working with the machinery themselves the youngsters connected with each other and demonstrated co-ownership with the initiative. None of the pioneers had prior knowledge of digital fabrication skills. Their shared learning experiences even strengthened their companionship. Participants started to help each other, which stimulated a cooperative way of working inside the lab, which can be seen in Fig. 7.4. The positive experiences were shared among friends, family, and school mates. In this way, the promotion of the new technology lab happened spontaneously and has ignited a flame of enthusiasm in the neighbourhood, leading to a large number of interested youngsters awaiting a place to participate (see for details Havenaar, 2016; Havenaar, Mulder, & van der Meer, 2016).

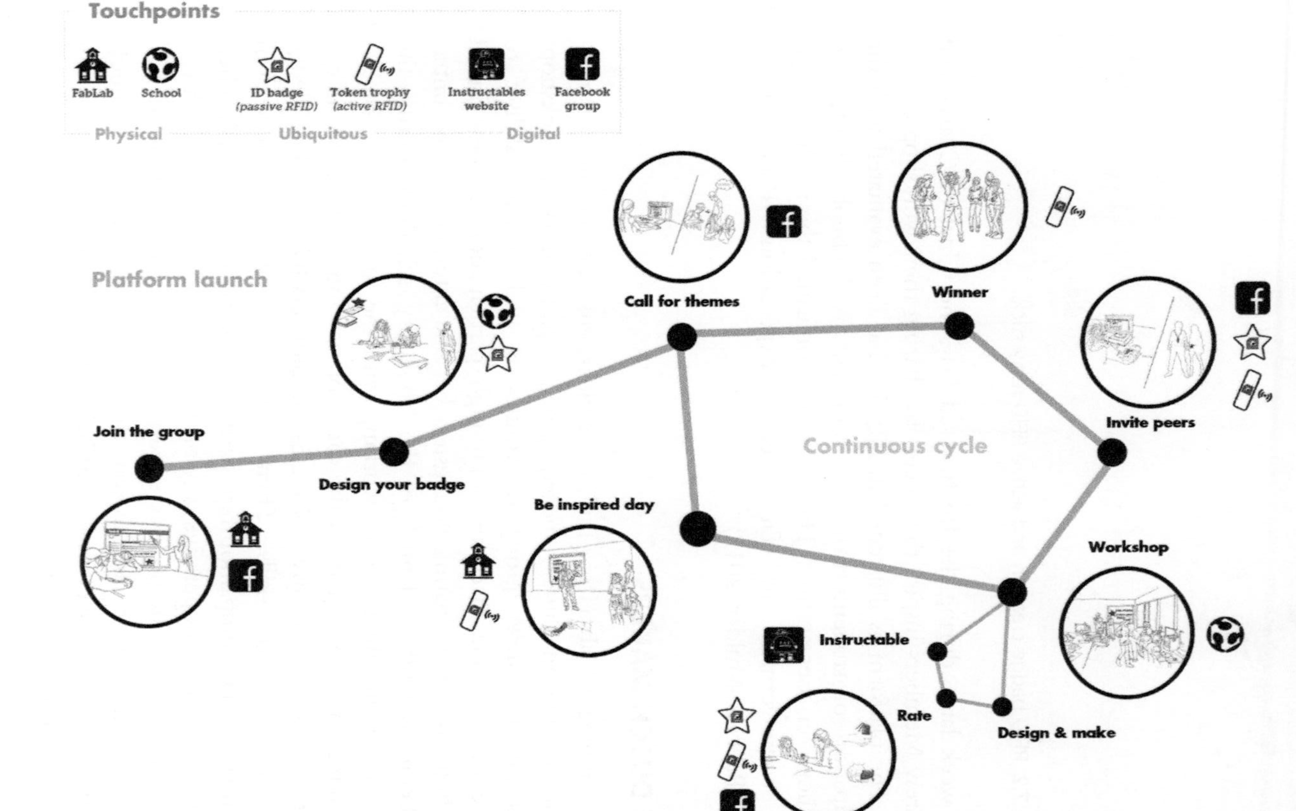

Figure 7.3 The workshop platform 'Star(t) to Shine'.

Figure 7.4 Participants learning with and from each other in the technological lab in the library.

Parallel to this, a name and a logo have been designed together with the first group of pioneers. Interestingly, the pioneers decided that the logo had to refer to a common factor in the neighbourhood in order to appeal to other participants as well. Hence, the Schilderswijk is known for closed and segregated groups. Consequently, the look of Ultimaker 3D-printer (ultimaker.com) was chosen as logo (see Fig. 7.5) aiming at sensitizing the youngsters, make them enthusiastic about the project and increasing co-ownership. The 3D-printer has proven to appeal to most; it offers seemingly endless possibilities and the resulting designs are tangible. The filament insert in the printer is of the colour orange, the Dutch national colour. The following rationale was presented by the young pioneers.

The Schilderswijk is named after the old Dutch masters. The name of artist painters like Rembrandt van Rijn and Peter Paul Rubens are found on the street signs, forming a connection with the Golden Age of fine art painting. Because of their Dutch heritage these artists and their work are something to be proud of. A brainstorm on the logo cherished the pride of these old craftsmen from 'their' neighbourhood. The difference, however, is that the Schilderswijk is named after old, deceased masters, while the current project aims to work with 'new masters'. Making a clear link to the maker movement, 'The New Dutch Makers' (NDM) was chosen as the new name. Fig. 7.5 shows the corresponding NDM logo.

Figure 7.5 New Dutch Makers logo.

Supporting Workshops to Empower Participants

In order to turn the technology lab into a living lab for personal development, a codesign approach was chosen to develop the setup of regular workshop into a self-sustaining way by the involved participants themselves. Since a large part of these youngsters has 'problems with authority' or with being told what to do, stimulating a proactive attitude towards determining themselves what to make inside the lab seemed to be a logical follow-up. As in the previous study, Self-Determination Theory (Ryan & Deci, 2000) has been used as a guiding principle, with a particular focus on co-ownership. A variety of creative sessions has been organized on 'how to create co-ownership', and how to ensure participation and devotion' among others. Other sessions, e.g., dealt with the different tools and techniques for the lab, what could be made by using these machines or for whom the participants could make things? A facilitator guided the participants where needed in order to come up with ideas that were less obvious. Among these ideas inspiring visions could be distinguished. One of the participants suggested making toys for children that were living in the recently opened refugee centre in The Hague, which was received as a very inspiring proposal. All ideas were rated on appropriateness and feasibility. After an initial selection had been made, these ideas were clustered to gain insight in the directions of topics that the participants are thinking about. Three different idea clusters have been constructed that incorporate all remaining ideas, which are explained in 'Biebboxes' section.

Biebboxes

The examples as referred to in 'Supporting Workshops to Empower Participants' section are intended to support further workshops aiming to provoke thinking about the content of the laboratory in a collaborative way. Appropriate support should allow for working with different topics, themes and ideas attached to the current way schools provide their education, and should avoid repetitive sessions to prolong participation.

The final design is called Biebboxes, and can be seen as a product-service-system, that supports different ideas, stimuli, workshops, topics and challenges that have been suggested by the participants in the previous session. Biebboxes are book-shaped containers that come in three different styles that stand for different subject-directions. These directions are derived out of the three clusters that could be distinguished in the communicated ideas that were created by the participants. Biebboxes communicate what kind of content can be found inside, and becomes the basis for a future workshop. The three different styles are: *Locality, Actuality* and *Diversity.* Within the Biebbox themed 'Locality', ideas to make are of benefit for local organizations, community houses and people inside the quarter. Think of ideas like 'making something meaningful for the inhabitants of an elderly home'. The 'Actuality' Biebbox contains ideas for workshops that attach to current affairs and topics from newspapers and/or local media. The idea to make something for the children of a refugee centre fits in this box. The last Biebbox, themed 'Diversity' incorporates many different ideas in many different directions. An example is a treasure hunt throughout several libraries of the Library The Hague to find out what to make during that workshop, or a score system that can unlock goodies when reaching a certain amount of points by making. The Biebboxes and their content are illustrated in Figs 7.6 and 7.7.

Repeatability of the Process

After the technology laboratory has been equipped with machinery and techniques, another group of young participants has been selected to work with the Biebboxes and refine the workshop process. The participants were provided with a common identity to associate with, many ideas on what to make, how to make it and for whom were generated by the participants. A design was formulated to support working with different ideas and idea directions inside the lab with a view to ensure the continuation of the project. The process of the current project has been

Figure 7.6 Three different versions of the Biebboxes.

Figure 7.7 Content of Biebboxes.

closely reviewed to determine which steps are of crucial value to assemble a group of participants that feel empowered due to the techniques they were able to work with inside the laboratory. These steps form the basis of a self-sustainable business model that can help the Library The Hague to continue and expand the New Dutch Maker labs across other locations of the Library The Hague. A small guide serves as a 'how-to', while

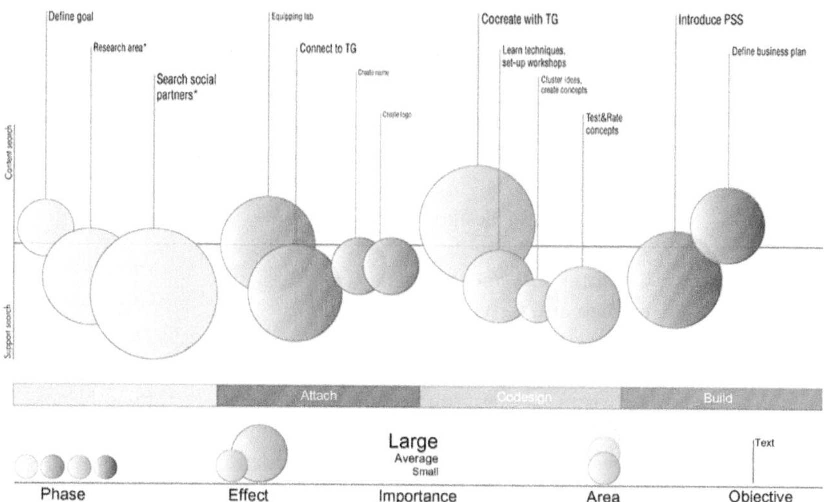

Figure 7.8 NDM business model enabling scaling of the NDM project.

setting up a new NDM lab. This model reminds library employees what steps are crucial and how the present laboratory setup can be improved (Fig. 7.8).

DISCUSSION

In the current section, we first look in more detail at the similarities and differences in both social living labs. Table 7.1 presents a brief overview.

Cocreation was a crucial element of both social living labs, allowing the designers to orient the design solution towards the actual needs of the local community and participants, while at the same time to enable the development of co-ownership among stakeholders.

Community Empowerment

The value of following this approach lies in its iterative nature, allowing initially broad assignments to develop into concrete design proposals aimed at fostering the talent empowerment of communities in need. The design solutions are not forced upon the recipient user group community, in an attempt to design 'for' them; instead they emerged from the context by embracing a participatory bottom-up view – designing 'with them'. A valuable part of this method is becoming a user of the context itself (Pucci & Mulder, 2015). In the exploratory phase of the *Star(t) to Shine*

Table 7.1 Overview of similarities and diversities in both social living labs

Project title	Star(t) to Shine (Pucci, 2013a)	New Dutch Makers (Havenaar, 2016)
Project	Design project (Delft University of Technology)	Design project (Delft University of Technology)
Duration	6 months	6 months
Initiative	Transdisciplinary design-inclusive research centre Creating 010 (including its FabLab and Citylab Rotterdam)	Library the Hague, location Schilderswijk
Goal	Design a hybrid community platform encouraging residents' active and cohesive participation to initiatives aimed at promoting their unique cultural, social and economic values within their neighbourhood	Deliver a technological laboratory for the library Schilderswijk with its corresponding Product-Service-System. In the lab, local youth can be empowered to contribute positively to their neighbourhood
Approach	Research through Design Codesign	Research through Design Codesign
Focus	Design for empowerment	Design for empowerment
Participants	Age of 15–24	Age of 9–19
Final design	A peer-to-peer talent development platform A workshop where youngsters are empowered by getting involved with modern-day technologies	A self-sustainable technological laboratory for local youth A working space constructed by and for local youth, where empowered occurs by modern-day technologies
Cocreative partners	Wijkschool Feijenoord Rotterdam Offensief, Creating 010	Library The Hague, NextProjecten

project, this was done by visiting the local market, engaging in casual conversations with shopkeepers and having lunch at local restaurants; these activities clearly contributed to immersion in the local ecology, getting in touch with its unique values and giving a face to its residents. When connecting with local organizations, the ambassadors or gatekeepers of the local communities, the most valuable connections were made by empathizing, respecting and sharing (opinions, information and coffee), enabling the establishment of trust and the creation of valuable partnerships for the projects.

It can be said that gaining trust and bonding with the local community, the search for local champions and the participation of culturally diverse array of residents have been a crucial strategy to build social capital throughout the whole process in a participatory, bottom-up approach. This approach allowed the design solution to come from within the community and not from outside, planting a seed for positive change in the local society. Fig. 7.9 shows the designs made by some students.

These insights have been used as a springboard in the New Dutch Makers project, and additionally extensive efforts have been made to immerse with the local context. Working with a key figure (as ambassador) in a neighbourhood with detached and hard-to-reach youngsters appeared to be an efficient way to get in contact. The key figure has the trust of the inhabitants and forms a solid connection. When the ambassador is enthusiastic about the initiative and the participants feel their input is appreciated, this acts as a sensitizing step, which is more likely to lead to participation. Instructions and procedures might contribute to less interest, and participation. Instead through facilitating a cocreation process, participants' creativity has been sparked, and it seemed to encourage bonding as well. Co-ownership leads to a steady number of participants, who likely act as ambassadors of the project. Since social circles tend to be tight and small in areas like the Schilderswijk, this mouth-to-mouth promotion guarantees larger interest of local youth in the project. This phenomenon leads to a steady growth of possible participants, making sure the laboratory is always used – now, and in the future.

Giving the initiative away, by supporting the youngsters to create their own objectives, goals and dreams to reach within the laboratory, the

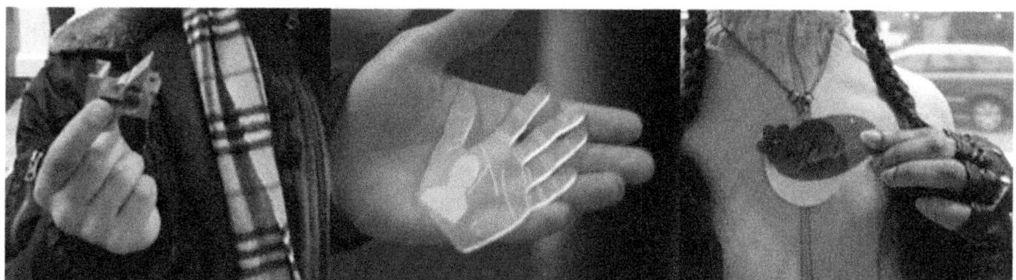

Figure 7.9 Afrikaanderwijk students with their work.

project will become self-sustaining. Input is being generated on a steady basis by the participants themselves, ensuring that there will always be renewing ideas to make. This again attaches to the current school model, bridging the gap to regular education. In a similar way, Bilandzic and Foth (2017) stress the value of connected learning spaces as an aggregation of individual experiences made through intrinsically motivated, active participation in and across various sociocultural, everyday life environments.

Creating a common identity for the youngsters to associate with will ensure a long-lasting bond with the project and will minimize the chances of fall-outs during the project. The project not only attaches the local youth to their own skills again, but also connects them to each other. Multicultural areas like the Schilderswijk tend to be segregated in smaller social groups, which are hard to enter by outsiders. The technological laboratory provided a place and a motive to come together and to feel and act as one. The common goal (making your dreams come true, finding your passion and being convinced of your own skills again) and common identity of the 'New Dutch Makers' made the group of participants feel alike. All differences fell away when entering the laboratory and a strong collective of cocreating youngsters was born. Ideas were made for local community houses, elderly homes, family that lived in the neighbourhood and so on. The technological laboratory seemed not only to have added value for the participants, but also contributed to the community's collective efficacy (Carroll & Reese, 2003).

The thread through the New Dutch Maker project was finding community support for a technological laboratory in the library Schilderswijk. The process to find this support has started through attaching to local social initiatives. This turned out to be a crucial step in gaining trust and respect of local community members. Being introduced by a key figure from the social network who has their respect provided the opportunity to get in contact with the target group: the youth from the Schilderswijk. The objective was to create, together with these youngsters, a technological laboratory in which the inhabitants from the Schilderswijk could experience (social) empowerment fuelled by the modern maker techniques. By letting the youngsters experience and try out a variety of techniques that were already at hand, they felt empowered and inspired immediately. This demonstrated the potential of the social living lab at start. When asking them to pledge themselves to the initiative a group of participants came together right away.

Already in earlier explorations, the risk of people dropping out was identified, jeopardizing continuity of the initiative. Interestingly, involving the youngsters in the development of a technological laboratory made them feel responsible and stimulated them to create input to work with. During different creative sessions, the participants provided a range of ideas on what to do with the lab, what to make and for whom to make. These ideas have been used as the basis of concepts that were created to evaluate in the laboratory. When the participants noticed that their ideas were used to think about a purpose for the laboratory ownership originated, they felt valued and were highly motivated to continue contributing to the development of the technological laboratory. This demonstrated the value of the codeveloping with local participants.

The empowerment that the participants experienced showed in various ways. Not only did the participants come to the laboratory on the days the lab was announced to be open, but several youngsters posted frequently at the library Schilderswijk, to see whether they could enter the lab at non-scheduled office hours. Another interesting observation was that through our network we have heard that various participants were promoting 'their' lab to friends and relatives. The participants who joined the initial cocreative session regarding the purpose of the lab, started to act as ambassadors of the social living lab, spreading the word and informing their neighbours about the opportunities in the lab. It seemed like the second objective, to make the lab self-sufficient as it comes to the contracting of participants was successful. Co-ownership had led to the feeling of being responsible. At the time that the lab started to run and workshops were given the participants felt proud to have been a part of setting-up the lab, making them proud ambassadors. By verbally promoting the laboratory a large number of motivated youngsters came to the library to see if there was a place for them as well to participate.

The Schilderswijk is frequently cited example of a place where people from all different cultures, educations and backgrounds live and work together within a limited area. The lab is a similar working environment, a place where everybody is welcome and people can collaboratively learn and explore. Differences among youngsters were seen as a strength, and turned into a collective optimism through desiring the same personal development and contributing to the (local) community. The fit of the 'New Dutch Makers' as the technological cornerstone is further ensured by a name that hints both to the past and future cultural heritage of the Schilderswijk and the Netherlands at large.

How to Sustain Social Impact?

Both social living labs clearly demonstrate the value of design for empowerment. It can be concluded that harnessing the most valuable assets in the local community, which are the young adults' passions and their digital literacy, and sharing these assets by rules of trust and reciprocity, enables a community to become cohesive and to empower its members. More specifically, the two presenting students at the 'Be Inspired Day' demonstrated in a convincing way, that it is indeed possible to transform from dropouts into engaged and successful individuals, who can become role models for their peers: 'stars shining bright in the local community'.

It was striking to see how Yussef, who made a medallion, was convinced that participating in the workshop was a mind-shifting activity for him. He clearly understood that he, too, could play a key role in this transformational change, by becoming an ambassador of the project. Clara, on the other hand, got accepted in a highly selective fashion design school. Her dream of becoming a fashion designer had always seemed far-fetched, but through participating in the workshop activities, she was able to design and make her own logo tangible, motivating her to create her own portfolio and apply for admission to the fashion design school. Breaking the autopilot of the status quo in the Wijkschool also proved to be an empowering experience for Sophie, the students' coach. Her passion for participatory educational approaches was not encouraged, and even hindered, by the school's management. Yet, she has been empowered by the collaboration with FabLab, since by facilitating her students' learning process with digital technologies, she could remain a relevant role model for them while learning new skills herself. Today, change goes faster than one can cope with, so it is not easy to remain relevant as an expert in a rapidly changing environment. Teachers need to learn how to teach in a different way.

The social living lab in Afrikaanderwijk empowers teachers as well to rapidly scale up their knowledge, allowing them to develop new skills so they can stay relevant for their students. By flipping the classroom, we can break the traditional divide between teacher/expert and student/recipient to create communities of colearners, subverting a mistake-averse teaching model into an environment that allows for experimentation and dynamic, lifelong and connected learning. In their new role of facilitators, teachers can become meaningful role models for their students, while at the same time training the students to become facilitators themselves. In this way, they can create a ripple effect on a wider societal scale. If we have the teachers and their colleagues on board, and they feel empowered to be ambassadors, we likely can scale the current practices, repeat them and have them embedded in the educational system, as well as making the platform self-sustaining.

The social relevance of the New Dutch Makers' social living lab is similarly multifaceted. It tackles the problem of youngsters who lost touch with their own ambitions, empowering them to start exploring their own talents again and developing their skills. Collaborating in a technology lab while using machines like a 3D-printer is more inviting than hanging around on the streets. Subsequently, the trend of the individualized society is being opposed by the collective aspect demonstrated in the social living lab: participants refer to themselves as being part of New Dutch Makers. Lastly, the social living lab puts the library on the map again in an original and contemporary way. It shows that the maker movement and the library have many things in common, though their joined forces can bring transformational change to the Schilderswijk.

The New Dutch Maker lab, equipped with the Biebboxes, can serve as a proof of concept for other libraries. The corresponding social business model enables other locations of the library to repeat the codevelopment process and to open more technology laboratories across the city of The Hague. After the first 6 months, the lab participants ran their sessions almost self-sufficiently, even though the designer initiated the sessions and was available to assist the process when required. The lack of a full-time available designer being the central point of contact within the technological laboratory has shown a great loss for keeping the momentum. The absence of such a contact person appeared to have created a threshold for the local youth to continue their participation. They felt less encouraged, and sometimes even neglected, just like they felt before they learnt from the opportunities in the laboratory. This observation shows that a (single) person of contact within such empowerment through making initiatives is key in sustaining community practices. Currently, only the empowered participants are visiting the laboratory, those that (still) need a role model have a hard time to enter the open doors of the New Dutch Maker laboratory again. Conclusively, a key issue remains how to design the designer out while sustaining the social impact.

CONCLUSIONS

The designed platforms as well as the intended interactions have been evaluated on empowerment, digital participation and social impact. It can be concluded that they lowered not only the threshold of access to digital fabrication in low social and economic status communities, they also activated participants to become active cocreators in a variety of workshops while collaboratively learning new skills. In keeping with Alsop and Heinsohn (2005), we view empowerment as someone's capacity to make effective choices and to transform these choices into desired actions and outcomes. The extent or degree to which a person is empowered is influenced by personal agency (the capacity to make purposive choice) and opportunity structure (the institutional context in which choice is made). The current interventions have established various degrees of empowerment, by providing opportunities to make choices, by enabling the participant to make choices, and has resulted in great achievements, oftentimes only dreamed of previously. Key to the success of both social living labs lies in leveraging technological skills and digital literacy by making digital participation and fabrication accessible and engaging them in an open codesign process. By making and sharing, they quickly acquired these so-called 21st century skills. The current work also showed the potential to build a thriving community of empowered individuals, serving as a 'best practice' for future interventions not only in similar sociocultural conditions (Sanders & Stappers, 2014). Next, the current work demonstrates the relevance of laboratories like FabLabs and makerspaces to reach out to underprivileged and uninitiated communities in a more inclusive way, empowering individuals to contribute to digital participation and open social innovation.

The following lessons can be learnt to sustain and scale community practices when embracing a participatory bottom-up approach to learning by making to promote digital participation:

1. Identifying the inherent learning potential of digital natives is important to transform reluctant learners or dropouts into empowered individuals;
2. Giving them shared ownership of their creative process ensures a more effective and lasting learning experience;
3. Enable participants to shape their own explorations and learning activities allows them to become colearners and cocreators of knowledge;

4. Next, a technology laboratory, like a FabLab, is an important node for establishing a physical and digital learning network to enhance empowerment and digital participation, while lowering the threshold of access to digital fabrication in education.

More work needs to be done to compare these and related initiatives on empowerment through making and the created social impact, and whether and how these social living labs have contributed to what kinds of empowerment, digital participation and social impact in a sustainable way. In our future work, we aim to gain more detailed insight in current practices and achievements on empowerment through making.

ACKNOWLEDGMENTS

The design interventions were part of two Master of Science graduation projects in Design for Interaction at Delft University of Technology. Emilia Louisa Pucci carried out *Star(t) to Shine* in Creating 010's program Meaningful Design in the Connected City in collaboration with Wijkschool Feijenoord and FabLab Rotterdam. The project has been nominated for the Dutch Design Awards 2013 and has been shortlisted for the Interaction 14 Awards as well. As a cherry on top, the TU Delft Student Inspiration Award 2014 was presented to Emilia Louisa Pucci, for being a role model herself for the TU Delft (student) community. Youri Havenaar elaborated upon this model in collaboration with the Library of The Hague to set up a maker laboratory in the Schilderswijk, resulting in the *New Dutch Makers* initiative. The findings of this project have been presented during the international IFKAD Conference 'Towards a New Architecture of Knowledge: Big Data, Culture and Creativity' in Dresden, Germany, 15–17 June 2016. Special thanks go to Sophie, Clara and Yussef, whose names are fictitious to ensure confidentiality in this chapter. We are grateful to all participants in the maker activities and in the codesign of the platforms, for their contribution in this great learning experience, we would have never dreamed of.

REFERENCES

Alsop, R., & Heinsohn, N. (February 2005). *Measuring empowerment in practice: Structuring analysis and framing indicators*. World Bank Policy Research Working Paper No. 3510. Available at SSRN <https://ssrn.com/abstract = 665062>.

Arnstein, S. R. (1969). A ladder of citizen participation. *JAIP, 35*(4), 216–224.

Bilandzic, M., & Foth, M. (2017). Designing hubs for connected learning-social, spatial and technological insights from coworking, hackerpaces and meetup groups. In L. Carvalho, P. Goodyear, & M. de Laat (Eds.), *Place-based spaces for networked learning* (pp. 191–206). Oxon: Routledge.

Blikstein, P. (2013). Digital fabrication and 'making' in education: The democratization of invention. In J. Walter-Herrmann, & C. Büching (Eds.), *FabLabs: Of machines, makers and inventors*. Bielefeld: Transcript Publishers.

Carroll, J.M., & Reese, D.D. (2003). Community collective efficacy: Structure and consequences of perceived capacities in the Blacksburg electronic village. In *Proc. of the 36th Hawaii International Conference on System Sciences (HICSS), Big Island, Hawaii.*

De Roeck, D., Slegers, K., Criel, J., Godon, M., Claeys, L., Kilpi, K., & Jacobs, A. (2012). I would DiYSE for it! A manifesto for do-it-yourself internet-of-things creation. In *Proceedings of NordiCHI'12, 14–17 October 2012, Copenhagen, Denmark*.

Frayling, C. (1993). Research in art and design. *Royal College of Art Research Papers, 1*, 1–5.

Havenaar, Y.M.P. (2016). *New Dutch makers: (Co-)designing a technological laboratory for the Library Schilderswijk* (Master thesis). Industrial Design Engineering.

Havenaar, Y.M.P., Mulder, I., & van der Meer, H. (2016). New Dutch Makers: (Social) empowerment through making. In *Proc. of IFKAD 2016, Towards a new architecture of knowledge: Big data, culture and creativity, Dresden, Germany, 15–17 June 2016* (pp. 820–831).

Honey, M., & Kanter, D. E. (2013). *Design, make, play: Growing the next generation of STEM innovators*. New York: Routledge.

Mostert-van der Sar, M., Mulder, I., Remijn, L., & Troxler, P. (2013). *FabLabs in design education. Proc. of E&PDE 2013, International conference on engineering and product design education, 5–6 September 2013* (pp. 629–634). Dublin, Ireland: Dublin Institute of Technology (DIT).

Mulder, I. (2015). A pedagogical framework and a transdisciplinary design approach to innovate HCI education. *Interaction Design and Architecture(s) Journal-IxD&A, 27*, 117–130, Winter 2015.

OECD (2011). *Towards an OECD skills strategy*. Paris, France: OECD Publishing.

Prensky, M. (2001). Digital natives, digital immigrants. *On the Horizon, 9*(5), 1–6.

Pucci, E. L. (2013a). *IK BEN STER(K)*. A peer-to-peer talent development platform empowering young adults *(Master thesis Design for Interaction, Faculty of Industrial Design Engineering)*. Delft, the Netherlands: Delft University of Technology.

Pucci, E.L. (2013b). IK BEN STER(K). *A peer-to-peer talent development platform empowering young adults (video)*. Retrieved from <http://t.co/0u1vGyP7KE>.

Pucci, E. L., & Mulder, I. (2015). Star(t) to shine: Unlocking hidden talents through sharing and making. *Distributed, Ambient, and Pervasive Interactions 2015*85–96. Available from http://dx.doi.org/10.1007/978-3-319-20804-6_8.

Rappaport, J. (1987). Terms of empowerment/exemplars of prevention: Toward a theory for community psychology. *American Journal of Community Psychology, 15*, 121–148.

Ryan, R. M., & Deci, E. L. (2000). Self-determination theory and the facilitation of intrinsic motivation, social development, and well-being. *American Psychologist, 55*, 68–78.

Sanders, E. B.-N., & Stappers, P. J. (2008). Co-creation and the new landscapes of design. *CoDesign, 4*(1), 5–18.

Sanders, L., & Stappers, P. J. (2014). From designing to co-designing to collective dreaming: Three slices in time. *Interactions, 21*(6), 24–33.

CHAPTER 8

Mapping a Connected Learning Ecology to Foster Digital Participation in Regional Communities

Ally Lankester, Hilary Hughes and Marcus Foth
Queensland University of Technology, Brisbane, QLD, Australia

INTRODUCTION

As physical and digital environments continue to fuse, individual and community wellbeing depends upon the ability to connect meaningfully and inclusively. Digital participation allows for all sectors of the community to build digital skills and confidence for improving economic opportunities and quality of life. This chapter proposes connected learning as a means to foster digital learning and participation. Connected learning is both ecology and pedagogy (Bilandzic & Foth, 2017; Ito et al., 2013). It colocates people and technologies in real-life contexts where purposeful learning occurs through idea sharing, experimentation, problem solving and creation. Outcomes can include fresh knowledge, social connection, a new process or product, or creative expression.

Based on the understanding that a learning ecology encompasses people, places, technologies and activities (Caldwell, Bilandzic, & Foth, 2012), this qualitative case study responds to the research question: *What is the nature of a connected learning ecology?* Set in Townsville, northeastern regional Australia, the case study maps an individual and collective connected learning ecology around different groups and contexts of digital access to identify opportunities for enhancing digital participation across these contexts. These cases included a group of young people learning game development at Townsville Creative and Technical College (TCTC), as well as a collective of artists, programmers and engineers involved in establishing a new makerspace and entrepreneurs with the Townsville Startup group (see Chapter 6: Mixhaus: Dissolving Boundaries With a Community Makerspace). The findings demonstrate

Digital Participation through Social Living Labs. DOI: http://dx.doi.org/10.1016/B978-0-08-102059-3.00008-3

the innovative potential of a methodological framework based on connected learning principles (Ito et al., 2013). Our study conducted a visual mapping of personal learning environments (Caldwell et al., 2012) to make visible the dimensions, links and gaps in a digital learning and innovation ecosystem to foster community-based learning and digital participation.

The chapter is in four parts. The first sets the scene by introducing connected learning as pedagogy and ecology and identifying the research gaps addressed by our study. The second part explains the case study methodology, while the third presents the individual and collective case study findings and maps the associated connected learning ecology. The chapter ends with a discussion of the study's findings.

SETTING THE SCENE

This study was part of the *Fostering Digital Participation* (FDP) project funded by the Australian Research Council. The project investigated social living labs methodology in Townsville, Australia (Hughes, Foth, Dezuanni, Mallan, & Allan, 2017). Living labs offer a dynamic environment for innovation and experiential learning where 'users are immersed in a creative social space for designing and experiencing their own future' (Schumacher, 2015, p. 4). Although living labs are increasingly applied to a range of community and market research settings, there is limited research that examines their nature and potential impact (Ballon & Schuurman, 2015) to enhance community digital participation. 'Social living labs' aim to fill this gap by providing contexts for researchers to work collaboratively with community members to identify particular digital participation needs, interests and opportunities and then cocreate and implement initiatives to build digital capabilities, social connectivity, community efficacy and confidence (see Chapter 1: Social Living Labs for Digital Participation and Connected Learning and Carroll & Reese, 2003).

The case study took place in Townsville, North Queensland, Australia. Townsville is situated on the coast of northeastern Queensland, Australia. It has a culturally diverse population of 192,038 (Queensland Government Statistician's Office, 2015). As a postmining boom regional city, Townsville faces an uncertain economic future and social challenges due to: the closure of nearby mines and refineries; high rates of unemployment and lack of new employment opportunities; increasing pressure on human services and infrastructure, including recreation and training; declining property values and slow population growth (Townsville City Council, Townsville 2011–2021; Wilson, 2016). Townsville was one of the first cities in Australia to be connected to the National Broadband Network (NBN) in 2010, a large Australian Government investment program to provide high-speed fibre optic cable Internet access across the country. However, access does not automatically translate into effective use (Gurstein, 2003). This study therefore sought to explore and map both existing and new digital participation opportunities in Townsville.

In a digitally mediated world of rapid technological innovation, digital participation is both a necessity and an entitlement to be involved 'socially, culturally, politically and economically in everyday life' (Hague & Williamson, 2009, p. 3). As an effect of the digital economy, around 40% of the Australian workforce is predicted to be replaced by computers and automation within 15 years (CEDA, 2015). Thus active digital participation is becoming essential to individual and community wellbeing. However, the effects of 'digital divide' (Perglut, 2011; Saunders, 2011) continue to exclude many from digital participation. Digital divide is a complex socioeconomic problem that extends beyond financial constraints and lack of connectivity or access to a personal digital device such as a smartphone (Notley & Foth, 2008). Physical and mental health, mobility, race and age can all impact on an individual's capacity to participate. Geographic location is also a significant factor, especially for residents in less advantaged rural and regional communities of Australia (Park, 2016). Moreover, the provision of network access to the Internet by itself does not ensure digital inclusion unless people are prepared to take up and use digital technologies (Gurstein, 2003; Williams, 2011; World Bank, 2016).

In addition to basic Internet access and device usage skills, digital participation requires knowledge about the affordances of digital technologies for communicating, using information, and learning (Armenta, Serrano, Cabrera, & Conte, 2012; Hague & Williamson, 2009). Digital literacy equips individuals and groups to confidently navigate digital environments and use a wide range of information and media effectively, critically, creatively and responsibly (Bruce, Hughes, & Somerville, 2012; Burgess, Foth, & Klaebe, 2006; Dezuanni, 2015). More than a static or discrete skill, digital literacy is an empowering process that ensures 'the life chances of individuals' (Walton, Kop, Spriggs, & Fitzgerald, 2013).

Connected Learning as Ecology and Pedagogy

Connected learning addresses the need to prepare people academically, emotionally and socially for change, while enabling boundary crossing between socioeconomic environments (Kumpulainen & Sefton-Green, 2012 and Chapter 6: Mixhaus: Dissolving Boundaries With a Community Makerspace). While the term *connected learning* has been used in various ways, this chapter brings together two recent perspectives of connected learning as *ecology* (Bilandzic & Foth, 2017) and *pedagogy* (Ito et al., 2013). The former highlights interpersonal and spatial relationships inherent in connected learning. The latter represents a set of pedagogical principles for designing environments conducive to connected learning.

As ecology, connected learning links people, places and resources across the community (Bilandzic, 2016). It fosters social, self-directed and collaborative learning. It is 'diversified and spread across digital and physical spaces' (Caldwell et al., 2012, p. 15) that include homes, schools, neighbourhoods and digital spaces. Intrinsically motivated communities of social learners, who share diverse capabilities for purposeful outcomes, populate the ecology. Digital technologies provide the ecology's vital links:

> *Like the distribution of water or electricity, the media and communication system underpins the spheres of work, education and commerce in ways that we increasingly take for granted.*
>
> ***Ito et al. (2013, p. 41)***

As pedagogy, connected learning fosters interest-driven practices and supportive relationships that open livelihood pathways through diverse forms of knowledge and expertise (Ito et al., 2013; Kumpulainen & Sefton-Green, 2012). It assumes that when young people (and other community members) focus on particular interests and forge connections for themselves, learning is likely to be powerful and sustainable:

> *. . .in order to develop these cross-cutting repertoires of practice, young people need concrete and sustained social networks, relationships, institutional linkages, shared activities and communication infrastructures that connect their social, academic and interest-driven learning.*
>
> ***Ito et al. (2013, p. 47)***

As an informal learning approach (Coffield, 2000), connected learning draws upon the empowering potential of trusted relationships and shared practices where the learner decides when, where and how they learn. It promotes social justice in and through learning to ensure that all learners, not only those who are educationally privileged, can take full advantage of learning opportunities that the digital world has to offer for personal, academic and career success (Livingstone, 2009). Thus connected learning enables individuals to flexibly develop a range of entrepreneurial skills for real-life contexts:

> *Connected learning is realized when the learner is able to pursue a personal interest or passion with the support of friends, caring adults and/or expert communities and is in turn able to link this learning and interest to academic achievement, career success, or civic engagement.*
>
> ***Kumpulainen & Sefton-Green (2012, p. 10)***

The connected learning framework (Ito et al., 2013; Table 8.1) supports the design of innovative learning approaches and environments. Integrating social constructivist (Vygotsky, 1978) and networked learning principles, the framework supports interest-driven production-centred learning that is mediated by digital technologies. A connected learning environment is a network that links learners, interests and technologies. It can exist across physical and digital spaces, which are intentionally inclusive, safe, challenging and supportive.

Although the connected learning framework was originally developed as a strategy to reengage disaffected young people in formal education, it has demonstrated potential to promote informal or self-directed learning in a variety of settings including other age groups and in public libraries (Bilandzic, 2016; Bilandzic & Foth, 2017; Martin, 2015). Thus in addition to educational reform it offers a foundation for community renewal:

> *If we are to pursue an approach to educational reform that is about elevating all young people, it is critical that we consider outcomes not only in terms of individual success and competitiveness, but in relation to the health of the groups, communities and institutions that build and support connected learning environments.*
>
> ***Ito et al. (2013, p. 47)***

This study addresses research gaps associated with connected learning, digital participation and social living labs. While connected learning is increasingly used to engage school students, there is limited research that explores its potential to support community-based learning and digital participation. In addition, there is a need for an appropriate methodology to develop theory and evaluate the processes and outcomes of connected learning for social living labs. While Caldwell et al.'s (2012) participatory method has proved effective for studying specific connected learning ecologies, this study provided an opportunity to test its transferability to

Table 8.1 Connected learning principles

Spheres of connected learning	Connected learning combines learning approaches that are: • Peer-supported • Interest-powered • Academically oriented
Core properties of connected learning	Connected learning experiences are: • Production-centred: active use of wide range of technologies and media • Shared purpose: support cross-generational and cross-cultural learning around common goals and interest • Openly networked: accessible, visible learning through social media
Design principles for connected learning environments	Connected learning environments intentionally allow: • Everyone to participate: low barriers to entry so individuals and groups with varying skills and knowledge can contribute in many different ways • Learning by doing: experiential, project-based 'messy' learning • Constant challenge: challenges create need to know and share • Everything to be interconnected: access to multiple learning contexts, technologies, ideas, peer learners and mentors across communities

Source: Adapted from Ito, M., Gutierrez, K., Livingstone, S., Penuel, B., Rhodes, J., Salen, K., & Watkins, S.C. (2013). *Connected learning: An agenda for research and design* (p. 78). The Digital Media and Learning Research Hub.

multiple community contexts and – as a visual participatory mapping tool – to complement participants' narratives of their learning experiences.

RESEARCH DESIGN

This research adopted a qualitative study approach to address the research question: *What is the nature of a connected learning ecology?* In order to explore connected learning ecology as a real-life phenomenon (Simons, 2009), the study focused on the cases of three groups of people (19 study participants in total) with broad common interests in using and learning about digital technology. A researcher (the lead author) used her local knowledge and contacts to identify suitable research sites and participants. The 19 participants were recruited via email and phone using convenience sampling (Patton, 1990).

The participant groups clustered around three different sites where digital learning occurs:

- Townsville Creative Technologies College (TCTC): a vocational education centre;
- Mixhaus: a mobile makerspace where community members gather intermittently on an ad hoc basis (see Chapter 6: Mixhaus: Dissolving Boundaries With a Community Makerspace) and
- Townsville Startup: a meet-up group where members meet online and in various public places.

Participants were recruited from these groups to capture a variety of perspectives that included students in formal education, active community members and entrepreneurs. While we considered each group as a separate case, we also recognized the likelihood of group members having connections with other individuals and groups across the Townsville community. Therefore, we combined the individual data to create a joint data pool for a collective case study that represents a wider and interconnected learning ecology.

To structure data collection and analysis, we used a participatory action design research method (Bilandzic & Venable, 2011; Sanders, Brandt, & Binder, 2010). This method allowed us to examine key elements of a connected learning ecology associated with links between work, play and learning and the convergence of the physical and the digital towards hybrid spaces in the context of urban public places (Bilandzic & Venable, 2011; Caldwell et al., 2012). Through narrative and visual methods we identified the places, activities and social networks where people are creative and productive (work), have fun and socialize (play), and develop digital and social knowledge and skills (learn).

The researchers intentionally avoided the term *connected learning* during interviews and focus groups. As a scholarly concept, it was unlikely to be meaningful to community participants. Moreover, as the research aimed to explore connected learning as a novel concept, it was important not to (mis-)lead participants through use of the term.

Case Study Sites and Participants

Townsville Creative Technologies College (http://heatleysc.eq.edu.au/Facilities/Campuses/Pages/Townsville-Creative-Technologies-College.aspx) (TCTC) is a digital trade-training centre that delivers nationally accredited vocational training in creative industry technology, business, design and production areas. The TCTC participants included nine students, two females and seven males – three were over 18, and six were school students aged between 13 and 18 years. Students were studying professional and academic computer game development or music and film production courses at TCTC separate to their school curriculum. As well as attending classes, individual students met informally before class on a regular basis at the college to generate and share ideas for their creative productions.

Mixhaus (www.mixhaus.com.au) is a mobile community makerspace (Educause Learning Initiative, 2013) in a refurbished shipping container. It was created in 2016 by a collective of Townsville community volunteers who fitted out the container with digital equipment for maker workshops with support from the ARC-funded FDP project. The Mixhaus is moved to different public locations for community events and workshops. The six Mixhaus participants were aged between 25 and 45 years: one female and five males. As volunteers, they contributed to the Mixhaus steering committee and/or in the design and construction. Their occupations ranged across the creative industries, community engagement, IT, video production, theatre, engineering, and higher education (see also Chapter 6: Mixhaus: Dissolving Boundaries With a Community Maker Space).

Startup Townsville (www.meetup.com/StartupTownsville/) is a regional entrepreneurship peer-support group for individuals with a passion for technology, business, social causes and community empowerment. The group promotes events and monthly meet-ups, teaches startup techniques and helps entrepreneurs find investment. The three Startup Townsville participants were regular attendees or organizers of Startup events and aged between 35 and 60 years: one female and two males. Their occupations spanned engineering, innovation, research and creative industries.

Data Collection and Analysis

Semistructured interviews were held with Mixhaus and Startup participants at workplaces or coffee shops. TCTC students participated in a focus group at the college.

To complement participants' narratives of their learning experiences, Caldwell et al.'s (2012) participatory design method provided a visual ecology of individual learning environments and the level of importance of different spaces and people in these learning environments. At the start of each interview or focus group the researcher asked participants to draw a map (diagram or mind map) of places where they engaged in learning about their particular digital-based interests. They were given the following instructions:

1. On a piece of paper, draw a diagram or map of places where you engage in learning and creating, starting out from TCTC, Mixhaus or Startup Townsville. Include: technologies and social networks used for learning; learning activities and physical sites of work, socializing and creativity.
2. List keywords describing creative work and learning/interests that you engage in at these places.
3. For each place, use one, two or three coloured dots to indicate the intensity of:
   - Your learning – green dots;
   - Productive creative work – yellow dots and
   - Relevance of people to your learning/creative work – blue dots.

   (1 dot = low, 2 dots = medium, 3 dots = high)

Some participants drew pictures; e.g., houses, or a vision for their community that connected the sites. Whereas others made circles or lists, e.g., of activities, names of people, online sites and/or activities with joining lines and arrows like a mind map. Some drew lines on their maps to show how places were connected for different learning interests; e.g., a dotted line for a weak link or low activity, a bold line for a stronger link or more regular activity, and sometimes arrows to identify the influence of the relationship between places. A few participants mapped places according to their main digital-based interest, while others drew detailed maps of their general personal learning environment. One map represented different stages of the learning process at different sites. Some maps separated more formal and informal areas, or social-physical and digital learning spaces. Some participants mapped out the 'Internet' as a place, whereas others listed digital activities they did in the different places. One participant's map (Fig. 8.1) showed his different learning sites as a vision for connecting the region's contexts.

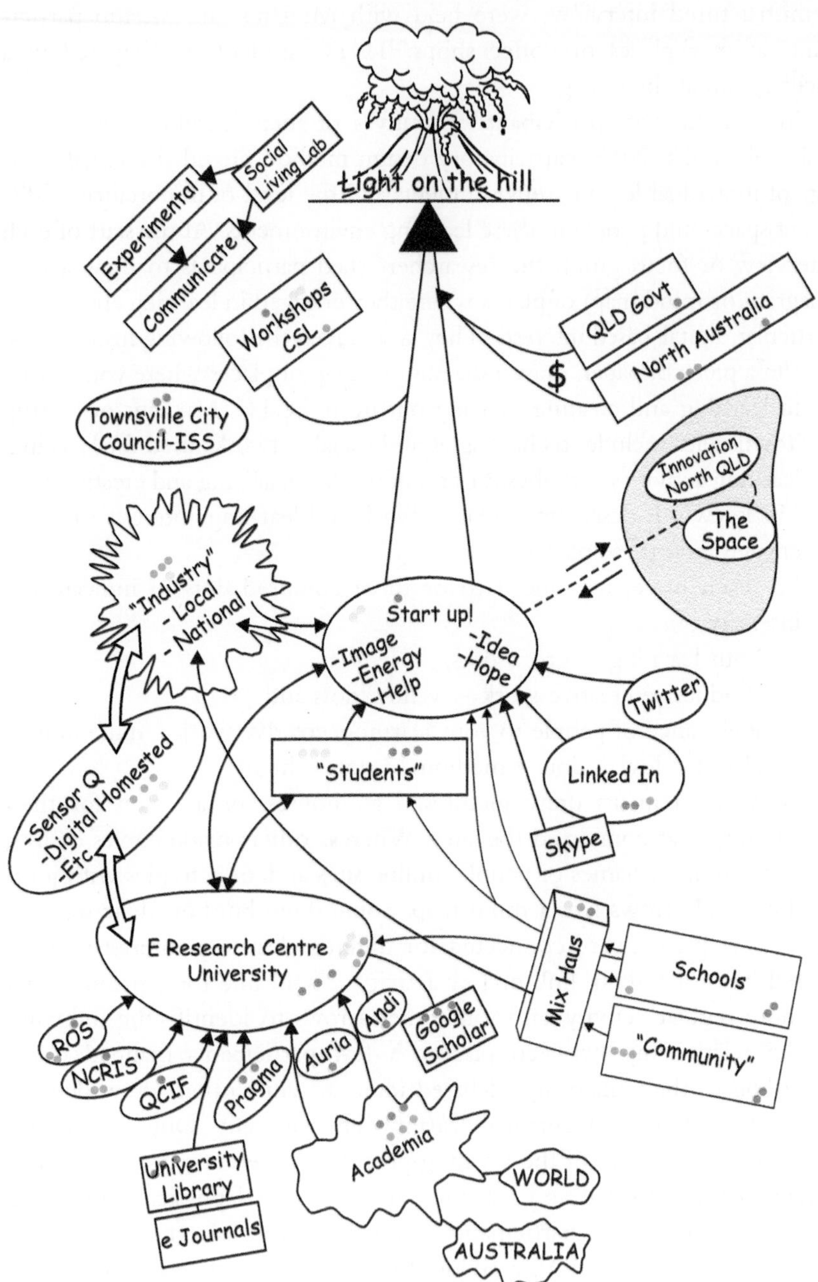

Figure 8.1 Example of a Startup participant's map.

Following the mapping activity, the researcher invited participants to explain their diagram and to answer a set of questions about perceptions of learning processes, challenges and opportunities and factors facilitating learning related to particular sites.

The lead author analysed the verbal and visual data thematically using frameworks of connected learning (Ito et al., 2013) and personal learning environments (Caldwell et al., 2012). Analysis related to the subresearch questions about the what, where, who, how and why of connected learning and involved:

1. Describing and comparing learning environments and processes with and across case study groups (TCTC, Mixhaus and Startup Townsville);
2. Identifying the range of sites (beyond TCTC, Mixhaus and Startup Townsville) where participants learnt, as well as the intensity (low, medium and high) of learning, creative productivity and the people of relevance;
3. Identifying and describing learning communities based on digital interests;
4. Relating the findings to relevant principles of connected learning and
5. Summarizing suggestions for enhancing learning and digital participation in the broader Townsville community.

The findings are presented in various ways, which collectively create a map of the connected learning ecology. We acknowledge that ecology is dynamic and changes over time, so this map is a snapshot. As well, it cannot be representative of the entire Townsville ecology, but is based on the data contributed by the 19 study participants. Tables and graphics describing different elements of the ecology are complemented by participants' first-hand commentary.

The main limitation of the study was the relatively small number of participants from similar backgrounds in one regional town. However, this was offset by the benefit of gaining rich and authentic first-hand insights of community-based digital participation and learning. Triangulation through visual and narrative data collection and analysis methods contributed to the trustworthiness of the findings.

INSIGHTS FROM THE THREE CASE STUDY SITES

Participants represented on their individual maps the range of sites where they engaged in digitally oriented activities and learning. These maps depicted particular interests and interconnections between physical–digital and formal–informal sites. They also indicated differing levels of complexity and varying emphasis on technology and people, as shown in the following sample maps from each research site. For example, one of the Mixhaus participant's map shows different sorts of social interaction and engagement that occur at cocreation sites in general (Fig. 8.2), whereas one of the TCTC participant's map shows different technical and social aspects of the game development learning process at particular sites (Fig. 8.3).

A Mixhaus participant mapped a variety of learning sites for engaging in community, academic and interest specific forums to explore new ideas through the cocreation of hardware and software (Fig. 8.2).

A TCTC participant mapped the main learning sites for learning, creating and playing games with friends that branch out from TCTC as a key learning site for game development (Fig. 8.3).

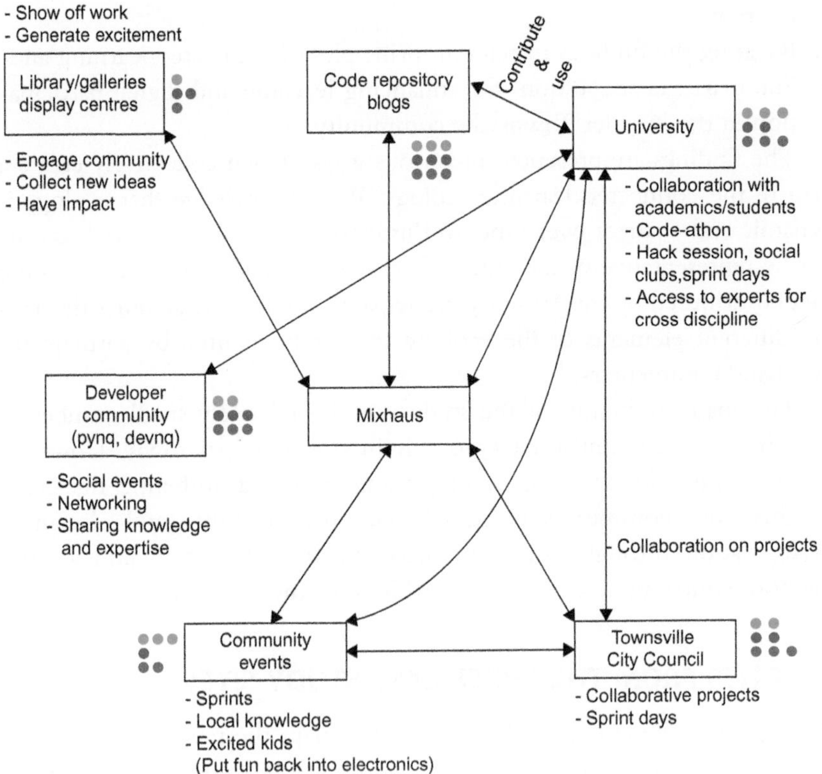

Figure 8.2 Mixhaus participant's map.

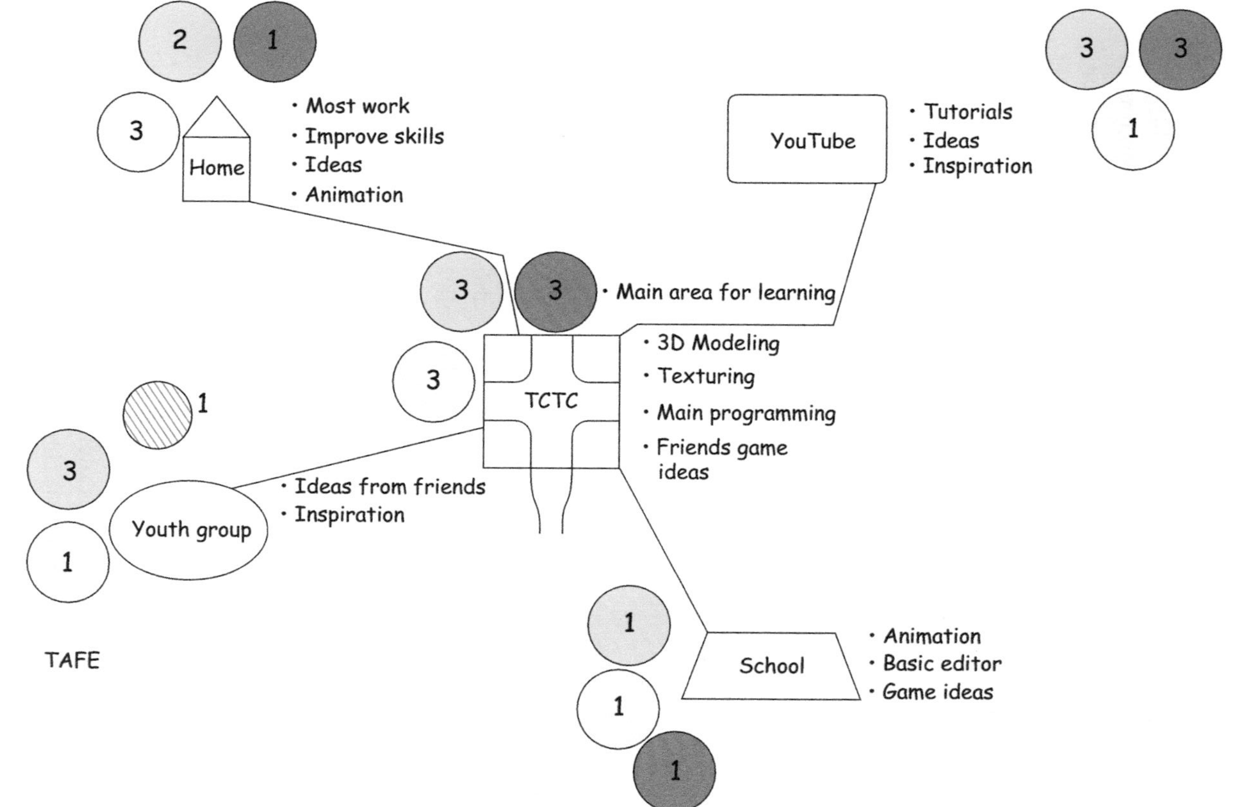

Figure 8.3 TCTC participant's map.

A Startup Townsville participant mapped different sites and the purpose and level of formality of these sites, for engaging in digital entrepreneurial learning activities (Fig. 8.4).

Shifting the focus from learning site to learners, it was evident in the case study that three distinct digital learning communities had formed around Mixhaus, Startup Townsville and TCTC. These communities principally appeared to support learning related to game development, software and coding and making. Defining characteristics for each community, with regards to member identity, interests, learning approaches and digital engagement are summarized in Table 8.2.

The game development community was centred around TCTC and mainly comprised TCTC participants. Members were connected in both formal and informal learning settings. More formal structured classroom learning occurred at the college that involved game development with teachers and peers, which appeared to be a springboard for further informal learning. Some members also collaborated with each other informally at TCTC as a peer group and in each other's homes. At home and at friends' places, members developed and fine-tuned animation creation, editing skills and game ideas learnt and created at TCTC.

Members of the community software and coding community often connected through Startup Townsville. They reported that meetups and idea generation forums (e.g., Start-up weekends) were important for connecting with others, having unstructured discussions and cogenerating ideas. Members said that they learnt with others about how to problem-solve, code computer programs and develop applications or platforms. While one person said that he also met face-to-face with others in meetups, most community members learnt and collaborated online to solve problems and create code in open-source code hosting sites such as Github and Bitbucket. At these sites, members reported learning code storage, reuse and collaboration, new programming languages and new technology and tools. They said they used code repositories such as Github for sharing code and hosting a project and finding other people who had worked on similar projects. While some community members described collaborative online learning as challenging and creative, several reported that sustained forums such as the Townsville Startup weekend were needed to connect people, ignite collaborations, be exposed to new ideas and perspectives and take risks in a safe, informal and supportive environment.

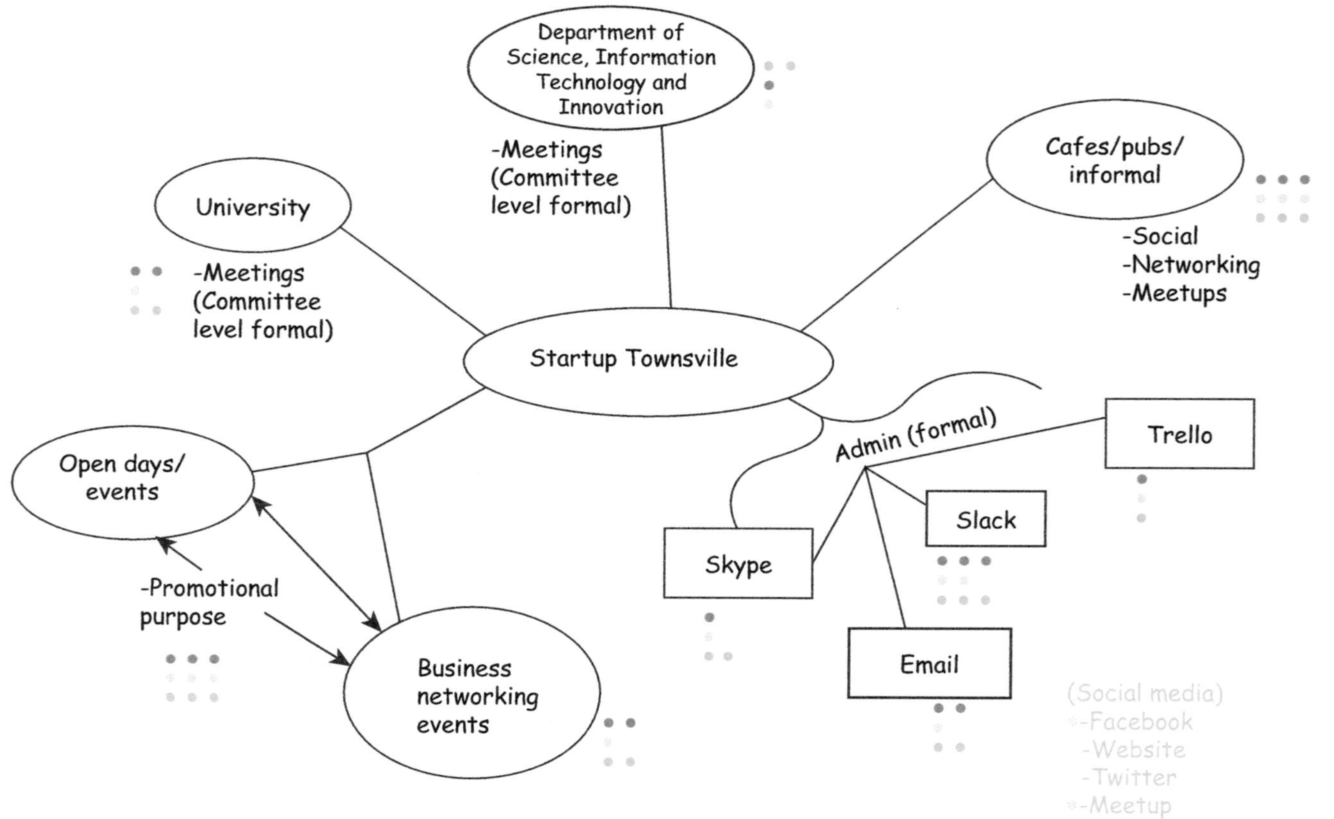

Figure 8.4 Startup Townsville participant's map.

Table 8.2 Defining characteristics of Mixhaus, Startup Townsville and TCTC digital learning communities

Digital community	Shared interests	Learning approaches	Digital engagement
Maker Site: *Mixhaus* Identity: *Digital creators*	Electrical engineering, visual arts, electronics, software and hardware development, DIY, video production and socializing	Social experiential learning: cocreating, trouble shooting in the workplace, at community events and informal gatherings	Tutorial videos, webinars, code repositories and host sites, collaborative forums, social media and networking sites
Software and coding Site: *Startup Townsville* Identity: *Digital entrepreneurs*	Entrepreneurism, innovation, creative industries and business acumen	Professional peer learning: sharing and generating ideas with peers and colleagues at formal and informal events and places	Digital networking and communication sites (e.g., Trello, Slack), social media, government data sites and information sharing
Game development Site: *TCTC* Identity: *Digital animators*	Gaming development and film and music production	Hands-on, peer learning: cocreation and production with peers and experts at college, informal gatherings and in homes	Animation/game development sites, tutorial videos, coding and programming

The maker community was made up of Mixhaus participants who collectively initiated and built a mobile makerspace. Members shared visions and desires of possible learning related to: connecting people, cocreating technology; bringing different interests together and enabling practical learning experiences (e.g., electronics), and facilitating politics and collaboration. They saw Mixhaus as a place for experimentation, cocreation and interaction with people on a similar intellectual level with similar interests, but also for mixing with people with different ideas to solve problems; and also as a platform for conversation and new ideas and feeling a sense of community. One participant said that the experience of 'learning by doing' helped them become more interested in the theoretical underpinning of technology. Another participant believed that the space had the potential to be an education tool for innovation and digital skill sharing, creating economic/revenue opportunities for people and building people's confidence through creating things with others.

Interpersonal links between the three communities were limited, although most participants reported connections with other learning places. Some members of the maker community interacted with the software and coding community to learn and collaborate informally – both face-to-face and digitally. They cocreated code and developed software with others at university and in the broader community.

There were some notable differences with regards to community members' connections with other learning places beyond Mixhaus, Startup Townsville and TCTC, as illustrated in Fig. 8.5. Some participants from each group showed a learning connection to public libraries, galleries and workplaces. However, only Startup Townsville members revealed connections to business networks and government. Mixhaus and

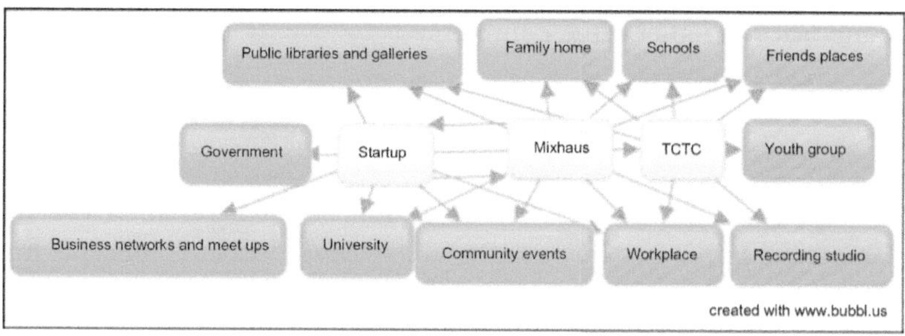

Figure 8.5 Map of connections between learning sites.

TCTC members indicated connections to a recording studio, friends' places, schools and the family home. Startup Townsville and Mixhaus members had connections to community events and the university. While Startup Townville and Mixhaus members had connections with each other, TCTC members had no connection to Mixhaus or Startup Townsville.

Mixhaus and Startup Townsville members were most similar in terms of the mix of learning places that they reported. Perhaps because of the older age group, they had connections to workplaces, community sites and networks (e.g., business, innovation and academic) that are associated with professional or 'expert' roles. The Startup Townsville participants mapped out more formal places concerned with entrepreneurial, academic and business interests. They mainly mentioned online networking and communication sites for collaborating with people in conjunction with physical meetings to share and develop ideas. Mixhaus participants included more creative, computer and electronic interests and a greater range of informal sites (e.g., home and friends). Mixhaus participants placed more emphasis on activities with a social purpose and included informal learning at sites such as community events, schools and public places (e.g., gallery), mostly in the role of 'expert' (e.g., STEM and STEAM (Science, Technology, Engineering, Arts and Maths)). In contrast, TCTC participants mostly mapped out TCTC, their home, friends' homes and school as their learning sites. Online learning was mostly to further learn and explore ideas and techniques that they had generated with peers and mentors at TCTC.

Face-to-face social interaction was emphasized by most participants across sites as a crucial part of their learning as it gave them opportunities to 'trouble shoot', have in-depth and serendipitous discussion, problem solve and learn together. One commented:

> *I do a lot of self-learning, but physical places to learn from with groups or teams is a much better way to get something happening and solve more complex issues (P1).*

However, participants also said they found online searching and networking to be important for learning about new ideas and concepts from experts and others in a variety of contexts that they could easily access and share.

MAPPING A CONNECTED LEARNING ECOLOGY

Combining participant data from all three case study sites, this section moves from individual to collective experience to define the wider connected learning ecology of the study's participants.

As summarized in Figs 8.6 and 8.7, participants engaged in productive/creative work and learning with varying intensity at a range of places in addition to Mixhaus, Startup Townsville and TCTC. The tables show the spread of participants who variously reported low, medium or high

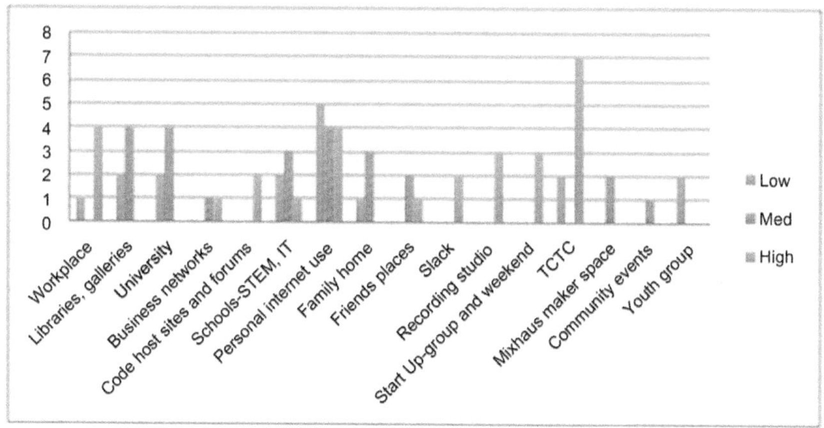

Figure 8.6 Intensity of productive/creative work at different places.

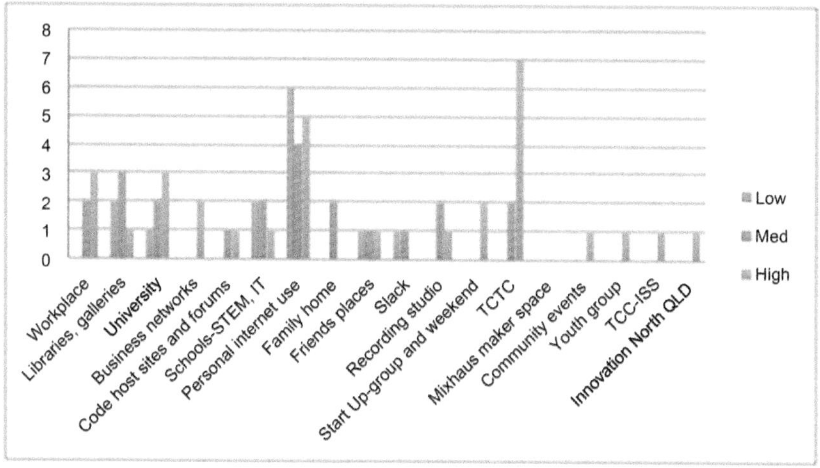

Figure 8.7 Intensity of learning at different places.

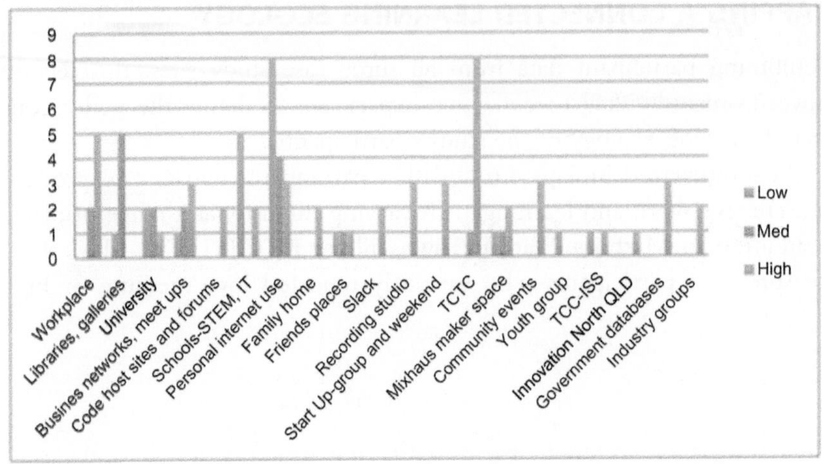

Figure 8.8 The relevance of people at different sites to participants' learning.

intensity of productive/creative work and learning at particular places. For example, as shown in Fig. 8.6, a total of 13 people mentioned the Internet, although five of these rated it as 'low intensity', while four people rated it as 'medium intensity' and four rated it as 'high intensity' for productive/creative work.

At most sites the participants considered people to be relevant to their learning, as shown in Fig. 8.8. It is notable that participants mentioned people were relevant to their learning in both physical and digital places, with TCTC as place of highest people-related relevance and personal Internet as most frequently reported people-relevant place.

Taken as a whole, the three digital learner communities represent a connected learning ecology. As shown in Table 8.3, key aspects of the digital learner communities can be mapped against principles of the connected learning framework (Ito et al., 2013). These aspects are distinguished (in the table's header row) as the What, Where, How, Who and Why of the ecology. Colour coding is used to indicate where particular principles are most evident:

- Dark grey – shading relates to *Spheres of connected learning* and learning approaches that are peer-supported and interest-powered;
- Light grey – shading relates to *Core properties of connected learning* and experiences that are production centred, shared purpose and openly networked and
- Grey – shading relates to *Design principles for connected learning* and environments that allow learning that happens by doing.

Table 8.3 Connected learning ecology for the three learning 'communities'

	What interests	Where the learning is happening	How the learning is happening	Who are the people most relevant to learning	Why – what is the purpose of the learning	Illustrative quotes
Maker community	• Electronics (e.g., sensor building), machinery, milling, robotics, 3D printing, visual and digital art • Community and school engagement, events, face-to-face digital technology-based forums INTEREST POWERED ACADEMICALLY ORIENTED	• Creative commons, Startup forums, school, university, council events, public library and galleries, community makerspace, community events OPENLY NETWORKED	• Cocreating, practical experimentation, problem solving and skill-sharing, technology and mixed-media initiatives and innovations • Cross-generational and multidiscipline contexts • Software/hardware/ visual art creations • Ideate and design • Socially SHARED PURPOSE LEARNING HAPPENS BY DOING	Schools, university, public library and gallery makerspace, community events, workplace PEER SUPPORTED	Innovation revenue opportunity Collaboration Social networking PRODUCTION-CENTRED	'Learning how to wire electronics and construct more things and build physical stuff with people who have different ideas and how that mixes and moulds together to come up with a final process' (P1)
Game community	• Game development, animation creation and production • Online gaming INTEREST POWERED ACADEMICALLY ORIENTED	• Open source, home, informal gatherings, TCTC, Internet game development sites OPENLY NETWORKED	• Cocreating new games (generating ideas, sharing skills) with friends at home and informally at college SHARED PURPOSE LEARNING HAPPENS BY DOING	Teacher/tutor, friends places, home PEER SUPPORTED	Making authentic games for entertainment and to solve problems PRODUCTION-CENTRED	'I am learning the most from the students around me – getting ideas, improving on ideas, 3D modelling, also doing home research on YouTube based on what I've learnt at TCTC first. We get together at friends' houses that have better resources and come up with ideas on how we can create things, online and face-to-face' (P2)

(Continued)

Table 8.3 (Continued)

	What interests	Where the learning is happening	How the learning is happening	Who are the people most relevant to learning	Why – what is the purpose of the learning	Illustrative quotes
Developer and coding community	• Software and hardware development-digital sites and forums and face-to-face gatherings • Business/ entrepreneurial acumen/reality • Community engagement INTEREST POWERED ACADEMICALLY ORIENTED	• Open source, Github, Bitbucket, Sparkfun, Aduino, instructables Pynq, Devnq, Start-up weekend, informal gatherings, workplace, university OPENLY NETWORKED	• Cocreating code and projects online and face-to-face • Sharing code, hosting and building on projects and cocreating code with others online SHARED PURPOSE LEARNING HAPPENS BY DOING	Friends places, mentors, Startup forums University, Community events, workplace, innovation space, government department, university PEER SUPPORTED	Developing software and computer-programming for entrepreneurial purposes PRODUCTION-CENTRED	'I am using someone else's code and making changes to improve my knowledge and experience and others can learn from my changes to the code' (P3)

SUGGESTIONS FOR ENHANCING DIGITAL PARTICIPATION AND LEARNING

The participants provided a range of suggestions in response to the researcher's question: 'What opportunities do you see for enhancing digital participation and learning in the Townsville Community?' Responses align with the same What, Where, How, Who and Why aspects addressed in Table 8.3.

As outlined in Table 8.4, the suggestions range from needs for informal practice-focused learning environments to more opportunities for learning from experts. There was a strong emphasis on creating opportunities for social connections, 'learning by doing' with others and building new and different skills to enhance economic opportunities and social cohesion. In addition, the participants suggested a need for places with people that create a feeling of comfort, inclusivity and safety with easy and free access to technology and equipment.

DISCUSSION

The study's findings provide real-life insights about connected learning in three digital learning communities. They also highlight the conceptual complementarity of connected learning ecology and pedagogy. While ecology focuses on learning spaces and connections between them, pedagogy focuses on the process of learning and interactions between learners. Key findings are summarized in relation to the study's main research question.

The connected learning ecology in this study is a complex web of people, places and technologies connected through digital technology interests. It brought together digital learners including school students, business people, academics and artists who supported each other's learning in various ways and contexts. The focus shift between places (the three sites) and people (the three learner communities) indicates that neither people nor places alone constitute a connected learning ecology; it is the synergy and discursive relationships between them that fosters creative, productive activity and outcomes.

Connected learning has no fixed abode. Rather than separating learners by educational context, there is the cocreation of knowledge based on interest and needs. A connected learning ecology merges digital and physical spaces, formal and informal approaches and academic

Table 8.4 Suggestions for enhancing digital participation and learning in the broader Townsville community

What needs to happen	Where it needs to happen	How it needs to happen	Who needs to be involved	Why it needs to happen	Illustrative quote
Cocreation, experimentation, social connection	Safe, comfortable, exciting, open, practice-oriented, physical, informal, flexible, less-structured, freeform, public spaces with free access to technology	• Egalitarian and nonhierarchical management • Mentoring and facilitation by passionate receptive, well-networked, knowledgeable and skilled mentors or teachers • Creation of an environment that encourages failing and risk taking and feels supported • Mixing of different demographics, institutions, disciplines and learning spaces	• A mix of experts for different interest areas • Mentors and teachers • University and other knowledge areas, industry and community	Innovation and connecting with others, solving problems creatively, active learning	'We need opportunities for connecting more. . .achieving the same outcomes but not in the same ways. . .so really looking at what the commonalities in what they want to achieve and what skills and experience and education and tools are needed to match them up that way. . .looking at those relationships (P4)'

and purposeful interests. While connected learning spans multiple sites, in this study it appears to thrive in a social, supportive and safe environment, thus, demonstrating the importance of a social context for digital learning. Connected learners evidently come together in different spaces as particular needs arise, interacting across educational, business, community and online boundaries that, generally, enable practical experimentation and cocreation, as well as the flow and exchange of ideas. Although digital technologies support interaction and collaboration, physical meeting places continue to be important for social interaction and connectivity.

Connected learners participate in multiple ways to enable productive outcomes, including sharing of ideas, collaborating practically on projects and mentoring. Thus, the study demonstrates *shared interest* to be a strong motivator for learning. The findings also show that formal learning promotes ongoing informal learning (and possibly vice versa) and there is an associated need to complement informal discussion with peers and learning from experts with more formal learning opportunities to extend essential knowledge. For example, the school students' participation in the game community extended beyond formal assignment work to extracurricular projects with peers in informal contexts.

Social interaction and 'learning by doing' is also revealed as important. In this study, practical experiences with others appear to facilitate challenge, information sharing, skill building and social support to develop interests. Conversing with others, sharing ideas and experiences supports social connection and motivation. Thus sustained collaboration can build trusted social networks with potential to expand the diversity and capacity of the wider ecology.

While digital technologies mediate connected learning, in this study they also constitute the participants' shared interest. Most cases showed productive, creative, entrepreneurial outcomes as being more important than academic ones. Participants engaged in a rich informed process of learning about and with digital technologies that fortuitously extended their digital literacy and participation (Bruce et al., 2012).

The connected learning principle *everyone can participate* is only partially fulfilled in this ecology, as the nature of membership varies across the digital learning communities. The maker community appears to be the most diverse and open to all-comers. While there is some interconnecting between Mixhaus and Startup Townsville members, the TCTC members seem as yet isolated from these two groups. As a result of these gaps, and in response to the suggestions by participants for ways to enhance learning, opportunities exist for providing cross-generational and cross-disciplinary learning experiences across the different groups and the whole ecology in informal, practice-focused learning environments. Digital participation could be enhanced through mixing different digital learning groups in informal, creative and open sessions (e.g., mini social living lab initiatives) with a focus on 'entrepreneurism and making' or 'entrepreneurism and gaming'. Furthermore, there is an opportunity to make the visual mapping of the Townsville connected learning ecology a public community project, which would allow different groups to find out about each other and connect if relevant.

The maker community's wide mix of interests and people appeared to give it vivacity. Applied to the whole ecology, this suggests that greater interaction between members of the three digital learning communities could advantageously increase social diversity, knowledge and expertise (Bilandzic, 2016). It could also extend opportunities for mentoring and peer-supported learning across traditional boundaries (Kumpulainen & Mikkola, 2014). For example, collaborative projects that connect younger game developers and more experienced business people could foster the kind of learning that productively fuses ideas and expertise for entrepreneurial success.

IMPLICATIONS OF THE FINDINGS

The findings of this research address the challenges of socioeconomic renewal faced by many regional communities in Australia and elsewhere. In the context of rapid social and technological change, there is a need for innovative strategies that not only foster digital participation across the community, but also ensure that all community members have the capacity to participate. This, in turn, calls for in-depth understanding of current digital activity and the identification of community-based learning needs.

Therefore, this Townsville case study provides evidence-based snapshots to inform the wider development of theory, policy and practice about connected learning ecologies in community contexts. By combining a participatory research design method (Caldwell et al., 2012) with the connected learning pedagogical framework (Ito et al., 2013) the study provides deeper understandings of what constitutes connected learning and its potential to empower people through digital participation. As a starting point for community renewal, connected learning provides a pedagogical model and environment for equitably building digital participation capacity, especially for those from less advantaged backgrounds.

As a contribution to connected learning theory, the findings support the development of a hybrid model of connected learning that integrates ecology and pedagogy. This integrative model would emphasize the synergy between people and places indicted by the findings and draw together the spatial elements that are emphasized in the ecology yet less evident in the framework. By addressing spatial elements of connected learning, the integrative model aligns with emergent thinking about the influence of learning environment as 'third teacher' (OWP/P Architects, VS Furniture, & Bruce Mau Design, 2010).

Applied to practice, the findings of this research extend the scope of connected learning from school-age students with academic intentions to community-based learning and digital participation. With its community focus, the proposed connected learning integrative model would support the design and evaluation of innovative informal learning, including social living labs. To enhance digital participation, the model promotes the digital literacy development that encourages thinking, creativity and confidence beyond particular skills or tools (Dezuanni, 2015). This model would encourage sustained learning as it is focused on learner interests and productive outcomes. It could also stimulate the creativity and productivity of self-directed learners when working collaboratively or side by side with others (Bilandzic, 2016; Bilandzic & Foth, 2017). Participation in such an environment could lead to entrepreneurial outcomes and enhanced employability.

This study also demonstrates the efficacy for community-based research through combining the visual participatory research approach (Caldwell et al., 2012) with analysis informed by connected learning framework principles (Ito et al., 2013). As described, the map activity is a useful way to contextualize the relationships, resources and practices that shape people's learning (Barron, 2006). The mapping and associated interviews enable participants to communicate a visual and verbal interpretation of their learning ecology. The connected learning framework draws out qualitative nuances in participants' narratives that, in turn, contribute deeper understanding about the experience of connected learning as ecology and pedagogy across different interest groups and sites. The emergent case study provides evidence of potential policymaking value about existing digital participation and further connected learning needs in regional areas (Notley & Foth, 2008). For example, such evidence might inform the provision of community-based learning that enables people to participate digitally in a world that is experiencing constant social, cultural, economic and technological change.

As connected learning ecology and pedagogy are relatively recent concepts, there is a need for further research to explore their potential for theory and practice. This includes development of the integrative model and related learning approaches that foster self-directed interest-driven learning. It is also important to explore additional community sites, beyond educational institutions and public libraries, where people can engage in this kind of learning as part of their daily lives, which will be more sustainable if they are self-directed rather than created (Bilandzic, 2016). Outcomes of this research could contribute to the creation of innovative learning and entrepreneurial opportunities in regional areas. In this way, further research could offer ways to reengage young people in formal education and enable community members generally to overcome social isolation and achieve economic security.

CONCLUSION

This study has revealed the complexity of a connected learning ecology and the potential of connected learning pedagogy to support interest-driven, peer-supported, productive learning. New understandings arising from this study about the nature and contexts of connected learning support further community-based initiatives and research to understand how connected learning interventions can support self-directed learning and enhance social connectivity and digital participation in communities that seek socioeconomic renewal. To this end, we propose the development of an integrative connected learning model to inform ongoing digital learning and participation, including through social living labs. The study also demonstrates the efficacy of visual and participatory design methodologies for community-based connected learning research. However, as this was a relatively small-scale study there is a need for further research of connected learning for digital participation in a wide range of contexts.

ACKNOWLEDGEMENTS

Complementing similar case study research work in Toowoomba, Queensland, this research project, 'Fostering digital participation through living labs in regional and rural

Australian communities', was supported under Australian Research Council's Linkage Projects funding scheme (project number LP130100469). Ethical clearance was approved by Queensland University of Technology (#1400000017). We thank the project partner organization, Townsville City Libraries, collaborating partners, James Cook University, La Luna Youth Arts, Jaycar Electronics Townsville and community members. We are also very grateful to the study participants for their time and contributions.

REFERENCES

Armenta, A., Serrano, A., Cabrera, M., & Conte, R. (2012). The new digital divide: The confluence of broadband penetration, sustainable development, technology adoption and community participation. *Information Technology for Development, 18*(4), 345–353.

Ballon, P., & Schuurman, D. (Eds.). (2015). Living labs: Concepts, tools and cases. Special issue. *Info, 17*(4). Available from http://dx.doi.org/10.1108/info-04-2015-0024.

Barron, B. (2006). Interest and self-sustained learning as catalysts of development: A learning ecology perspective. *Human Development, 49*, 193–224.

Bilandzic, M. (2016). Connected learning in the library as a product of hacking, making, social diversity and messiness. *Interactive Learning Environments, 24*(1), 158–177.

Bilandzic, M., & Foth, M. (2017). Designing hubs for connected learning: Social, spatial and technological insights for coworking spaces, hackerspaces and meetup groups. In L. Carvalho, P. Goodyear, & M. de Laat (Eds.), *Place-based Spaces for networked learning* (pp. 191–206). New York: Routledge.

Bilandzic, M., & Venable, J. (2011). Towards participatory action design research: Adapting action research and design science research methods for urban informatics. *Journal of Community Informatics (JoCI). Special Issue: Research in Action: Linking Communities and Universities*, 7(3).

Bruce, C. S., Hughes, H., & Somerville, M. M. (2012). Supporting informed learners in the 21st Century. *Library Trends, 60*(3), 522–545. Available from http://dx.doi.org/10.1353/lib.2012.0009.

Burgess, J.E., Foth, M., & Klaebe, H.G. (2006). Everyday creativity as civic engagement: A cultural citizenship view of new media. In *Communications Policy & Research Forum*, 25–26 September 2006, Sydney. <http://eprints.qut.edu.au/5056/>.

Caldwell, G., Bilandzic, M., & Foth, M. (2012). Towards visualising people's ecology of hybrid personal learning environments. In M. Brynskov (Ed.), *Proceedings of the media architecture biennale 2012* (pp. 13–22). Aarhus: Association for Computing Machinery (ACM).

Carroll, J.M., & Reese, D.D. (January 6–9, 2003). Community collective efficacy: Structure and consequences of perceived capacities in the Blacksburg electronic village. In *Paper presented at the 36th Hawaii International Conference on System Sciences (HICSS), Big Island, Hawaii.*

Committee for Economic Development Australia (CEDA). (2015). *Australia's future workforce?* Melbourne.

Coffield, F. (2000). *The necessity of informal learning*. Bristol: Policy Press.

Dezuanni, M. (2015). The building blocks of digital media literacy: Socio-material participation and the production of media knowledge. *Journal of Curriculum Studies, 47*(3), 416–419.

Educause Learning Initiative (ELI). (2013). *7 Things you should know about makerspaces*. <https://net.educause.edu/ir/library/pdf/ELI7095.pdf>.

Gurstein, M. (2003). Effective use: A community informatics strategy beyond the digital divide. *First Monday, 8*, 12.

Hague, C., & Williamson, B. (2009). *Digital participation, digital literacy and school subjects: A review of the policies, literature and evidence*. Futurelab. <http://www2.futurelab.org.uk/resources/documents/lit_reviews/DigitalParticipation.pdf>.

Hughes, H., Foth, M., Dezuanni, M., Mallan, K., & Allan, M. (2017). *Fostering digital participation through social living labs in Townsville: A qualitative case study from regional Australia*. Communication Research and Practice. https://doi-org.ezp01.library.qut.edu.au/10.1080/22041451.2017.1287032.

Ito, M., Gutierrez, K., Livingstone, S., Penuel, B., Rhodes, J., Salen, K., & Watkins, S. C. (2013). *Connected learning: An agenda for research and design*. The Digital Media and Learning Research Hub.

Kumpulainen, K., & Mikkola, A. (2014). Boundary crossing of discourses in pupils' chat interaction during computer-mediated collaboration. *Learning, Culture and Social Interaction*, *3*, 43–53.

Kumpulainen, K., & Sefton-Green, J. (2012). What is connected learning and how to research it? *International Journal of Learning and Media*, *4*(2), 7–18.

Livingstone, S. (2009). *Children and the Internet*. London: Polity.

Martin, C. (2015). Connected learning, librarians and connecting youth interest. *Journal of Research on Libraries & Young Adults*, *6*. <http://www.yalsa.ala.org/jrlya/2015/03/connected-learning-librarians-and-connecting-youth-interest/>.

NBN Co. (2010). NBN Co announces "first release" sites for high-speed network. Retrieved from <http://www.nbnco.com.au/content/dam/nbnco/media-releases/2010/first-release-mr-final-02-mar-10.pdf> Accessed 23.03.16.

Notley, T., & Foth, M. (2008). Extending Australia's digital divide policy: An examination of the value of social inclusion and social capital policy frameworks. *Australian Social Policy*, 7, 87–110.

OWP/P Architects, VS Furniture, & Bruce Mau Design (2010). *The third teacher: 79 ways you can use design to transform teaching & learning*. New York: Abrams.

Park, S. (2016). Digital inequalities in rural Australia: A double jeopardy of remoteness and social exclusion. *Journal of Rural Studies*, January, online

Patton, M. (1990). *Qualitative evaluation and research methods*. Beverly Hills: Sage.

Perglut, D. (2011). Digital inclusion in the broadband world: Challenges for Australia. In *Paper presented at the Communications policy and research forum Sydney, November 7, 2011*. <http://apo.org.au/files/Resource/digital_inclusion_donperlgut_0.pdf>.

Queensland Government Statistician's Office (2015). *Queensland regional profiles: Townsville City Local Government Area (LGA 2011)*. The State of Queensland (Queensland Treasury). <http://statistics.qgso.qld.gov.au>.

Sanders, E.B.-N., Brandt, E., & Binder, T. (2010). A framework for organizing the tools and techniques of participatory design. In *PDC10: Proceedings of the 11th biennial participatory design conference* (pp. 195–198). doi:10.1145/1900441.1900476.

Saunders, P. (2011). *Down and out: Poverty and social exclusion in Australia*. Bristol: The Policy Press.

Schumacher, J. (2015). *Alcotra Innovation Project: Living labs definition, harmonization cube indicators and good practices*. <http://www.alcotra-innovation.eu/progetto/doc/Short_guide_on_Living_Labs_and_some_good_practices.pdf> Accessed 23.03.16.

Simons, H. (2009). *Case study research in practice*. Los Angeles: Sage.

Townsville City Council. (Townsville 2011–2021). *Community plan: Leading, creating, connecting: Shaping a place to be proud of*. Retrieved from <http://www.townsville.qld.gov.au/council/publications/communityreports/Documents/Community_Plan.pdf>.

Walton, P., Kop, T., Spriggs, D., & Fitzgerald, B. (2013). Digital inclusion: Empowering all Australians. *Australian Journal of Telecommunications and the Digital Economy*, *1*(1), 9.1–9.17. Available from http://dx.doi.org/10.7790/ajtde.v1n1.9.

Williams, T. (2011). *A fair go for all in the digital era: Towards a digital inclusion roadmap.* Huwaei. <http://democracy.nationalforum.com.au/articles440.html>.

Wilson, J. (2016). In regional Australia, messages about fairness can't drown out the three-word slogans. *The Guardian, Thursday 19 May.* Retrieved from <https://http://www.theguardian.com/commentisfree/2016/may/19/inregional-australia-messages-about-fairness-cant-drown-out-the-threeword-slogans>.

World Bank (2016). *World development report 2016: Digital dividends.* Washington: World Bank. <http://dx.doi.org/10.1596/978-1-4648-0671-1> Accessed 12.02.16.

Vygotsky, L. (1978). *Mind in society: Development of higher psychological processes.* Cambridge: Harvard University Press.

CHAPTER 9

Connecting Digital Participation and Informal Language Education: Home Tutors and Migrants in an Australian Regional Community

Margaret Kettle
Queensland University of Technology, Brisbane, QLD, Australia

INTRODUCTION

A colleague shocked me recently with a question about the findings of the current social living lab. We were at a conference and presenting on another project about second language student achievement trajectories and factors that influence them. Our conference presentation focused on statistical analyses and measures of achievement at particular points in time. The shock of my colleague's question derived from its incommensurability with the goals and principles of social living lab research. Where the academic trajectory study prioritized manipulation of data and discrete time-points, the social living lab emphasized process and the duration of participation across time. As illustrated in this chapter, the lab was characterized by participant coconstruction, innovation and ongoing, cumulative change.

The chapter presents the social living lab that I developed with a group of community-based tutors helping adult second language learners in Oakey, a small town in regional Australia. The tutors were volunteers and enroled in a home tutoring program run by a Technical and Further Education (TAFE) college in the nearby city. The focus of the program was one-on-one English language support for migrant women employed as skilled workers in the local abattoir. The women had settled with their families in Oakey and worked with their partners and husbands in the same processing plant. The tutors were tasked with meeting the women in their homes and helping them with their English needs. The problem for the tutors was their own lack of English language teaching (ELT)

Digital Participation through Social Living Labs. DOI: http://dx.doi.org/10.1016/B978-0-08-102059-3.00009-5

qualifications and the frustration of how best to help their migrant 'clients'. The social living lab was a response to this issue and designed to augment the tutors' introductory TAFE training with tailored knowledge and skills for addressing their clients' language needs. An additional goal was to upskill the tutors in the use of digital technology as a resource for developing meaningful language learning activities. The emphasis on developing digital skills is aligned with the Australian Government-funded Fostering Digital Participation (FDP) project that housed the social living lab and is described elsewhere in this collection.

This chapter introduces the home tutors and the migrant women as well as the town of Oakey. It highlights the changing circumstances of the town as migrant families have settled and taken up skilled employment in the two local meat processing plants. It also introduces the methodological principles of social living lab research and the contingencies that arise in the negotiated, participatory design of a project that operates across a protracted period of time. Finally, the chapter concludes with thoughts on social change in the areas associated with the social living lab: digital participation, second language teaching and learning and migrant settlement in a rural community. It also proposes extensions to thinking on social living lab methodology that foreground the complex processes of creative coconstruction using concepts such as 'thinking through the middle' (Stengers, 2005) and research in a 'minor key' (Heimans, Singh, & Glasswell, 2017).

THE CONTEXT

A Rural Area in Transition

Oakey is a small rural town located 140 km directly west of the state capital of Brisbane. It is part of the Local Government jurisdiction based in the regional city of Toowoomba – known as the Garden City thanks to its cool, damp climate on top of a mountain range. Oakey lies 28 km to the west of Toowoomba and is drier, making it well suited to pastoral industries. In the Accessibility/Remoteness Index of Australia (ARIA+), the Toowoomba area is classified as Inner Regional Australia (The State of Queensland: Queensland Treasury, 2017). Over the past 10 years the region has experienced population growth of about 1.3% with a boom expected in the coming decade (Geoghegan, 2015). The reasons are economic and social: the economic expansion is expected to come from the proactive efforts of local companies especially farmers and food manufacturers to export internationally, especially to China (Courtney, 2017) and the social stimulus is being led by generous programs from the local government to settle refugees and migrants in the region (Geoghegan, 2015).

Oakey began as a white settlement in the 1860s, thanks to the expansion of the railway from Toowoomba. The main industries that developed around the town were mining and agriculture, especially dairying. The town was named after oaks lining creek banks in the area. During World War II, nearly 2000 defence personnel were stationed north of Oakey at a Royal Australian Airforce base that was established to repair and maintain military aircraft. The airbase still operates but has been a controversial source of concern since 2016 when its firefighting foam was found to have contaminated groundwater and soil in the area (Roe, 2016).

At the time of the 2011 Australian Government census, Oakey had a population of 4529 with slightly more males (51%) than females and a median age of 37 years across the population (Australian Bureau of Statistics, 2013). While the major country of birth was overwhelmingly Australia (86%), the other top birth countries were England (1.9%), New Zealand (1.1%), Brazil (1.0%) and the Philippines (0.6%). Other than English, Portuguese (the main language of Brazil) was the top language spoken at home followed by Tagalog, an Austronesian language spoken by people from the Philippines. The chief industry of employment was Meat and Meat Product Manufacturing which employed about 16% of people, followed by Defence with 5%. Nearly one-fifth of the people in Oakey indicated that they performed voluntary work through an organization or group (The State of Queensland: Queensland Treasury, 2017). In terms of access to the Internet, 74% of private dwellings in the Toowoomba area including Oakey were connected.

It is not surprising that the meat processing industry is a major employer in Oakey. Like much of the region, dairying has been replaced by beef as the key pastoral industry (The University of Queensland, 2015). The town has two large, export-focused meat processing plants: Oakey Beef Exports and Beef City. Oakey Beef Exports is owned by NH Foods Australia which is a subsidiary of NH (Nipponham) Group, a leading Japanese fresh meat, ham and sausage company (NH Foods Australia, 2017). Beef City is owned by the Australian operation of JBS Group – the world's biggest meat processing company headquartered in Brazil and named after its founder, rancher Jose Batista Sobrinho (Condon, 2016; JBS Australia, 2017). Both companies operate vertically across feedlots, meat processing and shipment with all operations occurring onsite in Oakey.

The two meat processing companies are large employers of local people. Oakey Beef Exports claims to employ 750 people in a range of positions including tertiary-educated engineers and microbiologists, skilled process workers for the slaughter floor and boning operations and unskilled labourers. JBS boasts a workforce of 8500 people across its 10 meat processing facilities (including Beef City), 5 feedlots and 7 distribution centres. The migrant women in the study were all Brazilian. They were skilled process workers who identified their job as 'slicer'. They were in Australia on a 457 visa – or more officially, the Temporary Work (Skilled) Subclass 457 visa.

Skilled Migration and Settlement in Australia

In terms of migration, Australia is known as a settlement country along with New Zealand, Canada and the United States (Organisation for Economic Co-operation & Development (OECD), 2014a). It has a three-streamed permanent migration programme: Skill, Family and Special Eligibility, with the Skill stream accounting for about 68% of the 2015–16 programme (Department of Immigration, & Border Protection (DIBP), n.d.). One of the biggest changes to Australian migration patterns in the past decade has been the increase in long-term temporary migration, with the largest categories being international students and temporary skilled migrants on 457 visas (Phillips, 2013). This visa category is skill-focused and intended to be demand-driven. It provides a means of attracting skilled workers from overseas and enables employers to sponsor skilled workers quickly and for a period of up to 4 years. While the category is designed to alleviate skills shortages, it has also on occasion been associated with worker exploitation, especially among migrants from non-English-speaking backgrounds (Phillips, 2013).

Managed labour migration has long played an important role in Australia (OECD, 2014b). Moreover, the country has a history of making migration contingent on settlement in regional and rural areas (Hugo, Khoo, & McDonald, 2006). Within the permanent Skill stream, numerous initiatives are available to encourage skilled migrants to work in state-based and regional schemes. Since the introduction of 457 visas in 1996, the numbers have reflected the economic conditions. For example, in the period of 2011–12, numbers increased to 125,000 with many skilled migrants working in industries associated with construction, health care and social assistance (Phillips, 2013). By June 2016, with the decline of the mining boom, the numbers were just under 95,000 (Wright, Sherrell, & Howe, 2017). In OECD countries including Australia recent figures show total temporary labour migration comprises about 2 million people (OECD, 2014a). These temporary migrants contribute to labour-market flexibility and tend to fill niches in fast-growing or declining sectors of the economy. The jobs are often unattractive to domestic workers and have few career prospects (OECD, 2014b). For many migrants, work in another country is a means of securing a more prosperous future for their families and they often look to converting temporary visa status into permanent residency in the countries where they find employment (OECD, 2014b).

The Brazilian women in the social living lab were on temporary 457 visas under the nominated category of 'skilled meat worker'. As noted earlier, they were identified as slicers; the slicer job description is determined by a meat industry labour agreement that includes duties such as 'cutting meat to separate meat, fat and tissue from around bones' (DIBP, n.d.). Skilled slicers are not permitted to do unskilled or labouring jobs. The agreement requires them to have a certain level of English language proficiency (an average score of 5 on the International English Language Testing System (IELTS) tests of speaking, listening, reading and writing) and mandates the provision by employers of at least two Workplace Health and Safety language measures such as the use of interpreters and the installation of multilingual signs. Workers on temporary 457 visas in the category of 'skilled meat worker' can progress to permanent residency in Australia after 3 years and 6 months if they meet the criteria for experience, qualifications and English language proficiency. They must also be under 50 years of age (DIBP, n.d.) (After this chapter was accepted – on 18 April 2017 – the Australian Government announced that the 457 visa subclass would be abolished and replaced by a new Temporary Skill Shortage (TSS) visa in March 2018 (DIBP, 2017). The new scheme will introduce a 2-year stream and a 4-year stream, the latter largely resembling the original 457 4-year program although with a new test to encourage employment of local workers. Within the announcement, concessions for the employment of skilled migrants in regional Australia were retained).

THE OAKEY SOCIAL LIVING LAB

The Oakey home tutoring project was one of a number of social living labs developed under the umbrella of the FDP project. The lab methodology was highly conducive to working with diverse stakeholders on the goal of building community and promoting competency in ELT and learning. The Oakey social living lab was designed by myself as an applied linguist from Queensland University of Technology (QUT). Dr Cherie Allan from the FDP project assisted with the implementation of the lab, recording field notes, audio-recording sessions and taking photographs. She also managed the bank of iPads from the FDP project that was available for use by the tutors and their clients.

Participants

The Oakey social living lab comprised the volunteer home tutors in Oakey, their migrant 'clients', the TAFE college Adult Migrant English Program (AMEP) Home Tutor Coordinator in Toowoomba and the researchers from QUT in Brisbane. The lab was conducted as a complement to the local AMEP run by the TAFE Queensland South West in Toowoomba. The AMEP is funded by the Australian Government and entitles migrants to 510 hours of English tuition as part of their settlement plan; home tutoring is one of their language learning options (Department of Education and Training, 2016). Volunteer tutoring is presented as an opportunity to help others and to make a valuable contribution to the settlement of migrants who have English as a Second Language (ESL). The program involves meetings in the student's home (or another convenient place) once a week to deliver 'a lesson tailored to that student's learning needs'.

The Oakey home tutors were a group of six women who had lived in the area for decades, either as farmers or as a result of their husbands' jobs. Some were retired, while others worked in part-time and volunteer roles in schools, aged care facilities and health clinics. They were often involved in church activities and very committed to the Oakey community. Most had travelled extensively in Australia and abroad, and had a strong sense of wanting 'to give back' to the overseas people who were now living in their town. Interestingly for a small town, some of the tutors did not know each other prior to the social living lab.

The migrant 'clients' were younger than the tutors and comprised a group of seven, all of whom knew each other well. The women were mostly married with children in the local primary and secondary schools which meant they worked shifts at the meatworks to fit in with school finishing times. They were skilled slicers and responsible for cutting fat off the meat as it came along the production line. For some of them, the work was heavy and their husbands had been relocated in the abattoir to help with lifting. The women worked under intense time pressure and were required to stay on their shift until their production quota was met. Most returned to Brazil during the Christmas holidays and maintained regular communication with family via social media and email. In Oakey they were part of a close-knit community that centred largely on their church. A visiting priest provided Portuguese-language church services as part of his ministry to Brazilian communities in rural towns.

The English language proficiency levels of the women varied. One had completed her meat inspector's exam and considered herself to be 'good at writing'. The issue for her was vocabulary and functional expressions:

> *Most of the time I know only the key words but I want to know the whole phrase. Like when I am talking to friends, sometimes I want to tell them something but I only know the key words but I want to know the whole phrase so that I make sure they understand me.*

Other women wanted help with speaking and comprehending English, while one older woman who had been in Australia for 10 years said that she wanted to be able to talk to her 'Aussie' coworkers on the production line: 'My job is I slice, my friend English, my (other) friend English talk talk talk, I understand a little bit'.

Social Living Lab Methodology

The social living lab approach was adopted for the project because of its emphasis on collaboration and coconstruction of innovations by users in a community setting (Ballon & Schuurman, 2015). The digital focus of the FDP project meant that some of the innovations would involve tutors learning to use online and digital technologies. Ballon and Schuurman (2015) maintain in their review of 15 years of living labs that most projects are practice-driven and orientated to user participation and real-life experimentation. Labs are seen as both research and an environment for innovation. Five key elements are present: (1) active user involvement that empowers users to impact the innovation process; (2) real-life contexts; (3) multistakeholder participation; (4) a multimethod approach and (5) cocreation involving iterations of design cycles (Ballon & Schuurman, 2015). These principles were useful in guiding the Oakey social living lab.

The socially oriented approach to living lab methodology advocated by Franz (2015) was also useful. Franz argues that technological and economic approaches traditionally associated with living labs need to be translated into the social sciences in order to stimulate cocreation and collaboration in social research questions. Socially oriented living labs can foreground the local context and take diverse social groups into consideration. As such, they provide a 'space of encounter' for participants that involves the implementation of a set of 'living methods that suit both the research design and the local requirements' (Franz, 2015, p. 53).

While living labs have become established as a part of innovation policy, especially in relation to Information and Communications Technology (ICT), they continue to be underresearched (Ballon & Schuurman, 2015). A theoretical and methodological gap exists between the research literature and the community of practice using living lab methodology. Schuurman, De Marez, and Ballon (2015) argue that the practice side of living labs is much more developed than the theoretical side. They call for the better grounding of practice in theory in order to advance the field. The ideas in 'Discussion' section are a response to this call.

The Process

The socially oriented living lab in Oakey was focused on experiences and interactions that scaffolded the tutors' learning of second language teaching and digital resource development. While I was able to provide 'expert' input on second language methodologies, my digital knowledge and skills were elementary and also in need of development. The key contributors to ICT knowledge in the lab were Dr Allan from the FDP project and the TAFE AMEP Home Tutor Coordinator. The objective of the social living lab was to move participant know-how from novice to more autonomous practitioner and digitally aware ESL tutor. In line with the steps outlined in Chapter 10, Pittsworth Stories: Developing a Social Living Lab for Digital Participation in a Rural Australian Community, the Oakey social living lab involved negotiations between the researchers and the local stakeholders. It included individual and focus group interviews with tutors and clients, as well as workshops, informal input sessions and feedback on second language teaching methods and ICT resource development. In this way, the project was both enquiry- and need-based. It was codesigned and coconducted by the tutors, migrant women, Home Tutor Coordinator and researchers.

That being said, the contingent nature of the project meant that the researchers had to be agile and responsive to the needs arising in each session. The codesign principle necessitated ongoing negotiation to determine the direction of the project, albeit within the FDP project framework and the principle of moving participation from initiation to independence. The argument in this chapter is that contingency, agility and responsiveness are parts of the researcher toolkit in a social living lab that need to be foregrounded in new theorizations of methodology. Concepts such as 'thinking through the middle' (Stengers, 2005) and research in a 'minor key' (Heimans, Singh, & Glasswell, 2017) can assist in understanding the complexities of conducting this type of research.

Events and Experiences

The Oakey living lab involved a number of face-to-face, or offline events, and online experiences that spanned 12 months and are ongoing. The use of social media and email has ensured the longevity of the lab. The initial negotiations for the research began between myself and TAFE Queensland Home Tutor Coordinator in late 2015. The focus of the discussions was English language support for growing numbers of migrants and refugees in the region. Of main concern were ways to develop the ELT capabilities of volunteers who worked directly with the migrants through the home tutoring program. The initial lab event was a professional development seminar that I conducted for home tutors at the TAFE college on 26 February 2016. The seminar was titled *Leading Low Proficiency Students from Reception to Production in Functional English* and designed to address the acknowledged lack of formal language training characterising the backgrounds of many home tutors (Barkhuizen, 2015). In addition, it highlighted the role that tutors can play in the low-structure context of clients' homes.

Attendance at the seminar – 60 instead of the predicted 20 – indicated the high level of interest in learning new knowledge and skills in second language teaching. Many of the attendees were volunteers with the AMEP as well as refugee and church organizations. Some were also TAFE employees seeking professional development in ELT. Key activities in the seminar included immersing participants in a second language learning experience via a German lesson and providing them with take-home activities such as using an iPad for teaching the spoken and written forms of vocabulary items. Three home tutors from Oakey had travelled to Toowoomba for the seminar and stayed behind afterwards to meet with the Home Tutor Coordinator, me and Dr Allan. The three tutors were excited about what they had learned in the seminar and keen to participate in the social living lab; indeed, they wanted technology tips for the next English lesson with their client. One woman was interested in downloading an audio-recording app onto her smartphone for modelling the pronunciation of English words for her client to practise. Another wanted to use her iPhone to take photographs of items in the home so her client could learn the words. The third borrowed an iPad to design a lesson using the example from the seminar. The tutors were highly motivated to try the new technologies, if also a little apprehensive.

A follow-up session was held in April 2016 on a Saturday morning in a large meeting room at the Oakey library. Six home tutors attended as did six Brazilian clients, and the daughter of one of the clients. Some of the tutors and clients were home tutoring pairs. The other participants in the session were the two QUT researchers and the TAFE Home Tutor Coordinator. This session was designed as an initial 'space of encounter' where both groups could meet and hear more about each other's lives. It also had two pedagogic aims: (1) to informally assess the English language levels of the clients and to elicit their perceived English language needs and (2) to model for the tutors how to communicate in English with their clients, including the low proficiency speakers. The point was that artificial 'foreigner talk' is unnecessary and unwelcome in language teaching encounters.

From a social living lab perspective, a key goal of the session was to form the two groups into a community. The initial spatial organization of the two groups had the Brazilian clients seated on one side of the room and the tutors on the other side. This seemed to reflect research showing that migrants and other English language learners often lack social contact with the wider community (Barkhuizen, 2015). They reside in an 'ethnic bubble' (Yates, 2011) that comprises members of their family and ethnic community but few people from the English-speaking population. English language tutors who access people in their homes often become a vital conduit to the mainstream community and its social and linguistic practices (Barkhuizen, 2015).

At the beginning of the session, I asked everyone to come to the table – literally – so that people could see each other clearly and address their introductions to the whole group. The intimacy of the space and the goodwill among participants meant that there was a lot of laughter and genuine interest in the stories. For the tutors, the session was an opportunity to meet not only each other but also the Brazilian clients of other tutors. As an applied linguist I was able to draw attention to second language issues as they arose during the session. For example, I acknowledged that the Brazilian members of the group were using English as a second language to speak to strangers who were native speakers. Such situations are stressful for ESL speakers who fear that their limited English proficiency will cause them to be misunderstood or conversely, that they will not be able to understand the questions of the native speakers (Horwitz, 2013). The conundrum was highlighted in one woman's comment: 'I understand (English) most of the time but I can't answer (laughs)'.

The session proceeded along social living lab lines in that the conversations were in-depth and dialogic across the group; the tutors were keen to ask questions about the migrant experience in Oakey and the clients were happy to answer. The home tutoring program was discussed in terms of the FDP project and the ways that digital technologies might be used to enhance English language home tutoring experiences for the client and the tutor. Many of the clients indicated that they had iPads and smartphones and were conversant with social media such as Facebook and communication technologies such as WhatsApp. The tutors – and myself – were the ones who were most unfamiliar with the different technologies.

Invoking principles of collaboration and iterative design, the three tutors from the Toowoomba seminar reported on their use of iPads and smartphones for photographing and audio-recording, and their varying levels of success. The other tutors, clients and researchers responded with feedback and tips for improvement. One of the tutors suggested starting a Facebook group as a means for both tutors and clients to share ideas and resources. The idea was welcomed enthusiastically although with reticence by some of tutors – and myself. The tutor assuaged people's concerns about privacy by explaining the settings and promising to email detailed instructions on how to join the group. One of the tutors admitted to not being on email and was offered suggestions on Internet providers and plans. Some tutors borrowed iPads from the FDP project and were given help on how to use them. The meeting concluded with one of the tutors requesting that the researchers return to Oakey with a session for tutors on specific ELT techniques. The invitation was happily accepted and a meeting date negotiated for the following month.

The request for expert input on ELT was an indication of the tutor's desire for more knowledge about how to design her teaching sessions. Her concerns were echoed by the other tutors. They wanted another face-to-face session and also had questions about the role of the Facebook group: should Facebook be for tutors only as a place to share resources? Or should it be a 'real learning experience' involving clients as well? This question was discussed both online and offline, with the decision to proceed with the second option. Eventually the participation of the Brazilian women in the Facebook group was resolved through attrition when the most active client returned to Brazil following a family emergency. While some tutors were more active on Facebook than others, all were comfortable with email and responsive to my requests for updates on progress. One tutor emailed: 'Thanks for sending app information. I have been using book creator with (client)'. Another wrote:

> *Since the very first time that the two of you (Dr Margaret Kettle and Dr Cherie Allan) came to Oakey, I feel a lot more satisfaction from my lessons. One, I went straight home with the iPad; I took pictures of my place and took them up. We used Google Earth; we looked at (student's name) place in Brazil from the street. So we were working together. It feels like you've got a real affinity with the students.*

A meeting in May 2016 was also held in the Oakey library on a Saturday morning. Prior to the meeting, my task was to design activities that answered the tutors' requests for teaching models while also taking into consideration the informal conditions of the lab. There was the sense that I should provide the structure to the session which raised questions for me about how to present second language teaching principles and associated activities in small, digestible chunks that could be easily adopted by the tutors. What could I present to the group that would help them with the highly differentiated needs of their respective learners? Instructively, the presentation that I developed for the session – with handouts and Powerpoint slides – was partially waylaid by a spontaneous lesson on using iPads initiated by some of the tutors, the FDP researcher Dr Allan, and the TAFE Home Tutor Coordinator. That impromptu lesson was in turn interrupted by the arrival of one of the Brazilian women with her baby and a large cake for the group to share.

Immediately apparent from the session was the need for myself as facilitator to be flexible and responsive to participant interests, as well as the sobering realization that as researcher participant, I was just one person among many. Another unplanned but powerful learning experience that arose organically in the meeting was the Question and Answer session between the Brazilian woman, the tutors and the researchers about the migrant experience in Australia. Echoing research on migrants' decisions to settle in regional areas (Griffiths, Laffan, & Jones, 2010), the woman reported some racism in urban areas but felt accepted in Oakey. For her a key motivator in learning English was her baby daughter:

> *I'd like to think in English, not translate ... when you learn to think in the language you want to learn, (it) makes easier... I like to learn English because when (her daughter) goes to school, I can't help her. She might say 'mum how I can do that' and I don't know.*

The next meeting in June 2016 was held in Toowoomba at the TAFE Queensland South West college. It was a professional development workshop conducted by the Home Tutor Coordinator and her colleague on useful technologies for home tutors. The coordinator's description of the workshop in an email to the researchers was as follows:

> *I will introduce Book Creator and illustrate with various ebooks, ie text/photo/video only, voice/photo/video only, combination of photo, text, voice and video etc. My colleague will introduce iMovie.*

The tutors and researchers met for coffee in the cafeteria of the TAFE college prior to the workshop. Subsequently, contact between the researchers and the social living labs participants has continued via email and Facebook with updates on progress. In response to a Christmas email, one of the tutors emailed the following:

> *Hi Margaret,*
>
> *Until you came on the scene we were flying blind. ... The opportunity that Cherie presented with the use of an iPad for my student was enormous. We were able to create albums and these lead into many sessions of grammar past and present. Thanks and hope to see you in the new year as I felt the students were acknowledged by yourself and Cherie.*

DISCUSSION

Innovation in Informal Language Education

Home tutoring inheres the principles of volunteerism, community and informal second language education. The Oakey social living lab added digital technology as an intervention with the aims of fostering participation among people in regional areas and building capabilities in ELT. The use of computer-assisted technologies in language teaching has a relatively long history, dating back to the 1960s when language labs were used for simple repetition exercises (Mao, Guardado, & Meyer, 2014). The more recent approach advocates combining technology use with cultural context and social interaction (Warschauer & Healy, 1998). Social interaction is a priority because of its links to meaningful language use.

For adult migrant learners, meaningfulness is directly related to their needs, i.e., the language needed to undertake social life in the new country; more often than not, these functions are associated with work, family and education (Murray & Christison, 2011). The Oakey social living lab provided an opportunity for the home tutors to learn first-hand the English language needs of their Brazilian clients. The needs ranged from literacy assistance to pass a meat inspector's exam to formulaic expressions for small talk on the production line. Addressing these needs was baffling to most of the tutors because of their lack of experience in second language teaching. Some of them were teaching food vocabulary using supermarket flyers (junk mail) in their letterboxes; others utilized the free local newspaper as a source of material. For many there was frustration in not knowing which authentic materials to access and how to employ them systematically in meaningful lessons; as the tutor above remarked: 'we were flying blind'.

The living lab provided the tutors with a pedagogic logic for designing lessons based on second language teaching principles (receptive skills to productive skills: listening to speaking to reading to writing) and the digital skills to develop relevant resources. iPads from the FDP project were loaned to the tutors for practice in the lab sessions and trialling activities with their clients at home. The FDP goal as it unfolded in the Oakey home tutoring project might be characterized as intensive input with incremental uptake. As the tutors gained confidence through the coconstruction experiences in the lab sessions, they reported increasing experimentation in the use of different technologies. One tutor was using WhatsApp to stay in touch with her client when she travelled interstate and another was working with her client to make a video of everyday life in the home. The video had commentary in English including the client introducing her husband and videoing him doing tasks such as changing a water filter.

The digital applications available in iPads and smartphones provide myriad possibilities for meaningful language teaching and practice. Need-based responses are enabled by the technology. The feedback from the tutors points to multiple benefits from the project: social, pedagogical, technological and cultural. From a researcher perspective, I also gained a great deal including growing competence and confidence in technology use. A further benefit was expanded understanding of the process of doing social living lab research. Section 9.4.2 conceptualizes this newfound knowledge in an attempt to contribute to the theorization of the field.

New Thinking on Social Living Lab Methodology

The genesis of the Oakey social living lab – with its roots in the local conditions of a regional town undergoing social and linguistic change – afforded the tutors and clients a particular legitimacy to cocreate the design of the experiences. Their commitment and participation sustained the interactive, durative nature of the social living lab. In facilitating the process as researcher, it soon became clear that this type of research is not a quest for enlightenment or one unerring Truth (Stengers, 2005); rather, it is orientated to creating a 'space of encounter' (Franz, 2015) in which stakeholders coconstruct experiences in the spirit of community and in the pursuit of knowledge and innovation. For those involved in the lab, participation was itself a democratic and empowering experience (Reich, 2011).

This social living lab approach to research can be conceptualized as 'thinking through the middle' (Stengers, 2005) in that – to be truly relevant – researchers need to incorporate the stakeholders' interests in the design. Otherwise the study is imposed and located only in the interests of the researcher; there is no ecology and sustainability in the practices of the research, meaning little orientation to ongoing change and innovation. Heimans, Singh, and Glasswell (2017) align with Stengers's position and argue for 'research in a minor key', i.e., enquiry which is multidirectional, multimethod with multiple stakeholders resulting in the researcher's expert knowledge always being subjected to the test of relevance.

Minor key research eschews the 'major key' in which the research takes 'what it will from situations, making them into something other than what practitioners are responsible to' (Heimans et al., 2017, p. 189).

Rather, the minor key approach demands a different responsibility; the responsibility of the researcher is 'response-ability' in that '*response-ability* ... requires ongoing readjustment and becoming – things and relations emerging out of reconstituting indeterminacies' (Heimans et al., 2017, p. 193). This need for response-ability aligns with Stengers's (2005) argument that research should involve an ecology of practice which begins with 'giving to the situation the power to makes us think' (p. 185). The job of the researcher is 'paying attention as best you can, to be as discerning, as discriminating as you can about the particular situation' (p. 188).

Following the call from Schuurman et al. (2015) for more theorization of living lab practice, the argument in this chapter is that the concepts of 'thinking through the middle', 'research in a minor key' and 'response-ability' can contribute to explanations of social living lab methodology. The concepts emerged in the practice of doing the Oakey social living lab and extend understandings of the processes and obligations of researchers engaged in this type of enquiry. The Oakey social living lab illustrates for researchers elsewhere how these concepts can be incorporated into their repertoire of practices. It also highlights researchers' responsibility to develop studies that are innovative, informed and iterative in design, while also being sensitive and responsive to stakeholders' interests.

CONCLUSION

This chapter has described a social living lab involving informal second language education with home tutors, their migrant clients, researchers and the AMEP provider in a small Australian town. A key dimension to the lab was the provision of experiences to support the uptake of digital technologies.

The outcomes of the project were not fixed-in-time findings as such. Rather they were process oriented and pointedly associated with the learning possibilities generated across time in the social living lab sessions. The lab provided a 'space of encounter' that was simultaneously enquiry- and need-based. It addressed the language teaching needs of the tutors while also fulfilling the wider objectives of the FDP project. These characteristics give social living lab methodology particular benefits that have been highlighted in this chapter.

REFERENCES

Australian Bureau of Statistics. (2013). *2011 Census Quickstats: Oakey.* Retrieved on February 24, 2017 from <http://www.censusdata.abs.gov.au/census_services/getproduct/census/2011/quickstat/SSC31262?opendocument&navpos = 220>.

Ballon, P., & Schuurman, D. (2015). Living labs: Concepts, tools and cases. *Digital Policy, Regulation and Governance, 17*(4), 12–25.

Barkhuizen, G. (2015). Learning English with a home tutor: Meeting the needs of migrant learners. In D. Nunan, & J. C. Richards (Eds.), *Language learning beyond the classroom* (pp. 282–291). New York: Routledge.

Condon, J. (November 15, 2016). *JBS suffers setback in third quarter financial results.* Beef Central. Retrieved on March 12, 2017 from <http://www.beefcentral.com/processing/jbs-suffers-setback-in-third-quarter-financial-results/>.

Courtney, P. (2017). *Toowoomba to Shanghai: Australian farmers head to China to turn promise into profit.* ABC News. Retrieved on March 19, from <http://www.abc.net.au/news/2017-02-04/toowoomba-farmers-take-off-to-china-to-learn-business-practices/8191468>.

Department of Education and Training. (2016). *Adult migrant English program*. Retrieved on March 5, 2017 from <https://www.education.gov.au/adult-migrant-english-program-0>.

Department of Immigration and Border Protection. (n.d.). *Meat industry labour agreement*. Accessed on March 5, 2017 from <http://www.border.gov.au/Trav/Work/Empl/Labour-agreements/meat-industry>.

Department of Immigration and Border Protection. (2017). *Abolition and replacement of the 457 visa: Government reforms to employer sponsored skilled migration visas*. Retrieved on April 28, 2017 from <http://www.border.gov.au/Trav/Work/457-abolition-replacement>.

Franz, Y. (2015). Designing social living labs in urban research. *Digital Policy, Regulation and Governance, 17*(4), 53–66.

Geoghegan, A. (2015). *Toowoomba opens arms to refugees as regional Queensland city faces economic boom*. ABC News. Retrieved on March 19, 2017 from <http://www.abc.net.au/news/2015-10-31/toowoomba-welcomes-refugees-as-city-booms/6899874>.

Griffiths, J., Laffan, W., & Jones, A. (2010). *Factors that influence skilled migrants locating in regional areas: Final report*. Institute for Social Science Research (ISSR). Canberra: Department of Immigration and Citizenship.

Heimans, S., Singh, P., & Glasswell, K. (2017). Doing education policy enactment research in a minor key. *Discourse: Studies in the Cultural Politics of Education, 38*(2), 185–196.

Horwitz, E. K. (2013). *Becoming a language teacher: A practical guide to second language learning and teaching* (2nd ed.). Boston: Pearson.

Hugo, G., Khoo, S.-E., & McDonald, P. (2006). Attracting skilled migrants to regional areas: What does it take? *People and Place, 14*(3), 26–36.

JBS Australia (2017). *Welcome to JBS Australia: A cut above the rest*. Retrieved on March 4, 2017 from <http://www.jbssa.com.au/>.

Mao, Y., Guardado, M., & Meyer, K. R. (2014). Integrating Chinese community into Canadian society: Podcasts, technology apprehension, and language learning. In J. E. Aitken (Ed.), *Cases on communication technology for second language acquisition and cultural learning* (pp. 459–483). Hershey: Information Science Reference.

Murray, D. E., & Christison, M. A. (2011). *What English language teachers need to know Volume II: Facilitating learning*. New York: Routledge.

NH Foods Australia (2017). *NH Foods Australia: Homepage*. Retrieved on March 4, 2017 from <http://www.nh-foods.com.au/>.

Organisation for Economic and Cultural Development (OECD). (2014a). *Migration policy debates: Who should be admitted as a labour migrant?* Retrieved on February 26, 2017 from <http://www.oecd.org/migration>.

Organisation for Economic and Cultural Development (OECD). (2014b). *Migration policy debates: Is migration good for the economy?* Retrieved on February 26, 2017 from <http://www.oecd.org/migration>.

Phillips, J. (2013). Temporary skilled migration and the 457 visa. Parliament of Australia: Parliamentary library. Retrieved on March 3, 2017 from <file:///C:/Users/Margaret%20Kettle/Documents/Articles%20and%20Publications%202017/Oakey_Social%20Living%20Lab/Temporary%20skilled%20migration%20and%20the%20457%20visa%20–%20Parliament%20of%20Australia.html>.

Reich, K. (2011). Diverse communities – Dewey's theory of democracy as a challenge for Foucault, Bourdieu, and Rorty. In J. M. Green, S. Neubert, & K. Reich (Eds.), *Pragmatism and diversity: Dewey in the context of late twentieth century debates* (pp. 165–194). New York: Palgrave Macmillan.

Roe, I. (2016). *Residents near Oakey Aviation base 'likely' ingested toxic chemicals, report finds*. ABC News. Retrieved on March 1, 2017 from <http://www.abc.net.au/news/2016-09-05/oakey-report-into-defence-base-contamination/7814204>.

Schuurman, D., De Marez, L., & Ballon, P. (2015). Living Labs: a systematic literature review. In *Open Living Lab Days 2015, Proceedings*. Presented at the Open Living Lab Days 2015.

Stengers, I. (2005). Introductory notes on an ecology of practices. *Cultural Studies Review*, *11*(1), 183–196.

The State of Queensland: Queensland Treasury. (2017). *Queensland Regional Profiles: Resident profile-people who live in the region*. Toowoomba (R) Local Government Area (LGA) compared with Queensland. Retrieved on March 7, 2017 from <http://statistics.qgso.qld.gov.au/qld-regional-profiles>.

The University of Queensland. (2015). *Queensland Places: Oakey*. Centre for the Government of Queensland. Retrieved on March 1, 2017 from <http://queenslandplaces.com.au/oakey>.

Warschauer, M., & Healey, D. (1998). Computers and language learning: An overview. *Language Teaching*, *31*, 57–71.

Wright, C.F., Sherrell, H., & Howe, J. (April 18, 2017). Australian government axes 457 visa: Experts react. *The Conversation*. Retrieved on April 28, 2017 from <https://theconversation.com/australian-government-axes-457-work-visa-experts-react-76321>.

Yates, L. (2011). Interaction, language learning and social inclusion in early settlement. *International Journal of Bilingual Education and Bilingualism*, *14*(4), 457–471.

CHAPTER 10

Pittsworth Stories: Developing a Social Living Lab for Digital Participation in a Rural Australian Community

Michael Dezuanni and Cherie Allan
Queensland University of Technology, Brisbane, QLD, Australia

INTRODUCTION

In this chapter, we discuss a social living lab established to foster digital participation in a rural Australian community. The living lab brought together residents, community institutions and university researchers to address the risk of digital nonparticipation, particularly for older people living in the community. Research (Warschauer & Matuchniak, 2010) illustrates the importance of digital participation initiatives for social participation and social mobility, particularly for individuals who may be identified as being 'at risk' of nonparticipation. The Pittsworth Stories social living lab aimed to find new ways to assist older residents to engage with digital technologies through interest-driven participation. The living lab challenged the typical 'computer class' model of technology education provision to identify ways that digital participation could enhance the residents' existing interests, passions and community involvement. The 'social' approach of this living lab adds a further dimension to the definition of living labs that emphasizes community participation, in contrast to other more technology and product-focused models:

> *Living Labs challenge us to examine new technologies in everyday contexts as used by people to achieve their goals. In this context, people from different areas of life explore innovative tools by interacting with them and discovering new ideas to expand their knowledge and to explore ways of acting.*
>
> ***Herselman et al. (2010)***

The social living lab described in this chapter demonstrates how 'ways of acting' can occur in a local community by bringing people together to address not only individual passions and concerns, but also the needs of

Digital Participation through Social Living Labs. DOI: http://dx.doi.org/10.1016/B978-0-08-102059-3.00010-1

the broader community. The Pittsworth Stories living lab encompasses the power of localism through harnessing volunteerism. These are important outcomes for a community that like many rural Australian towns is in transition due to rapid economic, social, political and technological change.

PITTSWORTH STORIES

Pittsworth Stories is one of the several social living labs established by the *Fostering Digital Participation through Living Labs in Regional and Rural Australia Communities* project, as described in Chapter 1, Social Living Labs for Digital Participation and Connected Learning. Following Warschauer (2003), we associate the risk of digital nonparticipation with the ability to harness technology's potential for meaningful social inclusion, rather than mere access to technology. Those 'at risk' may include residents with little or no technology experience or, equally, those with technology experience of a certain kind, but who are unable to take full advantage of technology due to a lack of access to specific kinds of knowledge and skill. The social living labs include a series of 'experiences' that initially involve in-depth conversations with residents, a codesign phase during which shared understandings are developed by the research team, local institution personnel and residents about the focus of the living lab, the technological and human resources required to implement it and the specific activities that will take place as part of the social living lab experiences.

For Pittsworth Stories, a group of older residents indicated they wanted to learn more about digital photography, video editing, recording local stories and sharing personal stories in digital formats. These residents were involved in a voluntary capacity with a number of town initiatives. For instance, members of the local Art group expressed a desire to explore ways to integrate local artists' work into the development of an ongoing record of the community. In addition, members of the Pittsworth Family and Local History Society actively record local history and they wanted to know how to use digital technologies to assist them. Following interviews with residents, members of the research team revisited the community to talk further with members of the Art Group and a local journalist about the possibility of developing a living lab with a theme such as 'Our Digital Community'. The research team decided to collaborate with these individuals, because they emerged from the interviews as likely living lab codesigners. Each of these people was already actively involved in the community and had access to a well-used community venue, the town Art Gallery.

Discussions between the research team and local residents led to a decision to develop a living lab in the later part of 2014 through documenting life in the town through digital photography, written stories and audio interviews with a small number of residents. In early September 2014, an evening community meeting was held in the town library to inform members of the community about the living lab proposal and to allow community members to provide feedback and make comments about the concept. Approximately 20 residents attended this meeting, including members of several community organizations, a church and other interested residents such as the local government representative. The research team pitched to the community the idea of using a platform called PlaceStories (http://placestories.com). This platform was chosen because it is a bespoke digital media space for recording local stories and the researchers were aware it had already been successfully used in a number of community-based digital media projects throughout Australia. The research team presented PlaceStories as an initial online tool to allow residents to capture and share digital stories. There was a great deal of support for the concept and a key local resident desire was that the space should enable a positive way to promote the town and its activities to the local community, town visitors and people from outside the community. It was decided to name the project *Pittsworth Stories*, to reflect this objective.

In the latter part of September, a digital media facilitator familiar with the local community was contracted and along with other members of the research team they implemented a series of living lab experiences at the community Technology Centre to provide residents with knowledge and skills in taking digital photographs, recording and editing audio recordings and writing digital stories. Community members were invited to create content to upload to PlaceStories. The initial living lab experience conducted in late September included 15 members of the community who, by the end of the session, had learned to take digital photographs and how to upload these to the Pittsworth Stories space on PlaceStories, accompanied by a short, written text to form a digital 'postcard'. A second living lab experience in mid-October included participants from the previous session as well as several newcomers. The participants from the September living lab experience engaged with audio recording by interviewing each other about local history and current events of interest. Several of the interviews were edited and then uploaded to *Pittsworth Stories*. The newcomers worked on digital photography and text creation and their 'postcards' soon joined those from the previous session.

Throughout October, a digital media facilitator was available in the community library for 2 hours each week to help participants create and share their content. This was an important support mechanism because it allowed living lab participants to gain access to ongoing support. In early November, *Pittsworth Stories* was launched at an exhibition opening at the Art Gallery. Two laptop computers were installed for visitors to access the *Pittsworth Stories* materials on PlaceStories. In addition, about 20 images from the digital postcards were chosen and printed in a large format and these were mounted as a small photographic exhibition in the gallery. Approximately 40 local residents attended the exhibition opening at the gallery.

The exhibition opening constituted the end of the first iteration of the *Pittsworth Stories* social living lab. In the next phase, residents extended their new knowledge of sharing digital stories online through the development of community organization websites using the Wix platform and through the use of Facebook groups. The range of people involved with the *Pittsworth Stories* social living lab expanded and digital participation for a number of the town's older residents was enhanced. Before going on to discuss the benefits of the first phase of the *Pittsworth Stories* social living lab for local residents, we provide some further background about how the social living lab addresses the needs of some Pittsworth residents dealing with significant changes in their community.

PITTSWORTH IN TRANSITION

The town of Pittsworth and its surrounds includes approximately 5500 residents (Australian Bureau of Statistics, 2014) and sits within an area of rich agricultural land in Southeast Queensland, Australia. It has, historically, been a relatively prosperous rural town with a stable population. The area surrounding Pittsworth is a particularly rich grain and cotton farming region known for its high-quality produce and the majority of farmers in the surrounding valley consider Pittsworth to be their local economic and government centre for goods and services. Over the last 20 years, however, there have been a number of changes presenting a threat to the town's identity and community cohesion. The continual upgrade of transportation links to the nearby regional city of Toowoomba and to the State capital, Brisbane, has been reassuring for the aging population who need ease of access to specialist medical and other services. The upgrade has also contributed, however, to a steady drift of young people from Pittsworth to Toowoomba, Brisbane and coastal communities for education and employment. This social mobility not only puts at risk local services and businesses such as banks and hardware stores but also changes the demographic composition of the town (Alston, 2004; McManus et al., 2012).

This demographic change was reinforced through the amalgamation of the local shire council with the larger Toowoomba City Council and several other smaller councils in 2008 to form the Toowoomba Regional Shire. The centralization of services to Toowoomba, the disbanding of the Pittsworth council and discontinuance of the Pittsworth Mayoral position has threatened Pittsworth's identity in a manner that reflects the experiences of residents in other Queensland communities and rural centres around Australia following amalgamation of smaller local councils into large council areas (Alexander, 2012). Pittsworth residents' concerns about their community's changing identity were reflected during our initial community interviews. Numerous people talked about their pride in the town and their desire to tell their stories so that other people could share in them. Following a focus group interview with two residents at the Pittsworth Technology Centre, we were shown a large mural artwork that had been created by Pittsworth Art Group members, including by one of our interviewees. The artwork was made to commemorate Pittsworth's history, including images of past councils, unique town buildings and colours reflecting the town's flora and representing a version of Pittsworth history.

The Artwork captures the era of Pittsworth's foundation as a civic and commercial centre during the late 19th and early 20th centuries and reinforces the romantic ideal of the region as the rural 'heart of the Darling Downs' (Pittsworth District Alliance, 2017). A significant recent threat to the fabric of the local community, however, is the intrusion of coal-seam gas exploration in Cecil Plains (50 km from Pittsworth) and proposed coal mining in Felton Valley (20 km from Pittsworth). Pittsworth acts as a commercial centre for Felton and the prospect of mining on Pittsworth's doorstep was of significant concern for residents. From 2012 to 2014 Felton residents undertook an ultimately successful campaign to stop mining exploration in the area. The Friends of Felton campaign was able to draw attention to the importance of the area as a centre for Queensland food production and the group gained political support for their position – the Queensland government declared in 2012 there would be no mining in the Felton Valley (see Newman quashes Felton mining plans, August 27, 2012). However, the events highlighted to Pittsworth residents the precariousness of their rural lifestyles and the rural economy. Just 170 km away on the Western Darling Downs is Chinchilla, formerly a small rural community that is now the centre of Queensland's Coal Seam Gas industry and the site of ongoing bitter disputes between the farming community and mining companies (Lloyd, Luke, & Boyd, 2013).

Digital technologies also have brought significant change to Pittsworth residents' communications and leisure activities and to the local business and farming sectors. The Internet, mobile and touch screen technologies, social media and the ready availability of digital production devices have all significantly changed the ways in which aspects of life occur in rural Australian communities (Warburton, Cowan, Winterton, & Hodgkins, 2014). Older residents have particularly been challenged by the increasing move to online banking and provision of government services. At the same time, several older residents spoke positively about their use of social and communications media, especially Facebook and Skype, to keep in touch with their children and grandchildren living in other parts of the country and overseas. Several parents we interviewed talked about the number of digital devices and gaming systems now available to their children and expressed concern about knowing how to best manage their screen time. We also heard from individuals working in the rural sector who are increasingly using digital technologies to assist them with their work. For instance, during the initial data collection phase in Pittsworth, one local business operator who sprays broad acre crops explained that he uses iPad apps to check the weather, especially the radar map which is essential knowledge for the efficient operation of his business as well as to access work-related emails while in the field. Other farmers spoke about the increasing move towards automation in the farming sector.

There is a sense of greater connection to urban centres through access to digital technologies, but simultaneously the unreliability of digital networks often leads to a feeling of disconnection for people living in and around Pittsworth. In an age when digital culture is associated not with rurality, but with cities and urbanization (Castells, 1996, p. 394), being disconnected from the network due to a lack of infrastructure potentially reinforces rural residents' isolation from the rest of the world. Several residents living on rural properties outside Pittsworth indicated their access to the mobile phone network and to the Internet was unreliable. Despite the imminent availability of the Australian Federal government's signature project the National Broadband Network (NBN), none of the residents we interviewed in March 2014 spoke about it in positive terms. There was much confusion about what high-speed Internet would allow and when it would be available. Even after the 'switching on' of the NBN in Pittsworth in mid-2014, there was little mention of the service by the residents involved in the social living lab. This contradicted the promise of the National Broadband Network for rural Australians that regardless of location, residents would have access to digital culture and the digital economy, fulfilling a vision that has been associated with technology and connectivity for the past 20 years:

> *The development of electronic communication and information systems allows for an increasing disassociation between spatial proximity and the performance of everyday life's functions: work, shopping, entertainment, healthcare, education, public services, governance, and the like.*
>
> **Castells (1996, p. 394)**

More than this collapsing of space, though, access to reliable networked technologies promises opportunities for individuals and groups living anywhere to participate in the digital economy in new ways. The claim is that physical location and access to specific resources and hardware are no longer the only determinants of economic opportunity in postindustrial communities.

> *The removal of the physical constraints on effective information production has made human creativity and the economics of information itself the core structuring facts in the new networked information economy. These have quite different characteristics than coal, steel, manual human labor, which characterised the industrial economy and structured our basic thinking about economic production for the past century.*
>
> **Benkler (2006, p. 4)**

In contrast, the older Pittsworth residents interviewed for our project had more modest proposals for the use of digital technologies in the town. The most common was a desire to see Pittsworth and its stories, historic and current, represented within digital culture. A sense of pride in Pittsworth was evident and several people we interviewed were volunteer members of a number of existing community organizations. This civic involvement seemed to be driven by a desire to provide opportunities for other local residents to take part in the community and to promote the town to the world.

In 'Pittsworth Stories for Digital Participation' section, we discuss how phase one Pittsworth Stories living lab aimed to enhance this local volunteerism and community activity by bringing a digital component to it and we outline the benefits for the participants. We particularly focus on how the project used interest-driven activity to build residents' digital capacities and how volunteerism helped to sustain the model.

Pittsworth Stories for Digital Participation

There are three ways in which the *Pittsworth Stories* social living lab experiences enhanced the digital participation of older residents in Pittsworth. The first is the development of digital skills and knowledge that a number of residents previously did not have access to or had no reason to acquire. The second is the opportunity to tell local stories and generate memories of value to the participants and the local community. The third is the opportunity to participate in the community through volunteerism in previously unavailable ways.

It was clear from the initial interviews with older Pittsworth residents that many were using digital technologies for basic services like making phone calls on smart phones, using computers to send emails and using Facebook and Skype to keep in touch with family and friends. A few participants in the social living lab had existing digital skills. For instance, one resident was an avid photographer who frequently uses a digital camera; another was a radio enthusiast who runs the local community radio station and uses sophisticated audio recording and mixing equipment and a third was a journalist for the local newspaper who uses some digital skills to write and submit stories. Despite these specific skills, none of these individuals considered themselves to be confident digital technology users and they all had significant gaps in their knowledge of social media and for using digital media in ways that would allow them to engage in meaningful social practices through digital technologies (Warschauer, 2003, p. 38). More generally, most of the older interviewees used digital technologies narrowly. Many residents suggested that although they had attended 'computer classes' from time to time, they mostly forgot what they had learnt as they did not have a reason to continue to practice their new skills. As one resident put it, 'over the years I have been to a number of classes but you forget it unless you are using it all the time'.

The Pittsworth Stories social living lab was codesigned with older local residents and, because there was input from the participants, the content was highly relevant and interest driven. Participants indicated they were much less likely to forget the new skills because there was a specific reason to keep practicing, which was their desire to continue to tell local stories. As the digital media facilitator suggested, 'they really have a sense of ownership and are really engaged in the process of creating the site'. It was also clear from discussions that took place during the social living lab experiences that the work meant a great deal to the residents. As the digital media facilitator said, 'we discussed in great detail the importance of this project to create story, raise dialogue, share in common interests and change the community's sense of culture – which was really impacting'.

In addition to being interest driven, the living lab experiences were developed as hands-on workshops rather than 'classes'. After the participants were provided with some initial information, the focus turned to learning through making (Gauntlett, 2011) and participants were encouraged to help each other to undertake tasks, in an attempt to develop a community of practice (Wenger, 1998). The research team believed developing situated learning within a community of practice was particularly important in recognition of the expertise that existed in the group in digital photography and digital audio recording. It was intended that participants with greater knowledge and skill would assist others to develop their digital literacies.

Perhaps the most significant challenge for fostering the digital literacies of the Pittsworth Stories participants, though, was developing both digital production skills to create stories and broader conceptual understandings not only about storytelling but about genres of digital participation (Ito et al., 2010, pp. 14–18). As Cope and Kalantzis argue (2000), multiliterate practice requires the development of genre knowledge, and in the digital arena genres continually emerge and rapidly change. One reason for using the PlaceStories platform in the first phase of the *Pittsworth Stories* social living lab was that it provides a series of story content templates of which only three were introduced to the participants, reducing the need for participants to develop extensive generic knowledge and skill. The first was the 'postcard', which enabled the creator to take a photograph and provide a brief written description. The postcard was the most popular type of story content uploaded to *Pittsworth Stories*.

The second type of story that participants were encouraged to experiment with was an audio story. This required the participants to record an audio story and then upload it to Soundcloud (soundcloud.com), a popular cloud-based audio sharing service. From there the audio could be embedded as a Pittsworth Story. The third type of content the participants were introduced to was a combination of the postcard and audio recording, which allowed participants to upload a photograph and then embed an audio recording so that when someone views an image, they simultaneously hear an audio recording. One participant involved in the community choir used this function to upload an image and recording of a local community choir performance, to great effect.

The main goal of the living lab participants was to tell local stories to add value to the community through sharing information about community facilities, groups, businesses and creative activities; preserving local memories to construct the broader Pittsworth narrative, and communicating ideas of value to the community and beyond. Two living lab participants were key members of the Pittsworth Art group and most of their involvement in the living lab focused on the activities of the art gallery and what they perceived to be a need to link up the various groups in the town. They believed it was necessary to keep reminding the local community about just how much was occurring in Pittsworth and they saw the PlaceStories platform as a space where this might occur. For instance, a PlaceStories Postcard about the Art Group stated:

> *Members have been busy preparing for our fifteenth Annual Spring Art Exhibition which has its official opening on Friday 2nd October at 7 pm, by Cr Sue Englart, Toowoomba Regional Council. The exhibition is open to the public from Saturday 3rd October until Sunday 11th October which ties in with the very popular Craft and Fine Food Spectacular. Visitors are most welcome to browse and see the all-new works by our local artists, potters as woodcrafters.*

This Postcard functioned not just as an advertisement for an event, but as a reminder to the local community about the civic-mindedness of the Art group volunteers and about the cultural activity of local residents. The digital postcard reflects the enthusiasm the social living lab participants have for their community and the work they undertake for the community.

Preserving local memories was also a significant focus of members of the social living lab. For instance, the President of the Pittsworth Returned Services League (RSL) and the previously mentioned local journalist worked together to record a story about the local 1929 built RSL building, using their audio recording skills, journalistic expertise and local history knowledge. The recording provides details about the opening of the building, the spaces available in the building, including their functions, and the future, unrealized plans for the building. The 'Soldiers Memorial School of Arts Hall' played a significant role in the town's history and is the site of cultural memory production for residents, central to local collective identity and particularly pertinent in the face of the rapid social and technological change discussed earlier. The construction of shared memory around the RSL building ties local Pittsworth history into the national story about sacrifice during war time of young men and women. Across the country the buildings constructed in honour of those who sacrificed their lives in war take on special significance in the establishment of national- and community-based *lieux de mémoire* (Nora, 1989). Such buildings and monuments are sites that hold great significance for remembering particular events and which have become part of the community and nation's collective cultural memory.

The development of particular cultural memories often occurs over many years and, in some cases, several generations. However, as Douglas (2010, p. 23) points out, cultural memory is never stable but is in a constant state of flux as interpretations of past events and counter-memories are offered, accepted or rejected, only to come under further reconsideration at some point in the future. The story of the RSL building for Pittsworth Stories is one iteration of this which ties into the creators' passion for preserving and retelling local historical stories for the contemporary digital context. The living lab provided them with an opportunity to recast their memories in a digital context blended with the immediacy of recording the story 'face-to-face' in journalistic fashion. Winters (2012, p. 3) suggests we now have a plethora of new media through which to record, transmit and recreate sounds and images thereby creating 'mediated memories'. Douglas (2010, p. 24) argues new technologies have provided greater opportunities for documenting our lives through blogs, online photograph albums and social networking sites.

Certainly, *Pittsworth Stories* provided the opportunity to preserve memories, including personal memories, which were highly meaningful to the participants. Winters (2012, p. 3) contends that the stories we tell about our personal past define who we are in the present. Part of the success of the *Pittsworth Stories* social living lab was that it linked digital participation to the important work of local and personal memory construction. The digital component of the living lab, combined with the exhibition in the art gallery provided an opportunity for memory generation and sharing about the community, which articulates to the construction of the community in the present in new and important ways. As Douglas (2010, pp. 16–17) suggests, memory is 'the collective ways in which the past is remembered, constructed, and made intelligible within culture'. *Pittsworth Stories* blended the present and the past, relating to both historical sites and current personal interests and activities, depicting past and present aspects of the community that came together easily in the digital context. From the perspective of fostering digital participation, the development of stories/memories and the associated personal and community identity work gave purpose to the social living lab due to the value of participation.

In addition to being a space for the preservation of memories, *Pittsworth Stories* also provided a location for residents to participate in the community in ways that were previously unavailable to them. As mentioned earlier, the living lab participants were not using social media for civic engagement. Although a few of the participants use Facebook on a regular basis, they mostly used it to connect with family and friends rather than to stay in touch with community activities. This is of interest particularly because other members of the town's community had established a very well-used Facebook group where information about happenings in the town was regularly exchanged, but which was unused by these older residents. Several living lab members regularly read the local newspaper – and as indicated, one of the living lab participants was a journalist for the newspaper. These older residents were much more familiar with the more traditional news media than they were with social media, particularly for knowing about community activities. It was suggested to the research team more than once that we should have stories about the project in the newspaper to let the community know about our project. Indeed, there was a story in the local paper about the *Pittsworth Stories* exhibition opening and PlaceStories was used to tell stories about the exhibition itself. Facebook was not, however, used to promote the event or to share photographs from the event.

In effect, PlaceStories became a 'safe' social network space to ease the older residents into digital civic participation – the tagline of the site is 'Create, Communicate, Collaborate' and it invites locally based and interest-driven social participation. The site functions as a social network in the sense that each participant creates a profile to become a member of the 'folk' in the space. Each project then has its own home space, and folks can post 'stories' to the project, including postcards, embedded audio and video recordings, PDF files and more. Each story can be tagged for searchability and participants can comment on each others' stories. In this sense, PlaceStories introduced the participants to the generic characteristics of social sites like Facebook, YouTube and Flickr, which promote the sharing of creative content and social communication. There were some initial concerns from the group about the possibility that community members from outside the living lab might post to the space and that it would be difficult to regulate the content. Despite these concerns, though, the participants' response was very positive. The research team's observations suggest the participants were surprised by how easy it was to share content. In addition, as the digital media facilitator reflects, the participants were 'excited at the potential of PlaceStories to be a 'place' now, not only where they share story, but to discover other voices, stories, images and videos from other individuals and communities of people across the world'.

As the Pittsworth Stories living lab has evolved since the PlaceStories experiences, key members of the group have gone on to develop other, related content. For instance, in a new phase of Pittsworth Stories, a small group worked with the project's digital media facilitator to develop a website for the Family and Local History Society (located at http://pittsworthhistory.wixsite.com/localfamilyhistory). Furthermore, a number of participants began to weigh up the affordances of websites in comparison to Facebook Groups to support local community activities. During a living lab experience to showcase various digital platforms a number of community groups and businesses, including representatives of the Pittsworth Art Group and the owners of a cattle stud concluded that a website would best serve their purposes. However, members of the Tennis Club and the owner of a local business that already had a website decided that a Facebook account would work better for them. In this sense, the social living lab experience opened up new possibilities for digital participation for the residents.

CONCLUSION

The Pittsworth Stories social living lab was codesigned by university researchers, Pittsworth residents and a digital media facilitator to address the 'problem' of older residents' underparticipation in digital culture. The social living lab made connections between local institutions such as the Pittsworth branch of the Toowoomba Regional Library Service, the Pittsworth Technology Centre, the Pittsworth Art Group and the Family and Local History Society. It achieved its aims because it enabled its participants to learn new ways to use digital media that were previously unavailable to them, and particularly to enhance community activities for which they already had enthusiasm and passion. In this sense, the social living lab enhanced the local community by developing social capital, the 'social networks, the reciprocities that arise from them, and the value of these for achieving mutual goals' (Schuller, Baron, & Field, 2000, p. 1). In particular, the social living lab provided residents with new ways to tell stories and preserve memories through digital media participation.

The Pittsworth Stories social living lab had inevitable limitations. It necessarily met the needs of a relatively small group of older residents in Pittsworth. If a social living lab with a storytelling focus was established with a different group in the town, teenagers for instance, it would necessarily tell very different stories about the town and would need to draw on a different version of the local digital learning ecology. The 'Pittsworth Stories' told by this group of residents constructed one version of the town and the digital participation needs of this group of residents were very specific to the group who codesigned the experience. One of the significant limitations of conducting research for a relatively short period of time with limited resources is that the digital participation needs of many residents in Pittsworth were not addressed. We are confident, however, that the social living labs approach provides a viable and highly responsive approach to fostering digital participation in ways that genuinely meet the needs of the participants who have the opportunity to take part.

REFERENCES

Alexander, D. (2012). Crossing boundaries: Action networks, amalgamation and inter-community trust in a small rural shire. *Local Government Studies*, *39*(4), 463–487.

Alston, M. (2004). You don't want to be a check-out chick all your life: The out-migration of young people from Australia's small rural towns. *Australian Journal of Social Issues*, *39*(3), 299–313.

Australian Bureau of Statistics. (2014). *Pittsworth SA2*. Retrieved on January 24, 2017 from <http://stat.abs.gov.au/itt/r.jsp?RegionSummary®ion = 307021182&dataset = ABS_REGIONAL_ASGS&geoconcept=REGION&datasetASGS=ABS_REGIONAL_ASGS&datasetLGA=ABS_REGIONAL_LGA®ionLGA=REGION& regionASGS = REGION>.

Benkler, Y. (2006). *The wealth of networks: How social production transforms markets and freedom*. New Haven; London: Tale University Press.

Castells, M. (1996). *The rise of the network society*. Oxford: Blackwell Publishers.

Douglas, K. (2010). *Contesting childhood: Autobiography, trauma, and memory*. Piscataway: Rutgers University Press.

Gauntlett, D. (2011). *Making is connecting: The social meaning of creativity, from DIY and knitting to YouTube and Web 2.0.* Cambridge: Polity.

Ito, M., et al. (2010). *Hanging out, messing around, and geeking out: Kids living and learning with new media.* Cambridge: MIT Press.

Kalantzis, M., & Cope, B. (2000). *Multiliteracies: Literacy learning and the design of social futures.* London: Routledge.

Lloyd, D. J., Luke, H., & Boyd, W. E. (2013). Community perspectives of natural resource extraction: Coal-seam gas mining and social identity in Eastern Australia. *Coolabah, 10,* 144–164.

McManus, P., Walmsley, J., Argent, N., Baum, S., Bourke, L., Martin, J., ... Sorensen, T. (2012). Rural community and rural resilience: What is important to farmers in keeping their country towns alive? *Journal of Rural Studies, 28*(1), 20–29.

Newman quashes Felton mining plans. (August 27, 2012). *The Chronicle.* Retrieved on December 7, 2015 from <http://www.thechronicle.com.au/news/newman-quashes-felton-mining-plans/1519905/>.

Nora, P. (1989). Between memory and history: Les Lieux de Memoire. *Representations, 26,* 7–25.

Pittsworth District Alliance. (2017). Pittsworth, Queensland. Retrieved on January 24, 2017 from <http://pittsworth.org.au>.

Schuller, T., Baron, S., & Field, J. (2000). Social capital: A review and critique. In S. Baron, J. Field, & T. Schuller (Eds.), *Social capital: Critical perspectives.* Oxford: Oxford University Press.

Warburton, J., Cowan, S., Winterton, R., & Hodgkins, S. (2014). Building social inclusion for rural older people using information and communication technologies: Perspectives of rural practitioners. *Australian Social Work, 67*(4), 479–494. Available from http://dx.doi.org/10.1080/0312407X.2013.834064.

Warschauer, M. (2003). *Technology and social inclusion: Rethinking the digital divide.* Cambridge: MIT Press.

Warschauer, M., & Matuchniak, T. (2010). New technology and digital worlds: Analyzing evidence of equity in access, use, and outcomes. *Review of Research in Education, 34,* 179–225.

Wenger, E. (1998). *Communities of practice: Learning, meaning, and identity.* Cambridge: Cambridge University Press.

Winter, A. (2012). *Memory: Fragments of a modern history.* Chicago: University of Chicago Press.

FURTHER READING

van Dijck, J. (2004). Memory matters in the digital age. *Configurations, 12*(3), 349–373.

CHAPTER 11

Urban Communities as Locations for Health, Media Literacy and Civic Voice

Angela Cooke-Jackson
Emerson College, Boston, MA, United States

INTRODUCTION

Urban communities have been known for their dynamic scaffolding of racially and ethnically diverse people groups where access to care or compromised infrastructures only perpetuates multilayered health risk and disparities. Pearcy and Keppelp (2002) describe 'Health disparities' as 'a marked difference or inequality between two or more populations groups defined on the basis of race or ethnicity, gender, educational level or other criteria' (p. 274). For example, Boston's urban communities, which are similar to other urban communities in the United States, has a large representation of immigrants and people of colour that report their race and ethnicity as African American, Hispanic, Haitian, Cape Verdean, Asian Pacific Islander, African and West Indian (Guyanese), respectively. Of these groups many would be defined by terms like, 'at-risk' or 'marginalized' and they would come from neighbourhoods with low levels of educational achievement and families who live below the federal poverty level. While research can be found, there is a deficiency of scholarly research on nontraditional health models that accent how access to care and disparities can be informed by creative, innovative approaches that address health gaps and emphasize the rich contextualization of a community's resilience and agency.

While admittedly difficult, numerous nonprofit organizations are working tirelessly to address health inequalities using unique community-initiated models. These models – two of which we will investigate later – have been successful towards advancing health information and resources while impacting health behaviours. As well, the models have been useful to illustrate how health and media literacy along with civic engagement can empower diverse populations living in Boston and other

Digital Participation through Social Living Labs. DOI: http://dx.doi.org/10.1016/B978-0-08-102059-3.00011-3

urban communities across the United States. With marked advances in technology more research scholarship has advanced which addresses different types of digital participation and how it can advance media literacy (Cooke-Jackson & Barnes, 2013; Hobbs, 2010). Furthermore, scholarship acknowledges that individuals who feel capable and confident using different types of digital platforms have been shown to have more competencies that foster media literacy skills when accessing health information. As society negotiates new technology and the ubiquitous impact of the Internet we move from an individual-use model to a value in societal skills and cultural competencies in media. It is at this juncture that we can help address literacy and health challenges in a new way by offering innovative forms of learning. As Hobbs (2010) notes, 'for people to take social action and truly engage in actual civic activities that improve their communities, they need to feel a sense of empowerment that comes from working collaboratively to solve problems' (p. viii).

This chapter highlights two organizations, both located in urban communities in Boston, Massachusetts, which are using innovative models and methodologies to empower diverse individuals and collective communities – *The Family Van* and *Community Conversations: Sister-to-Sister, A Women's Health Initiative.* The author spotlights two real-world cases in which civic engagement, new technologies and modalities as well as collaborative teams can advance health and media literacy. The goal is to underscore these often-unacknowledged programs that celebrate the diverse urban communities, while simultaneously seeking to understand how transformative experiential engagement can shift health behaviours and enrich marginalized groups.

BACKGROUND: UNDERSTANDING HEALTH COMMUNICATION, HEALTH AND MEDIA LITERACY

In the United States approximately 9 out of 10 adults struggle with understanding health information available on a day-to-day basis, whether in health care facilities, media or in the community (U.S. Department of Health and Human Services, 2014).

A trend which has become more applicable for the field of health communication is the investigation of the intersection of health and media literacy. Traditionally, scholars have looked at these constructs independently; however, the emergence of different modalities and new technologies offer an important intersection for investigation between health, media literacy and digital participation.

Numerous definitions of Health Communication, a multifaceted and multidisciplinary discipline, have emerged that are based on the ways different health sectors address their fundamental goals and objectives which focus on reaching different populations and groups. The goal is: to exchange health-related information, ideas, and methods in order to influence, engage, empower, and support individuals, communities, health care professionals, patients, policymakers, organizations, special groups and the public so that they will champion, introduce, adopt, or sustain health or social behaviour, practice or policy that will ultimately improve individual, community and public health outcomes (Schiavo, 2007, p. 7).

Health communication has been studied from varying perspectives. Typically it investigates communication strategies and their impact on individuals' and communities' ability to enhance health. This applied research discipline examines topics such as patient—physician communication, health care and health promotion, risk behaviours, and health narratives (Kreps, Bonaguro, & Query, 1998). Often, the goal is to understand health behaviours and motivate behaviour changes using messages that target specific populations and health disparities (Kreps et al., 1998).

As the Health Communication field expanded and prominent organizations like the Centers for Disease Control (CDC) or the National Institute of Health (NIH) saw the importance and value of research in the field many adopted their own definitions of health communication to reflect their specific goals. This provided a space for health specialists, practitioners and scholars to understand health behaviours and motivate behaviour changes using messages that target specific populations and health disparities. As such an area in the field of health communication that has become increasingly more valuable and accessible is health literacy.

As we attempt to dissect and understand health and media literacy, we must first understand the differences between the terms. Defined by The Patient Protection and Affordable Care Act of 2010, Title V, health literacy is 'the degree to which an individual has the capacity to obtain, communicate, process, and understand basic health information and services to make appropriate health decisions' (Health Literacy, 2016). It's the ability to distinguish quality bodily information from the frauds, and apply it to our own well-being as it pertains to us; becoming our responsibility to utilize our informative, connective, means to move information along.

Not only is health literacy an important means of dispersing health information, it introduces a participatory dialogue between public health discourse and public health action, inviting people to engage in evaluating and attaining health information (Mihailidis, 2014).

Literature on health literacy is extensive (Zarcadolas, Pleasant, & Greer, 2005). The National Academy of Sciences has reported on literacy in medication usage and the ability to read prescription labels (Committee on Health Literacy, 2004). Additional research looks at health literacy and racial and ethnic inequalities in health outcomes (Smedley, Adrienne, Stith, & Nelson, 2003). Importantly, health literacy implies that individuals and communities can weigh risks and benefits and then make informed decisions and take action. As such, it seems obvious that the Department of Health and Human Services believes that a person's culture has major implications for how individuals communicate and understand health information. Furthermore, the concept means that health practitioners must take steps to be culturally and linguistically competent so that positive health outcomes are accessible and useful among diverse groups.

More than 90 million adults in the United States have low health literacy levels, meaning the complex language used in health care has implications for families, communities, and national health systems (Smedley et al., 2003). Health literacy does not simply affect an individual; it has implications for policy, the environment, industry and disease prevention (Zarcadolas et al., 2005). It reaches into families, communities and society, and has distinct connectivity globally. Moreover, it does not just mean an individual has the reading skills to understand language used by health professionals and in health policy. To be health literate, individuals must be able to analyse general health information – text, charts, symbols, abbreviations and other sociosemiotic features – as it pertains to them specifically. Health literacy implies that individuals and communities can weigh risks and benefits and then make informed decisions and take action (Clear Communication: A NIH Health Literacy Initiative, 2016).

In turn, media literacy refers to the training of individuals in 'sharing information in integrated spaces of hypermedia activity', and aims to engage people in more active civic lifestyles (Mihailidis, 2013). Media literacy is grounded in the development of critical thinking skills and being able to find, interpret and evaluate relevant information (Mihailidis, 2013). Using that as a foundation, individuals are then able to build skills around creative idea generation, health promotion and leadership through civic engagement (Mihailidis, 2013). Fluency or the ability to discern information in the media allows for critical thinking and judgement among consumers helping individuals transition from simply being consumers to becoming engaged citizens. It gives individuals the capacity to evaluate media or new technologies around them and to create meaningful parallels and content when necessary (Thoman & Jolls, 2004). As we consider health and media literacy in tandem with the new challenges in the digital era, the implications of digital technology and digital participation are critical. More studies report the value of technology in patients' understanding of health procedures, dosage and diagnosis (Xiao, Sharman, Rao, & Upadhyaya, 2014). Research also addresses the rapid accessibility and value of disease diagnosis via Google for physicians. We also know that sites like WebMD and ZocDoc have influenced the layperson's ability to not only self-diagnosis but even schedule doctor's appointments online. One article notes when teens serve as creators of health information via digital vignettes on sexual health information, they become more literate in their own endeavour to find accurate sexual health information on the Internet (Cooke-Jackson & Barnes, 2013). While there is a paucity of empirical data that weds health and media literacy with digital technology and digital participation, more and more anecdotal evidence has emerged that this model should involve literacy skills along with cultural competencies to enhance the learner's experience (Jenkins, 2006).

For this chapter, an understanding of media literacy and its relationship to health literacy is valuable because the author believes it plays a key role in how individuals garner health information via various outlets and how that information is understood and used.

URBANITY

Historically, urban communities have been known for their dynamic scaffolding of racially and ethnically diverse people groups where access to care or compromised infrastructures only perpetuates multilayered health risk and disparities. The term encompasses the spatial nature of 'urban' but has equal significance for the characteristic of individuals living in these spaces that represent the mecca centre of all things cultural and modernized.

Urban areas like Boston are very developed, which means there is a density of human structures such as houses, commercial buildings, roads, bridges and railways. While this lends itself to vibrant city life, it also creates pockets of exclusion where low-income populations must struggle to pay high rent cost, and access quality food and health care. These characteristics mean that marginalized and disparate individuals are among a high quota of people living in urban spaces. As an urban community Boston is known for some of the best teaching hospitals in the country and some of the most prestigious academic institutions in the world. Even in these rigorous academic and medical spaces a segregation of culture, race and ethnicities prevails. Hence, there are significant pockets of poverty among these hallowed buildings and institutions. For instance, residences in sections of the city like Roxbury, Dorchester, Roslindale and Mattapan are geographically isolated and racially divided, lacking access to basic medical services (A People Movement, 2016).

Boston's segregation is most notable in the number of low-income African American and Latino teens who do not graduate from high school which can result in patterns of truancy and leads to gang violence, incarceration and even homicides (Urban Violence in the Commonwealth, 2017). Neighbourhood violence is also prevalent in Boston urban communities. One report found that in 2015 one in four girls in Boston had been in a physical fight, 51% reported that a family member or close friend was murdered, and 67% reported gunshots or shooting as problems in their neighbourhoods (The 2015 Report on the Status of Women and Girls in Boston, Massachusetts, 2017). Importantly, new research from the Massachusetts Youth Services found that juvenile female offenders were more likely to be in an environment or a victim of abuse-effective creating a cycle of abuse and violence (The 2015 Report on the Status of Women and Girls in Boston, Massachusetts, 2017).

The Family Van and Community Conversations are both exemplar models of community participation at a grassroots level. My role as a research partner, health communication trainer and health behaviour consultant offer first-hand insights on the various steps they have taken to build strong alliances in the urban Boston communities. My connection with The Family Van began as a health communication educator in training session with their Harvard graduate and doctoral student volunteers. Over time this relationship transformed into training a small cohort of teens from the Boston community in a 6-week summer program called The Emerson Literacy Education and Empowerment Program (eLEEP) that I direct at Emerson College. Using a peer-to-peer participatory learning model, this program focuses on giving urban at-risk teens an opportunity to use new technology to address issues of health and media literacy in their respective communities.

In 2013 the director of *Community Conversations: Sister to Sister* approached me with a request to provide a methodological protocol to chronicle their community involvement whereby African American women meet with African American health care experts at a local beauty salon in Cambridge, Massachusetts. The sole objective of the conversations was to improve the health outcomes of information sharing among Black medical professionals and lay-women as they sought to navigate the medical system. Among other responsibilities, a primary goal was to assess the program and then create a qualitative questionnaire that could be used to gain information from participants on the program's usefulness. The intent was not only to create a more robust program and digital content for their website but to have grounded research findings to apply for foundation and government grants.

MOBILE CLINICS

Motivated to eliminate health disparities in urban Boston communities The Family Van, a mobile clinic established in 1992, has played a critical role in providing tangible care by 'carrying out curbside testing, health coaching and care referrals to individuals in underserved communities' (Song, Hill, Bennett, Vavasis, & Oriol, 2013). Research has proven that 'mobile clinics provide an important safety net for disease prevention and management in urban communities with poor health status and high emergency department usage' (Song, Hill, Bennett, Vavasis, & Oriol, 2013). Based on data from Mobile Health Map, 548 mobile clinics receive on average 3300 visits annually and an estimated 2000 mobile clinics nationwide collectively receive 6.5 million patient visits per year. Typically they are staffed by community health workers and health educators, and sometimes by physicians and nurses.

Customized to meet the specific needs of rural and urban communities, these custom vehicles deliver a variety of services, like primary and preventive care, cancer screenings, dental screenings and specialty care (Hill et al., 2012).

While scholars acknowledge that even though the mobile clinics are on the rise, research of their impact and cost effectiveness, and support for larger medical establishments is minimally analysed. The Department of Health and Human Services Office of Minority Health (2011) set up funding to advance scholarship and nationwide research partnerships to evaluate the impact of mobile clinics which began to shed light on the mobile world (Department of Health and Human Services, 2011). Even acknowledging the shortcomings of research and lack of access to patient outcome data in this area, it is worth noting that mobile clinics have been impactful towards improving health disparities and access to care through community-based education and prevention, chronic disease management and promotion of public health infrastructure (Hill, 2012; Song et al., 2013). One of the novelties of mobile health clinics is their ability to move through the malaise of health disparities in communities where individuals are not comfortable seeing medical doctors. For this reason, they have made a major impact on the health sector in the United States.

THE FAMILY VAN

Dr Nancy Oriol, the founder and current Dean of Students at Harvard Medical School had a vision to change access to care in poor Boston communities. Her vision was the impetus for *The Family Van*, a large urban mobile clinic based in Boston, Massachusetts. In 1992 Boston's Beth Israel Hospital established the van and in 2001 the Harvard Medical School created a program whereby the van's mission set out to improve access to care, increase healthy behaviour, and help people prevent and manage chronic diseases in Boston's underserved neighbourhoods. The Van, which is financed by federal, state and philanthropic supporters, serves six neighbourhoods (Dorchester, Mattapan, Roslindale, Roxbury, Mission Hill and East Boston) with poor health and high emergency department use. The Van also collaborates with neighbourhood health centres and other partners so they can provide referrals to hospitals, clinics and other healthcare systems. Beyond addressing health issues they work tirelessly to address different social determinants of health, like unemployment, parenting and different health behaviour dynamics (Song et al., 2013).

While the team provides health screening, monitoring, coaching and referrals, it does not diagnose or treat. Rather, when needed, it refers patients to local neighbourhood health centres and other partners for definitive diagnosis and treatment using a 'Knowledgeable Neighbor' model, which aims to remove all barriers to services and create a social space for wellness in the community (Hill et al., 2012). The staff on the van are deeply knowledgeable yet extremely accessible to those who frequent it. Typically there are health educators, a registered dietitian and HIV counsellors with free drop-in services providing ease for all patients. This team, which is led by executive director Jennifer Bennet, is multi-ethnic, multicultural and multilingual, so they can discuss health issues with patients in their primary languages. One of the unique aspects of the Van is that patients lead the encounters. Basically, they decide how often to attend and what services to use. Some patients use the clinic for acute concerns, and some for monitoring chronic diseases, blood pressure and blood sugar levels. Others, particularly those without insurance, use it as the main point of access into the health care system (Song et al., 2013).

With very little scholarly research on the use of Mobile Vans in Massachusetts one body of scholarship does a thorough assessment of the Van's impact. Song et al. (2013) used an exclusive dataset of 5900 patients that visited the Family Van at least 10,509 times during 2010–12. The primary focus was to examine the effect of screenings and counselling provided by the clinic on blood pressure. They found that a large percentage of those who used the Van 'did not speak English as their primary language, with the top non-English languages being Spanish and Haitian Creole' (Song et al., 2013, p. 40). Moreover the majority 'were black or Hispanic people with educational attainment at or below twelfth grade' (Song et al., 2013). As expected, most of the patients were uninsured and had gone at least 2 years without having a physical examination. Notably, these individuals avoid emergency room visits and are not comfortable with the traditional medical encounters one would have with a primary care physician. Song et al. (2013) also observes that those who returned to the Van were more likely to be female, older and African American.

One challenge that the Van faces has been attempting to increase the number of teens and young adults who might use the services offered on the Van. Through impromptu face-to-face conversation with teens in the community the executive director and staff members found that most teens viewed the van as a space that serviced older adults and elders (i.e., their parents and/or grandparents). This among other issues makes the Van feel nonaccessible for this population. In collaboration with The Family Van we were able to enlist a group of teen leaders to create digital media and educational information to spread the knowledge of ways that teens could find the services more useful for their specific needs. A select few teens attended a summer training program on civic engagement and health-media literacy with the goal to take health information to their

Figure 11.1 The Family Van is wrapped in colours to capture the diversity of its communities. *Jennifer Bennett, Executive Director of the Family Van.*

respective communities and share the narratives of the Van's impact and usefulness.

Inviting teens to participate in the cocreation of the Van's narrative and public image, particularly as it relates to the use of digital media, was useful. The teens were able to simultaneously learn about media literacy while creating short videos that would be viewed by peers from their communities on the usefulness of the Van.

Above all other efforts the Van has been able to academically and pragmatically demonstrate the fact that mobile clinics are not only cost effective but can work in tandem with large medical facilities to deliver primary and secondary care, deter unnecessary emergency department visits and improve health information and behaviours among high-risk and marginalized communities (Fig. 11.1).

BARBERSHOP AND BEAUTY SHOP AS LOCATIONS OF HEALTH INFORMATION

African American beauty salons and barbershops have been the cornerstone of Black communities dating back to the 19th century. Barbershops specifically were initially spaces of servitude that catered to white patrons like wealthy businessman and politicians (Mills, 2004). Over time as the white clientele decreased barbershops not only become gathering spaces patronized by blacks of all ages but they served as locations to understand what was transpiring in the black community. Numerous Black barbershops and hair salons have capitalized on using these gathering spaces to promote health information and share personal narratives on topics like prostate cancer, breast screenings and mental health (Mills, 2004; Shabazz, 2016). One model that has been successfully growing in Boston has made a major impact on health behaviours of women living in Cambridge neighbourhood – Community Conversations.

The model seeks to expand and adapt a well-recognized Barbershop/Salon model long employed in public health by bringing providers and consumers together to share information and strategies. It has successfully addressed a broad spectrum of health issues among Black women, families and community members with the intent to form a new 'health care team' of consumers and faculty.

Community Conversations: Sister-to-Sister, A Women's Health Initiative: Community Conversations: Sister to Sister, A Women's Health Initiative was officially founded in Cambridge, Massachusetts in 2009. One of the cofounders, Dita Obler said she, 'often found herself engaged in rich, deep and not infrequently challenging and profound conversations that occur daily at her local Cambridge hair salon' (Community Conversations, 2016). As a genetic counsellor with experience navigating the complex maze of medical systems in Metro Boston she found the conversations often touched on medical questions or concerns. She found herself offering health resources or guidance to interested patrons at the salon who broached different topics of health. She soon realized that most of the conversations revealed a true desire for more health knowledge, comprehensive information and accessibility of informative resources.

The main stylist and salon owner, Erinn Pearson, was thrilled with the idea of using her salon as a location to bring Black women together for conversations. *Simply Erinn*, the name of the salon had been a cornerstone business in Cambridge bringing together different members of the diverse community. Along with her lifelong friend Ms Flaherty, who was also a patron of the salon, Dita shared her idea with Erinn to host a series of dialogues to explore health challenges, information and issues that affect Black women, families and communities. Typically the patient-provide relationship can be difficult and awkward so a primary goal was to bring Black female health care providers, practitioners and specialists across different health sectors (i.e., gynaecologist, general practitioners, cancer researchers, mental health, public health, etc.) together with African

American adult females to explore all sorts of health services. By levelling the playing field the core value of the model was to bring a sense of understanding to women who saw themselves being on the peripheral of their health care and well-being.

In a candid interview Dita observes with her model:

> *Health challenges are placed in context, allowing our consumers to develop a more holistic picture of how to work toward health and wellbeing. While up-to-date health information is exchanged at each conversation, we also provide each participant with tools to create individualized health scaffolding. Developing health literacy skills to evaluate the validity and applicability of health information requires becoming familiar with health related language and concepts.*
>
> ***Community Conversations (2016)***

The community of women of colour who attends the conversations is from varied educational, socioeconomic and ethnic backgrounds including but not limited to Black women who are American-born, Caribbean and African, as well as other nationalities. Practitioners are from the Cambridge community and health care system with professional careers in medicine, science and public health. They come together to learn about each other breaking down the normative myth of the role of the medical doctor and the information that lay people should have to negotiate the difficult medical terrain. The holistic circular conversational format puts everyone on an equal playing field and encourages a candid and open dialogue. From their data they have learned that the 'emphasis on a shared role as the "keepers" of important health information and medical decision-making has the potential to reduce some barriers to improved access to and uptake of health care resources' (Community Conversations, 2016).

The forum has been diligent in recognizing that Black women see themselves as the keepers of their families and the community, thus helping them explore their own stressors. The place and importance of balance offers them order. As they attempt to address their role as 'Chief of Family Health' it also increases their sense of empowerment and preservers of their own health (Community Conversations, 2016).

The conversations at the salon transpire month-to-month and the topics are vast and often represent the issues that the women feel are most valuable. For instance, during 2016 the forum has addressed the following topic:

- *Podiatry – Feet Don't Fail Me Now* where the women discussed foot anatomy and physiology, common foot specific issues and prevent and modifiable risk factors with a Doctor of Podiatric Medicine (DPM) and a medical doctor from the Cambridge Health Alliance.

- *Elder Care: The Physical, Mental & Emotional Challenges (Balance for them and Us)* where the women discussed how to support independence and new relationship roles, managing challenging behaviours and social connection and isolation with a Chief of Geriatric Medicine at Atrius Health, a Licensed Counselor & Social Worker (LCSW) and trained therapist and a Registered Nurse (RN) who is a State Home Care Nurse Manager for an Elder care service in Cambridge, Massachusetts.
- *Righteous Anger: How to Harness Anger to Empower Black Women & Families* where the women unpack and discuss the meaning of anger, how to recognize anger that serves as the catalyst for change and understanding differences in anger and depression, sadness and anxiety with a Medical Doctor, a Psychologist and a college professor in a Psychology department at a large university in Boston, Massachusetts.

Currently the forum is doing more qualitative and quantitative data-driven research to capture and understand the implications of the conversations on the women who attend, their families and eventually their communities. This has been a twofold process whereby one set of data has been administered to garner in-depth interviews of the participants' experiences and a second data collection has been instituted to garner the experiences of practitioners and physicians that participate. The implications of this forum have been far reaching over the past few years. Currently the pilot has nearly 500 health care consumers, providers and community partners (Community Conversations, 2016) and has been rigorously seeking national grant funding to capture the model but also make it adaptable for other scenarios like Latina or immigrant communities (Fig. 11.2).

CONCLUSION

The Family Van and Community Conversations are exemplary models of projects that serve Boston's high-risk and disparate communities of colour. In an effort to advance positive health behaviours, each has a primary goal of promoting resilience and agency among respective community members and Black women. The contributions have been successful at targeting specific needs related to different health issues and both have local and even global ramifications. The ability to infuse health and media

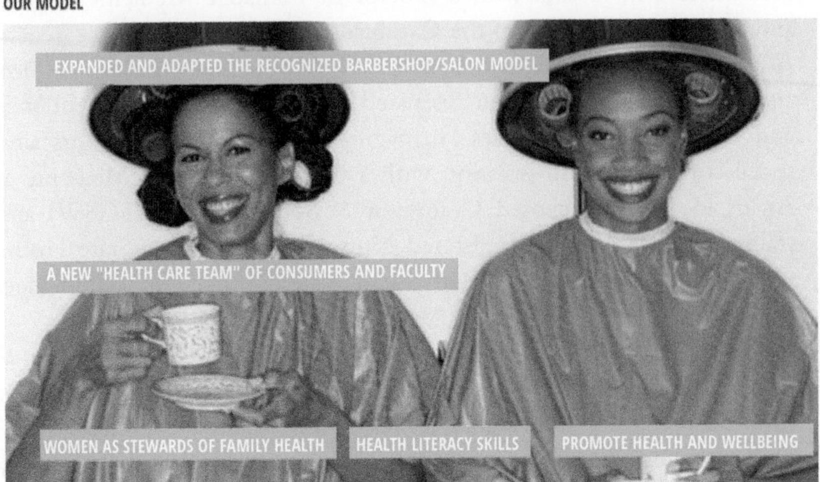

Figure 11.2 The Sister-to-Sister model of holistic empowerment. *Dita Obler, co-founder of Sister-to-Sister Community Conversations*

literacy into each model makes the work of The Family Van and Community Conversations even more poignant because it means that health information is not only disseminated to individuals who access the services but information reaches into a number of different relational contexts promoting self-efficacy, empowerment and community health.

ACKNOWLEDGEMENTS

Thanks to The Family Van and Sister-to-Sister for the opportunity to collaborate and partner with them in their growth and community impact.

REFERENCES

Clear Communication: A NIH Health Literacy Initiative. (2016). Retrieved from <https://www.nih.gov/institutes-nih/nih-office-director/office-communications-public-liaison/clear-communication>.

Committee on Health Literacy. (2004). Health literacy: A prescription to end confusion. In: L. Nielsen-Bohlman, et al. (Eds.), Committee on health literacy, board on neuroscience and behavioral health, Institute of Medicine.

Community Conversations. (November 10, 2016). Retrieved from <http://www.ccsister2sister.org/whoweare>.

Cooke-Jackson, A., & Barnes, K. (December 2013). Peer-to-peer mentoring among urban youth: The intersection of health communication, media literacy and digital health vignettes. *Journal of Digital and Media Literacy.* Retrieved on November 10, 2016 from <http://www.jodml.org/2013/12/01/peer-to-peer-mentoring-among-

urban-youth-the-intersection-of-health-communication-media-literacy-and-digital-health-vignettes/>.

Health Literacy. (November 10, 2016). Retrieved from <https://nnlm.gov/outreach/consumer/hlthlit.html>.

Hill, C., Zurakowski, D., Bennet, J., Walker-White, R., Osman, J. L., Quarles, A., & Oriol, N. (2012). Knowledgeable neighbors: A mobile clinic model for disease prevention and screening in underserved communities. *American Journal of Public Health, 102* (3), 406–410. Available from http://dx.doi.org/10.2105/AJPH.2011.300472.

Hobbs, R. (2010). *Digital and media literacy: A plan of action.* Washington: John S. and James L. Knight Foundation and Aspen Institute.

Jenkins, H. (2006). Confronting the challenges of participatory culture: Media education for the 21st century. In *An Occasional Paper on Digital Media and Learning*. John D. and Catherine T. MacArthur Foundation.

Kreps, G. L., Bonaguro, E. W., & Query, J. L. (1998). The history and development of the field of Health Communication. In L. D. Jackson, & B. K. Duffy (Eds.), *Health Communication Research: A guide to developments and directions* (pp. 1–15). Westport: Greenwood Press.

Mihailidis, P. (2013). *Exploring global perspective on identity, community and media literacy in a Networked age.* Retrieved from <http://www.jodml.org/2013/02/01/perspectives-identitymedia-Literacy/>.

Mihailidis, P. (2014). *Media literacy and the emerging citizen: Youth, engagement and participation in digital culture.* Bern, Switzerland: Peter Lang Inc.

Mills, Q. T. (2004). Truth and soul: Black talk in the barbershop. In M. Harris-Lacewell (Ed.), *Barbershops, bibles, and BET: Everyday talk and black political thought* (pp. 162–203). Princeton: Princeton University Press.

Pearcy, J., & Keppel, K. (2002). A summary measure of health disparity. *Public Health Reports, 117*(3), 273–280.

A People Movement: Massachusetts community health centers' historic fight for access. (November 13, 2016). Retrieved from <http://www.rchnfoundation.org/?p = 3986>.

The 2015 Report on the Status of Women and Girls in Boston, Massachusetts (February 26, 2017). Retrieved from <https://www.cityofboston.gov/images_documents/2015%20Report%20on%20Women%20and%20Girls_tcm3-51854.pdf>.

Schiavo, R. (2007). *Health Communication from theory to practice* (2nd ed).). San Francisco: Jossey-Bass an Imprint of Wiley.

Shabazz, D. (2016). Barbershops as cultural forums for African American males. *Journal of Black Studies*, 1–18. Available from http://dx.doi.org/10.1177/0021934716629337.

Smedley, B. D., Adrienne, Y., Stith, A. Y., & Nelson, A. R. (2003). *Unequal treatment: Confronting racial and ethnic disparities in health care.* Washington: The National Academies Press.

Song, Z., Hill, C., Bennett, J., Vavasis, A., & Oriol, N. A. (2013). Mobile Clinic in Massachusetts associated with cost savings from lowering blood pressure and emergency department use. *Health Affairs, 32*(1), 36–44. Available from http://dx.doi.org/10.1377/hlthaff.2011.1392.

Thoman, E., & Jolls, T. (2004). Media literacy – A national priority for a changing world. *American Behavioral Scientist, 48*(1), 18–29.

Urban Violence in the Commonwealth. (February 26, 2017). Retrieved from <http://www.jfox.neu.edu/Documents/AG%20report.pdf>.

US Department of Health and Human Services, Agency for Healthcare Research and Quality. 2011. National healthcare disparities report. Available from: <http://www.ahrq.gov/qual/nhdr10/nhdr10.pdf> Accessed 11.07.17.

U.S. Department of Health and Human Services. (2014). Web site retrieved from <https://health.gov/communication/literacy/quickguide/factsbasic.htm>.

Xiao, N., Sharman, R., Rao, H. R., & Upadhyaya, S. (2014). Factors influencing online health information search: An empirical analysis of a national cancer-related survey. *Decision Support Systems*, *57*, 417–427.

Zarcadolas, C., Pleasant, A., & Greer, D. S. (2005). Understanding health literacy: An expanding model. *Health Promotion International*, *20*(2), 195–203.

FURTHER READING

National Geographic. (2016). Retrieved from <http://nationalgeographic.org/encyclopedia/rural-area/>.

CHAPTER 12

Including the Rural Excluded: Digital Technology and Diverse Community Participation

Hilary Davis and Jane Farmer
Swinburne University of Technology, Melbourne, VIC, Australia

INTRODUCTION

Public workshops and meetings, committees, surveys and focus groups are often used to obtain consumer and/or community views for input to policy and local decision making, as are more established technologies such as websites. However, given the challenges and potential costs of citizen partnership efforts, there is a gap in research that examines the role that new, emergent and innovative technologies, including online forums, social media, digital stories, apps, texting, crowdsourcing and geographical technologies might play in engaging people traditionally absent from partnerships with health services. Australian health services are required to partner with consumers, the public and communities in designing and providing safe, quality and needed services. Industry standards highlight that services should tailor partnering methods to ensure inclusion of people from diverse backgrounds (ACSQHC, 2014). However, partnering with people from diverse backgrounds is particularly challenging in remote, rural and regional areas. People are located often across vast areas, public transport is limited, technology connections are variable, and there is high turnover in the public sector workforce. Despite this, rural communities are identified as producing innovation. While partnerships are beneficial in delivering improved health outcomes (Rathert, Wyrwich, & Austin Boren, 2012), community capacity and better services (Doyle, Lennox, & Bell, 2013), consumer participants in traditional partnering events (such as public forums) tend to be white, middle class and more highly educated. A wider diversity of participants is needed to include those defined as hidden or hard to reach, such as homeless, transient, indigenous people, marginalized young people and people with disabilities.

Digital Participation through Social Living Labs. DOI: http://dx.doi.org/10.1016/B978-0-08-102059-3.00012-5

Using findings from literature in the social science and Human Computer Interaction (HCI) fields, and drawing upon our own research in this space, we explore the role of new technologies for supporting consumer and community partnerships with health services, particularly in regional and rural communities. We examine and outline opportunities and challenges afforded by technology for identifying and recruiting participants (particularly from diverse backgrounds) in order to capture peoples' experiences, and potentially support ongoing partnership with services. Further, we present an account of some of our own experiences with socially isolated housebound people. We do not seek to provide an exhaustive account of all diverse and marginalized communities, nor of all types of technologies which might help. Rather, we seek to recognize and engage others in a discussion of some of the challenges and opportunities of using new and existing technologies for partnering with people from diverse backgrounds in rural and regional Australia.

BACKGROUND

The Australian Commission on Safety and Quality in Health Care states, 'There is evidence to show that the involvement of consumers in service planning, delivery, monitoring and evaluation is more likely to result in services that are more accessible and appropriate for users' (p. 6). Holman (2014) notes there has been a 'participatory turn' in government and public services over recent decades. There are multiple, interconnected explanations of why this has occurred. In health, on the one hand, there is a provenance in the World Health Organisation Alma Ata Declaration (1978) (see http://www.who.int/publications/almaata_declaration_en.pdf) where it was proposed that involving citizens and communities in decision making about services and initiatives would empower them. This would occur through the empowerment of being involved with other stakeholders in decision making, interactions with the research evidence-base providing health literacy and extension of social networks, and growing community social capital. Simultaneous with this empowerment strand, the growth of neoliberal politics has led to an ideology which values skilling individuals to self-care and to increasingly understand individual and community responsibility to use public health services appropriately and even to get involved in health and care provision (e.g., through volunteering and caring responsibilities) (Farmer, Hill, & Munoz, 2012).

A further movement has emerged from service design, marketing and quality improvement disciplines. This suggests that consumers are well placed to inform service providers about what services they want and how to consume them; and that, if consumers are involved in designing services, they will use them appropriately and perceive them as high quality as they will have been designed to meet consumer needs. While these ideas are widely promoted, indeed now to an extent taken for granted in health policy, there is very little specificity about how to involve people, for how long and what to expect as short or long-term outcomes for individuals and services, and how to identify and measure that (Attree et al., 2011). While the literature on consumer participation in health has been relatively unsophisticated to date, it is developing (Milton et al., 2011). Some literature suggests that participation by consumers and the public in health service decision making leads to better individual and community health and wellbeing and a growth in community capacity. In particular, it has been linked with improved health outcomes, better recognition of community capacity and improved services (NICE, 2014) (A brief version of the report can be found here: https://www.nice.org.uk/guidance/lgb16/resources/community-engagement-to-improve-health-60521149786309. A summary of the evidence for the role of community engagement in improving health outcomes can be found here: https://www.nice.org.uk/guidance/ng44/evidence.).

Terminology

In health, there is discussion of consumer participation (which suggests involvement of interested people with experience of service use – these might be patients, carers, families and friends), public participation (which suggests a much broader involvement of those who use services, but also those that pay for public services through taxation) and community participation (which suggests a particular link between services and the place location they are provided). There is also some discussion of receiving input from communities of interest that might have particular knowledge or perspectives. Communities of interest (Henri & Pudelko, 2003) are defined as a group of people who share a common interest or passion. Communities of interest are not bounded by a particular place or location, and members of that community may know little or nothing of each other. Rather they are assembled around a topic of common interest. Members 'take part in the community to exchange information, obtain answers to personal questions or problems, to improve their understanding of a subject, (and) to share common passions or to play' (Henri & Pudelko, 2003, p. 478). Classically, Arnstein (1969) suggested that interest in involving citizens and consumers in public sector decision making is really about including marginalized people. It is frequently commented that those that get involved in public meetings and forums in community decision making are 'the usual suspects' – i.e., middle class, educated, mobile, healthy and employed. Indeed, one study (Munoz, Farmer, Warburton, & Hall, 2014) found that those who participated formally in rural community activities, management and governance tended to fall within these broad categories. One reason for this is that it is very difficult to attract a range of participants to become involved in public or community participation exercises. Participants are generally not interested unless they can see something in it for themselves, it is related to their job or another interest. Farmer, Currie, Kenny, and Munoz (2015) found that people in rural areas are reluctant to share views about the future of health services in public, and are more interested in confidential methods where they can express opinion in community votes, confidential surveys or by iteratively responding to plans.

Consumers of health services are a diverse group and communities are increasingly multicultural (e.g., see, Queensland Health, 2012). It is important to strive to find ways to include diversity in health partnerships and participation exercises, to help improve service acceptability, efficiency, effectiveness and equity; to support contributions to quality services and to target services towards community needs and priorities. If health service managers merely want to consult or gain views, this could be done via methods that avoid public gatherings. However, if elements of deliberative decision making are required, it is necessary to gather people together in some way. For example, decisions might be about what new or existing services should be prioritized or upgraded. People will gain capacity from learning new information, sharing information, exchanging views and, through interactive processes, arrive at decisions. Technology can help. It can assist to support the voices and views of people who are, may be, less visible in rural communities including people who are homeless, housebound, mobility challenged and those who are refugees. It may allow people to participate who cannot physically access particular places and spaces such as health services, because of distance, cost or social limitations (e.g., agoraphobia and anxiety). For example, text-based technologies allow people to engage anonymously, without including visual imagery.

Participation exercises lead to shared learning. That is, both citizens and health service representatives work together and learn from each other. This shared learning and the extension of social networks it creates is a source of community capacity created through partnership (Taylor, 2015, p. 350). If there is no element of meeting together as a group or sharing of information (whether in a physical or 'virtual space'), then participation is merely an instrumental gathering, by health services, of one type of information (i.e., consumer's initial thoughts) to feed service design decisions.

Diverse Types of Health Services

There are different types of health service organizations across Australia. They include publically funded health services and community health services, private hospitals, metropolitan health services, regional health services, subregional services and private hospitals. The Australian Commission on Safety and Quality in Health Care (ACSQHC), amongst other Australian health policy measures, is seeking to encourage health services to be responsive to patient, carer, consumer and public input. Some areas in which the ACSQHC aims to facilitate this include encouraging consumer *partnerships* in governance and in the improvement of patient experiences and local health outcomes. Consumers and carers may receive information on a local health service's performance and may be sought to contribute to the ongoing monitoring, measurement and evaluation of performance to try to impact on quality improvement, as suggested in hospital (ACSQHC, 2014) and regional health commissioning guidance. We recognize that there is no single proven, evidence-based approach to partnering with consumers, but that partnering should reflect the organizational context, purpose of partnership, desired outcome and the external environment (e.g., place, community, health system and so on). In line with this, suggested strategies for health services to recruit and encourage consumer participation are made available to health services (see e.g., https://www.safetyandquality.gov.au/our-work/patient-and-consumer-centred-care/national-safety-and-quality-health-service-standard-2-partnering-with-consumers/).

All health services are assessed and accredited on how well they meet these standards. According to reviews of this accreditation process, it is clear that at least 30% of respondents are struggling to meet their ‘partnering with consumers’ requirements (see http://www.ravencg.com.au/images/documents/Health-Services-Partnering-with-Consumers-Survey-Summary-Report.pdf?utm_source=LTU+Hospital+Study&utm_campaign=d725a5c13b-EMAIL_CAMPAIGN_2017_06_21&utm_medium = email&utm_term=0_89fd73b0d7-d725a5c13b-226973153). This report suggests involving consumers in governance, the training of clinicians, service codesign and consumer training are the actions most health services find difficult to implement. The least difficult area was cited as involving participants in providing feedback on publications about health services. Some of the reasons given for poor consumer partnerships with health services include: evidence that health services are unsure how to locate consumers; the belief that consumers do not have sufficient knowledge to contribute to partnerships or that consumers are only interested in their own health issue or focus.

REGIONAL AND RURAL CONTEXT

Consumer, public, community participation and partnership is particularly important for disadvantaged people living in remote, rural and regional places (Preston, Waugh, Taylor, & Larkins, 2009), but it is still highly problematical (Kenny, Farmer, Dickson-Swift, & Hyett, 2015). Rural places are particularly challenged in terms of access to amenities and services associated with health. For example, some health services are less accessible (such as dental services), there is less choice of providers, and there is high staff turnover. In Australia, rural and remote communities tend to have higher place-based socioeconomic disadvantage. This is related to fewer employment opportunities, lower incomes and a lower proportion of the population with higher education compared with urban Australia. Indeed it has been reported that in the past decade, income inequality has worsened for people in rural and remote areas. This has exacerbated challenges to health, housing, education and work (National Rural Health Alliance, Inc., 2014). It is suggested that coproduction of health services (i.e., involving local people) could make vital services more accessible. Involving local people in designing and providing locally appropriate services could build capacity in skills, experience, confidence and networks; and by association, social capital – which is also associated with increasing health status. At the same time, rural populations are often seen to be more amenable to community participation initiatives because people traditionally have greater social connections and higher levels of volunteering (Hofferth & Iceland, 1998).

In terms of traditional methods of community participation that involve bringing local people together in public consultations, rural Australia is challenged. Firstly, rural people in a single health service catchment might be dispersed across a large distance. Distances to travel to a community event could be considerable. Road travel in rural Australia can be dangerous due to weather hazards and the monotony of long distance driving; and there is poor access to public transport. As previously highlighted, there may be cultural disconnects that make it difficult to have diverse people come together; e.g., Shubin (2010) has highlighted entrenched divisions between relatively more affluent and poorer people in small communities in Europe. While technology might provide a way to afford greater accessibility to participation initiatives, the Australian Digital Inclusion Index shows a significant disparity between many parts of rural Australia and Australian cities in terms of access to Internet connection and digital literacy (Thomas et al., 2016a, 2016b).

TRADITIONAL PARTNERING METHODS

There are a range of well-used methods for including consumers' views in aspects of health services provision. These include having a consumer representative on health services committees, establishing specific consumer advisory groups, and seeking to engage 'critical friends' groups in health services consultations.

Other strategies include employing surveys in feedback on patient experiences, and engaging service users in one-to-one discussions. Participants for these activities are often sourced through existing service provision, such as people sitting in waiting rooms, or residents or visitors to hospital wards and clinics. These established methods have the benefit of being relatively low cost and easy to deploy, and access an existing 'captive' population (e.g., a form is handed out when a visitor approaches a reception desk, or is mailed-out postvisit). Further, the use of paper-based forms aligns with existing organizational and cultural norms, such as nursing procedures (Davis, 2001). However, there are limitations with these methods including that the consumer pool is limited to existing service users, and, while a useful tool, surveys typically do not capture depth of experience. Focus groups are a method for capturing more depth in consumer feedback, however they have limitations. As noted earlier, recruitment of people from diverse backgrounds may be difficult, people may have to travel long distances, and within the focus group itself, time is limited, the group is small (typically 4–6 members) and dissenting voices (particularly voices which are less articulate) are less likely to be heard (Smithson, 2000). New technologies offer the potential to address some of these challenges. We now provide a contextual overview of some of the ways in which technology might support increased consumer engagement in health service provision in Australia, particularly for people from disadvantaged and diverse backgrounds.

MEDIATING CONVERSATIONS THROUGH NEW TECHNOLOGIES

Websites

One of the most obvious ways in which health services seek to engage consumers is via their websites. The websites of health services range in sophistication. Typically, they might include strategic plans, historical information, details of the Board or Executive, basic demographic information such as contact details, job vacancies, services provided and so on. Health services websites typically provide simple background information, while others include news items, and videos (including information about services provided, volunteers, community leaders or successful programs). Some health services tap into social media platforms. Consumers may 'follow' the health service on Twitter, or Instagram, or visit their Facebook pages. Regular 'tweets' from the Health Service may also feature on the website; e.g., information about key activities such as days dedicated to local events (such as Open Days), health campaigns. These may include Movember or International Initiatives such as World Diabetes Day.

There are other nonspecific health services websites, which seek to support consumers in different ways. The National Health Services Directory is an Australian government initiative, delivered by Healthdirect Australia, which aims to provide health professionals and consumers with reliable and consistent information about health services. Consumers use the directory to find a service (whether allied health, hospital, community service or other) by entering in simple search terms such as the type of service, service preference (e.g., no appointment, telehealth capable, free parking and wheelchair access) and a postcode. The search results include a list of services in the local area, their contact details and hours, distance from the postcode and a google map link flagging the location of relevant services. The 'healthdirect app' is a free app used to find health services, check symptoms and receive trusted health information (Health Direct App, 2017). Other examples include a service navigation and networking app for rural people with dementia, their families and service providers. Currently on trial in regional Victoria, Australia, this app seeks to ease challenges to navigating services, connecting dementia service providers and users and providing opportunities to review services (Blackberry, Wilding, & Farmer, 2016). The Clickability website supports reviews of disability services such as these (Clickability, 2017).

Internet Forums

Internet forums or simply 'forums' are becoming more popular due to their flexibility, i.e., they can support a range of activities including individual posts or messages and 'threads' (a series of responses to a post). Some forums are 'moderated' by the users or employees of the forum who seek to keep the forum clean from spam or abuse. One specific example is the Consumers Health Forum of Australia (2017). This forum is hosted by a nonprofit, consumer advocacy organization. Its aims are to help consumers find their way to useful information and health services, and to encourage consumers to share their healthcare experiences and the ways they would like these to change. At the time of writing, this was the only one of its kind that we could locate, in Australia. It provides an example of technology facilitating direct patient to health service interaction, and facilitation of feedback from health services to consumers. The forum supports a range of activities including an electronic newsletter, an 'Ideas Wall' on which people may post ideas (similar to a virtual noticeboard), and other activities such as connecting consumers with local health services and organizations through an interactive map, and online polls on topical issues. The forum hosts a blog and digital stories. The Consumers Health Forum supports direct consumer interaction with health services through a 'patient opinion' page, on which people who have used a health service can comment on their interactions with nurses, clinicians and other health professionals. The names of services and people working within them are included on the site after independent moderation to check for use of language and accuracy of the story. The health service is then notified and given a right to reply, which is also posted on the website. In this way, the dialogue continues, the consumers' concerns are addressed and the health service may reflect on and consider ongoing changes to their services. Thus the site could be viewed as facilitating conversations between consumers and health services, providing the latter with potentially important information about user experiences. These may be experiences which consumers are not comfortable sharing *in situ*, at the time of a visit.

Up to this point, we have discussed a range of formal top-down health organization-led initiatives. These seek to obtain information about consumer experiences with health services in Australia. Alongside, there are consumer-driven initiatives that seek to report on, engage and educate health professionals in turn.

Blogs

There is evidence that creating personal narratives can be of therapeutic benefit to people who have experienced trauma or who are living in difficult circumstances (Pennebaker & Seagal, 1999), as well as providing a useful source of information about experiences of consumers that health services could use. A blog (short for a weblog) is a means by which people can share their views with interested others, usually via a personal website. Entries often take the format of diarised entries. Typically, they are presented in a reverse chronological timeline (e.g., newest entries at the top), recounting a story over time, such as the progression of an illness. There are many health blogs originating from Australia, which often focus on issues of diet and exercise (e.g., Blog Chicks, 2017).

Some blogs recount personal experiences with the health system. One of the more well known in Australia is written by a young woman with a serious skin and health conditions. She writes of her experiences with health professionals and the health system, and analyses how different models of disability inform the way in which healthcare providers treat people with disability (Findlay, 2017). She views her role as educating others and has gained some influence, appearing as a guest speaker on television and in other media. Some health and wellness blogs are part of larger blogging sites, which contain a collection of health blogs, such as Nourishing Hub (2017) and Australian Counselling (2017).

In principle, blogs appear to provide the opportunity for people from diverse and marginalized backgrounds and communities to share their experiences with others, and to comment on everyday interactions with health services. However, there is potential for bias in relation to blogs; while there is gender balance in blogging (49.1% men to 50.9% women), typically bloggers are young 21–35 years old (53% of bloggers) or below 20 years (20.2%). There are far more American bloggers than of any other country (Sysomos, 2017). Blogs tend to preclude people with low levels of literacy, or from backgrounds or cultures where stories are visually based. Furthermore, while blogs are widely available, health services staff would usually only learn about them if they were brought to their attention, or if they specifically searched for blogs around a specific issue. Even then, blogs which do not discuss local issues of concern may not provide any insights as to how a condition or illness was experienced in a local context. What is needed, therefore, is direct dialogue between local bloggers with concerns of interest to specific regional or rural areas, and local health services.

Social Media

There are a range of other technologies which may be appropriated by either health services, individual consumers (or both) to share information, stories and experiences. In particular, Social Networking Services (SNS) such as Facebook, Twitter, Instagram, Snapchat and MySpace (amongst others) have become an integral aspect of many young people's lives in Australia and overseas. These technologies support a range of methods for connecting with other individuals and groups of people including messaging, texting, sharing photos, stories and videos. There are many studies which highlight the negative aspects of social media use, particularly for vulnerable or marginalized young people, such as those with mental health issues. However, SNS can also be used for a range of positive purposes including building connections, sharing stories, connecting people to support and health services and influencing change. Collin, Rahilly, Richardson, and Third (2011) provide a literature review of the use of SNS by young Australians, including a discussion of some of the ways in which SNS can facilitate a sense of community and belonging, particularly through functions such as Facebook 'Groups' and 'fan' pages and groups, and Twitter 'hash tags' (p. 19). Further they discuss how technologies are often appropriated for civic engagement and political participation purposes. One recent example of this can be found in the work of Larson, Nagler, Ronen, and Tucker (2016) which examines Twitter activity during the 2015 Charlie Hebdo protests in Paris. Larson speculates on a theory of participation in which an individual's decision depends on his or her exposure to others' intentions, and that networking position determines exposure. Larson finds that, relative to comparable Twitter users, protesters are significantly more connected to each other via direct, indirect, triadic and reciprocated ties. Other studies have examined how nonprofit organizations are engaging stakeholders through Facebook and other SNS (Waters, Burnett, Lamm, & Lucas, 2009). Such findings about behaviour of SNS users are of relevance to health services in that such evidence could be applied to engaging social media users and their exchanges to inform health services priorities and developments.

Mobile Apps

With increasing pressure on health services, one response has increased use of mobile health 'apps' for consumers' self-care. There remains a paucity of research into consumer engagement with electronic self-monitoring. Some exceptions include Anderson's research which uses a qualitative approach to explore how consumers use health apps for health monitoring, identify benefits from using them and suggests improvements to apps (Anderson, Burford, & Emmerton, 2016). In addition, there are a variety of apps which are used in health services and hospital settings to better engage consumers with services (Mobile Smith, 2017). However, it is important to recognize that apps which are commercially available and of use to people within the general population are not always helpful for people from diverse backgrounds and communities. For example, Sarkar et al. (2016) investigate the usability of existing 'apps' for diabetes, depression and caregiving, to facilitate the development of future patient-focused apps for diverse populations. Using a mixed methods approach, with interviewing and direct observation, he found that participants were only able to complete 43% of tasks without assistance. Participants noted a lack of confidence with technology, frustration with design features and navigation, but still had a desire to use technology to support self-management of their health. Overall, Sarkar et al (2016) argue that technology developers should employ participatory design strategies when designing apps for vulnerable and diverse populations. Common in the HCI space, participatory design methods have been used successfully to engage marginalized rural people in technology design. This includes people who emphasize 'primary orality', or direct face-to-face unmediated communication, due to distance, low levels of technology and cultural antecedents (Bidwell & Hardy, 2009). Further, the use of proxies (people who advocate for, or support people in interactions with designers and others (Brereton et al., 2015)) has had some success with engaging people with cognitive and sensory impairments, people who may be nonverbal, have an intellectual disability or a particular disorder such as autism. Other research has used codesign techniques with people with visual impairments (Metatla, Bryan-Kinns, Stockman, & Martin, 2015) and autistic adults (Gaudion, Hall, Myerson, & Pellicano, 2015). These are techniques/ technologies which health services may use to engage with people from diverse or marginalized communities.

CROWDSOURCING

While we have discussed a range of personal technologies, other technologies can call on the power of collectives to help solve individual problems which health services find challenging. For example, CrowdMed (2017) is an online platform which supports the sharing of individual health symptoms, and diagnosis by a large group of Doctors. In essence, it uses the 'wisdom of crowds' to help find a diagnosis. Sickweather (2017) is the largest crowdsourcing app of its kind. It scans social media sites such as Facebook and Twitter for indicators of illness. These data are then shared with app users so that they can get real-time alerts when they enter a 'sick zone', people can share forecasts and reports with friends and Sickweather groups, and track recent illnesses nearby on a live map. Sometimes, it might be difficult to discern how helpful this information is: how useful is it to know if that people near your home or work have reported an illness? Or is this illness biological, viral or simply allergy related – in which case, there is no chance of catching the illness anyway. Nevertheless, the app may be useful for people who are immune suppressed, or very young or old, and therefore potentially more at risk.

Crowdsourcing has been used successfully to recruit volunteers in times of disaster (Ludwig, Kotthaus, & Pipek, 2016) and to support disadvantaged populations. For example, in the United States it has been applied to help blind and low-vision users better access the world around them (Bigham et al., 2010). Crowdsourcing is a technology with promise for health services as local people could be asked to crowdsource on feedback to services or to participate in health events. However, recruiting participants can be difficult, unless specific interest groups are targeted. Commentary might be crowdsourced at gatherings of people with collective interests such as racing meets, swimming carnivals or annual agricultural shows. This has been a strategy used to target hard-to-reach men for specific health checks or Health Pitstops. The PitStop program has been distributed to a range of organizations throughout Australia and overseas, including those servicing rural, remote populations such as farmers (Kuhns, 2009), the Royal Flying Doctor Service (Harvey & Hill, 2006) and others (Russell, Harding, Chamberlain, & Johnston, 2006). However, for rural health services targeting people living in rural or remote areas, or for those servicing areas with small, sparse populations, the large numbers of people usually targeted through crowdsourcing apps may be difficult to attain.

DIGITAL STORIES

While keeping a written personal account of life experiences is known to provide benefit, visual communication provides additional unique properties, particularly for sharing stories or experiences that might be difficult to express through words alone (Gubrium, Hill, & Flicker, 2014). Recognizing the power of the visual, and building on the increasing availability of digital technologies to support visual communication, the digital storytelling movement began in the mid-1990s (Edmonds, Chenhall, Arnold, Lewis, & Lowish, 2014). Digital storytelling typically involves small group workshops where amateur storytellers learn to use technology to create short narratives, using digital photographs and video footage and sometimes a voice-over from the storyteller. Digital stories have been used to empower and give voice to marginalized people and to build connections through the power of shared experiences (Clarke et al., 2013; Gubrium et al., 2014; Vivienne, 2014). For example, digital stories have been utilized as a means of supporting people with intellectual disability and complex needs to overcome barriers to societal participation and inclusion. FACS (The Family and Community Services Department, New South Wales, Australia) has employed a codesign approach to produce three different kinds of videos that convey client experiences: Introductory Videos, which convey a personalized impression of a client to new acquaintances and support services; Individual Support Videos which convey key aspects of the person's support needs and Clinical Support Videos which aim to capture specialized practices essential to a person's health and wellbeing (Woelms & Anderson, 2016).

There is a form of digital storytelling where people create and share personal and confessional-style videos online. The advent of video-sharing websites such as YouTube and Vimeo have given voice to a subculture of YouTube video bloggers (or 'vloggers') who share visual diaries of their experiences living with serious or chronic illness, such as cancer, HIV or diabetes. Liu, Huh, Neoghi, Inkpen, and Pratt (2013) research examined how these health vloggers share personal videos on YouTube that chronicle their illness trajectories, and advocate for particular treatments, providing an outlet for connecting with others who are experiencing similar difficulties. Their research, which involved analysing YouTube videos posted by health vloggers, found that vloggers used a variety of techniques to express specific messages to viewers, and explicitly sought interaction with viewers.

Typically digital stories seek to share personal experiences or important events. The development of publically available video-sharing websites, such as YouTube and Vimeo, have provided a potentially global audience for the sharing of digital stories. Potentially, digital stories are an easily accessible tool for anyone with a video camera or a smart phone. Indeed, with support, they have been used by marginalized communities, such as Pacific Youth living in New Zealand (Pacific Youth, 2016) to share stories of health and wellbeing. However, issues arise in terms of quality and ease of use, particularly for people living with disabilities who may have cognitive or other issues, lack of access to a reliable Internet connection for uploading the video (which may be an issue in regional and remote areas) and so on. Australians from low-income backgrounds, including the unemployed, are at a higher risk of digital exclusion due to the costs associated with digital technology (Thomas et al., 2016a, 2016b). Yet the importance of technology for these groups should not be underestimated. For example, some young homeless people use them for staying connected with others, managing identity, finding employment and creating videos which recount their experiences living on the streets (Woelfer & Hendry, 2010, 2011).

Digital Stories and Housebound People

While there are a range of ethical and practical challenges associated with creating digital stories with housebound people (Davis & Waycott, 2015; Waycott, Davis, Warr, Edmonds, & Taylor, 2017), further concerns arise in terms of how and with whom we share the stories of people who may be from marginalized communities, vulnerable, living with obvious physical or intellectual disabilities or have mental health concerns.

While many health bloggers receive positive comments, video-sharing sites such as YouTube potentially expose people to unkind or insensitive commentary (Huh, Liu, Neogi, Inkpen, & Pratt, 2014, p. 23). Seasoned vloggers may use a variety of strategies to manage negative comments including flagging them as spam, arguing back, defining boundaries 'this is MY video' or seeking support from others within their vlogger community.

One of the authors of this chapter was involved in a study with housebound people living in Victoria, Australia. During this study, we had to carefully consider the most appropriate means for sharing our participant's stories given they were socially isolated, vulnerable and not familiar or comfortable with online forums. Participants were referred to the study by their local community health service. Ultimately we (participants, staff and researchers) felt that local empathetic audiences might be more supportive of housebound people's digital stories, than global online audiences. Further we were concerned to leverage opportunities to develop connections between housebound participant's and their local communities. To this end, we developed an interactive digital display to share the stories. The display was lightweight and portable and could easily be deployed in any community facility (such as a library, school or neighbourhood house). The display supported audience feedback via personal mobile devices – similar to leaving a comment on a YouTube video. Once checked for moderation and approved, this feedback appeared at the bottom of the digital story when played.

The stories were displayed at the community health centre's Open Day, and at a staff training day (both in 2015). The digital stories evoked emotional responses including empathy and admiration from audience members (Davis, Waycott, & Zhou, 2015), reflection on their own practice from community health workers, and a shared sense of relief from housebound people that they were not alone in their experiences. This work shows promise for other marginalized individuals or groups wishing to share their stories and reconnect with their local community. Community health services and other community organizations could help. Digital stories could be shown at Open Days, or to local interest groups or at targeted library events. Digital stories such as these could feature in staff training events, as a means of educating community health workers such as Occupational Therapists and social workers about the lived experiences of people who are housebound, socially isolated or marginalized. Further, the digital stories could be hosted on local health services websites (Our Stories, 2014). Digital stories such as these might be repurposed as a recruitment tool for volunteer or befriending services. In this way, people who are physically absent may still contribute to and build capacity in their local community.

CONCLUDING DISCUSSION

In this chapter we have discussed the requirement for Australian health services to partner with consumers, the public and communities to design and provide safe, quality, appropriate and accessible services. We have highlighted the significance of challenges inherent within the rural context, and the importance of including people from diverse backgrounds and communities. We have not provided an exhaustive account of diverse and marginalized communities, indeed we recognize that we have not included people who are excluded due to gender or sexual orientation, such as the LGBTI community. Nor have we discussed refugees, transient populations, or recognized the diversity of ethnic groups in Australia, or people with mental health issues. Further, we have not provided an exhaustive account of all technologies. Chatbots, virtual reality, augmented reality and gaming are some other potential areas of development beyond the current reach of this chapter. Rather, what we have sought to do is provide a general account of some of the challenges and opportunities of using new and existing technologies for partnering with people from diverse backgrounds in rural and regional areas.

We note that recognizing, designing for and partnering with diverse community groups is challenging, and that to date most health services have called upon more traditional partnering methods like public consultation meetings. However, we argue that there is a role for new, emergent and innovative technologies, including online forums, social media, digital stories, apps, texting, crowdsourcing and geographical technologies to engage people generally absent from citizen and community partnerships with health services.

We suggest that some of the ways in which health services may recruit and engage people are through local connections and existing service provision. In particular, recruitment and ongoing engagement could be a regular feature of home visits, volunteering services, neighbourhood houses and local service use (people attending shelters, food banks). Further, health services in regional and rural Australia could advertise their presence to collective audiences (e.g., on large screens and billboards) and individual attendees (e.g., on the back of entry tickets and in booths). Health services could then crowdsource consumer feedback at country fairs, racing meets, sporting events, farmers' conventions and the like.

What is obvious is that all the technologies are not going to be useful to all health services, at all times. Rather, what is needed is to utilize the most appropriate technologies for each particular consumer group, in a particular context. For example, digital stories may lend itself as a method for sharing the lived experiences of people who may be housebound, might have difficulty with written responses or are uncomfortable meeting other people face to face. Health services could capture consumer feedback by training those that visit consumers in their homes (e.g., community caregivers) to work with consumers to create digital stories *in situ*. These could then be viewed by health service workers and other members of the public.

Other less intensive mechanisms include the use of SMS or texting. For example, building on the model used for Text4baby (2017), where health service sets up an SMS link and engages in two-way personalized interaction with pregnant women and new mothers. Consumers can then trust that this information is up to date and reliable, as it was developed by expert practitioners, and is supported by local community services. Further, they have a contact in times of crisis.

Finally, consideration should be given to spaces where people who are uncomfortable meeting face to face can have anonymity from others, while still sharing their stories and opinions (e.g., such as in private booths, in the virtual world or in gamification). These safe virtual spaces – where people cannot be physically seen or heard might also help to mitigate issues of social stratification that can be pertinent in rural areas in particular, as well as overcoming the tyranny of distance.

REFERENCES

Anderson, K., Burford, O., & Emmerton, L. (2016). Mobile health apps to facilitate self-care: A qualitative study of user experiences. *PLoS One*, *11*(5), e0156164. Available from http://dx.doi.org/10.1371/journal.pone.0156164.

Arnstein, S. (1969). A ladder of citizen participation. *Journal of the American Institute of Planners*, *35*, 216–224.

Attree, P., French, B., Milton, B., Povall, S., Whitehead, M., & Popay, J. (2011). The experience of community engagement for individuals. *Health & Social Care in the Community*, *19*(3), 250–260.

Australian Commission on Safety and Quality in Health Care (2014). *National Safety and Quality Health Service Standard 2: Partnering with Consumers—Embedding partnerships in health care*. Sydney: ACSQHC.

Australian Counselling. (2017). Retrieved March 23, 2017, from <https://www.australia-counselling.com.au/mental-health-articles/best-bloggers-mental-health/>.

Bidwell, N., & Hardy, D. (2009). Dilemmas in situating participation in rural ways of saying. In *OzCHI '09, Nov 23–27, Melbourne Australia*.

Bigham, J., Jayant, C., Ji, H., Little, G., Miller, A., Miller, R., ..., Yeh, T. (2010). VizWiz: Nearly Real-time answers to visual questions. In *UIST'10, October 3–6, New York City, USA*.

Blackberry, I., Wilding, I., & Farmer, J. (2016). SENDER: A smartphone app for carers and service providers of people with dementia. In *Digital participation: engaging diverse and marginalised communities, an OZCHI workshop, Nov 29, Launceston, Australia*.

Blog Chicks. (2017). Retrieved March 23, 2017 from <http://blogchicks.com.au/australian-health-blogs>.

Brereton, M., Sitbon, L., Haziq Lim Abdullah, M., Vanderberg, M., & Koplick, S. (2015). Design after Design to bridge between people living with cognitive or sensory impairments, their friends and proxies. CoDesign: International Journal for Co-Creation in Design and the Arts, 11(1).

Clarke, R., et al. (2013). *Digital portraits: Photo-sharing after domestic violence. Proc. CHI 2013* (pp. 2517–2526). ACM Press.

Clickability. (2017). Retrieved March 23, 2017, from <https://clickability.com.au/>.

Collin, P., Rahilly, K., Richardson, I., & Third, A. (2011). *The benefits of social networking services: A literature review*. Melbourne: Cooperative Research Centre for Young People, Technology and Wellbeing.

Consumers Health Forum of Australia. (2017). Retrieved March 23, 2017 from <https://ourhealth.org.au/>.

Crowdmed. (2017). Retrieved March 23, 2017 from <https://www.crowdmed.com/>.

Davis, H. (2001). *The social management of computing artefacts in nursing work: An ethnographic account (Ph.D. thesis)*. UK: Sheffield University.

Davis, H., & Waycott, J. (2015). *Ethical encounters with housebound people: Location, timing, and personal storytelling. Proc. CHI 2015 Workshop on Ethical Encounters in HCI.* Research in Sensitive Settings.

Davis, H., Waycott, J., & Zhou, S. (2015). Beyond YouTube: Sharing personal digital stories on a community display. In *Proc OzCHI, Melbourne* (pp. 579–587).

Doyle, C., Lennox, L., & Bell, D. (2013). A systematic review of evidence on the links between patient experience and clinical safety and effectiveness. *British Medical Journal Open, 3*, e001570. Available from http://dx.doi.org/10.1136/bmjopen-2012-001570.

Edmonds, F., Chenhall, R., Arnold, M., Lewis, T., & Lowish, S. (2014). *Telling our stories: Aboriginal young people in Victoria and digital storytelling*. Melbourne: Institute for a Broadband-Enabled Society, University of Melbourne.

Farmer, J., Currie, M., Kenny, A., & Munoz, S.-A. (2015). An exploration of the longer-term impacts of community participation in rural health services design. *Social Science & Medicine, 141*, 64–71.

Farmer, J., Hill, C., & Munoz, S.-A. (2012). *Community co-production: Social enterprise in remote and rural areas*. Northampton: Edward Elgar.

Findlay, C. (2017). Retrieved from <http://carlyfindlay.blogspot.com.au>.

Gaudion, K., Hall, A., Myerson, J., & Pellicano, L. (2015). A designer's approach: How can autistic adults with learning disabilities be involved in the design process? *CoDesign: International Journal for CoCreation in Design and the Arts, 11*(1), 49–69.

Gubrium, A., Hill, A., & Flicker, S. (2014). A situated practice of ethics for participatory visual and digital methods in public health research and practice: A focus on digital storytelling. *American Journal of Public Health, 104*(9), 1606–1614.

Harvey, D., & Hill, W. (2006). A flying start to health promotion in remote North Queensland, Australia: The development of Royal Flying Doctor Service field days. *Rural and Remote Health', 6*, 485.

Health Direct App. (2017). Retrieved March 22, 2017 from <https://www.healthdirect.gov.au/health-app>.

Henri, F., & Pudelko, B. (2003). Understanding and analysing activity and learning in virtual communities. *Journal of Computer Assisted Learning, 19*, 474–487.

Hofferth, S., & Iceland, J. (1998). Social capital in rural and urban communities. *Rural Sociology, 63*(4), 574–598.

Holman, D. (2014). The relational bent of community participation. *Community Development Journal, 50*(3), 418–432.

Huh, J., Liu, L. S., Neogi, T., Inkpen, K., & Pratt, W. (2014). Health Vlogs as social support for chronic illness management. *ACM Transactions on Computer-Human Interaction (TOCHI)I, 21*(4), 1–29.

Kenny, A., Farmer, J., Dickson-Swift, V., & Hyett, N. (2015). Community participation for rural health: A review of challenges. *Health Expectations, 18*(6), 1906–1917.

Kuhns, S. (2009). Men's health pitstop. A nurse coordinated program to bring health screening to rural farmers. *AJN, 109*(7), 58–60.

Larson, M., Nagler, J., Ronen, J., & Tucker, J. (June 15, 2016). Social networks and protest participation: Evidence from 93 million Twitter users. In *Political networks workshops and conferences 2016*. Retrieved from <https://ssrn.com/abstract = 2796391>.

Liu, L. S., Huh, J., Neoghi, T., Inkpen, K., & Pratt, W. (2013). *Health vlogger-viewer interaction in chronic illness management. Proc. CHI 2013* (pp. 49–58). ACM Press.

Ludwig, T., Kotthaus, C., & Pipek, V. (2016). Situated and ubiquitous crowdsourcing with volunteers during disasters. In *UbiComp/ISWC'16, September 12–16, Heidelberg, Germany* (pp. 1441–1447).

Metatla, O., Bryan-Kinns, N., Stockman, T., & Martin, F. (2015). Designing with and for people living with visual impairments: Audio-tactile mock-ups, audio diaries and participatory prototyping. *CoDesign: International Journal for CoCreation in Design and the Arts, 11*(1), 35–48.

Milton, B., Attree, P., French, B., Povall, S., Whitehead, M., & Popay, J. (2011). The impact of community engagement on health and social outcomes. *Community Development Journal, 47*(3), 316–334.

Mobile Smith. (2017). Hospital apps. Retrieved March 23, 2017 from <https://www.mobilesmith.com/hospital-apps/>.

Munoz, S.-A., Farmer, J., Warburton, J., & Hall, J. (2014). Involving rural older people in service co-production: Is there an untapped pool of potential participants? *Journal of Rural Studies, 34*, 212–222.

National Rural Health Alliance, Inc. (October 15, 2014). *Submission to the Senate Inquiry into the extent of income inequality in Australia, 2014*. Retrieved from <http://ruralhealth.org.au/document/income-inequality-experienced-people-rural-and-remote-australia-submission-senate-inquiry>.

NICE National Institute of Health and Care Excellence. (2014). *Community engagement to improve health*. Retrieved from <http://publications.nice.org.au/lgb16> March 2017.

Nourishing Hub. (2017). Retrieved March 23, 2017, from <www.nourishinghub.com.au>.

Our Stories. (2014). Retrieved March 23, 2017 from <https://ourhealth.org.au/stories?page = 1>.

Pacific Youth (Mobile Storytelling). (2016). Retrieved March 23, 2017, from <https://youtu.be/UgXs5L3UVYY>.

Pennebaker, J. W., & Seagal, J. D. (1999). Forming a story: The health benefits of narrative. *Journal of Clinical Psychology, 55*(1), 1243–1254.

Preston, R., Waugh, H., Taylor, J., & Larkins, S. (2009). *The benefits of community participation in rural health service development: Where is the evidence? 10th National rural health conference.* Cairns: National Rural Health Association.

Queensland Health. (2012). *Health care providers' guide to engaging multi-cultural communities and consumers.* Retrieved from <https://www.health.qld.gov.au/__data/assets/pdf_file/0037/158599/com-engage-guide.pdf>.

Rathert, C., Wyrwich, M. D., & Austin Boren, S. (2012). Patient-centered care and outcomes: A systematic review of the literature. *Medical Care Research Review, 70*(4), 351–379. Available from http://dx.doi.org/10.1177/1077558712465774.

Russell, N., Harding, C., Chamberlain, C., & Johnston, L. (2006). Implementing a 'Men's Health Pitstop' in the Riverina, South-west New South Wales. *Australian Journal of Rural Health, 14,* 129–131.

Sarkar, U., Gourley, G. I., Lyles, C. R., Tieu, L., Clarity, C., Newmark, L., . . . Bates, D. W. (2016). Usability of commercially available mobile applications for diverse patients. *Journal of General Internal Medicine, 31*(12), 1417–1426.

Shubin, S. (2010). Cultural exclusion and rural poverty in Ireland and Russia. *Transactions of the Institute of British Geographers, 35,* 555–570. Available from http://dx.doi.org/10.1111/j.1475-5661.2010.00402.x.

Sickweather. (2017). Retrieved March 23, 2017 from <http://www.sickweather.com/>.

Smithson, J. (2000). Using and analysing focus groups: Limitation and possibilities. *International Journal of Social Research Methodology, 3*(2), 103–119.

Sysomos. (2017). *Inside blogger demographics: Data by gender, age etc., June 2010.* Retrieved from <www.sysomos.com>.

Taylor, J. (2015). *Working with communities.* Oxford: Oxford University Press.

Text4Baby. (2017). Retrieved March 23, 2017 from <https://www.text4baby.org/>.

Thomas, J., Barraket, J., Ewing, S., MacDonald, T., Mundell, M., & Tucker, J. (2016a). *Measuring Australia's digital divide: The Australian digital inclusion index 2016.* Swinburne University of Technology, Melbourne, for Telstra. Retrieved from <www.dx.doi.org/10.4225/50/57A7D17127384>.

Thomas, J., Barraket, J., Ewing, S., MacDonald, T., Mundell, M., & Tucker, J. (2016b). Measuring Australia's digital divide: The Australian digital inclusion index 2016. Swinburne: University of Technology for Telstra, Melbourne. Retrieved from <https://digitalinclusionindex.org.au/wp-content/uploads/2016/08/Australian-Digital-Inclusion-Index-2016.pdf>.

Vivienne, S. (2014). Mediating influences: Problematising facilitated digital self-representation. *Conjunctions. Transdisciplinary Journal of Cultural Participation, 1*(1), 1–25.

Waters, R., Burnett, E., Lamm, A., & Lucas, J. (2009). Engaging stakeholders through social networking: How non-profit organizations are using Facebook. *Public Relations Review, 35,* 102–106.

Waycott, J., Davis, H., Warr, D., Edmonds, F., & Taylor, G. (2017). Negotiating participation: Ethical tensions when 'giving voice' through digital storytelling. *Interacting with Computers, 29*(2), 237–247.

Woelfer, J. P., & Hendry, D. G. (2010). *Homeless young people's experiences with information systems: Life and work in a community technology center. Proc. of CHI '10* (pp. 1291–1300). ACM.

Woelfer, J. P., & Hendry, D. G. (2011). Designing ubiquitous information systems for a community of homeless young people: Precaution and a way forward. *Personal and Ubiquitous Computing, 15*(6), 565–573.

Woelms, T., & Anderson, G. (2016). The Digital Life Project. Digital Participation: Engaging Diverse and Marginalised Communities, an OZCHI workshop, Nov 29 2016, Launceston, Australia. Retrieved from <https://digital-participationhci.files.wordpress.com/2016/07/digital-life-project-facs-nsw-18112016-woelms.pdf>.

FURTHER READING

Australian Government (2015). *PHN Commissioning: Needs assessment guide.* Canberra: Department of Health.

Movember Foundation. (2017). Retrieved March 23, 2017 from <https://au.movember.com>.

RUOK. (2017). Retrieved March 23, 2017 from <https://www.ruok.org.au>.

CHAPTER 13

Digital Storytelling for Community Participation: The *Storyelling* Social Living Lab

Cherie Allan, Michael Dezuanni and Kerry Mallan
Queensland University of Technology, Brisbane, QLD, Australia

The emergence of digital storytelling over recent years (Lambert, 2002) as a popular practice for sharing personal and community stories and artefacts is an example of how digital participation is occurring with individuals and groups for different purposes, such as learning how to use a digital tool to create and edit images, telling or writing a story in multiple formats or simply as a way of connecting with others. In this regard, digital storytelling is an embedded humanistic practice that relies on information and communication technologies for creating a digital space that supports personal and community interests. While digital technology plays a critical role in the process of representation, so too does human participation. The two are codependent in achieving a desired outcome.

The purpose of this chapter is to provide an account of how a social living lab approach was used to support a group of young people realize their goal to create a digital storytelling website in order to share their community's stories. The initial social living lab and its generative activities occurred in Toowoomba (a regional city in southeast Queensland) throughout 2015, as part of the Fostering Digital Participation (FDP) project (see Chapter 1). Toowoomba is an important regional city in Australia with a population of 163,323 as of June 2015 (Australian Bureau of Statistics, 2016). The city serves as an educational and business centre for the rich agricultural and, more recently, mining region of the Darling Downs. It has a small but vibrant arts scene centred around the University of Southern Queensland (USQ), the Toowoomba Regional Council's Empire Theatre and Art Gallery along with a number of

Digital Participation through Social Living Labs. DOI: http://dx.doi.org/10.1016/B978-0-08-102059-3.00013-7

independent community arts groups and initiatives such as The Grid and First Coat. These arts and cultural milieux provide spaces and opportunities for various creative endeavours and social interactions. The four young people who developed the digital storytelling site they named (with punctuation) 'storyelling.' were all emerging artists (refer to Chapter 14 for an interview with two of the creators of the website). How this process unfolded and its outcomes form the basis for what follows in this chapter.

Initially we discuss storyelling as a social living lab and how this particular approach to digital participation in a community ensured that the activity was participant-led with researchers and other professionals providing support, resources and advice at different stages. This is followed by a profile of digital participation within the Toowoomba community with respect to this particular living lab community. We then outline the social living lab experience which culminated in the creation of the storyelling website and provide analysis of the stories produced on the site. In the final section we offer reflections about how the social living lab was a success yet also presented difficulties, challenges and insights that can inform future practice.

STORYELLING: A SOCIAL LIVING LAB

In order to achieve the FDP project's aims and objectives around fostering digital participation of rural and regional Australians through interest-driven activities, the research team adapted the European model of industrial/commercial living labs (see Eriksson, Niitamo, & Kulkki, 2005; European Network of Living Labs, 2014) to better suit a *social* living labs approach (Franz, 2015). This involved collaboration with interested community participants in the cocreation of a 'product' or service (Hronszky & Kovács, 2013, p. 97), in this case, a website. While Ballon and Schuurman (2015) argue that the concept of living lab is gaining more clarity, living lab practices are still underresearched. Franz (2015, p. 54) describes a social living lab as a 'conceptual translation from technologically centred to socially centred living labs [...] based on asking socially centred research questions'. In developing a social living lab approach we found Franz's definition helpful as it aligns with our notion of human-centred participation.

A key research method we used was participatory observation in which the dual roles of the researcher—participant were transparent to the other participants. At varying times, we were involved in discussions, collaborations and cocreation with community participants while also keeping observational notes. Other methods of data collection included informal and semistructured interviews, written and/or recorded reflections and photographs. As outlined in Chapter 1, the project over time developed a more *socially* inclusive and connected living labs methodology. While retaining some key living lab principles with respect to user-centred activities, the focus was on the expressed needs and interests of the residents and provided opportunities for them to engage with these by following a three-step process:

1. Work with residents to define digital literacy needs and interests.
2. Implement a series of social living lab experiences to respond to those needs and interests and provide opportunities.
3. Provide short-term support for emerging social living labs as they become more self-sustaining.

These steps provided the implementation strategy for the Toowoomba social living lab storyelling as discussed in the following sections.

Work With Residents to Define Digital Literacy Needs and Interests

The FDP project conducted an initial data collection in March 2014 in three centres, namely the Empire Theatre in Toowoomba and the public libraries of the nearby towns of Pittsworth and Oakey. During the data collection at the Empire Theatre 28 people were interviewed to determine their current use of technology, any challenges to digital participation they had experienced and their desires for future use. Included in this cohort were 10 young people aged between 15 and 20 years who could be described as frequent and adept digital technologies users. They were largely secondary school and university students involved in a range of creative arts practices such as media, music, ceramics and art installations for the purposes of both study and leisure. They were all actively engaged in digital technologies such as social media, visual design, blogging, gaming, programming and hacking.

While the interviewees generally regarded themselves as accomplished and independent users of digital technologies, they also wished to further develop their digital skills around animation, recording and mixing music, video editing and YouTube. They raised a number of challenges to their digital participation: costs of equipment and/or software, cost and difficulties of Internet access, slow Internet connections and opportunities to learn from people who had the kinds of skills they lacked – professional sound mixing, website development and video production. As a result of this initial feedback, the research team, along with recruited DMFs connected to the Empire Theatre, organized a meeting to gauge interest in a digital participation project for digitally savvy young people. This initial social living lab experience took place at the Empire Theatre in mid-January, 2015.

To address the social dynamics of everyday life, Mulder (2012) recommends that living lab methodologies provide an open attitude and a human-centred mindset to enable user-driven and cocreative innovation. In accordance with this notion and to encourage a sense of ownership in the participants, the Empire Theatre, a community-based space, was the venue for the first meeting of the social living lab, with participants drawn largely from the Empire Theatre's youth program. The nature of this space aligns with Franz's direction to 'go where targeted residents already are and interact' (2015, p. 58) as the recruited members all had been or were currently involved with programs at the Empire Theatre. These so-called 'spaces of encounter' (Franz, 2015) provide familiar settings in which participants can feel confident that their lived experiences and opinions would be valued. However, the research team also wanted to challenge (and support) the group that came together at the Empire Theatre to expand their digital participation beyond mere computer skills by using the affordances offered by National Broadband Network (NBN) connectivity, and taking advantage of the equipment and expertise available through the FDP project.

The 12 participants included young people who took part in the initial data collection phase in 2014, and others who were members of the Empire Theatre's youth programs. Three DMFs led a series of ice-breaker activities with the group as a whole while a member of the research team acted as a visible observer/researcher. The value of the researcher—participant role lies in its ability to give first-hand access to the moment in which participants give meaning and expression to their experiences and ideas, with the researcher in full view recording the observations (McKechnie, 2008). Following this activity, the aims of the FDP project were explained to the young people and they were then divided into three groups with a DMF in each to facilitate discussion.

The aim of the small group discussions was to determine a project involving digital participation that the young people would like to undertake. This included discussion of three topics: current digital participation, barriers to participation and future desires. However, as it was important that ideas came from the participants, the research team adopted an organic process rather than impose an agenda. As each of the groups reported on their discussions to the whole group, we noted how the outcomes were very similar. As one DMF observed: 'Our discussions began to form a common dialogue between all of those present' (C, 14/01/15). Each group indicated that they wanted to tell the untold stories of Toowoomba, the people, characters and events that otherwise go unremarked. As one group expressed it: 'We [. . .] are intrigued by the people who live here and [. . .] where the treasures are hiding'. Ideas for creating and publishing these stories included: a radio segment along the lines of 'What's on in Toowoomba', an app for accessing stories and events, and a virtual gallery showcasing people, their stories and events. Enthusiastic discussion ensued and it was eventually decided that the app idea was the most achievable option.

Plans were made for another meeting in February 2015 to follow up on the enthusiasm evident during the discussion groups. In the meantime, the research team pursued the app option but it was found to be too expensive and too labour intensive to be viable. After looking at a range of alternative ideas, the consensus of opinion between all stakeholders was to create a website using the Wix platform. After a session of brainstorming, the name *storyelling* was suggested for the project. The group readily adopted this name (later including the full stop for emphasis), and they subsequently became the 'storyellers'.

Implement a Series of Social Living Lab Experiences

A series of meetings followed throughout March, April and May 2015 and, in keeping with the digital participation aims of the project, a closed Facebook page was established to serve as a channel for communication between participants, DMFs and the research team. It also served as a record of dialogue and debate. During these early months of the project much discussion, high hopes and planning took place but very little actual progress on the website eventuated. Attendance at meetings became more sporadic as the demands of study and part-time work escalated. At this point the research team identified a core group of four, still-enthusiastic storyellers who were emerging as the project's 'digital champions' – a term that the Queensland Government (2016) employs to describe individuals who will 'demonstrate the benefits' and 'inspire others' to take part in digital technologies.

Due to the stasis of the project at this point, we decided to intervene rather than see the project lose momentum. This intervention entailed inviting the four storyellers to a two-day living lab experience in Brisbane at Queensland University of Technology (QUT) and The Edge, part of the State Library of Queensland (SLQ). The first day was spent in a media room at the QUT Kelvin Grove library workshopping aspects of the website design with the assistance of a marketing expert. On the second day the group met at QUT Gardens Point campus where they were introduced to The Cube (a hub for digital exploration, learning and display) and then attended a session learning how to create their own podcasts using GarageBand. The afternoon was spent at SLQ's innovative space The Edge on future planning around the website and the storyelling project. These varied experiences provided what Herselman, Marais, and Pitse-Boshomane (2010, p. 18) describe as 'novel approaches and strategies' that are designed to foster innovation skills, learning by doing, critical thinking and creativity.

Feedback from the storyellers following the trip to Brisbane was extremely positive. They felt validated by the fact that the research team was prepared to support a trip to Brisbane so that they could experience 'big city' facilities such as those offered by QUT and SLQ in order to further their digital literacy skills and see the website become a reality. Their enthusiasm is reflected in one storyeller's words: 'While this is fun, I can't wait to start writing for the website' (T, 07/05/2015). The experience reinforced the message that the FDP project was serious about the storyelling project and that the research team valued their input as both participants *and* collaborators.

Building on the success of the trip to Brisbane, the research team organized a series of workshops as the next phase of the social living lab to equip the group with additional skills to complement and extend their current digital skills. The project also supplied equipment to assist the storyellers: initially, one digital SLR camera, three pocket digital cameras and two voice recorders. These proved invaluable tools for when they formed the editorial team in the subsequent workshops and preparation of the stories for the storyelling website. Later, a digital production studio was assembled to enable the storyellers to produce their own podcasts, record interviews and edit and record music to accompany their stories (podcasts and photo stories for instance) on the storyelling website. The studio was initially located at the Empire Theatre but later relocated to the Arts Council, Toowoomba, for use by a community organization called Story ARC, involving members of the storyelling team.

Each workshop followed a similar pattern whereby an expert in the field was employed through the project as a DMF to provide particular skills and understandings to the group and to guide practice of the newly acquired skills as well as to critique their initial efforts. For instance, while the storyellers were adept at taking digital photographs and uploading them to various social media platforms, a professional photographer was able to introduce them to techniques such as lighting, colour, perspective and framing, and demonstrate the different effects these might achieve. At another workshop, a local journalist not only gave them pointers on how to prepare and conduct successful interviews, but reminded them of their responsibility to respect both the interviewees and the stories they shared. The group's understanding of the importance of social connection over technical skills was reflected in a comment made by one of the storyellers during an interview with ABC Open (2015): 'We began to understand the privilege we are being gifted in hearing people's stories'. Another workshop, conducted by an ABC Open journalist, built on the earlier session on using GarageBand at QUT and focussed on recording audio stories and publishing them as podcasts.

Throughout this period each of the storyellers began to work on their initial stories for the website. These included a recorded interview, a photostory and a podcast. It was at this point that the core group of four storyellers decided upon the title 'editorial team' and the research team welcomed it as a sign that they were growing in confidence and taking control of the creative output. At the same time, planning was underway for the launch of the storyelling website. This event took place at the Empire Theatre on Friday evening 16 October 2015 with approximately 50 local civic leaders, representatives of a range of community organizations (including some with whom the FDP Project was working on other FDP projects), librarians, family and friends in attendance. The regional newspaper, *The Chronicle,* ABC Open radio and other local media outlets covered the launch. The success of both the launch and the website concept was evident by the enthusiasm of the attendees and the storyellers as well as people who came forward on the night with ideas for future stories. Subsequently, an open access Facebook page, separate from the closed group, was created to draw attention to the storyelling website. It was time to enter the third stage of the social living lab experience.

Provide Short-Term Support for Emerging Social Living Labs

Following the launch of the website the aim was for the storyelling project to become self-sustaining. To that end the FDP project members progressively reduced their involvement and control by handing over the organization of the social living lab to the digital champions. Members of the research team, however, remained available to the storyellers via email and the storyellers' Facebook page. To support the young people during this transitory stage the project also allocated funds to put in place one of the original DMFs to meet regularly with the editorial team of the storyelling project throughout the first half of 2016 to assist with transition to a sustainable model beyond the FDP project's involvement. The research team maintained regular contact with the DMF to ensure that the young people were adequately supported while, at the same time, allowing them opportunities to develop their independence from the FDP project. Despite these processes, during 2016 the storyelling project began to lose momentum and was in danger of becoming inactive. There were a number of reasons for this (see interview in Chapter 14: Storyelling from the Inside). However, in the living lab spirit of innovation and collaboration, the editorial team has recently forged connections with an artist-run collective in Toowoomba called StoryARC, and it is envisaged that the storyelling website will become an arm of this group's artistic and creative endeavours, thus ensuring greater audience reach and sustainability.

THE STORYELLING WEBSITE

The storyelling project serves as a reminder as to how digital phenomena generally, and social living labs specifically, can be enablers of collaboration and participatory practices that can occur within and across different demographics, as well as inside and outside communities. The preceding discussion provided our account of the implementation steps of a particular social living lab. In this section, we consider briefly some of the stories that were created for the storyelling website. In particular, we consider the way the storyellers were able to apply the digital skills, editorial practices, knowledge of design, as well as display a sense of responsibility towards their participants. It was also important for the group to develop what they regarded as their own 'artistry, aesthetics and personal style' (ABC Open, 2015).

CREATING THE STORYTELLING AESTHETIC AND STYLE

The melding of digital technology and personal expression through words, images and design in the storyelling website illustrates how the group was able to bring together their own personal style and their developing knowledge of editing, design and digital skills. While acknowledging that they wanted to do something that would benefit the community, it was also important for them to improve their 'arts practice' (see interview in Chapter 14: Storyelling from the Inside). The storyellers wanted to convey through the website their sense of identity and community. A functional way of achieving this was through a form of 'we-speak' that occurs under the 'Our People' navigational button – 'We tell. We share. We play' (see Fig. 13.1). In announcing who 'we' are, the group included four black and white photographs and short bios of the editorial team as a way of overcoming the anonymity of many community websites. Another navigational tool is an invitation to 'Say Hello' by making email contact, attempts to construct the community symbolically by making the site a resource and a repository of stories, biographical sketches, photos,

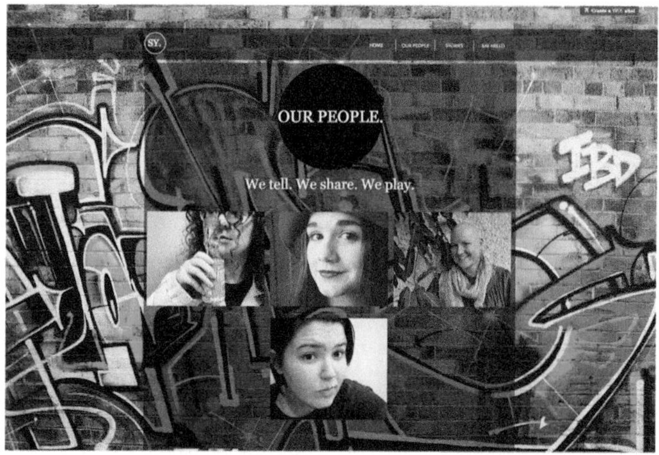

Figure 13.1 Screenshot of 'Our People'.

interviews, that residents of Toowoomba (and beyond) could choose to read, revisit and add to over time.

The storyelling site was created using the Wix online publishing template. However, the visual aesthetics, arrangement and design features were created by the storyellers. The experience of working with Wix was positive and as Rosie comments: 'It's not complicated. It was easy for me ... someone who doesn't know how to create website ... to upload my content to a template' (interview in Chapter 14: Storyelling from the Inside). The group's artistic abilities and growing confidence working with the Wix platform resulted in very upbeat background images and graphics which give the site its own character.

The image that appears on the homepage shows a cityscape of Toowoomba, despite the fact that there are no identifying signs to indicate that it is indeed that city (see Fig. 13.2). The scene is also largely industrial, not residential, and there is no visible human presence. For the (urban) viewer there is a double identity at play that speaks to both identification and distance, as the familiar urban space is also defamiliarized by the almost confrontational rhetoric and aesthetic of the image. These rhetorical and aesthetic elements connote a rather detached community which can be seen as either working ironically against, or confirming the need for, storyelling's stated mission: 'Bringing Toowoomba together...'. The edgy, urban aesthetics of the homepage – its muted, sombre colours,

Figure 13.2 Screenshot of homepage.

Figure 13.3 Screenshot of graffiti laneway backdrop.

vertical lines of the tall buildings that form the background, the texture of the wire mesh fence and the thick vertical bars of the bright yellow fencing in the foreground – suggest that this is not a romantic storytelling site. Rather, it yells, shouts, announces its presence and performative function – STORYELLING!

A similar urban rhetoric and aesthetic is evident in the 'Stories' screen whereby the paradoxical language of the subtitle – 'Yelled Whispers' – refuses a quiet tone, but is contrasted by images that are almost serene in their capturing of the various storytelling subjects. A further juxtaposition of sensory representation is made through the textured backdrop of a differently coloured brick wall adorned with graffiti (Fig. 13.3). The graffiti-decorated walls and laneways are part of Toowoomba's street art scene that was given official approval by the Council in 2013. (A similar graffiti backdrop is used for the 'Our People' screen, as noted earlier.)

RECORDED INTERVIEWS

Of the 12 stories on the site, 3 are written responses to questions asked by one of the storyellers, 1 is a personal narrative, 1 is an essay about a past family member, 2 are photo stories, 3 are recorded video interviews and 2 are sound interviews with images. One interview with Jayden Blaxland who is listed as storyelling's 'resident composer' offers an interesting insight into how a subject ventriloquizes his feelings through music. Jayden explains his preferred mode of communication: 'I can't talk... But I can speak through my music'. Jayden plays the piano to illustrate how he communicates his feelings, how he 'Fights the sad', and when words fail, his language is 'the sounds, notes and harmony' that he plays on his piano. The sound interview is a mixture of the voices of Jayden and the interviewer, and Jayden's piano playing. The piano represents a 'voice' and thereby contributes to the listener's understanding of Jayden's personal story. It also animates and illustrates his words by giving a different interpretation to everyday words (e.g., he plays greetings such as 'hello' and 'goodbye') and for communicating emotions (sounds of anger and joy).

Another composer–musician, Ayden Roberts, quietly explains to interviewers, Sarah and Rose, how he uses his music to tell stories of a personal nature: 'I tell intimate things in a way that I hope they [audience] will connect with'. Harry Paroz (at the time of the interview was a 15-year-old busker) finds that through his music he too is able to connect with people. His interview took place at a specific, named location – Wangsa Walk, Toowoomba. The specifics of this locatedness speak to the intersections of place, people and everyday life in a community. Harry resembles the ideal 'storyeller' as he describes himself as 'very very loud'. He explains how he finds busking 'strange and confronting', especially for someone his age; however, he enjoys how he is able to entertain people, earn some money for his busking and meet 'special characters' such as the group of young musicians who were visiting Toowoomba during one Easter weekend. These three interviews display multimodal properties – visual and auditory – that contribute to their material and aesthetic representation and appreciation.

PHOTOSTORY

A different kind of visual aesthetic from the other stories on the storyelling site is presented in the photostory format. The group's expressed desire to learn more about photography was realized in many of the stories that appear on the website. While some include only a colour photograph of the teller or interviewee, others such as *A day in the life of ... Fred Wilks* rely on the arrangement of colour photographs to tell a story.

This photostory offers images of interior and exterior domestic scenes that show Fred Wilks doing everyday things around his home – filling a bucket with water, tending to a garden, sitting at a table (see Fig. 13.4). We can understand these incidental actions and scenes as stills that capture the moments and 'micromovements' of a life at a particular time and place (Rancière, 2006, p. 2).

One of the storyellers was the photographer, observer, chronicler and editor of this photostory but her presence is rightly invisible. The decision to

Figure 13.4 A screenshot of selected images from 'A Day in the Life of Fred Wilks'.

not include a narrative or captions with the photographs makes for a more open interpretation by the reader. The photos present moments in time but they also invite speculation about the subject's identity through the clues of the visible accoutrements and setting. The arrangement of the images conveys a sensitive treatment of the subject and an artful sense of design.

The storyelling website offers a definition of storytelling as: 'The act in which stories are told, shouted, yelled, smashed, dropped, announced or crafted'. This definition underscores the storyellers' coining of a neologism – 'storyelling' – which issues a challenge for a different kind of storytelling community; one that is prepared to shout, yell, smash, drop, tell and craft their stories. The vocal and physical elements of these words demonstrate the multimodality that characterizes storyelling with its mix of photos, sounds, texts, embedded links to Facebook, websites and videos. These modalities of digital stories contribute to meaning and understanding of place, individuals and community, and underline the specific strategies of representation, design and technical skills that the storyellers developed and refined over the course of the project.

Reflecting on Storyelling

Central to the social living labs methodology is ongoing reflection on how to continue to address the issue, problem or concern that catalysed the establishment of the living lab in the first place. Chapter 14, Storyelling from the Inside, provides an example of this kind of reflection from the perspective of two key participants in the storyelling living lab. In this final section, we provide some additional thoughts about what we have learnt from our experience of storyelling as researchers with an interest in using the methodology in future to promote digital participation in new contexts. Aspects of the living lab worked well, but other aspects were less successful and this has implications for ongoing theorization about social living labs and for the practicalities of implementing them.

NEW REPERTOIRES OF SKILLS, KNOWLEDGE AND PRACTICES

The most successful aspect of storyelling was how it extended the knowledge and skills of the editorial team to enable them to participate socially and culturally in ways that were previously unavailable to them. As noted, from the outset of the project, the storyellers already possessed a range of digital abilities that enabled them to participate in digital culture through their mobile phones and the use of social media, particularly Facebook. The social network platform was utilized by the group from an early stage of the project to share thoughts, organize meetings, circulate images and to stay connected. It was evident from the group's early discussions, though, that their digital literacy repertoires did not extent to knowledge about how to create a digital presence in a cohesive way, for instance, through an app or website.

The series of living lab experiences undertaken by the group successfully built upon each individual's existing knowledge to enable them to make a significant contribution to achieving the goal they set for themselves of building a website to share the stories of the people of Toowoomba, and the website analysis in the previous section indicates the sophisticated representation of these stories. The storyellers did not merely extend their technical skills, they also learnt new ways to participate, including new rhetorical practices in the storytelling process as contributors to the ongoing construction of Toowoomba as a place of meaning in their lives. The launch of the storyelling website was a significant community cultural event for both the storyellers and members of the community who attended and the experience allowed the group to make new social connections and to contribute in a significant way to their community. In these ways, storyelling, as a social living lab, achieved much of what it set out to do. There were aspects of the project, though, that presented challenges and new insights into the process.

NEED FOR INTENSIVE FOCUS AND LOCAL CONNECTIONS

As a research team, we underestimated the extent to which we initially had to intervene to ensure the living lab gained and maintained momentum. As explained earlier, despite a lot of initial input from the academic researchers and DMFs, there was a significant risk that storyelling would not get off the ground. The decision to bring the core editorial team to Brisbane for an intensive training period provided the impetus necessary to reignite the project. We are well aware that most community groups would not be able to resource such an intensive intervention, and we had always hoped to keep the living lab 'local' to explore what was possible at the immediate community level. In hindsight, it was somewhat naïve to assume that if we provided some of the resources usually only available in Brisbane to young people in Toowoomba then this would suffice for a successful social living lab experience. We had hoped that the visit to Brisbane with its 'special attractions' of The Cube and The Edge would provide the motivation for the storyellers to commit to the project. We are hopeful that a major aspect of the success of the trip was simply the time we provided for intensive focus on the project, rather than the novelty of visiting a large city. A key learning for us as researchers is that some social living labs may require an intensive focus or intervention at a key point of implementation.

Another learning for us was the extent to which there was a lack of existing connectedness across the community's public institutions and services in Toowoomba. One of the theories that informed our approach is connected learning, which argues that the local learning ecology is central to fostering digital participation at the community level (see Chapter 8 in this collection by Lankester, Hughes, & Foth). Toowoomba has a range of exemplary services and initiatives that provide opportunities for young people to extend their creative practices through digital participation and we had hoped to leverage these to support the storyelling team. We underestimated how much work and time would be required to optimally draw on these resources for the benefit of storyelling. The academic researchers, locally based research assistants and DMFs worked hard during the development and implementation of the living lab to involve key local stakeholders in the project, without much success. Later, it proved difficult to find a 'home' for storyelling beyond the life of our project, although significant resources and a successful ongoing community project were offered as part of the arrangement. This suggests a need for the academic researchers to be even more connected to the community and its activities than we were. If we had another opportunity to work in a community in a similar way, we would spend even more time than we did identifying, connecting to, and drawing upon the key people and institutions in the local connected learning ecology.

CONCLUSION

As has been regularly articulated throughout this book, *social* living labs are still underresearched and their potential to enhance community digital participation has not yet been fully explored. This chapter has documented one particular experience of fostering digital participation with a cohort of young people who were already quite savvy and frequent users of readily available digital technologies like mobile phones and social media. Despite their level of digital know-how, they were also keen to push the boundaries of their knowledge to further develop their creative endeavours and promote the stories of their regional city. The social living labs methodology proved to be a successful approach to fostering digital participation for this group of young people who learnt new skills, expanded their repertoires of storytelling practice and made new connections with their community. This was achieved, though, with more intervention from the research team than was initially imagined or intended. A key learning for us is that social living lab success is likely to result from intensive and ongoing community engagement, beyond the living lab participants, to understand the kind of support (equipment and advice) necessary to ensure the best chance for success. A genuinely shared community understanding of the need for a social living lab should be a priority for researchers who wish to undertake social living labs work.

REFERENCES

ABC Open. (2015). Retrieved from: <https://open.abc.net.au>.

Australian Bureau of Statistics (ABS). (2016). *Toowoomba: Estimated Residential Population (ERP)*. Retrieved November 3, 2016 <http://profile.id.com.au/toowoomba/population-estimate>.

Ballon, P., & Schuurman, D. (2015). Living labs: Concepts, tools and cases. *Info, 17*(4). Available from http://dx.doi.org/10.1108/info-04-2015-0024.

Eriksson, M., Niitamo, V.P., & Kulkki, S. (2005). *State-of-the-art in utilizing living labs approach to user-centric ICT innovation – A European approach*. Retrieved February 9, 2014 <http://www.vinnova.se/upload/dokument/Verksamhet/TITA/Stateoftheart_LivingLabs_Eriksson2005.pdf>.

European Network of Living Labs (ENoLL). *About us: What is a living lab?* Retrieved February 25, 2014 from <http://www.openlivinglabs.eu/aboutus>.

Franz, Y. (2015). Designing social living labs in urban research. *Info, 17*(4), 53–66. Available from http://dx.doi.org/10.1108/info-01-2015-0008.

Herselman, M., Marais, M., & Pitse-Boshomane, M. (2010). Applying living lab methodology to enhance skills in innovation. In P. Cunningham, & M. Cunningham (Eds.), *eSkills summit 2010 proceedings*. IIMC International Information Management Corporation. Retrieved from <http://researchspace.csir.co.za/dspace/bitstream/10204/4628/1/Herselman3_2010.pdf>.

Hronszky, I., & Kovács, K. (2013). Interactive value production through living labs. *Acta Polytechnica Hungarica: Journal of Applied Sciences, 10*(2), 89–108.

Lambert, J. (2002). *Digital storytelling: Capturing lives, creating community*. Berkeley: Digital Diner Press.

McKechnie, L. E. F. (2008). Participant observation. In L. M. Given (Ed.), *The SAGE encyclopedia of qualitative research methods*. SAGE Publications. Retrieved from <http://www.ebrary.com>.

Mulder, I. (2012). Living labbing the Rotterdam Way: Co-creation as an enabler for urban innovation. *Technology Innovation Management Review, 2*(9), 39–43.

Queensland Government. (2016). *Advance Queensland community digital champions*. Retrieved January 8, 2017 from <http://godigitalqld.dsiti.qld.gov.au/godigitalqldchampions>.

Rancière, J. (2006). *Film fables (talking images)*. London: Berg.

FURTHER READING

Fostering Digital Participation Project (November 23, 2016). *Fostering digital participation [video file]*. Retrieved from <https://www.youtube.com/channel/UC7nP27btCtuznTAWJGTq-yQ>.

Leminen, S., Westerlund, M., & Nystrom, A.-G. (2012). Living labs as open-innovation networks. *Technology Innovation Management Review, 2*(9), 6–11.

Storyelling. (2015). Retrieved from <http://toowoombaconnect.wix.com/storyelling>.

CHAPTER 14

From the Inside: An Interview With the 'Storyelling.' Group*

Roger Osborne[1] and Sarah Peters[2] With Rosie O'Shannessy[3]
[1]Queensland University of Technology, Brisbane, QLD, Australia
[2]Southern Queensland University, Toowoomba, QLD, Australia
[3]The Storyelling Project, Toowoomba, QLD, Australia

INTRODUCTION

The city of Toowoomba is a large regional centre approximately 125 km west of Brisbane. It is the gateway to the rural Darling Downs and, at the same time, it is a destination for young people from the region who attend the University of Southern Queensland or seek a wider range of cultural and employment opportunities. Dr Sarah Peters is a playwright and academic, who completed her PhD in Verbatim Theatre at the University of Southern QLD in 2016. Rose O'Shannessy is a digital storyteller whose practice includes photography and podcasting. Rose is currently expanding her practice into the field of documentary. They are both founding members of the storyelling group which formed in 2015 as part of the Fostering Digital Participation project to help young Toowoomba residents develop skills in digital storytelling. This project culminated in the launch of the storyelling website in October 2015 as detailed in Chapter 13. To provide a record of these activities and to contemplate future opportunities, this interview was conducted at the University of Southern Queensland on 30 September 2016.

* The formatting of the group's title is deliberate. The lack of capital letters and the full stop appealed to the creative aesthetic the group was looking to achieve. They had participated in workshops on marketing and on 'knowing their audience', and felt that this more alternative style would attract the audience they were looking for. The group was also driven by a desire to embrace diversity and disrupt the status quo – so a lot of decisions were informed by a discourse of 'breaking the rules' and going against the norm.

Digital Participation through Social Living Labs. DOI: http://dx.doi.org/10.1016/B978-0-08-102059-3.00014-9

HOW THE STORYELLING GROUP CAME TOGETHER

ROGER *I am interested in the original storyelling group. How did* members *come together? How did you recruit participants to tell their stories?*

SARAH When people from QUT first came to Toowoomba to find out how people from our community were engaging with digital technologies, we were one of the groups that was identified with youth programs that were organized through the Empire Theatre. And so Ari Palani, Cassie Kowitz and I facilitated a workshop. We basically met with this group of youth from all over, around twenty people from diverse backgrounds, but with common interests with something to do with the arts . . . it was an arts community, really. And from there it was just this, 'if you had the opportunity to learn something new, and at the same time create a project, what would that be?' A couple of ideas came out of that, including podcasts and a radio station idea, a "humans of Toowoomba" idea. But the idea that resonated most with the group was a place where people could tell stories in a digital context . . . learning how to tell stories in that context.

ROSIE A little while after we received an invitation to see who was still interested in participating, and 5 or 6 accepted, and we went to Brisbane for an intensive workshop. That was when we really decided what we were going to be. We were going to have a website. We were going to tell the stories of the people of Toowoomba. We didn't really have a name then.

SARAH Yeah, we proceeded from this desire to tell people's stories along with a recognition that there was a whole bunch of people in Toowoomba doing fabulous things, but that they didn't know one another. We had a desire to connect people in our home town.

ROSIE And all of these people are doing fabulous things. Not everyone does things like climb Mt Everest or crazy things. People in our community might not do those things, but they have some amazing views of the world, and stories to tell. We wanted to tell the big stories, but we also wanted to talk about people in Toowoomba. We all have interesting stories to tell.

SARAH That desire was coupled with an interest in improving our arts practice.

ROSIE Yeah, we wanted to benefit personally from the experience, but we also wanted our community to benefit.

DEVELOPING DIGITAL STORYTELLING SKILLS

By providing the opportunity to develop new digital skills, the storyelling project went some way to realising these envisaged personal and community benefits.

SARAH So then this storyelling group came together to spearhead the project. That's when we came down to Brisbane for this intense session learning about the WIX website and how you can go about creating one. The group already had discussions about what storyelling is, its brand, what it was meant do, what they were going to do. And so this weekend that we had down in Brisbane was for upskilling with the website and a way to give some devoted time to the project.

We're all busy people living busy lives. I guess this weekend provided help with achieving the goal of the launch of the website. The weekend helped us to know what we needed to learn, because none of us had any experience with this type of thing before. Some of that was that we really needed to focus on podcasts, how to create podcasts. That was something that we were really interested in doing. We wanted to learn more about podcasts, interviewing and written stories and photo stories, which became the three mediums for storyelling. Michael Dezuanni (from QUT) came to give a tutorial on Garage Band.

CHALLENGES FACED BY THE STORYELLING GROUP

ROGER What were some of the challenges you faced?

ROSIE I know for me and some of the other people, time management and other human things got in the way. Specifically, for me, being able to tell the difference between a series of photos and an actual succinct photo story.

SARAH For the project, a challenge was when we were working towards the launch, we had an idea of a 'production' because of our performance background, and we had regular meetings, and the launch went well, but, after the launch, we lost a reason for meeting and the project kind of fell by the wayside. And so the challenge was learning how to maintain momentum, or considering whether we needed more events or exhibitions to accompany stories uploaded on the website, to provide opportunities for people to meet up in a tangible space and not just connect through the digital format.

Another challenge was connecting people in Toowoomba, many of our stories are very white and there is not a lot of diversity in the stories themselves. We were drawn to the people we know and a challenge was figuring out ways to move beyond our immediate circle of familiarity.

ROSIE For me, connecting was hard because approaching strangers is awful. Not a good time. After we have approached people, usually Toowoomba people are very accommodating, but the initial approach was incredibly hard.

THE EVOLUTION OF THE STORYELLING PROJECT

As a project directed by the needs and desires of participants, the storytelling project evolved.

SARAH I think that the project is morphing into something new now, which is very exciting. This is in direct response to some of these challenges. We had been saying that storyelling was sleeping and it's now evolving and one of the biggest factors in how it is changing is in the network of people who are contributing to it. Storyelling will become just one arm of an artist-run collective in Toowoomba called StoryARC, and that will enable the networks and enable the connections that the project is currently lacking.

In the build up to the launch of the website, one of the workshops was run by Ben Tupas when he was employed by ABC Open. Because of that connection, he has come on board to help take storyelling in its new direction. Brilliantly, he has also seen the project for the potential it has. He has the skillset and knows the people. This links into one of the questions about local knowledge. For a project like this, the passion and interest is there, but it's about connecting with the right people in the community and that there is a community need. While we saw the need, we couldn't place our puzzle piece in the bigger puzzle of Toowoomba. But there is a potential space opening up. For Some artists who want to share their work, but don't have a platform, the storyelling website can be a home for their stories and the work they are doing. This connects us with those artists, expanding the arts network and simultaneously enabling us to learn new skills, such as videography and sound design.

STORYELLING METHODS AND STYLES

ROGER *Storyelling used different genres and styles of storytelling available – interviews, written stories, photo essays, music. Were there any particular styles that worked best? Why? Did you encounter any difficulty?*

ROSIE The first group was enthusiastic about podcasting and audio stories, which was what we needed most help with: How to use the equipment, and simple shortcuts on the computer to make the process more succinct. The set out of written stories, I think that was one thing that didn't click straight away. Everyone was enthusiastic about podcasting. I was enthusiastic about photo stories. But we didn't know enough about styles of writing or how we wanted to present them.

Michael Dezuanni (from QUT) taught us to use Garage Band. This is how we edited our stories. Then Ben Tupas (from ABC Open) came in to show us examples, and showed the more emotive side or the writing side of those things.

SARAH In the lead up to the launch, we realized there were gaps in our knowledge and we organised workshops to fill in those gaps. Kate Stark (journalist) taught us about written stories; Tammy Law (professional photographer) about photo stories; Ben Tupas (ABC Open) about podcasts. The written works were most difficult. As audience members of online content we were aware of what people like us would engage with. We would look at photos, and listen to something fairly short, but we didn't think written works would engage visitors. But in saying that there are written stories on the website. But I don't think anyone has ever read them in their entirety.

BENEFITS OF THE LIVING LAB APPROACH

ROGER *The Fostering Digital Participation Project used a Living Labs approach to encourage community participation and knowledge sharing. What were some practical benefits of this approach for you? What is it about the living lab approach that you found conducive to encouraging community participation in something new (like storyelling)?*

SARAH The most successful Living Lab we had was with photos with Tammy Law (professional photographer) because the day was set aside as a full day to learn how to use the cameras. She taught us something and we applied that knowledge straight away. We walked around Toowoomba with an agenda. We sat around and looked through the images. We discussed their quality and how they could be used. In that sense, she came in to teach a skill, but we were walking around the back streets of Toowoomba, taking photos about our town; upskilling but in relation to our own community.

ROSIE With Tammy Law, she taught us, we did the practice, and then we got feedback. There was less contact in the other living labs.

SARAH Our own working process ended up mirroring the structure of the workshops with Tammy Law. Whenever the group got together and worked on stories for the website, Rosie would bring in something and we would all give critical feedback and make suggestions and do some editing and collaboratively use our own knowledges that we were all bringing together to enhance each individual work. So the workshop days gave us a good idea of a framework to use later on. It showed us the fluid nature of living labs. We change and respond to things in the past; either positive or negative. Reframing them to move forward. At this moment, we are reframing once again as we look forward to the next step. Many times, it took critical reflection as a group to work out what the next steps are. How can we use new skills on current and future projects? We often taught each other. Sometimes we were teachers and other times we were learners.

SARAH In terms of managing a project my confidence has grown. There is a wonderful irony that I feel like I have steered the group, but I often have to ask Rosie how to use the technology. Like 'How do I use this thing on WIX again?'

ROSIE I probably wouldn't be able to facilitate a class on Garage Band, but I can help remind people of how to use it. I'm probably more comfortable as a collaborator with one or two people than teaching a group. But I think this might reflect the nature of the living lab.

SARAH Yes, you did just sit down with me to remind me of the basic functions of Garage Band. If we think back to before we have done anything, we are now much more familiar with the technology and software. Working together like this enabled us to make decisions about what we wanted to do.

DEVELOPING DIGITAL SKILLS

ROGER Tell me about your experience using the Wix templates. Did you find it stifling? Or liberating? Or something else? What was it about Wix that was 'stifling' or 'liberating'? Did you look at other templates?

ROSIE Personally, I wouldn't say it was stifling. At the start, I had very limited knowledge of website creation. I didn't know anything about coding or things like that. If someone were to come to me, I'd tell them to use Wix because once you get the hang of the controls it's very drag and drop and you don't have to worry about coding. It's not complicated. It was easy for me ... someone who doesn't know how to create website ... to upload my content to a template. It's already made for me. You can just edit it a bunch and make it your own new website. I found it a very good experience.

SARAH Same. I remember at the first workshop being very excited about making my own website. There seemed to be enough choice and variety that we felt like we were doing what we wanted to do anyway. That it wasn't prescribed.

ROSIE For our website we started with a template, but our website is now unrecognizable in relation to that template.

SARAH For most of us at the workshop, it was that we didn't even know that it was possible to do this. I had some engagement with another program ... Place Stories ... Cassie and Ari and I had talked about that platform and what it could and couldn't do. In comparison, Wix seemed to be much freer, and had more possibilities for tailoring to a specific vision. These guys spent a long time talking about the aesthetic ... the look, feel, vibe of the whole thing as an overall website.

ROSIE The stories are very specific to the author a lot of the time. We couldn't find a template for each story, but it was important for us to have the overall look of the website seamless.

LESSONS LEARNED

More than just acquiring digital skills, participants in the storyelling living labs learned about organization, communication and sustainability.

SARAH To have enough in common to fit in with the storyelling aesthetic, but individual enough for the artists to express themselves in their work. We were introduced to WIX on the weekend, and came back to Toowoomba. This workshop was in June and the launch was in October. Between June and October we met once a fortnight and had these other workshops, and so it was all growing in between then. We learned more about WIX between that time. We worked on it as a group, coming together to edit and move things around. At the time it seemed like the most liberating thing for me. For people who have no skills in website building I would totally recommend it. But now ... when we realise that people never go to our website ... they go to our Facebook page, and they go to the website through the Facebook page and we named our link Toowoomba connect ... storyelling is only at the end .... as it has evolved it has evolved beyond what a free WIX can offer. And so now, Ben's in the throes of thinking about having a different platform for a website that has a link to the WIX for storyelling and that we can improve access to the website that way ... or in fact, changing the platform.

The one thing that was identified before was our understanding that at a point WIX wouldn't hold any more stories ... that there was a capacity to it. That was something that we knew at the time. I don't think we came up with a solution. That was a limitation we came aware of when we started to upload the podcasts, but not something that we looked elsewhere to try and rectify.

ROSIE From what I've been hearing, storyelling is a good prototype to tell our experience to the rest of the gang that are getting involved.

SARAH I feel like it has been the seed of the idea. Ben and other artists have seen it and the equipment we've been working with, and gone, "the concept is great". In a slightly different shape it's something we'd like to be involved with.

We are a group who is about digital storytelling, but for the launch these guys all wanted to have the tangible printed invitations that we posted to people. There is something about the human engagement that was really important. I think that, ironically, that that is something that was missing from the storyelling project, and that's what it needs to maintain momentum, to be sustainable, and whether that is through ... every six months there is an exhibition where human beings come together to share in an actual physical space the stories that are online. For it to have been such a genuine desire for you guys to have these actual printed invitations to people to come to the event ... the human factor ... I think is something that now I can reflect on and see as something that we need to maintain.

ROGER *In the various activities you participated in over the course of the project, what did you learn about what you didn't know?*

SARAH I didn't know how quickly you can forget a new skill if you don't apply and engage with it regularly, because after that first weekend of learning WIX I thought it was so easy. And then, if you don't engage with it . . . .

ROSIE Practicing your acquired skill is ridiculously important. I had some knowledge of how to do music things on Garage Band, but when it came time to create a story I didn't know what I was doing.

SARAH It's important to try things and fail. That's something I have learned. I have tried to get over this idea of giving something a go that might be a bit crap . . . risking failure.

ROGER *What were the most beneficial aspects of the activities for you personally? (e.g. experience, skill development, people, networks)?*

SARAH I think, for me, the people I've been able to meet because of this project has been one of the best things . . . whether that's people involved in it or the people I've met because you guys have done a story on them. I've met people I've never heard of, and that's really nice. Straddling the position of being involved in the storyelling group and a research assistant of the project, and observing and facilitating sometimes what the group is doing, and kind of straddling that position of being a project manager towards the launch, and then finding a way to step back from that to be a contributor, has been, for me, the most personally rewarding experience of the whole thing. To see an idea go from a concept on a piece of Butcher's paper on the floor of the Empire Theatre to 'hey, we've created a website'. To have seen it through this process and learning the nitty gritty such as writing an agenda for a meeting. It's all something that you know, but I've been reminded of how important this was to have an agenda, to delegate tasks, to network with people at the launch event, to create connections with the people who printed our invitations . . . all of this kind of project management skills has been one of the most rewarding things.

ROSIE For me, all of the above. Most of my arts practice was just me doing self-teaching and stuff like that, and so developing my skills with industry professionals was a great experience, and then by writing stories gathering the experience through all of the things they taught us . . . Creating networks was also good for me, because, technically, I'm not a local of Toowoomba. I don't know very many people here. Getting to meet people like Ben and getting to know Cassie and Ari better . . . If I ever want to do anything like an exhibition, then I know now who to contact, and who can help me organize that.

I was recently approached. Someone had seen our website, and I had applied for a job, and they had seen some of the work I've done. It didn't get me the job, but it got me an interview in the artistic field, which is the dream.

SARAH And to think that it's a platform that we have created to showcase our arts practice. That's pretty fantastic. Artists are often faced with gatekeepers who decide who gets to see their work, whether that be institutions who decide on what shows get to tour, or galleries on what exhibitions get to be shown. We've removed the gatekeeper between us and the general public. Now we just need the general public to know that we exist. That's a cool thing.

KEEPING IT LOCAL

ROGER What do you see are the benefits and challenges of tapping into local knowledge? Has your experience shown you how to make the most of available networks; and how to identify and map local knowledge in the community? Do you need help with strategies to record and share these networks with others?

SARAH It's definitely a challenge we've had in the past. As an example, we had attempted to tap into our local community by advertising storyelling through a local newspaper article around the time of the launch. We had some responses from people who said they had a story to tell. They got in touch, shared their story, but one of the connections that never eventuated was someone from a school who wanted us to talk to her students.

ROSIE She was from a learning college associated with TAFE. We tried to organize a time that suited a majority of our group and her to come a facilitate how to tell stories ... to share this knowledge ... and to see if anyone from her class wanted to tell their story through storyelling, but we could never figure out a time and the communication ended.

SARAH It was one of those things that may have been a great network to connect with. If we had been thinking more strategically we would have tried to find a way to make it work.

ROSIE I think that the majority of us were young people transitioning from high school to university, and living adult lives. Everyone just got too busy with university.

SARAH Everybody was in a position of 'cuspiness' ... transitioning ... Interestingly, Ben and the artists coming into evolve the project are more established artists who have found a space in their work life balance who want to expand their arts practice and act as mentors. At a recent meeting with Ben and others, they all expressed their desire to connect with and mentor younger artists. It would be good to bridge this age gap, enabling mentorships for these younger people who are on the cusp of exploring what they want to do. This would help with the sustainability of the project ... we tried to build in sustainability by saying we'll have an editorial board and freelance contributors. Freelancers could be mentored into an editorial role, but it all happened too quickly. The rate of change and growth when you are young ... 17 ... 18 ... 19 ... too fast for the project to keep up with. Now we are connecting with more people who have a desire to connect with youth who are on the cusp of their arts practice and life after high school.

SARAH About tapping into local knowledge, I think that's the only way to go. If there have been any challenges, it has usually been imposed from outside. But if it is an organic need and an organic desire to tell their story or we genuinely wanted to know about how to make podcasts. Maybe written stories were imposed. But maybe there wasn't a genuine desire there in the first place. It's funny to say what are the benefits of tapping into local knowledge, because to me the *only* way forward is through local knowledge.

The newly evolved group is more diverse than the original group: videographer, dance, multimedia, projections. Ben recently exhibited in the "Unframed exhibition". These are some of the new arts practices that will be a part of the new collective. But the thing that brings it all together is stories and digital media, these are the connecting points.

If you want a project to be genuinely sustainable and to have meaning beyond the project ... what it is to be valued by the community, to meet your greater visions and greater goals, then you have to connect with your community.

One of the things that came out of our most recent conversation was the importance of audience, and so we need to cultivate spaces for audiences to embrace the stories. They become just as important as the stories and the medium ... is the people you share it with. We genuinely believe there is something powerful in storytelling ... that being exposed to diverse stories can build our community ... so I think that in terms of what it gives back ... that is what it gives back. Connection and community.

Of course there are challenges with that because we identify things that we don't know. Some of the people who came in for our living labs are not from Toowoomba. Ben is from Toowoomba, but Kate's based in Brisbane. Tammy's based in Brisbane. We could have identified photographers or journalists from Toowoomba that we could have connected with, but at the time we tended towards this idea that if you come from somewhere else it's kind of cool. It's cool to be from somewhere else.

APPLYING NEW SKILLS TO FUTURE PROJECTS

ROGER *Would you approach new digital storytelling projects differently after this experience?*

ROSIE I really enjoyed the way we started off. I really enjoyed it up until it became just me and Sarah. I still enjoy it, but it has become a lot harder. So if I was to do another thing like this ... I mean there is no real way to guarantee commitment ... If I could be assured that there would be people to help this project ...

SARAH I think if we were to start from scratch, and the thing that the learning that I'm taking into this new evolution would be to be more strategic ... to identify the people I wanted to connect with ... and then connect with them. In Toowoomba we spent an afternoon filling a whiteboard with the names of people we'd like to tell stories about. 'We need to highlight the fabulous things this person is doing and share this story'. We didn't come up with a plan to contact those people. I think in contrast to have a bit of strategy ... ok, well, if I have the opportunity to tell eight stories this year, then I want to push myself to connect with people and schedule that in: in July I'm going to approach this person; and then connect with the art gallery; and then designate ... if I have eight stories ... have some room for flexibility, but a more strategic approach ... let's move from a brainstorm on a whiteboard to scheduling a calendar with specific dates. I suppose there was more focus on the artistry then the organization of the content, and that's a balance I would try to strike more effectively.

ROGER *Following this experience, what would you do differently if you organized your own living lab?*

SARAH I think having the opportunity to learn a skill or concept or something practical and make sure there is time to apply that skill with the equipment the professionals use. As we talked about earlier with Tammy's workshop, that was important. We've kind of been in this position where the equipment hasn't necessarily been in a space that is accessible to us ... or didn't align when we were free to access the equipment. Being in a space that was open not only to us, but open to the broader community who knew they would be assisted, allowing us to mentor them - this would be important for any future living lab ... enabling people with a skill, but with the knowledge that they can return to immerse themselves and upskill ... not a hit-and-run.

In the new phase of development I'm also picking up a new lexicon from Ben, an awareness of how you converge the different interests of stakeholders.

STORYELLING FUTURES

ROGER *Now that Storyelling is live, where to now?*

SARAH It really has gone through stages. Storyelling was one thing up to its launch. Post-launch it became a different thing; and now it's into its third life.

At the time of the Living Labs Symposium in July 2016 we hadn't reconnected with Ben. We didn't have the key to reigniting the project; and probably thought it could exist unchanged. We might see it now as a prototype; seeing the seed of the concept; there are people interested in the seed, but not necessarily the shell that surrounds it.

Something that was learnt was how our audience could interact with us. We set up an email account, but only a few people contacted us. By and large the most feedback we received was comments on the Facebook posts. What is most interesting is which stories get more traction. Which stories are shared more than any of the others. Beautifully Facebook has some functions that tell you what is going on. How many people are engaging with it. Highlighted by the fact; one of Rose's recent stories on a student from Barcaldine has received the most views and the most engagement than any other story that we've put up; again it comes back to the people factor. There are stories on storyelling that we would think are big names that you would think would get more traction, but I love that it is Luke's story. He is surrounded by a community of people . . . And it was a written story.

ROSIE I enjoyed interviewing Luke and writing it, but I didn't expect it to have that impact.

SARAH So now I guess storyelling is really progressing into its new phase, as one supporting arm of the larger StoryARC project. We're applying our knowledge and addressing some of the challenges that caused us to lose momentum in the earlier iteration of the project. It's exciting, because we're connecting with more artists from the community, but also feel like we have something genuine to contribute and share with them as well.

SUMMARY AND CONCLUSION

Social living labs have the potential to foster 'spaces of encounter' where structured or unstructured 'phases of interaction' emerge as real or conceptual spaces for knowledge exchange and cooperative learning experiences (Franz, 2015). The history of the storyelling group demonstrates that social living lab experiences can provide a variety of benefits to the community by fostering digital participation and activating or consolidating local networks of expertise. With some initial guidance and support from project mentors and instructors, the storyelling group took ownership of the project to face and overcome the technical and social challenges posed by sustainable digital storytelling in a large regional centre. They engaged directly with the local community to establish and consolidate relationships that evolved from one-directional exchanges of skills and information to a collaborative exchange of ideas amongst peers. Sarah and Rosie aim to draw on their experience with storyelling to foster similar experiences for others, highlighting the sustainability of social living lab experiences through the identification, support and encouragement of digital champions.

REFERENCE

Franz, Y. (2015). Designing social living labs in urban research. *Digital Policy, Regulation and Governance*, *17*(4), 53–66.

CHAPTER 15

Vancouver Youthspaces: A Political Economy of Digital Learning Communities

Stuart R. Poyntz
Simon Fraser University, Burnaby, BC, Canada

While amateur youth cultural production has a long history in many countries, youth media production really began to find its footing in the 1960s and 1970s, before moving through fits and starts in the 1980s and settling into a global mode of informal cultural production from the 1990s onwards. With the addition of mobile phones, the reach of informal digital learning networks and practices crosses the globe. The result is community youth media initiatives are part of the collection of resources present in cities that aid youth transitions by creating participatory spaces to negotiate citizenship and address digital divides in highly mediated cultures in late modern global capitalist life.

Informal youth media production is typically organized around a range of groups and associations that together form a nonformal learning community linked to larger cultural economies. The youth media learning community operates under a system of provision for socially excluded youth now proffered by states and nongovernment actors. Yet creative youth media spaces have rarely been examined structurally, as sites of social living shaped by policy, funding structures, technology change and related forces (Blum-Ross & Livingstone, 2016). A similar observation is made by Sefton-Green (2012). In a related study, Vadeboncouer (2006) offers a helpful account of the characteristics and practices of informal learning, but her analysis is concerned with the *participatory frameworks* established in different contexts of informal, not-school learning. She is less interested in the structures or sectors that shape learning contexts.

In this chapter, I offer a structural account of a youth media production community as a space of social living in the global city. The site of

Digital Participation through Social Living Labs. DOI: http://dx.doi.org/10.1016/B978-0-08-102059-3.00015-0

my account is Vancouver, Canada, a mid-sized city with a global population and a history of alternative (youth) media production. Youth media groups now impact the culture of cities by territorializing urban spaces in ways that produce cultural friction (Poyntz, 2013, 2017). I develop this analysis here and address the ways policy, funding structures, technology change and labour practices have shaped the political economy of community digital learning in Vancouver. I link this analysis to the rise of neoliberalism and draw on a concept of neoliberal governmentality (Foucault, 1991; Rose, 1993) to situate the work of policy and organizations in Canada's third largest city. Governmentality is an instructive concept for mapping how the conduct of conduct has been produced in Vancouver's youth media community and other national settings (Blum-Ross, 2016; Blum-Ross & Livingstone, 2016). This process has not gone on without negotiation and strenuous objection from groups whose commitments 'exceed the confines of governmental projects' (Ilcan & Basok, 2004, p. 132). But the contemporary era of neoliberal governance has shaped digital learning communities as part of a parallel learning economy that is state supported and increasingly encouraged to operate with entrepreneurial guile to support, train and produce citizen learning for youth in increasingly risky times. Developments in Vancouver exemplify this new global cultural form. Youth media is part of the space of social living and learning for socially excluded youth in the global city, and here I explore the tensions and possibilities that shape this field.

ALTERNATIVE YOUTH MEDIA IN VANCOUVER

Vancouver has a history of media reform movements and alternative media scenes. Located far from historic news and information metropoles (New York, Washington and Toronto), yet long integrated into the Hollywood film industry as a branch plant production centre set just north of Los Angeles, Vancouver has been a site of consumer media production and independent media experimentation and invention since the early days of film (Leys, 2000). In the present moment, commercial television and film production, animation, gaming, software, social media, live action and related industries comprise a creative industries and information sector that is deeply connected to Vancouver's image as a global city linked to international capital, migration, tourist and information markets. Yet since the earliest days, this sector has included other, less hegemonic media communities and forms of semiotic production.

Alternative media organizations and scenes have a long history in Vancouver and are interwoven with the development of public media and arts communities in the city (Douglas, 1991). Since the 1970s, for instance, Vancouver has been home to Co-op Radio, one of the largest listener-sponsored stations in the country. It was the birth place of AdBusters, the international anticonsumerist magazine and group widely linked to the Occupy Movement, and was one of the first cities to see an Independent Media Centre burst on the scene in the 1990s (Hackett & Carroll, 2006). Since the early 2000s, the Media Democracy Day Project has been held every October or November and has fostered similar events across the country (cf. Media Democracy Days Regina 2015; Media Democracy Days Ottawa 2013; Media Co-op, 2012 and Viva la Feminsta 2009, etc.), (Skinner, Hackett, & Poyntz, 2015). In a related vein, a host of independent and social movement-driven media organizations (i.e., Discourse Media, The National Observer, DeSmog Blog, The Global Reporting Centre, The Tyee, Rabble Media, Richochet Media, OpenMedia and Hakai Magazine) have together fostered a Vancouver school of journalism that foregrounds advocacy and 'solutions-oriented' journalism focused on investigating and contesting the status quo (David Beers, personal communication).

Alternative media and arts institutions are tied to the emergence of the youth media community in Vancouver. A political shift in federal policy orientation in Canada in the 1960s and 1970s actually set the stage for the role media and arts groups would play in the development of youth media. Throughout the 1960s, in response to growing social unrest and flourishing resistance movements, among Quebec nationalists, feminists, and those fighting for First Nations sovereignty, a new policy orientation and an array of social policies emerged from the federal government to extend the reach of state administration and create new modes of citizen representation and participation (Druick, 2007). In arts and media policy this led to a shift from a concern for high arts to support for community arts and media and citizen participation programs. The development of community arts funding intended to bring 'arts to the people' (Canada Council for the Arts, 2007, para 5) followed at the country's largest arts funding body, the Canada Council for the Arts (CCA). The first recipient of this funding was the Vancouver-based Intermedia Society, an artists' collective that brought together practitioners from across art disciplines to explore new media and examine the role of artists in sociopolitical life. The collective dissolved in 1972 but not before a series of media-related organizations developed from its ashes, including: Pacific Cinémathèque (now The Cinémathèque), Western Front, Satellite Video Exchange, Video Inn and the Canadian Filmmakers' Distribution West (now Moving Images Distribution). Among these groups, The Cinémathèque (and to a lesser extent, Video Inn) has played a formative role in shaping the youth media community.

So too has the legacy of the National Film Board's (NFB) Challenge for Change (CFC) program, an initiative that arose in conjunction with the turn to community media and arts policy in the 1960s. Canada's NFB has a well-established international reputation for innovation and experimentation with realist media forms. In this tradition, a turn to community oriented media funding in the 1960s led to the introduction of the NFB's celebrated CFC program. CFC was innovative in its time and looks frankly radical from a contemporary perspective. From 1968 to 1980, CFC extended training and the use of portable media (in this case, film cameras) to marginalized groups to enable communities to engage more directly with government and government policy. CFC would eventually oversee the development of more than 80 productions that eventually toured schools and communities across the country. While impressive, CFC demonstrated how social justice pedagogies could be married to new media technologies to promote social activism and change. In the 1990s, not-for-profit groups working with youth in Vancouver would take up this agenda.

As in other places, the 1990s is a kind of watershed for youth media production in Vancouver. Between the 1990s and today, creative media learning in community (and school) settings has grown as technology change and social sharing networks have made available to youth the kind of media production and circulation resources previously only available to professional creators (Poyntz, 2008). In the mid-1990s, The Cinémathèque introduced a series of media education and digital video production programs under the direction of the author. Two other successful Vancouver-area programs, the Gulf Islands Film and Television School and Access to Media Education Society began during this period. All three programs were motivated by broad conceptions of youth empowerment and critical media education, extending the legacies of the NFB's CFC program. Over the next two decades more than 40 digital media learning organizations (e.g., Peace It Together, Check Your Head, Reel 2 Real: International Film Festival for Youth, Reel Youth, Miscellaneous Productions and Out in Schools) would develop in the city, fuelled by technological possibility and the prospect of new modes of youth engagement. The development of this community is the subject of the Youth Digital Media Ecologies (YDME) project, which examined the youth media creation sector in Canada's three largest cities (Toronto, Montreal and Vancouver) over the past two decades (Poyntz, 2013, 2017). Drawing on data from extensive and iterative web scans conducted throughout 2012, a series of follow-up telephone interviews, a 1-day research forum with participating youth media groups in Vancouver, and a series of interviews with key program coordinators and directors, the YDME project explored the history, funding, primary objectives, primary media, target demographics and so on, of participating organizations.

On first blush the outcomes from this research are interesting for the plurality they reveal in Vancouver's digital learning community. There exist many institutional forms (i.e., after-school programs, initiatives connected to art galleries and stand-alone institutions and projects) that address a range of objectives (i.e., media education and film literacy; youth violence prevention; global education and democratization; participatory digital policy; peace activism; health and risk prevention and the promotion of youth voice for urban aboriginal teenagers, recently immigrated youth, and queer youth). A diversity of media, including video, music, photography, radio, web design and blogging, are common in the community and projects extend across genres, from news and documentary to narrative storytelling and experimental filmmaking. Youth media organizations engage approximately 12,000–15,000 youth per year, which represents about one-sixth of the local public high school population. To do this, they draw on organizational networks to share personnel, students, equipment, space and sometimes funding. Project participants tend to be between 13 and 25 years of age and while attendance is typically voluntary, more than 80% of organizations work largely with low-income youth and young people of colour make up the majority of participants in two-thirds of organizations. More than half of all media groups do at least some work with LGBTQ youth and while gender participation is about equal across programs, 1 in 10 groups produce media with young people who lack citizenship or permanent residence status in Canada. The community is best represented as a pyramid in which most groups are small players in a mediatized learning economy of youth provision.

Within this community, different styles of address, minority or ignored behaviours and diverse lifeworlds constitute a space of social living and cultural friction organized around creative youth expression in the city. Through a plurality of form and content often made by and for socially excluded youth, media groups territorialize Vancouver with a rich mix of media, institutions and people, adding to the reservoir of conflicting and competing stories, images and performances on Canada's west coast (Amin, 2008; Arendt, 1958; Silverstone, 2007). Digital learning organizations contribute to the media democracy movement in Vancouver (Poyntz, 2017) and add to cultural difference in the city by involving young people in agonistic encounters with others over matters of public concern, thereby helping to support a culture of belonging and access to the public realm (Banaji & Buckingham, 2015, p. 13; Dahlgren, 2003).

A PRECARIOUS INCUBATOR OF CREATIVE EXPRESSION

Against this backdrop, a sense of vulnerability and precariousness remain structural features of digital media learning in Vancouver. Capturing this dimension of the political economy of the sector is complicated by the fact that the structures of cultural sectors in Canada can be difficult to see. Murray (2005) tells us that conflicting policy paradigms across the cultural field mean that the boundaries of any one cultural sector are rarely clear. They intersect and blur and in general make for an ambiguous object of analysis. Bellavance (2011) notes further that visual and media arts are often addressed as part of various sectors, including education and economic development, meaning the impact of media learning communities can be unclear across jurisdictions. Added to this, the broader context of neoliberalism confounds our work. Neoliberal policy orientations tend to focus attention on the role of innovation and individual entrepreneurial leadership over and above the setting or structural conditions where these practices emerge. This is a function of the narrow lens neoliberalism casts over social life. By prioritizing markets, individual actors and business models of development, neoliberalism obscures the social life of communities, blurring the structural forces and drivers shaping spaces of social living like youth media communities even as non-governmental organizations and struggles within civil society have grown in significance in a neoliberal era (Harvey, 2005).

In response, in what follows, I build on research from the YDME project and work with a concept of neoliberal governmentality to situate the structural conditions undergirding youth media in Canada's third largest city. As is widely known, neoliberalism is associated with a shift and sometimes a contraction in the role of the state in social relations as compared to the era of Keynesian welfare state capitalism that preceded the contemporary period. By privileging private life over public accommodation, everyday life has increasingly been recruited for market activity and regulation for socially sanctioned ends. In the process, neoliberalism has emerged as a system of governance that operates through a governing rationality of 'regulated choices' for individual citizens (Rose, 1993, p. 285). Neoliberal subjects are expected to become self-governing in ways that support and extend the interests of the state. An increasing sense of individuation and self-reliance thus come to be hallmarks of neoliberal governance, and institutions that exist at arms-length from the state, including youth media groups, become key players in the development of 'individuals who do not need to be governed by others, but will govern themselves, master themselves, care for themselves' (Rose, 1993, p. 285). The resulting social imaginary prioritizes the interests of markets and economics over public life, with the consequence that matters of public concern are increasingly come to be subsumed by a governing rationality of individualism, entrepreneurialism and social enterprise (Brown, 2015; Hertz, 2001).

In Vancouver, a neoliberal governing rationality began to take hold following a period of significant economic, social and political upheaval in the 1980s. In the aftermath of a brutal commodity recession in the early 1980s, Vancouver's cultural and economic orientation turned outwards, shifting from a focus on regional resource development and economic services, to a focus on global networks linked to international migration, foreign direct investment in Vancouver's property market, new opportunities for technology and information-led growth, and the development of international global fairs (including Expo '86). In the 1990s, Vancouver's global embrace led to increased migration, the development of new employment clusters, the expansion of centres of higher education and the rezoning of the inner city to support the development of new media industries (Murray & Hutton, 2012). Much of this work took place under the auspices of the City Planning Department (1991), the most important strategic policy initiative in the postwar era in Vancouver. By the 2000s a distinct and pervasive knowledge-intensive orientation came to dominate economic development alongside real estate and 'the growing ascendancy of creative industries and of information-based, contract-intensive industries' (Murray & Hutton, 2012, p. 313). From

2010 onwards, an identifiable cultural economy emerged organized around new sites of media and information production, opportunities for spectacle (including the 2010 Winter Olympics), and new housing options in the downtown core, following a road map of neoliberal development common in cities around the world (i.e., London, Toronto, Brisbane and San Francisco) (Murray & Hutton, 2012, p. 313).

The digital learning community in Vancouver emerged in this context and would be fueled by a broad interest in information and digital literacy training in formal schooling (Goldfarb, 2002; Poyntz, 2008). The call to learn and equip oneself with digital media skills has been linked to the development of information societies and the resourcing of creative industries to develop a globally competitive work force. Alongside these forces, however, new funding structures, an emphasis on social enterprise, new labour practices and audit cultures have combined to shape the growth of digital learning in Vancouver. Drawing on anonymized interviews with youth media program directors and key policy shifts, I address these drivers in turn, link them with the emergence of neoliberal governance, and conclude by speculating on how they impact the role of community media learning in shaping social stratification and opportunity for youth.

STRUCTURAL BURDENS IN THE CULTURAL ECONOMY

The changing cultural economy is the backdrop for the emergence of Vancouver's digital learning community. Amidst these developments, beginning in the 1990s, two federal austerity budgets (1994 and 1995) dramatically altered the funding landscape for nonprofit community groups in Canada. A key feature of both budgets was the downloading of federal funding responsibilities to provincial and local authorities, undoing decades of federal support for culture and the arts and releasing the federal government of responsibility for various program areas. The localization of funding has been a common tactic across jurisdictions where neoliberalism has taken hold, as part of efforts to reduce the size of the state and expand the field of market activity. In Canada, the effects of shifts in federal funding support have been pronounced. Federal per capita funding for culture in British Columbia (BC), for instance, is now among the lowest in the country (Murray & Hutton, 2012). Moreover, because provincial funding for the arts in BC is notoriously modest (as compared with other provinces in the federation) and efforts by municipal authorities to raise funds are limited by Canada's Constitution, the impact of the federal government's restructuring of arts support has been especially acute. In Vancouver, it has left behind a legacy of tighter funding allotments, a more competitive funding environment and fewer instances of stable, long-term support. And this has occurred at a time when the number and service responsibilities of civic, not-for-profit groups, including youth media organizations, have grown.

Project-Based Funding

Since the late 1990s digital media learning groups have operated in a highly competitive funding environment where project-based models have largely replaced long-term core operational funding support. Project-based funding is targeted to new, short-term initiatives that may or may not be part of an organization's primary operations. A director from one youth media group in Vancouver points to this development:

> *I state emphatically that a lot of [funders] that used to fund for core [operations] and support ... ongoing operations now have changed their mandate so that they only fund new projects.*

Another director from a youth media group confirms this and alludes to key implications:

> *Very few [agencies] do core funding. In fact, a lot of applications will specifically say that they don't fund core projects, or don't fund staff time, or some don't fund travel.*

The consequence is that organizations – including those with a long track record of program development – are left to operate in an environment of enforced precarity. Project-based funding regimes typically exclude support for administration, communication and marketing, and core staffing costs, meaning they compromise the development of long-term programming, even when such programing has proven to be successful and meaningful for participants. Moreover, while core-funding tends to afford organizations with a level of flexibility to manage their programs and operations, project funding tends to allot more control to the funder because it is short term and focused on specific results (Gibson, O'Donnell, & Rideout, 2007). Because it is short term, the pressure to produce more and more grant applications is immense, even when this means initiating a program to serve the grant rather than an organization's fundamental aims. Witness for instance, the reflections of another program director:

> *Some people will say [project funding] encourages innovation[.] I ... disagree ... because you're innovating for the grant and not innovating [to address] what you need. I think every organisation has done that ... you see a grant that is close, and think: How can you tweak what you do to fit that?*

In this way, project funding is a crucial feature of neoliberal governance. Financially, organizations are left with less structured forms of support and the conditions of project funding ensure organization programming is ever more dependent on acquiescence to the goals and ambitions of state and philanthropic funding agencies.

In this context, youth media groups have been under increased pressure to diversify their funding base to develop more flexible and entrepreneurial funding models, emulating the practices of business start-ups. In a competitive project funding environment, entrepreneurial astuteness is as important as competency in media education and digital learning. The same director quoted in the first citation above, for instance, went on to observe:

> *It's much more competitive [now]. And I think that's one of the trends I've noticed ... There are more people applying for the same amount of funds, and in some cases, for less grants than were previously available.*

Gibson et al. (2007) emphasize a similar point, noting that this pattern is not unique to Vancouver. 'Because project-funding is not sustained "across the community non-for-profit sector," directors find themselves constantly applying for more funding in a climate of steep competition among organizations' (Gibson et al., 2007, p. 432). The work of applying for more and more funds in turn produces a high stakes competition for support among groups, the effect of which is to encourage organizations to work in silos. We discovered in the YDME project, for instance, that while groups actually share a host of resources, including people, equipment, space and sometimes funding (Poyntz, 2013), they are generally unaware of these connections. When asked why, directors and workers explained that there simply is not enough time to take account of the larger youth media scene in which they operate. This is probably unsurprising but the tension revealed here points to an important contradiction in the community. Creative, collaborative ambitions may drive many digital learning organizations, but the structural conditions under which they operate undercut these ends. The structural burden that results weighs on the future of digital learning in Vancouver and elsewhere.

Specialization as Governance

Of the 40 or so groups in the city, most emerged after 2000, meaning the current funding regime has been the norm throughout much of the community's history. Program directors and administrators are charged with the work of negotiating this regime and not surprisingly, are aware of the pressures they face to align programs with funder priorities and the need to manage these pressures where and when possible. In reflecting on the role of high stakes funding competitions, another youth media director noted:

> *I think the wariness of crafting a program or shaping a program specifically for a funding opportunity is that you don't want to compromise the quality or the content solely for the money. And I think that's always ... the heart of [the matter:] are we offering something relevant? Is it impactful? Is it meaningful? Are teens and youth looking for this? ... We want to make sure that those things are in balance.*

If not quite critical of this context, an interviewee from another youth media organization noted that:

> *I think a creative grant writer can make [anything] work, but it's never fun [and] wouldn't it be great instead to just have the opportunity to have the organisation funded and be able to pursue your mandate freely ... It mainly ends up ... that you ... spend a lot of time explaining to someone else some new thing that looks like something new, that is kind of similar to what you've already been doing anyway. So, you kind of have to play the game ...*

One can appreciate the need to 'play the game' to get on with the project at hand, and yet, the problem with structural constraints is that intention alone is not enough to counter their impact.

One of the significant effects of the system of governance under which digital learning now operates in Vancouver is that the time commitments and conditions of dependency produced by competitive project funding regimes encourage groups to specialize and to avoid unfunded work. This may help to explain the incredible diversity of small media groups in Vancouver and other cities. Specialization supports small, agile, short-term projects. Less time for unfunded work also means less time for training and development, policy advocacy, and activism (Gibson et al., 2007; Kwon, 2013). But this marks a significant change in the way youth media groups pursue their work, particularly if we recall the ambitions that drove the NFB's CFC program. CFC aimed to equip communities with the media resources to contest and respond to government policy, not simply to implement that policy. The aims of the CFC program were not unambiguously progressive (cf. Druick, 2007), yet comparatively speaking, this program aimed to generate community-led policy activism and advocacy and it is often these very objectives that are now discouraged under the structural conditions under which media groups operate. It is in this sense that a neoliberal governance regime regulates conduct by normalizing a less ambitious and critical mode of practice, one that serves the state and the status quo, rather than civil society and citizen learning.

Fundraising and Structural Disadvantage

Since the 2000s, youth media organizations have responded to changing funding environments by developing flexible operations that allow them to access support from a cross-section of sources, including private and community foundations, government programs, private donations and fee-for-service programming. Flexibility and entrepreneurialism are cardinal features of neoliberal adjustment, and for organizations that have the necessary infrastructure and board composition to nurture corporate and private sponsorship, this adjustment can be productive. Over the past decade, for instance, one of the largest arts and media learning associations in the city has mostly moved away from government support and has developed an enviable fundraising program. In commenting on this move, a director notes:

> *It's probably not a bad thing that we have minimal government funding . . . I think sometimes . . . if you're an organisation that's solely dependent on government funding, that you really are in a much riskier position because changes in governments and changes in policies can happen rather quickly, and then you can be in a bit of a precarious situation.*

The director goes on to explain why and to identify how a diverse and flexible funding formula has helped their association:

> *There are organisations that have three funders; if you lose one of them that is a third of your budget gone, what do you do? You close your doors or you have to downsize by a third. For us . . . some years we have [had] 40 funders so if we lose one, depending on who the funder is, it could be one fortieth of our budget, or it could be more like ten percent of our budget, depending on how much they give.*

These sorts of reflections point to the way a small minority of groups have adapted to new funding environments over the past two decades.

Yet, this story does not fully capture the impact of changing funding practices on the digital learning community.

To make sense of the broader impact, recall that most organizations in this community are small- to mid-sized groups. More than half of the organizations working in Vancouver have budgets of less than $100,000 and 84% of groups have annual budgets of less than $250,000. In comparison, the budget of the aforementioned fundraising organization is more than $1 million. Most groups are not in a position to adapt to models that require intensive fundraising strategies, in other words, for a host of reasons. The director of a mid-sized youth media group noted, for instance, that:

> *[W]hen folks are deciding who they're going to donate to, they're tending to go for larger organisations [and] brand recognition, things that they see. A lot of small organisations, we don't spend any money on advertising, we don't spend any money on public awareness, partially because we just couldn't ... So folks don't necessarily know what the smaller organisations are doing.*

Beyond the 'return' organizations can provide to sponsors, successful fundraising programs depend on robust digital networks that leverage technical resources alongside professional skill sets to draw in corporate and private support. Yet, because youth media groups typically draw on project-based funding they lack for the time, resources or technical and professional expertise to develop such fundraising networks. This leads to a paradox: digital learning organizations offer programs in digital literacy and training, yet they struggle mightily to develop the digital resources (i.e., computer infrastructures and databases), staff training and equipment to support and sustain this work.

Added to this challenge, corporate sponsorship is highly selective and is not necessarily available for media education organizations that address critical issues (i,e., peace advocacy, climate change activism, or issues of justice for indigenous youth, recently immigrated or queer youth, etc.). Research in fact indicates that fundraising for marginal populations is hugely challenging. Boucher (2015) notes that when organizations focus fundraising efforts on the rights and needs of marginalized women, for instance, they are much less likely to be successful: '... [When] women's organizations focus their work on marginalized populations and issues [and] experiment with alternative structures ..., they are less likely to successfully attract prestigious private funding' (p. 39). While fundraising campaigns may succeed for a select group of organizations, in other words, it is hardly clear that these practices are transferable across the youth media community. Fundraising and fee-for-service models are in fact likely to undermine the ability of groups to address the needs of the most vulnerable members of society (MacIver, 2010), the consequence of which is that digital learning organizations are compromised in their ability to impact issues of equity and social change.

A Policy Crutch?

In response to these and other challenges impacting youth participation in civic life, Vancouver's Office of Cultural Affairs developed the Olympic Youth Legacy program in 2004 to foster youth engagement by encouraging youth participation in 'the development, design and implementation of arts, sports, recreation and cultural activities' (Masters & Anderson Eng, 2006, p. 3). Initiated as part of Vancouver's pursuit of the 2010 Winter Olympics, the Get Out! Youth Legacy Program Grants (2004–07) were the most important policy intervention to emerge from this context. Get Out! grants were designed in consultation with youth communities to foster civic participation and to resource groups with funding support, especially in their early years of development. Intentionally designed to be 'youth friendly' and to foster civic engagement among inactive youth through creativity and cultural expression, the grants program reflects a tradition of participatory civic cultural policy in Vancouver (Brunet-Jailly, 2008; Murray & Hutton, 2012; Weiler & Mohan, 2009). Cultural policy has been driven by the social policy department in Vancouver's municipal bureaucracy and as a consequence, formative participatory values and a history of civic consultation in arts and culture policy (i.e., 1987 Cultural Plan, 1992 Vancouver Arts Initiative, 2006 Creative City Conversations, 2008 Culture Plan and 2009 Culture Infrastructure Plan) have moderated the impact of neoliberalism in the cultural and economic life of the city. The Get Out! grants might be seen in this light, reflecting a pattern of relatively generous municipal funding for the arts in Vancouver, where the city spends 25% more on recreation and culture than the Canadian average (Murray & Hutton, 2012, p. 315). Yet the Get Out! program was short-lived and largely focused on start-up and project grants that helped to increase the number of youth media projects in the city. Get Out! may have helped to mitigate funding pressures, in other words, yet the policy hardly changed the nature of the youth media field.

In fact in the years following the end of the Get Out! program, other pressure points would emerge, further consolidating the impact of neoliberalism within the youth media community. The lure of global fairs and opportunities for spectacle are a key feature of the way culture is integrated within and shaped by a system of neoliberal governance. In keeping with this pattern, in Vancouver the arrival of the 2010 Winter Olympics coincided with a reorganization of provincial funding for the arts to encourage cultural initiatives and arts and culture '"incubators" to generate economic benefit' (BC Ministry of Finance, 2010, para. 3). This in turn led to the introduction of the 2010 Sports and Arts Legacy Fund, which replaced the British Columbia Art Council's more broad-based program of digital media and arts funding. The Arts Legacy fund prioritized cultural entrepreneurship in funding decisions (Beale & Murray, 2011, p. 15) and the impact of this shift coincided with the suspension of less targeted funding (i.e., the British Columbia Gaming Grants program) and the reorientation of cultural work in BC towards Olympic celebrations, cultural enterprise and training in the service of economic growth. The impact of this shift for digital learning groups was exacerbated by previous cuts to provincial funding that arose in the aftermath of the global financial crisis of 2008–09 (Beale & Murray, 2011). Together, these developments forced youth media groups to juggle programming in such a way as to adapt to a system whose that prioritized focused on institutional self-sufficiency and cultural entrepreneurship.

Social Enterprise and Unpaid Labour

To encourage the move towards funding and operational self-sufficiency, a broad emphasis on social enterprise models of support emerged in late 2010 and 2011 in conjunction with an increasing focus on the role of volunteers and unpaid labour in nonprofits. Again, this turn reflects a broader impulse within neoliberalism to privilege market-based models of management and self-governance alongside an interest in the use of low cost, precarious labour.

In Vancouver, support for social enterprise models of organization aligned with efforts to encourage entrepreneurial conduct within not-for-profit communities. To further this agenda, the City of Vancouver developed the Vantage Point Workshops initiative in 2010 (the program remains in place) to encourage organizations to become self-sustaining, 'abundant' not-for-profits through an emphasis on board development, performance management and recruitment of volunteer labour. The book, *The Abundant Not-for Profit*, from which the program drew inspiration, captures the enthusiasm driving the Vantage Point Workshops:

> *The abundant not-for-profit finds ways to focus on what is available: talented people. The abundant not-for-profit examines all the resources around the organization, and attracts people with skills and talent. This is a different strategy to effectively deliver your mission: you can engage people with professional skills. You can pay these people differently. You do not have to pay them money.*
>
> **Gerty and Kelly (2013, p. 30)**

The BC provincial government accelerated this trend in 2011 with the BC Partnerships for Social Impact program, which encouraged nonprofits to develop an entrepreneurial focus in new initiatives. The gist of each of these policy actions was to invest in programs that support self-reliance through fee-for-service programming to encourage nonprofits to move away from paid labour and publicly funded support. More than that, these initiatives urged organizations to focus on the development of entrepreneurial cultures and the promotion of program directors, staff and participants as autonomous, creative, job-ready subjects. For one program director the result is that youth media organizations are now hamstrung by their need to multitask:

> *We are basically masters of multitasking, where our social media coordinator, for example, she's not just our social media coordinator, she's also our board operator, she's also our graphic designer, she also knows how to do marketing and news ...*

Gollmitzer and Murray (2008) confirm that a pattern of precarious and overburdened labour is common across the cultural sector and a report by the Vancouver Foundation (2011) indicates that this reliance has only grown among the majority of youth organizations in the city. For our purposes, it is key to note that this leads to instability in youth organizations (something to be addressed more explicitly in conclusion), even as they have tried to adapt to an emerging system of neoliberal governance.

Audit Culture and Normalized Conduct

The challenge of adapting to changing expectations, policies and funding resources in the digital learning community has been further aggravated throughout the 2000s by an imposing audit culture that has brought to bear a broad focus on accountability and measurable outcomes among youth media organizations. The challenge here is that teaching creative media expression with young people does not easily lend itself to rationalization and the quantification of outcomes. Gidley and Slater (2007) explain why:

> *Participatory media must be seen as a process ... This process can be uneven – like participants' own lives, it does not follow a set, linear pathway – but it almost always requires duration, a long-term investment. Similarly, an emphasis solely on measurable outcomes, whether in terms of hard skills or employability, would miss the point of the impact of the work on people's lives, including the development of their personal and creative skills, their civic engagement, and the stories they can tell through media (p. 42).*

Audit cultures tend to force media groups to become accountable to the funding regime rather than to the community of people they serve. Not surprisingly, while organizations have attempted to appease this system, as one program director indicates, they have also tried to negotiate less restrictive forms of accounting and reporting:

> *When you're talking about changing a person, it's very difficult to have hard outcomes. In terms of how many attend the festival, how many people go to workshops, all of that kind of thing. We have been trying to do a lot from the testimonials from the youth and their parents.*

Such efforts are part of the negotiation youth media groups have learned to engage in the current context. And yet the effects of an audit culture endure through the conduct they normalize in the community. More intensive systems of management and outcome-based reporting encourage organizations to self-monitor and limit the kind of work they do. Governance practices shape the conduct of conduct in organizations and threaten to compromise how digital learning groups produce cultural friction in the global city. Youth media organizations are now charged with the work of addressing a host of risk conditions in youth lives – related to health, job training, sexuality, identity and so on – and are leaders in using art and culture to nurture identities, creativity, and social and aesthetic skills and literacies. Yet, the introduction of new mechanisms of management and financial oversight throughout the course of the 2000s has produced a structural burden that threatens to undo the plurality and culture of belonging the youth media community brings to the city.

CONCLUSION

In 2017 there are in fact signs that the structural burdens shaping the digital learning community in Vancouver have begun to take their toll. The community remains an incubator of creative expression and social belonging with a substantial number of projects that engage a large and diverse range of youth. Yet, precariousness and vulnerability seem ever present. Since 2015, three key organizations – PeaceitTogether, the Summer Visions Film Institute and the Purple Thistle Society – have ceased to operate. While the community continues to produce a remarkable range of media, more than ever informal digital learning in Vancouver resembles a sharply drawn pyramid, with a few large and relatively healthy organizations at the top and a host of smaller, shorter term organizations making up the base. Youth media groups continue to bring young people into the city at a time when gentrification and land values are pushing low-income youth further afield to underresourced and underserved suburbs in the surrounding regions. Yet, the architecture of governance shaping the youth arts learning community appears to make it more difficult than ever for groups to secure the resources to support youth transitions in a time when the risk conditions encountered by young people are intensifying.

A space of social living must account for and respond to the cultural, social, economic and citizen needs of a community. It is a space of rich and productive friction, where belonging and exchange with the signs and symbols of others enables plurality and a mix of stories, images and performances to flourish. In the global city, the work of digital learning groups and projects are vital to nurture public space. They are part of the infrastructure of democratic living that support and foster youth transitions in inequitable times. As a site of social living shaped by policy, funding structures, technology change and related forces, informal digital learning communities are bending under the pressures and strains of neoliberalism. Even as these communities have emerged as part of a global mode of informal cultural production over the past two decades, in other words, what matters now is how such youthful media spaces will persist as core components of the civic conditions that shape the future of urban space and democratic cultures.

ACKNOWLEDGEMENTS

I wish to thank Sophie Daviau Dempsey for her contributions to this work. She has explored related themes in her unpublished MA Thesis, *Reflecting on Vancouver's current youth media funding trends in the context of neoliberalism* [2016]. Vancouver: Simon Fraser University.

REFERENCES

Amin, A. (2008). Collective culture and urban public space. *City, 12*(1), 5–24.

Arendt, H. (1958). *The human condition* (2nd ed.).). Chicago: University of Chicago Press.

Banaji, S., & Buckingham, D. (2015). *The civic web: Young people, the internet, and civic participation*. Cambridge: MIT Press.

Beale, A., & Murray, C. (2011). British Columbia's place-based approach: Policy devolution and cultural self-determination (1952-2008). In M. Gattinger, & D. Saint Pierre (Eds.), *Les politiques culturelles provinciales et territoriale de Canada. Origines, évolutions et misses en oeuvre* (pp. 449–498). Quebec: Presses de l'Université Laval.

Beers, D. Personal Communication. March 8, 2017.

Bellavance, G. (2011). *The visual arts in Canada: A synthesis and critical analysis of recent research*. Montreal: Institute National de la Recherche Scientifique, Centre-Urbanisation Culture Société.

Blum-Ross, A. (2016). Voice, empowerment and youth-produced films about "gangs". *Learning, Media and Technology, 42*(1), 54–73.

Blum-Ross, A., & Livingstone, S. M. (2016). From youth voice to youth entrepreneurs: The individualization of digital media and learning. *Journal of Digital and Media Literacy, 4*(1–2).

Boucher, M. (2015). *Negotiating a neoliberal funding regime: Feminist service organizations and state funding (unpublished Ph.D. dissertation)*. Toronto: York University.

British Columbia Ministry of Finance (2010). *Backgrounder: A new emphasis on sports and the arts*. Victoria: Government of British Columbia.

Brown, W. (2015). *Undoing the demos: Neoliberalism's stealth revolution*. Cambridge: Zone Books. Retrieved from <http://site.ebrary.com/lib/alltitles/docDetail.action?docID=11031965>.

Brunet-Jailly, E. (2008). Vancouver: The sustainable city. *Journal of Urban Affairs, 30*(4), 375–388.

Canada Council for the Arts (CCA). (2007). *The evolution of the Canada Council's support for the arts*. Retrieved from <http://canadacouncil.ca/council/about-the-council/the-evolution>.

City Planning Department. (1991). Central area plan: Goals and land use policy. Vancouver: City of Vancouver Planning Department.

Dahlgren, P. (2003). Reconfiguring civic culture in the new media milieu. In J. Corner, & D. Pels (Eds.), *Media and political style: Essays on representation and civic culture* (pp. 151–170). London: Sage Publishing.

Douglas, S. (1991). Introduction. In S. Douglas (Ed.), *Vancouver anthology: The institutional politics of art* (pp. 11–22). Vancouver: Talonbooks.

Druick, Z. (2007). *Projecting Canada: Government policy and documentary film at the National Film Board*. Montreal and Kingston: McGill-Queen's University Press.

Foucault, M. (1991). Governmentality. In G. Burchell, C. Gordon, & P. Miller (Eds.), *The Foucault effect* (pp. 87–104). Chicago: University of Chicago Press.

Gerty, L., & Kelly, C. (2013). *The abundant not-for-profit: How talent (not money) will transform your organization*. Vancouver: Vantage Point Press.

Gibson, K., O'Donnell, S., & Rideout, V. (2007). The project-funding regime: Complications for community organizations and their staff. *Canadian Public Administration, 50*(3), 411–436.

Gidley, B., & Slater, I. (2007). *Beyond the numbers game.* London: Goldsmiths, University of London.

Goldfarb, B. (2002). *Visual pedagogy: Media cultures in and beyond the classroom.* Durham: Duke University Press.

Gollmitzer, M., & Murray, C. (March 2008). *From economy to ecology: A policy framework for creative labour.* Presented at The Centre for Expertise on Culture and Communities and the Canadian Conference of the Arts, Ottawa, ON. Retrieved from <http://ccarts.ca/wp-content/uploads/2009/01/CREATIVEECONOMYentiredocument.pdf>.

Hackett, R. A., & Carroll, W. K. (2006). *Remaking media: The struggle to democratize public communication.* New York: Routledge.

Harvey, D. (2005). *A brief history of neoliberalism.* Oxford: Oxford University Press.

Hertz, N. (2001). *The silent takeover.* London: Heinemann.

Ilcan, S., & Basok, T. (2004). Community government: Voluntary agencies, social justice, and the responsibilization of citizens. *Citizenship Studies, 8*(2), 129–144.

Kwon, S. A. (2013). *Uncivil youth: Race, activism, and affirmative governmentality.* Durham; London: Duke University Press.

Leys, C. (2000). Fugitive events: A history of filmmaking in British Columbia, 1899–1970. In J. MacGregor (Ed.), *Cineworks Independent Filmmakers Society 1980–2000* (pp. 86–120). Vancouver: Cineworks Independent Filmmakers Society.

MacIver, M. (2010). *Through a neoliberal lens: How a Canadian community media program for at-risk youth operates today (unpublished Masters thesis).* Vancouver: Simon Fraser University.

Masters, C., & Anderson Eng, D. (2006). *Get out! Youth Legacy Program – Evaluation and next steps. [Administrative Report]* (pp. 1–68). Vancouver: City of Vancouver.

Murray, C. (2005). *Cultural participation: A fuzzy cultural policy paradigm. Accounting for culture: Thinking through cultural citizenship* (pp. 32–54). Ottawa: University of Ottawa Press.

Murray, C., & Hutton, T. (2012). Vancouver: The enigmatic emerging cultural metropolis. In H. Anheier, & Y. R. Isar (Eds.), *Cities, cultural policy and governance* (pp. 310–321). London: SAGE Publications.

Poyntz, S. R. (2008). *Producing publics: An ethnographic study of democratic practice and youth media production and mentorship (unpublished dissertation).* Vancouver, BC: University of British Columbia.

Poyntz, S. R. (2013). Public space and media education in the city. In P. Fraser, & J. Wardle (Eds.), *Current perspectives in media education: Beyond the manifesto* (pp. 91–109). London: Palgrave Macmillan.

Poyntz, S. R. (2017). Remediating democracy: Participatory youth media scenes, cultural friction and media reform. In B. De Abreu, P. Mihailidis, A. Lee, J. Melki, & J. McDougall (Eds.), *International handbook of media literacy.* New York: Routledge.

Rose, N. (1993). Government, authority and expertise in advanced liberalism. *Economy and Society, 22*(3), 283–299.

Sefton-Green, J. (2012). *Learning at not-school: A review of study, theory, and advocacy for education in non-formal settings.* Cambridge: MIT Press.

Silverstone, R. (2007). *Media and morality: On the rise of the mediapolis.* Cambridge: Polity Press.

Skinner, D., Hackett, R., & Poyntz, S. R. (2015). Media activism and the academy, three cases: Media democracy day, openmedia, and newswatch Canada. *Studies in Social Justice, 29*(3), 285–297.

Vadeboncouer, J. (2006). Engaging young people: Learning in informal contexts. In J. Green, & A. Luke (Eds.), *Rethinking learning: What counts as learning and what learning counts* (pp. 239–278). Washington: AERA.

Vancouver Foundation (2011). *Vital signs*. Vancouver: Vancouver Foundation. Retrieved from <www.vancouverfoundationvitalsigns.ca>.

Weiler, J., & Mohan, A. (2009). *Catalyst, collaborator, connector: The social innovation model of 2010 Legacies Now-Case study commissioned for the International Olympic Committee*. Vancouver: 2010 Legacies Now Corporation. Retrieved from <www.2010legaciesnow.come/media-centre-downloads/?tx_2010media>.

FURTHER READING

Browne, C. (2000). Fugitive events. In J. MacGregor (Ed.), *Cineworks 2000: Twenty years of independent filmmaking in British Columbia* (pp. 85–120). Vancouver: Cineworks Independent Filmmakers Society 1980–2000.

CHAPTER 16

Policy Experiments and the Digital Divide: Understanding the Context of Internet Adoption in Remote Aboriginal Communities

Ellie Rennie
RMIT University, Melbourne, VIC, Australia

As anthropologist Faye Ginsburg (2008) has observed, when it comes to the digital divide, remote-residing Aboriginal people are often depicted as existing in a different time, not just place, as though caught in a perpetual past. Reports on the digital divide have tended to reinforce the view that Aboriginal people have been left behind on the digital timeline, even when pointing out that rates of adoption are increasing faster than for other segments of the population (for instance, Australian Communications & Media Authority, 2006, p. 35; Daly, 2005). Statisticians have also overlooked the fact that significantly uneven patterns of access are observable across different remote communities it was intended to inform policy development by enabling statistics to be easily grouped into categories that share common characteristics.), including communities in the same region and those with similar socioeconomic profiles (Ewing, Rennie, & Thomas, 2014).

This chapter discusses a project that set out to understand the factors that were leading to extreme digital exclusion in smaller remote Aboriginal communities. The project involved a 4-year collaboration between three communities in the central Australia region, two Indigenous organizations, Australia's peak body for consumer representation in communications, and university-based researchers. The majority of households in each community chose to participate (20 of 30

Digital Participation through Social Living Labs. DOI: http://dx.doi.org/10.1016/B978-0-08-102059-3.00016-2

total dwellings), receiving computers and Internet connections, as well as support in the form of hardware maintenance and basic training (see Rennie et al., 2016).

The project was not trialling a new technology, but rather a regime of access – home Internet – and the underlying policy assumptions associated with it. When the project commenced in 2010, household Internet was the norm for other Australians and the goal of national communications policy, but was assumed to be unviable or unsuitable for very remote communities. Home Internet adoption rates remained the lowest in the country, despite consumer subsidies for satellite infrastructure and subscriptions, intended to keep the costs of Internet comparable to ADSL connections in the city. When we commenced, only one house in the three communities had an Internet connection (That connection happened to be in the only house within reach of mobile reception, and had been achieved by mounting a prepaid mobile broadband dongle on a pole on the roof of a house.). Over the course of the project, participating households received commonly available equipment, enabling them to access satellite Internet services for free for 2 years.

By the end of the project, we had gained a detailed understanding of the ways in which policies, programs and providers were neglecting the needs of remote community households, particularly in areas where satellite Internet was the only available option. We found that home Internet was viable, and home connections were desired by a significant number of households, but many struggled to acquire and maintain services through standard arrangements. Rather than assuming that Aboriginal households had no need or capacity for Internet services, our research found that if the services were more appropriately structured (particularly payment systems), home Internet adoption would likely increase.

This chapter focuses specifically on the trial approach and how it enabled us to understand the cultural, social and economic context of remote communities as it relates to Internet services. Issues such as culturally specific rules of ownership, household and individual mobility, and the relationship of Internet and computing hardware to other infrastructures were revealed through our engagements with the residents. From this knowledge base we were able to better interpret patterns of Internet access and use, and to suggest alternative policies and programs. The final section of the chapter discusses some of the traps of establishing valid evidence for the purposes of policymaking and programs, and particular considerations when undertaking research with Indigenous communities.

THE DIGITAL DIVIDE IN REMOTE AUSTRALIA: POLICIES AND ASSUMPTIONS

The digital divide matters because residents living in remote communities face significant obstacles undertaking everyday activities such as banking and shopping, and can face high costs for transactions (for instance, Altman, Dillon, & Jordan, 2009). As technological change brings with it new services and applications – including government services – it is likely that those not connected now will face further disadvantages as the benefits for others increase. While it is possible that people may choose not to take up online opportunities even when they are available, in communications policy terms, the issue of equal access remains a valid concern regardless (see Rennie et al., 2016 for further discussion).

The Australian government has implemented various measures to ensure that those living in remote areas are not overly disadvantaged in terms of affordability when it comes to Internet services. From 2007 to 2011, the Australian Broadband Guarantee (ABG) provided subsidized satellite Internet services to households and businesses where no other means of accessing the Internet were available. Australia's National Broadband Network (NBN), which superseded the ABG, was initiated to provide fast broadband services to all Australians, with the vast majority accessing fibre-to-the-node services. Satellite Internet was incorporated into the NBN to serve the 3% of the population in very remote areas. The model of a national wholesale infrastructure provider was also intended to benefit those in less densely populated areas by providing a wholesale price base that would be consistent as far as possible across the country, rather than being strictly costed at the local level. Pricing was designed to ensure that entry-level prices remain at pre-NBN levels for low-income consumers (Ewing et al., 2014).

While mainstream policies, including the NBN, assume that households will acquire Internet services of their own accord, the Australian government has also introduced a range of programs to address the digital divide in areas where that has not occurred, including remote Aboriginal and Torres Strait Islander communities. These programs have typically been in the form of Internet facilities and informal group training, and more recently, public Wi-Fi (Featherstone, 2013). Census data from 2011 shows that in central Australia, home Internet was around 4% in areas where satellite Internet was the only option. Where mobile Internet was available, Internet adoption was significantly higher at around 30% (Australian Bureau of Statistics, 2011). The 2015 National Aboriginal

Torres Strait Islander Survey, which provides a representative sample of Aboriginal households in remote Australia, revealed that 5 out of 10 of Aboriginal households in remote and very remote Australia had an Internet connection at the time of the survey (Australian Bureau of Statistics, 2015), which is still significantly lower when compared to almost 9 out of 10 Australians nationwide.

While the provision of shared Internet facilities would seem to make sense in this scenario, when we commenced our research only communities with a population of over 300 people were eligible to apply for funding for shared facilities (telecentres). Those living in smaller communities (80% of remote Indigenous communities have a population under 100 people) would need to commute to access the Internet. In 2009 we conducted a survey of 34 remote communities in the central Australia region (accounting for two-thirds of the Aboriginal population of the region outside of Alice Springs), and found that of these less than half had community Internet access (see Rennie, Crouch, Thomas, & Taylor, 2010). The computers were located in council offices, training centres, welfare services offices, remote Indigenous media organizations and schools. Many facilities were only semiactive, operating with part-time or no supervision, or waiting on maintenance and upgrades. So while home Internet was not viewed as viable, community centres clearly faced limitations. Moreover, we had no evidence that those living in small communities were travelling to larger communities to access the Internet. Understanding the barriers to home Internet was therefore important.

Our review of policy literature related to these programs revealed a range of assumptions and ideas. One was that the communal lifestyle of remote communities meant that shared facilities were considered more culturally appropriate (Telecommunications Action Plan for Remote Indigenous Communities, 2002). Another was that remote community homes were inadequate for housing computer equipment, and that environmental conditions, such as heat, dust and vermin, would result in the untimely destruction of equipment. Between 2007 and 2011 (under the Northern Territory Emergency Response legislation) laws intended to stem the flow of pornography into remote communities required that any publicly funded computers be supervised and audited, reflecting the Commonwealth Government's protectionist stance towards communities at the time. In addition, during our encounters with remote community workers (teachers, government service workers and others), some expressed the opinion that our trial would not last long, suggesting that the equipment would be stolen, or taken out of the homes and not returned, either due to demand sharing practices (see 'Findings From the Home Internet Trial' section) or theft. We observed a generally low priority given to Internet access in remote communities by non-Indigenous government workers, possibly stemming from a view that Internet is only viable or important when other needs have been met. As Mazzarella writes, the 'insistence that computers come later' (2010, p. 797) perpetuates the assumption that technology should be evaluated in terms of a hierarchy of needs that can be known in advance. From this perspective, digital exclusion is assumed a subset of other social exclusions.

In sum, reasoning behind these mostly well-meaning programs and policies was that home Internet was either not suitable for Aboriginal communities, not practical or not desired. We decided to treat this as a falsifiable proposition by undertaking a trial of home Internet in three small communities. The trial approach was made possible through the work of an Indigenous-owned research and training organization, the Centre for Appropriate Technology (CAT) and the Central Land Council (CLC, the representative body for traditional owners in the region). As discussed below, these organizations work with communities to understand how services and infrastructures can be better delivered. The Australian Communications Consumer Action Network initially funded us to conduct a baseline study in the three communities, and remained involved in the project throughout the trial.

From the start, we accepted the possibility that the model of Internet provision we were testing might fail. If home Internet succeeded, then it would suggest there was scope for alternative policy approaches. If the equipment did not withstand the conditions, or if people chose not to use the computers or Internet, we would at least have a better understanding of the factors influencing Internet adoption and use.

THE HOME INTERNET PROJECT TRIAL

Our research in the three outstations incorporated input from end-users, within their social environments, in order to understand how commonly available systems and hardware would be used in remote community households. We used a quasiexperimental approach in that we created the intervention, including providing infrastructure, training and maintenance, but sought to understand context, not just the outcomes of the intervention itself.

CAT was formed in the 1980s when Aboriginal people began moving back to their traditional lands, and much of their work remains focused on the sustainability of small communities. In CAT's definition, appropriate technologies meet the economic, cultural, environmental and social needs of the people, and design and development occurs through consultation and collaboration with communities (Mayne, 2014). The CLC's interest in communication technologies spans unequal access to services for remote residents, as well as communication affordability issues, rights to services and increasing the choice of communication options for remote communities. In the CLC's view, access to communication technologies is compatible with the determination of traditional owners to remain living on or near their country. Both organizations were therefore motivated by an interest in the overall wellbeing of those living in small communities.

The research consisted of three phases. In the first phase, CLC and CAT made initial contact with a number of communities and consulted with community members, at which time the elders in the three outstations gave permission for the project to proceed (including through formal ethics procedures). During our early meetings with the residents, we carefully documented their prior use of ICTs, and tried to ascertain what they perceived to be the barriers to ICT uptake, and the opportunities available through having computers and Internet access.

CAT provided a total of 20 computers and associated satellite services connecting all computers to the Internet in Kwale Kwale (4), Mungalawurru (5) and Imangara (11). Across the three outstations, approximately 50 individuals took part in the project, although not all participated for the duration. Structured interviews with residents were carried out 3–4 times a year. Interviews were conducted either one-on-one or in groups were intended to capture changes over time. Topics included who was living in the house, who used the computer, what they used it for and how usage of the computer was managed. We also discussed events that affected the use of the computers, such as people moving in and out of the community, or the ways in which death rites impacted on use. Much of our time during our research visits was spent visiting houses, checking up on the computers and responding to requests for on-the-spot training in ICT skills and applications. These ad hoc house visits were as informative for us as they were for the residents, giving us a snapshot of how different individuals were learning how to use the equipment, how they maintained the computer and what these factors might say about the relative value of ICTs in the outstations. Residents provided input on the location and relocation of computers, and suggested that lockable boxes be built for the computers for security purposes. Our documentation of these and other requests formed part of the research findings, accrued through short visits of a day or two in each community.

Aside from the research fieldtrips, CAT researchers also carried out regular ICT training and maintenance support in the communities for 2 years from the commissioning of the facilities, resulting in 1458 event records (see Crouch, 2014). Midway into the project, we extracted usage data from a small number of computers (with the owners' permission) to confirm that the computers were in fact being used in the ways described by the residents. We also carried out research in two larger communities, one with a successful shared Internet facility (Papunya), and the other with mobile coverage (Ali Curung) in order to compare home satellite Internet with other infrastructures.

In the third phase, from the end of 2013, we assisted the residents in setting up Internet services (where desired), and documented the transition to household-controlled accounts. Participants were given the choice to either maintain Internet access by paying for their own plans under the NBN Interim Satellite Solution, or share services and costs with others in the community. We continued to visit the communities in 2014 in order to understand how the households were faring with their own Internet services. That final stage of the research was revealing, providing important insights into how the government's solution to providing Internet to remote areas was failing this particular group.

FINDINGS FROM THE HOME INTERNET TRIAL

Despite some equipment failure, loss and damage, 17 of the 20 computers installed by early August 2011 were still operational by the end of the first year. By the end of the project, only two computers had been lost or taken out of the community.

Although non-Indigenous people often associate a 'caring and sharing' ethic with Aboriginal culture, and therefore assume that shared or communal Internet facilities are most appropriate, we found that individuals wanted to identify as the owners of the computers. At the start of the project, the few individuals who possessed laptops told us that they would hide them from others to keep them safe. After the computers arrived, people attempted to use padlocks and passwords to regulate others' access to the household computers, often without success. Virtually all households experienced visitors to their community using their computer, in some instances by cutting off the padlocks on the computer covers. During interviews, people spoke of taking steps to limit access to their computer when they were out of the community, including locking the room of the house where the computer was kept (in houses that were otherwise left unlocked). One woman said she only allowed nonhousehold members to use her computer in emergencies. Such an emergency, she stated, might be someone arranging a funeral who needed to use Facebook to contact relatives. Another woman took the computer cords with her when she travelled to stop others using her computer. Residents cited Internet data and power usage among the reasons why they did not want others using their computers, as well as people potentially accessing content that they felt was inappropriate.

The Aboriginal system of demand sharing, a mechanism for the distribution of goods and the maintenance of social relationships (underpinned by an ethic of helping each other), seemingly negates individual ownership (Schwab, 1995). However, as some anthropologists have observed, there is a tension between relatedness and autonomy, and individuals may use strategies to look after some items rather than part with or share them (Macdonald, 2000). This may explain why Internet access, and by extension, usage, was largely restricted to the household/immediate family members, with the owner determining who could use the computer. At the same time, avoidance relationships between families (part of the kinship system), and the emphasis on discrete family ownership and use of ICT, resulted in certain family groups often dominating access to computers that had been located in shared spaces and excluding others, a finding that was corroborated at the telecentre at Papunya. At one community's request, we placed two computers in a shared community facility for those who did not have a computer in their own house, but also for the couple supervising the facility. In time, it became apparent that the couple considered the computers to be 'theirs', restricting access mainly to themselves and some of their family members.

These findings on location and access have implications in considering models for the provision of ICT and Internet access in remote communities. Shared Internet arrangements, such as telecentres run by Indigenous community members, may not be the most suitable mechanism for providing equitable access to the broader community, owing to family and other cultural obligations. For example, in one of the larger communities we visited, the death of a young man who had been supervising a computer centre meant that some others in that kinship network were unwilling to use it.

While in theory the home computing model provided ICT access for the whole family, the dynamics of interfamilial, gender and age relationships influenced community members' access to and use of the ICTs. Women were high users of the computers in the home: when asked who was the most frequent user of the computer in the house, two-thirds of those identified were women. The higher profile and level of participation of women in the home computing model suggests that locating computers and Internet access within household spaces might lead to a stronger association of digital technology with a female-coded domain and technical activities, with positive flow-on effects in facilitating greater ICT usage by women and children. By contrast, at the Papunya telecentre, the main room became so closely identified with young men for a time that a separate space had to be created for women to access computers and the Internet. Non-Indigenous staff observed that some boys would still enter the women's space and that this discouraged some women from being there. Local Papunya female staff members were unable to get the boys to leave because of interfamily relationships, demonstrating how certain family relationships, as well as age and gender groups, can influence who feels comfortable using shared ICT centres.

We also found that residents' degree of mobility, both within and outside the community, can have implications for ICT provision in relation to access, ownership, management of billing and sustainability. ICT arrangements need to be flexible in response to residential mobility, and some devices and equipment may be more suitable than others depending on community members' degree of mobility. For instance, residents moved houses within the community for a range of reasons, including available housing stock, maintenance issues in some houses, the cost of power and cultural customs surrounding death. Such intercommunity mobility has consequences for fixed infrastructure costs such as satellite dishes. However, the high level of mobility does not necessarily equate to a preference or requirement for mobile devices. Personal computers can be easier to manage in the domestic setting, whereas there is a high degree of sharing (and possibly demand sharing requests) for mobile devices.

By the conclusion of our research, we saw that there were clear reasons for the digital divide that were specific to Aboriginal communities, rendering any simple comparison with mainstream adoption inadequate. Although there was a significant digital divide, the reasons for the divide were primarily based on practical obstacles to acquiring home services, as well as retail mechanisms that did not correspond to the household economies of many remote-living Aboriginal families. In particular, postpaid billing – the only billing option for satellite Internet customers at the time – was deemed intolerable by many. Despite the willingness of some community members to allocate a portion of household budgets to Internet services, navigating and managing the ISP's billing systems was difficult. At the conclusion of the project, about half the computer owners struggled over the first 6 months to maintain sufficient balances in their nominated bank accounts to support the monthly payments when they became due, resulting in temporary or permanent loss of Internet access in some cases. For others, direct debits of large, unexpected amounts occurred if bills had been unpaid in previous months. Our research in Ali Curung (The research involved interviews with approximately 100 people in Ali Curung in late 2013, with representation from half of all households.), a community with mobile coverage, confirmed that people are prepared to pay for the Internet if it suits them. All interviewees who were paying for Internet access were paying for prepaid mobile broadband, even though satellite Internet was available at cheaper rates.

The research enabled us to see why the strikingly uneven patterns of Internet adoption between remote communities correspond to the availability of mobile broadband and other government programs. As Indigenous households in many of these communities share a similar socioeconomic profile, causal links between social exclusion and digital exclusion should be treated with scepticism. Understanding the digital divide requires close examination of people's preferences, capacities and the relationship of use to community norms (see also Rowse, 2010).

DISCUSSION

While the aim of our project was to test an alternative policy approach, the extent to which such an approach can produce generalizable results needs to be considered. Can a study of three small communities provide evidence that will satisfy the requirements and expectations of policymakers?

Researchers from the fields of social innovation and development economics have advocated for experimental research using randomized controlled trials (for instance, Banerjee & Duflo, 2011; Grissmer, Subotnik, & Orland, 2009). In this research design, an intervention is applied to a statistically significant group, selected randomly, and compared to a nontreatment group. Randomization is considered important for overcoming variables that might influence the outcomes of the intervention. Such approaches seek to show definitively if an intervention works, and can provide strong evidence that can be used to support and justify particular policy responses.

A small-scale trial of the kind that we embarked upon does not meet these standards of evidence (including replicability), as the results are specific to the time, place and people involved. However, qualitative or quasiexperimental research has the advantage of showing *why* a particular approach works (not just whether it works), and of providing insight into complex social dynamics that are otherwise difficult to know (Pawson, 2002). In the Indigenous research context, the processes of consent and consultation can preclude random selection, and projects need to be adaptive to accommodate community concerns and needs. The model we implemented was expensive and time-intensive, and is not necessarily what we would recommend for Indigenous digital divide programs. But it did reveal merits and drawbacks of other arrangements, including the use of satellite for community Wi-Fi (see 'Conclusion and Future Directions' section). The research thus enabled theory building (meaning the development of ideas to explain a set of occurrences) to evolve throughout the research project rather than testing one theory from commencement.

Moreover, the media landscape was changing rapidly during the course of our research. Attempting to control the context would have risked missing exactly what we were seeking to understand (including the launch of two new NBN satellites and the extension of mobile broadband into more communities). The need for flexibility also arose when tablet devices and smart phones arrived in the communities over the course of the research, indicating new options for private ownership, as well as a new suite of considerations around practices and affordability (Donner, 2015). As one researcher from the realist school of evaluation writes:

> *The external validity of experiments will be limited as long as the unit of analysis remains the program and will be problematic whenever researchers attempt to control for the effects of context, rather than embrace context as determining whether mechanisms are activated and generate outcomes.*
>
> ***Hawkins (2014, p. 49)***

It is also important to acknowledge that while policymakers might demand irrefutable proof, in reality this is not necessarily how policy change occurs (Mulgan & Puttick, 2013, p. 4). Effective innovations often go unrecognized even when there is evidence of their success, while ineffective ones continue to be funded. Many innovations in remote communications have occurred 'prepolicy' and in an ad hoc fashion through the efforts of the Indigenous sector, requiring the buy-in and ideas of local people, without which they would most likely have failed. Indigenous-owned organizations, together with local leaders, have carried out these initiatives, aided (and in some cases generated) by non-Indigenous workers from the research and education sector and the media sector. The work of Eric Michaels (1986) in setting up a pirate television station in Yuendumu has been influential. The contemporaneous EVTV media in Ernabella (established with key involvement from two educators working in the community at the time), the Tanami videoconferencing network of the 1990s, PY Media's high frequency radio network and the establishment of Indigenous community television (ICTV) in the early 2000s also deserve recognition for raising issues of remote community communication needs in ways that were responsive to remote Indigenous sociality, including cultural requirements and expectations. The enterprises and infrastructures of remote media and communication have thus arisen from two cultural traditions operating together within the one settler state (Hinkson, 2004).

Christie and Campbell write that, when working with remote communities, knowledge needs to be conceived as action and as performative, rather than representational (2014, p. 155). They observe that those undertaking the work of implementing programs are often doing so through an act of good faith, and will bend the rules and go out of their way to make sure that participants experience benefits from the work. This was the case in our project, in that the two Indigenous organizations were motivated to develop solutions that would work within the specific context of small remote communities.

CONCLUSION AND FUTURE DIRECTIONS

The findings of the Home Internet Project contradict the idea that remote households are simply 'behind' other Australian houses. Instead, the findings suggest that the decision not to acquire home Internet can be explained as one of lexicographic choice, whereby the options on offer fail to meet certain targets set by the consumer, causing the consumer to go without rather than suffer a less-than-ideal arrangement. The project produced tangible recommendations related to infrastructure, as well as how to assist households to acquire services, and the retail arrangements most likely to succeed. We concluded that if this particular divide is to be resolved, then more flexible and user-friendly arrangements and administrative processes for satellite Internet will need to be investigated.

CAT is now installing mobile hotspots in outstations, as well as highway stops and at other key locations where the terrain allows. These nonelectrical, low-maintenance structures use a satellite dish to amplify mobile reception from distances of up to 40 km out of mobile range. The infrastructure was designed and tested by CAT towards the end of our project.

Another response that appears to be gaining traction among policymakers is the provision of public Wi-Fi in communities. As discussed in this chapter, the experiences of the outstations suggest that government investment in faster satellite speeds – as has been the focus with the NBN – is unlikely to make a difference for Aboriginal families living in small, traditional communities, as it does not address the problem of account set-up and billing. However, NBN satellite connections can be used as the basis for community Wi-Fi to positive effect. In 2016, the Northern Territory Government announced 34 such projects to be administered by Northern Territory Libraries. There are limits to public Wi-Fi, in that NBN satellite plans are capped at 150 gigabytes of downloads a month even for public Internet premises (with Wi-Fi managers generally capping individual device usage between 100 and 300 megabytes per day). Individuals who wish to consume over-the-top-video services, for instance, still require home Internet connections. However, as a basic level of access, Wi-Fi has practical advantages, especially now that mobile device ownership is becoming common.

Both of these approaches suggest new directions for remote Indigenous communications, the first seeking to provide greater access via mobile Internet to small settlements, the second providing free local access points. If restrictive satellite download caps were removed, prepaid mechanisms for public Wi-Fi could possibly evolve. A further issue that is yet to be addressed in government policy, but that is worthy of consideration, is whether some government and other key services should be provided unmetered, including on prepaid mobile broadband, for those living in disadvantaged areas and as government services implement 'digital first' strategies. Although such issues of access continue to evolve, the home Internet project demonstrated that when the digital divide is approached and investigated as a matter of digital choices rather than social exclusion, policies and programs can emerge that provide acceptable systems and incentives for participation.

ACKNOWLEDGEMENTS

The research discussed in this chapter was a collaborative effort. The author acknowledges the knowledge, time and generosity of the residents of Kwale Kwale, Imangara, Mungalawurru, Papunya and Ali Curung. The research partners were the Swinburne Institute for Social Research, the Centre for Appropriate Technology, the Central Land Council and the Australian Communications Consumer Action Network. The research team consisted of Ellie Rennie, Eleanor Hogan and Julian Thomas (based at Swinburne University of Technology at the time), Andrew Crouch and Robin Gregory (Centre for Appropriate Technology) and Alyson Wright (Central Land Council). The research was funded through three grants: Australian Communications Consumer Action Network Research Grant 2010; Aboriginals Benefit Account grant 2011 and Australian Research Council Linkage Project 2011. Additional support was provided through the Australian Research Council Centre of Excellence for Creative Industries and Innovation.

REFERENCES

Altman, J. C., Dillon, M. C., & Jordan, K. (2009). *Submission to the House of Representatives Standing Committee on Aboriginal and Torres Strait Islander Affairs Inquiry into community stores in remote Aboriginal and Torres Strait Islander communities*. Canberra: ANU Centre for Aboriginal Economic Policy Research, (CAEPR Topical Issue No. 04/2009).

Australian Bureau of Stastics. (2011). *Census of Population and Housing, QuickStats search by Indigenous location*. Retrieved from <www.abs.gov.au/websitedbs/censushome.nsf/home>.

Australian Bureau of Statistics. (2015). *National Aboriginal and Torres Strait Islander Social Survey 2014–15 (No. 4714.0)*. Retrieved from <http://www.abs.gov.au/ausstats/abs@.nsf/mf/4714.0>.

Australian Communications and Media Authority. (2006). *Telecommunications in remote Indigenous communications*. Retrieved from <http://www.acma.gov.au/theACMA/telecommunications-in-remote-indigenous-communities>.

Banerjee, A. V., & Duflo, E. (2011). *Poor economics: A radical rethinking of the way to fight global poverty*. New York: Public Affairs.

Christie, M., & Campbell, M. (2014). Aboriginal contributions to the evaluation of housing (and to postcolonial theory). *Learning Communities: International Journal of Learning in Social Contexts*, *14*, 154–165.

Crouch, A. (2014). *Home internet for remote Indigenous communities: Technical report*. Alice Springs: Centre for Appropriate Technology.

Daly, A. E. (2005). *Bridging the digital divide: The role of community online access centres in Indigenous communities (DP273)*. Canberra: ANU Centre for Aboriginal Economic Policy Research.

Donner, J. (2015). *After access: Inclusion, development, and a more mobile Internet*. Harvard: MIT Press.

Ewing, S., Rennie, E., & Thomas, J. (2014). Broadband policy and rural and cultural divides in Australia. In K. Andreasson (Ed.), *Digital Divides: The new challenges and opportunities of e-inclusion* (pp. 107–124). London: Taylor and Francis.

Featherstone, D. (2013). The Aboriginal invention of broadband: How Yarnangu are using ICTs in the Ngaanyatjarra Lands of Western Australia. In L. Ormond-Parker, A. Corn, C. Fforde, K. Obata, & S. O'Sullivan (Eds.), *Information technologies and Indigenous communities* (pp. 27–52). Canberra: AIATSIS Research Publications.

Ginsburg, F. (2008). Rethinking the digital age. In P. Wilson, & M. Stewart (Eds.), *Global Indigenous media* (pp. 127–144). Atlanta: Duke University Press.

Grissmer, D. W., Subotnik, R. F., & Orland, M. (2009). *A guide to incorporating multiple methods in randomized controlled trials to assess intervention effects*. Washington: American Psychological Association.

Hawkins, A. (2014). The case for experimental design in realist evaluation. *Learning Communities: International Journal of Learning in Social Contexts, 14*, 46–60.

Hinkson, M. (2004). What's in a dedication? On being a Warlpiri DJ. *The Australian Journal of Anthropology, 15*(2), 143–162.

Macdonald, G. (2000). Economies and personhood: Demand sharing among the Wiradjuri of New South Wales. In G. Wenzel, G. Hovelsrud-Broda, & N. Kishigami (Eds.), *The social economy of sharing: Resource allocation and modern hunter-gatherers* (pp. 87–111). Osaka: National Museum of Ethnology.

Mayne, A. (2014). *Alternative interventions: Aboriginal homelands, outback Australia and the Centre for Appropriate Technology*. Adelaide: Wakefield Press.

Mazzarella, W. (2010). Beautiful balloon: The digital divide and the charisma of new media in India. *American Ethnologist, 37*(4), 783–804.

Michaels, E. (1986). *The Aboriginal invention of television in central Australia, 1982–1986: Report of the fellowship to assess the impact of television in remote Aboriginal communities*. Canberra: Australian Institute of Aboriginal Studies.

Mulgan, G., & Puttick, R. (2013). *Making evidence useful: The case for new institutions*. London: Nesta.

Pawson, R. (2002). Evidence-based policy: The promise of "realist synthesis". *Evaluation, 8*(3), 340–358.

Rennie, E., Crouch, A., Thomas, J., & Taylor, P. (2010). Beyond public access? Reconsidering broadband for remote Indigenous communities. *Communication, Politics and Culture, 43*(1), 48–69.

Rennie, E., Hogan, E., Gregory, R., Crouch, A., Wright, A., & Thomas, J. (2016). *Internet on the outstation: The digital divide and remote Aboriginal communities*. Amsterdam: Institute of Network Cultures.

Rowse, T. (2010). Re-figuring "Indigenous culture". In J. Altman, & M. Hinkson (Eds.), *Culture crisis: Anthropology and politics in aboriginal Australia* (pp. 153–178). Kensington: UNSW Press.

Schwab, R. G. (1995). *The calculus of reciprocity: Principles and implications of Aboriginal sharing*. Canberra: Centre for Aboriginal Economic Policy Research.

Telecommunications Action Plan for Remote Indigenous Communities (2002). *Report on the strategic study for improving telecommunications in remote Indigenous communities*. Canberra: Department of Communications and Arts.

CHAPTER 17

Effective Digital Participation: Differences in Rural and Urban Areas and Ways Forward

Long Pham and Beth Massey
University College Cork, Cork, Ireland

Our world is becoming increasingly electronically connected. Mobile broadband penetration in the OECD surpassed 90% by the end of 2015, increasing nearly 10% from 81.6% at the end of 2014 (OECD, 2016). Fixed broadband coverage reached 30% in OECD countries. The term Information Communication Technology (ICT) embraces technology including computer hardware and software, digital broadcast and telecommunications technologies such as mobile and smart phones, and electronic resources such as the World Wide Web, the Internet and CD-ROMs (Selwyn, 2004). ICT is inevitable for social and economic progress in the OECD (Selwyn, 2004) and the developing world and is regarded as a fundamental aspect of citizenship in the information age (Dahalin, 2016).

Many governments have chosen to stimulate citizen interaction with public services and elected officials using ICT tools such as social media alongside traditional communication media (television, radio, newspapers and magazines). To ensure inclusiveness, governments initiated ICT-based programs to ensure that citizens have connectivity and utilize ICT as a business-as-usual model (Selwyn, 2004). This business-as-usual model is trending in both urban and rural areas. However, despite the many initiatives in place, work to date has shown that digital citizen participation in both rural and urban areas still has limitations. The digital divide between rural and urban areas is one of the limitations and a part of the emerging wider theme: social inclusion. Utilizing ICT as a transformative enabler to overcome existing social divisions and inequalities (D'Allesandro & Dosa, 2001; Katz, Rice, & Aspden, 2001), the key conditions of digital

Digital Participation through Social Living Labs. DOI: http://dx.doi.org/10.1016/B978-0-08-102059-3.00017-4

access, participation and skills became the emerging themes in many discussions and research.

This chapter explores the three key conditions of access (i.e., usage, ICT infrastructure and information); participation (i.e., practices and willingness) and skills in using key digital tools. The authors attempt to identify key drivers and barriers that thwart progress, and forms of rural–urban digital variations. The ultimate goal of this exercise is to discover how individuals engage in the digital world, while providing governments with evidence and insights to guide their policy strategies. The researchers' perspective is that digital participation is an important path towards stronger social inclusion.

DIGITAL ACCESS, PARTICIPATION AND SKILLS

Achieving digital access is both a technology and nontechnology issue. The technological covers physical devices, software and training (Wise, 1997), while the nontechnological involves policy, users' digital skills, knowledge of how systems work and support to use them effectively. The complexity of ICT systems extends to social infrastructure and governance (Clement & Shade, 2000), and nonaccess issues (Wilhelm, 2000). ICT access is mixed and unequally distributed socially and spatially (Warf, 2001); lack of access is often associated with socioeconomic status, ethnicity, income, gender, levels of education, age and geography. Rural areas suffer from 'double jeopardy' (Park & Kim, 2015); low population density increases costs in installing and improving connectivity while low-income rural residents pay more for services (Eardley, Bruce, & Goggin, 2009). Rural residents require less from online services (Horrigan, 2010), causing the ICT model based on economies of scale to falter, reinforcing the cycle of inadequate rural digital access. Urban areas tend to use more mobile devices (Park & Kim, 2015).

Researchers have demonstrated positive benefits of Internet digital participation, including reshaping citizens' expectations and interactions with government. Others have examined issues that interfere with participation such as race and socioeconomic status, participation via computers at home or in public places, social groups, education levels, ages, gender and the role of the local government in driving participation (Light, 2001).

Local governments are key drivers in planning long-term strategies for digital inclusion involving all residents and multiple stakeholders. Officials, often accustomed to disseminating information downwards, are learning to use digital spaces for civic participation and open dialogues with citizens (Light, 2001). One result, Freeman (2016) wrote, is that greater government receptivity and responsiveness enables civic participation to inform local decision making and facilitates citizens developing a sense of connection with their local government. Genuine engagement is a coproduction of policy and services that requires a major shift in negotiation and in the collaborative culture within government (Barricelli et al., 2016; Bartoletti & Faccioli, 2016; Zappalà, Parker, & Green, 2000). It also demands that citizens be willing to engage and to develop capabilities for deliberative participation in a spirit that focuses on the public good (Holmes, 2011). Gordon (2011) showed that digital participation enlarges the audience by including those unable to attend physically and others who prefer to choose how and when they participate. It reduces labour, costs and spaces for stakeholders, especially local governments (Fredericks & Foth, 2013).

From the citizen's perspective, digital participation provides platforms, space and convenience for staying in touch, being connected and facilitating interactions not always possible in the physical sphere (Foth, Bajracharya, Brown, & Hearn, 2009). Digital participation facilitates two-way citizen communication through accessing information, networks and communities, but also through contributing their ideas and skills. It also provides an opportunity to access information, networks and communities, which in turn enables the participants with diverse knowledge to add to the process. People's participation in informal online networks and communities can create learning opportunities that contribute to their wellbeing, personal growth and collective activities and outputs (Ala-Mutka, 2010). When people participate more online with higher frequency and in more activities, Wei (2012) argues that they have the tendency to engage in more sophisticated and participatory uses, as well as enhance their own personal creativity. Helsper, Deursen, and Eynon (2015) showed that participatory and creative behaviours can lead to a tangible outcome in the offline world in economic, cultural, social and personal spheres.

Despite the positive gains reported in research on digital participation, there are on-going challenges that need further investigation. One of the challenges is the digital skills of citizens, who are both the end users and the driving forces for engagement in any digital participation platforms.

The digital skills issue is still in its infancy, especially with the emergence of newer platforms and applications. Certain skills are required for effective utilization of ICT applications, including the basics of Internet access. In some studies, measurements of digital skills of various population groups were on technical and operational levels, while others focused on critical and social skills in working with the communication technologies (Deursen, 2010). Park and Kim (2015) researched the skill issues between urban and rural users and found large skill gaps in using e-government services and email between the two groups. The skills to use those newer social media platforms, the newest form of ICT applications, are also important for citizen engagement, especially in the more disadvantage groups such as young people with disabilities.

Building on the knowledge gained regarding digital access, participation and skills and the disparities between rural and urban areas, this chapter examines research performed in a small European city (Cork) to see how policymakers, key stakeholders and residents can benefit from ICT-based opportunities, engagement and outcomes. Instead of 'pundit suppositions, travellers' tales and laboratory studies' (Wellman, 2001, p. 2031), this research utilizes robust survey-based work to take a step towards unpacking the complexities of the digital divide and promoting effective digital participation in both rural and urban areas (DiMaggio & Hargittai, 2001).

METHODOLOGY

Cork Profile

Cork is a half million population county, including the 123,000 residents of Cork City, located in the southern most region of the Republic of Ireland. Being the second largest county in Ireland, Cork has been a destination for investment by the world's leading companies, generating jobs and demands for higher education and skills training provided mainly by the two world-class educational institutions: the University College Cork and Cork Institute of Technology. While economic growth is making Cork a good place for investment, job opportunities, educational and training activities along with other urban amenities, these place enormous pressure on the infrastructure systems. Cork Smart Gateway (CSG) was initiated as one of the solutions to meet the sustainable growth demands for the area. The CSG utilizes technologies and technology-enabled management to boost cities' competitiveness, promote sustainable development and enhance the quality of life of citizens. The overall aim of the CSG Initiative is improving the region's economy, environment and quality of life.

Among other technological projects, CSG initiative focused on the fundamental question of how to effectively engage with Cork citizens and involve them in consultation, feedback, decision making and implementation processes. The project researched key characteristics and indicators to come up with the idea of establishing baseline citizens' engagement data, thus identifying channels, platforms and practices for the real engagement and involvement between Cork local authorities and their citizens.

SURVEY DESIGN AND IMPLEMENTATION

Achieving baseline data collection with a limited budget mandated collaboration, a key engagement strategy indicated in the literature review. CorkCitiEngage, the short name for the Cork Smart Gateway Citizen Engagement project, demonstrates the collaborative character of successful smart city (SC) projects (Schuurman, Baccarne, De Marez, & Mechant, 2012). The project focused on three key categories of participation in public issues: digital skills, access and usage (Alawadhi et al., 2012; Giffinger et al., 2007) that align with the objectives of the Cork Smart Gateway Initiative.

To collect data, five sets of surveys were deployed. They measured citizens' understanding of SC projects in Cork; current practices and willingness to engage/participate in public issues; digital skills; preferred means of communications and access to and use of hardware, broadband Internet and public transport (i.e., buses). The surveys targeted five groups: representative general public, nonrepresentative general public, youths from 15 to 18 years old, seniors and local authorities working in the two councils. Figs 17.1 and 17.2 show the survey sets, their corresponding survey methods and the final numbers of collected respondents. Details on the methodologies of this project are presented in a crowdsourcing paper (Pham & Linehan, 2016).

Figure 17.1 Survey methods.

Outcomes

Representative	950	Senior	141
Non-Representative	1301	Youth (15-18)	768
Mallow	87	Official	352
3599 respondents			

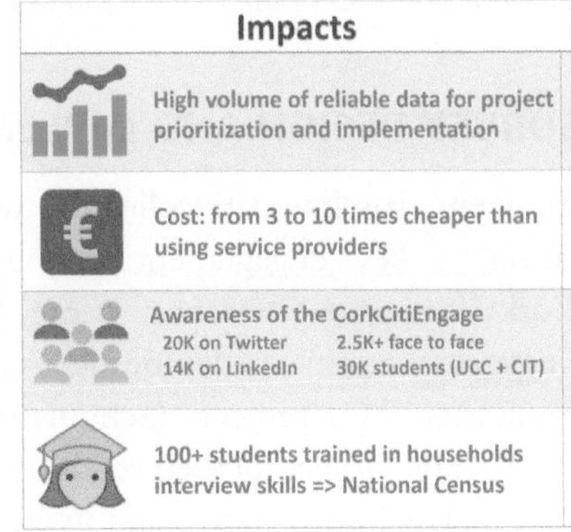

Impacts
High volume of reliable data for project prioritization and implementation
€
Cost: from 3 to 10 times cheaper than using service providers
Awareness of the CorkCitiEngage
20K on Twitter
2.5K+ face to face
14K on LinkedIn
30K students (UCC + CIT)
100+ students trained in households interview skills => National Census

Figure 17.2 Number of respondents in each survey and totals.

RESULTS AND DISCUSSIONS

The descriptive analysis provided some evidence on the differences between urban and rural respondents in Cork to test the presumption that urban respondents were more engaged and comfortable with the concept of SC and that they have some technology advantages. The main gaps are in digital skills and access. This section presents results and discusses those gaps under the three key themes of access, participation, and skills to shed some light on how best to promote sustained citizen engagement. Another question regarding conditions to help people to better use public services over the Internet was also framed as an access issue.

Access

Social media emerged as important sources of information that urban and rural people use on a daily basis (Table 17.1). Radio and television use averaged about 45%. The percentage of urban respondents using television as their primary source of information was significantly higher than those in the rural areas. Online newspapers and news sources were popular source of information. Point 1 in Table 17.1 shows that the percentage of respondents depending on online sources from rural areas was significantly higher than their peers in the urban areas. Print newspaper and magazines use shows the global readership decline trend in both rural and urban areas, although since most online newspapers originate in the print

Table 17.1 Access

1	**Primary sources of information used on daily basis**	**Urban ($n = 1582$) (%)**	**Rural ($n = 655$) (%)**
	Television	47.20	40.90*
	Radio	45.4	47.0**
	Online newspapers/news sources	47.2	53.0*
	Social media	50.3	53.3**
	Print newspapers/magazines	26.1	16.6*
2	**Access the Internet**	**Urban (%)**	**Rural (%)**
	Anywhere with free Wi-Fi	41.70	45.60**
	Work	37.2	36.9**
	Home	75.5	82.9*
	Public offices	3.7	2.7**
	Other	12.0	9.5**
3	**Interactions with public services/ authorities via the Internet**	**Urban (%)**	**Rural (%)**
	Obtain information	51.00	57.60*
	Download forms	45.50	55.70*
	Submit completed forms	32.60	37.30*
	Make online payments (i.e., property tax and motor tax)	48.60	66.10*
	Didn't have to	25.00	12.20*
4	**Willingness to use specific local smart phone app**	**Urban (%)**	**Rural (%)**
	Yes	74.8	82.3*
	No	25.2	17.7**

Mean values of measured access topics in Cork compared between rural and urban groups
$^{*}\chi^2 < 0.05$; $^{**}\chi^2 > 0.1$.

product, the assumption can be made that the 47.2% and 53% of urban and rural people who read online newspapers and magazines should be counted as depending on print products for information.

Regarding access to the Internet, the home was the most popular place for the respondents in both urban and rural areas (Point 2 in Table 17.1). The percentage of the respondents in the rural areas was significantly higher than their peers in the urban areas. The access rate of the rural areas was closer to the national figure, which estimated 85% of households had home Internet access in 2015. Nearly 43% of people responded that they accessed the Internet from 'anywhere with free

Wi-Fi'; meanwhile, Internet access at workplaces was at 37%. Rural respondents also outdid their urban counterparts at significantly higher percentages in all online services provided by local governments; 66.1% used online payments, compared with 48.6% of urban respondents (Point 3 in Table 17.1). The respondents in the rural areas were also frequent users in obtaining the information and downloading forms.

The demand for a local Cork smartphone app was high at 77% of all respondents, which included a significantly higher percentage of the respondents in rural areas. The percentage of those who didn't want a special Cork app was at 23%, and most of the 'no' respondents were over 60 years old. Meanwhile, answers to an open-ended question soliciting ideas for improving Internet use yielded a range of suggestions: better website layout and design; phone contact with offices is still important; safer, reliable and available free Wi-Fi; discount on computer/tablet; more public service providers on the Internet/social media; incentives for using public services on the Internet and better websites and more services offers.

The above results demonstrate the access issues on physical ICT infrastructure such as computers, Wi-Fi, public services online and 'beyond access' issues including the demands for information and preferred means of communications. Three key points emerge.

First, both urban and rural information users use social media sources (Point 1 in Table 17.1). This is becoming a particularly important channel for people, hence, local governments can use this channel to push local information, especially since 65% of people in Cork responded as Facebook users and other less popular platforms including YouTube and Twitter. This aligns with an increasing practice of local governments in the OECD (2009), of which Ireland is a member. Both Cork City and County Councils have their Facebook and Twitter accounts and they are operating as information dissemination tools rather than interactive tools with timely response and two-way feedback. Television, radio and online newspapers/new resources are each used by less than 50% of people. These traditional means are still important sources of information, especially for the older groups of population. Therefore important information regarding local development, social welfare, changes in policies that would impact many people should come to people via those media.

Second, the high percentage of people using mobile phones provides a unique opportunity for local governments to consider the adoption of mobile government or m-government, a subset of e-government. The m-government platforms enable citizens to access and use government information and services whenever they want and wherever they are (Ahmed, 2006). Cork City has provided a service of weather alert via text message to mobile phones of registered residents/citizens. However, there are many other applications that could be added such as reminders to renew licenses, tax returns, tax and fee payments, public health alerts, special health care and social welfare schemes and others.

Third, the overall home usage of the Internet is a little lower than the national average, 77.6% on average in Cork (Point 2 in Table 17.1) versus 85% nationwide. The Internet usage is related to the coverage of broadband and mobile phone penetration. While those in the rural areas reported their Internet use closer to the national level, at 83% versus 85% nationally, the more broadband connectivity, the better urban and rural people can leverage the advantages of the information and knowledge economy. Research has found that there are strong links between the availability of connectivity (i.e., broadband and mobile penetration) and rural socioeconomic development (Erdiaw-Kwasie & Alam, 2015).

We found that Internet access at public offices was extremely low, 3.4% (Point 2 in Table 17.1). This reflects both the current computer/hardware and Wi-Fi availability in the public offices. Accordingly, there is a strong demand for hardware access; nearly 30% of people want access to computer/tablet at public offices, 35% asked for access to computer/tablet at public libraries and 22% would choose to access to computer/tablet at community centres. Improving the access to hardware and Wi-Fi (connectivity) would help the residents to engage stronger and use the information for their personal decision making, thus improving their quality of life in the area. Access to online public services is also an important measure for both citizens' participation and service delivery. Over 50% of people in Cork are obtaining information, downloading forms, submitting completed forms and making online payments for their property tax, motor tax and the like (Point 3 in Table 17.1). While the percentage reflects some improvement in using online services, 86% of people are using their smart phones (Deloitte, 2016), therefore, there is even more chances to increase the use public services via smartphone apps.

Participation

Measurement of the involvement and willingness aspect was derived from five potential SC projects that Cork City may include in its initiative. They are: report of public issues, use of city's open data, efficient use of

Table 17.2 Participation

1	**Involvement willingness in future smart city projects**	**Urban ($n = 1582$) (%)**	**Rural ($n = 665$) (%)**
	Strong involvement	46.5	45.1
	Some involvement	22.7	28.7*
	No involvement	30.8	26.1
2	**Volunteer activities in the last 12 month**	**Urban (%)**	**Rural (%)**
	Sport/recreation	26.1	32.5*
	Community service	21.3	24.4**
	Disadvantaged people	10.9	12.2**
	Faith/religious	8.2	12.1*
	Academic	22.9	28.1*
	Didn't volunteer	41.2	31.3*
	Other	6.0	6.6**
3	**Communication methods preferred in interactions with public offices**	**Urban (%)**	**Rural (%)**
	Email	67.10	74.00*
	Mobile phone	45.40	44.10**
	Land phone	16.90	12.20*
	Text	20.70	19.40**
	Post	34.50	33.30**
	Apps	6.80	7.30**
	Social networks	8.70	8.40**

Mean values of measured participation topics in Cork compared between rural and urban groups
$*\chi^2 < 0.05$; $**\chi^2 > 0.1$.

energy, efficient use of water and use of shared-payment car rides. Table 17.2 shows that there was little difference between the urban and rural respondents in their willingness to be involved in such SC projects. Over 70% of the respondents in both rural and urban areas indicated interest in future involvement as 'strong' or 'some involvement' (Point 1 in Table 17.2). However, rural respondents expressed significantly greater willingness to have 'some involvement' in future projects, with 28.7% of rural residents choosing that option compared with 22.7% of urban respondents (Point 1 in Table 17.2).

Volunteer activities questions measured one area of participation. Point 2 in Table 17.2 shows that rural area respondents volunteered significantly more in all categories measured than those in urban areas. More rural respondents volunteered in activities, including sport/recreation, faith/religious and academic activities. In these categories, rural residents were significantly higher (at the 0.05 level), while in other volunteer categories measured, rural residents were significantly more active at the 0.1 level. The percentage of urban respondents was significantly higher only in the 'Didn't volunteer' category. Overall, about 60% of respondents in urban areas participated in volunteering activities, compared with 70% of rural respondents. Most popular volunteer activities for both groups were in sport/recreation, community service and academic activities.

Preferences for being contacted by public officers was led by email, mobile and post, in that order, as preferred means (Point 3 in Table 17.2). Email was preferred by nearly 70% of the respondents, and the percentage of rural respondents preferring emails (at 74%) was significantly higher than their urban peers (at 67%). Text and land phone followed as the officers' preferred means of communications with urban respondents. The percentage of urban respondents was significantly higher than among rural residents in preferring to be contacted by land phone. In summary, email and mobile were the most popular means of communications between the public and public officers. Even so, the percentage of respondents who preferred email as their primary means of communication was lower than at the national level, which was at 85% (http://www.cso.ie/en/releasesandpublications/er/isshh/informationsocietystatistics-households2015/).

Overall, the people in Cork were willing to participate in public issues, and they believed their participation would have a positive impact on their living environment. In Cork, 70% of the respondents were intended to participate in the surveyed public issues, while 63% of them actually volunteered (Point 2 in Table 17.2). This was one of the measurements for civic participation (Putnam, 2000). Literature demonstrated that those who said they intended to participate had a high possibility to actually participate (Carpini, Cook, & Jacobs, 2004). This suggests that public issues such as efficient use of water or energy could be incorporated in volunteer activities.

Cork has a number of academic, social and civil organizations which are great nodes for organizing volunteer initiatives that promote public participation in local issues using different formats of recreational, academic and community service activities. Also, the improvement of access issues (i.e., hardware availability and connectivity) mentioned earlier can help to facilitate the participation of people in civic activities and gradually recruit them for other public activities.

A local city app or other e-government or m-government platforms could integrate a dedicated function for volunteer activities with some forms of rewards and incentives for the participant. Through those activities, local governments can groom residents towards e-participation, helping them to experience the openness, inclusiveness and ease of access to local government. Consequently, local government can ensure that information is not only flowing from the government to the people but also from the people to the governments and among the citizenry themselves (Chun, Luna-Reyes, & Sandoval-Almazán, 2012). Furthermore, research found that a more open and accessible government was a factor that promotes greater e-participation because people believe they have an influence on policymaking processes (Macintosh, 2004; Reddick, 2011).

Skills

Regarding skills in using the key digital tools, respondents self-assessed themselves high for text and email and good in online services, mobile apps and social networks (Point 1 in Table 17.3). Rural respondents rated themselves significantly higher than their urban peers in skills, using all of the five measured digital tools. Among the newest of the communication vehicles, social media, Facebook was the most popular, and again rural users outdistanced their urban peers (Point 2 in Table 17.3). The percentage of rural Facebook respondents (69.2%) was significantly higher than their urban peers (62.8%). Video platform YouTube was the second most popular social media tool used by respondents in both the urban and the rural areas. Other tools, including Twitter and LinkedIn, were used by fewer than 20% of the respondents, while the image-sharing tool Instagram was used by 14% of the respondents, mostly those under 25 years old. Responses to questions about improving Internet use for public services were similar in urban and rural residents (Point 3 in Table 17.3). Improving access at public libraries appealed to about one-third of both groups, while other offers (skills assistance, access at public offices and community centres) appealed to fewer people.

While respondents rated themselves as quite proficient in using digital tools (i.e., email, text, mobile apps, online services and social networks), gaps exist between people in rural and urban areas. Residents in urban areas were found to be less skilful than their peers in rural areas in using

Table 17.3 Skills

1	**Skills in using key digital tools**	**Urban (n = 1582) (%)**	**Rural (n = 655) (%)**
	Email	72.20	80.60*
	Text	78.30	84.40*
	Mobile apps	62.80	69.60*
	Online services	65.30	71.30*
	Social networks	60.80	64.40*
2	**Social media used most**	**Urban (%)**	**Rural (%)**
	Facebook	62.8	69.2*
	Twitter	19.0	22.3**
	YouTube	23.9	27.0**
	LinkedIn	14.0	15.6**
	Tumblr	2.4	1.5**
	Instagram	13.8	14.4**
	Google +	15.1	12.5**
3	**Conditions for better use of public services over the Internet**	**Urban (%)**	**Rural (%)**
	Access to computer/tablet at public libraries	35.30	33.30**
	Computer skills assistance	18.8	15.4*
	Access to computer/tablet at public offices	26.3	31.5*
	Access to computer/tablet at community centres	22.6	20.6**
	Other	25.5	29.8*

Mean values of measured digital skill topics in Cork compared between rural and urban groups
$^{*}\chi^2 < 0.05$; $^{**}\chi^2 > 0.1$.

those key digital tools. The results from the access and use of public services (Point 3 in Table 17.3) over the Internet were also consistent; those in the rural used more than their peers in the urban areas. The question was framed as an access issue over the Internet rather than skills; however, people who use those services must have the required skills for using computers/tablets/the Internet, apps and other applications such as security verification and online payment validations. Thus the higher percentages of those in the rural areas used the public services online reflected their actual practical skills.

Computer skills assistance was one of the key variables that magnified the specific need of people in urban and rural areas. Again, it was those in the urban areas who responded higher in this demand than their peers in the rural areas. Also, there are skill gaps among elderly groups, who find it difficult to catch up with the new tools. The results of the CorkCitiEngage overall surveys showed that one of the most popular activities for youth and secondary students' engagement is volunteering. For example, young 'computer geeks' could provide computer and Internet skills to special need groups, senior citizens and those who need digital assistance in urban areas. A few secondary schools in Cork and other civil groups have tried to set up similar activities for transition-year students, who are 15 to 16 years old, and are required to have either volunteer or practical experience in their fourth year of secondary school. A locally focused social media app, which could be dedicated to people and organizations to share their needs and find those who could help, is another example of sustained youth volunteerism.

CONCLUSION AND THE WAYS FORWARD

This work has identified drivers in digital access, participation and skills in rural and urban areas towards digital participation via the adoption of e-government or m-government under a SC approach. The skill gaps can be addressed by using participation practices such as volunteering and collaborations among similar-interest stakeholders. Key drivers emerge in people's current practices in accessing information and other public services. The data also underlines rural and urban preferences in using different digital tools and their perceptions about connectivity and hardware access issues, thus helping local governments devise strategies that provide people with vehicles to improve their quality of life. The research also has implications for leveraging community-based resources to narrow digital skill gaps and increase access. The end result is that cities and regions – especially those who are considering adopting the Smart City approach – have tools and incentives to capture the full strength and energy of the places and their people in both rural and urban areas.

Local governments consider the targeted audience, i.e., rural, urban or both users, to design communication strategies for the programs that they want to promote. Overall, local governments can utilize a multiple-channel approach in pushing information to the right audience, thus creating more opportunities for their awareness and participation. Clear findings on communication styles expected from those groups could be stratified as cities have diverse population groups with a variety of needs and expectations, and the SC with the ICT enabler can ease the process. The findings also have some implications for technology application within the SC agenda and technology diffusion literature even though influences of the attributes may differ substantially across citizen segments.

Research discussed in this work was generated in a specific area in Ireland, but results are applicable to similar areas. The data reveals needs of residents useful in guiding governments in designing and developing systems and applications that reflect people's needs and goals, whether they use traditional or electronic media (Luna-Reyes & Gil-Garcia, 2011). This study contributes to the rare literature that quantitatively assesses the needs of citizens for the selection of design and implementation of ICT infrastructure in the public sector.

Governments want to garner trust with constituents, and one way to earn trust is being transparent and efficient in their actions, whether in the policymaking, service delivery or in openness and availability to people via popular channels that they actually use. Governments can also use citizens' voices by collecting and reflecting them to transform existing government policies or introduce new ones. The discourse can promote collaborative decision making by including the voice of the people as new or changed policies are considered (Chun et al., 2012).

The data presented in this work had a specific focus and may contain sample bias in the way some survey sets were deployed in online data collection. Subsequently, the descriptive analyses represent a specific context-based setting and challenge. The surveys were conducted in Cork respecting the boundary constraints of a particular cultural and sociopolitical context (Venkatesh, Brown, & Bala, 2013). Future research can examine the potential of the attributes and general drivers in different settings.

REFERENCES

Ahmed, N. (2006). An overview of e-participation models. In *UNDESA workshop: E-participation and E-government: Understanding the Present and Creating the Future* (pp. 27–28). Budapest, Hungary.

Ala-Mutka, K. (2010). *Learning in informal online networks and communities.* Seville: European Commission-Joint Research Centre-Institute for Prospective Technological Studies.

Alawadhi, S., Aldama-Nalda, A., Chourabi, H., Gil-Garcia, J. R., Leung, S., Mellouli, S., … … Walker, S. (2012). *Building understanding of smart city initiatives. Electronic Government*. Berlin, Heidelberg: Springer.

Barricelli, B. R., Fischer, G., Fogli, D., Mørch, A., Piccinno, A., & Valtolina, S. (2016). *Cultures of participation in the digital age: From have to want to participate. Proceedings of the 9th Nordic conference on human-computer interaction, October 23–27, 2016* (p. 128). New York: ACM.

Bartoletti, R., & Faccioli, F. (2016). Public engagement, local policies, and citizens' participation: An Italian case study of civic collaboration. *Social Media + Society*. July–September, 1–11. http://dx.doi.org/10.1177/2056305116662187.

Carpini, M. X. D., Cook, F. L., & Jacobs, L. R. (2004). Public deliberation, discursive participation, and citizen engagement: A review of the empirical literature. *Annual Review of Political Science*, 7, 315–344.

Chun, S. A., Luna-Reyes, L. F., & Sandoval-Almazán, R. (2012). Collaborative e-government. *Transforming Government: People, Process and Policy*, *6*, 5–12.

Clements, A., & Shade, L. (2000). The access rainbow: Conceptualizing universal access to the information/communication infrastructure. In M. Gurstein (Ed.), *Community informatics: Enabling communities with information and communications technologies* (pp. 32–51). Hershey: Idea Group Publishing.

D'Alessandro, D. M., & Dosa, N. P. (2001). Empowering children and families with information technology. *Archives of Pediatrics & Adolescent Medicine*, *155*, 1131–1136.

Dahalin, Z. M. (2016). ICT as a transformative driver for socio-economic development. *Journal of Theoretical and Applied Information Technology*, *89*(1), 71–77.

Deloitte. (2016). Global mobile consumer survey 2016. Retrieved in February 2017 from <https://www2.deloitte.com/ie/en/pages/technology-media-and-telecommunications/articles/Mobile-Consumer-Survey-2016.html#>.

Deursen, A. J. A. M. (2010). Internet skills: Vital assets in an information society *(Unpublished doctoral thesis)*. The Netherlands: University of Twente.

DiMaggio, P., & Hargittai, E. (2001). *From the 'digital divide' to 'digital inequality': Studying Internet use as penetration increases*. Princeton: *Center for Arts and Cultural Policy Studies, Woodrow Wilson School, Princeton University, New Jersey, United States*.

Eardley, T., Bruce, J., & Goggin, G. (2009). *Telecommunications and Community Wellbeing: A review of the literature on access and affordability for low-income and disadvantaged groups*. Sydney: Social Policy Research Centre. University of New South Wales.

Erdiaw-Kwasie, M. O., Alam, K., & Shahiduzzaman, M. (2015). Towards understanding stakeholder salience transition and relational approach to 'better' corporate social responsibility: A case for a proposed model in practice. *Journal of Business Ethics*, 1–17. Available from http://dx.doi.org/10.1007/s10551-015-2805-z.

Foth, M., Bajracharya, B., Brown, R., & Hearn, G. (2009). The Second Life of urban planning? Using NeoGeography tools for community engagement. *Journal of Location Based Services*, *3*, 97–117.

Fredericks, J., & Foth, M. (2013). Augmenting public participation: Enhancing planning outcomes through the use of social media and web 2.0. *Australian Planner*, *50*, 244–256.

Freeman, J. (2016). Digital civic participation in Australian local governments: Everyday practices and opportunities for engagement. In J. Freeman (Ed.), *Social Media and Local Governments*. Switzerland: Springer International Publishing.

Giffinger, R., Fertner, C., Kramar, H., Kalasek, R., Pichler-Milanovic, N., & Meijers, E. (2007). *Smart cities-Ranking of European medium-sized cities*. Vienna University of Technology. *Centre of Regional Science*. Retrieved from <http://www.smart-cities.eu>.

Gordon, E. M. (2011). Augmented deliberation: Merging physical and virtual interaction to engage communities in urban planning. *New Media and Society, 13*(1), 75–95. Retrieved from <http://nms.sagepub.com/content/13/1/75.abstract>.

Helsper, E.J., Deursen, A.J., & Eynon, R. (2015). *Tangible outcomes of internet use: From digital skills to tangible outcomes project report.* Available at <www.oii.ox.ac.uk/research/projects/?id=112>.

Holmes, B. (2011). *Citizens' engagement in policymaking and the design of public services. Canberra: Department of Parliamentary Services*, Parliament of Australia.

Horrigan, J. B. (2010). *Broadband adoption and use in America. Federal Communications Commission.*

Katz, J. E., Rice, R. E., & Aspden, P. (2001). The Internet, 1995–2000 access, civic involvement, and social interaction. *American Behavioral Scientist, 45*, 405–419.

Light, J. (2001). Rethinking the digital divide. *Harvard Educational Review, 71*, 709–734.

Luna-Reyes, L. F., & Gil-García, J. R. (2011). Using institutional theory and dynamic simulation to understand complex e-Government phenomena. *Government Information Quarterly, 28*, 329–345.

Macintosh, A. (2004). Characterizing e-participation in policy-making. In *System sciences, 2004. Proceedings of the 37th annual Hawaii international conference on 5–8 Jan, 2004* (pp. 10).

The Organisation for Economic Co-operation and Development (OECD). (2009). *Focus on citizens: Public engagement for better policy and services.* Retrieved from <http://www19.iadb.org/intal/intalcdi/pe/2009/03785.pdf>.

The Organisation for Economic Co-operation and Development (OECD). (2016). OECD broadband statistics update. Retrieved in October 2016 from <http://www.oecd.org/sti/broadband/broadband-statistics-update.htm>.

Park, S., & Kim, G. (2015). Same access, different uses, and the persistent digital divide between urban and rural Internet users (March 21, 2015). In *TPRC 43: The 43rd research conference on communication, information and Internet policy paper.* Available at SSRN <https://ssrn.com/abstract=2582046>.

Pham, L., & Linehan, C. (2016). *Crowdsourcing: Tackling challenges in the engagement of citizens with smart city initiatives. Proceedings of the SEACHI 2016 on smart cities for better living with HCI and UX.* San Jose: ACM. Available from http://dx.doi.org/10.1145/2898365.2899799.

Putnam, R. D. (2000). *Bowling alone: America's declining social capital. Culture and Politics.* Springer. Available from http://dx.doi.org/10.1007/978-1-349-62397-6_12.

Reddick, C. G. (2011). Citizen interaction and e-government: Evidence for the managerial, consultative, and participatory models. *Transforming Government: People, Process and Policy, 5*, 167–184.

Schuurman, D., Baccarne, B., De Marez, L., & Mechant, P. (2012). Smart ideas for smart cities: Investigating crowdsourcing for generating and selecting ideas for ICT innovation in a city context. *Journal of Theoretical and Applied Electronic Commerce Research*, 7, 49–62.

Selwyn, N. (2004). Reconsidering political and popular understandings of the digital divide. *New Media & Society, 6*, 341–362.

Venkatesh, V., Brown, S. A., & Bala, H. (2013). Bridging the qualitative-quantitative divide: Guidelines for conducting mixed methods research in information systems. *MIS Quarterly, 37*(1), 21–54.

Warf, B. (2001). Segueways into cyberspace: Multiple geographies of the digital divide. *Environment and Planning B: Planning and Design, 28*(1), 3–19.

Wei, L. (2012). Number matters: The multimodality of Internet use as an indicator of the digital inequalities. *Journal of Computer-Mediated Communication, 17*(3), 303–318.

Wellman, B. (2001). Computer networks as social networks. *Science, 293*, 2031–2034.

Wilhelm, A. G. (2000). *Democracy in the digital age: Challenges to political life in cyberspace.* New York: Routledge Press.
Wise, J. M. (1997). *Exploring technology and social space.* Thousand Oaks: Sage Publications.
Zappalà, G., Parker, B., & Green, V. (2000). *Social exclusion and disadvantage in the New Economy, Working Paper no. 2. Research & Advocacy Team, The Smith Family.* Retrieved from <http://www.orfeusresearch.com.au/web_images/workingpaper%20no2.pdf>.

FURTHER READING

Pham, L. (2014). *Resident Engagement as a necessary component for Smart City Programmes. White Paper.* Cork: *International Energy Research Centre.*

CHAPTER 18

Gateways to Digital Participation: The Rhetorical Function of Local Government Websites

Kerry Mallan
Queensland University of Technology, Brisbane, QLD, Australia

The rhetoric of digital participation occurs in diverse contexts such as education, town planning, civic engagement, personal lifestyle, financial management and local governance. Alongside the increased availability of mobile computing devices and other Internet usage there is a corresponding increase in public expectation for quick and easy access to all that these technologies can offer, especially information, entertainment and social networking, regardless of where people live. Historically, the city has been regarded (and privileged) as the hub of connectivity, productivity and consumerism in relation to commerce, industry, employment and the arts. However, with the expansion of urbanization and exurbanization, and increasing access to the Internet through Broadband, the idea of proximity to infrastructure that supports social-economic-cultural development is no longer a driving force behind the lure of urbanity.

Defining exactly what is meant by 'urban', 'nonurban' or 'exurban' is often conflicted, especially among ecologists, urban planners and even residents of these areas (MacGregor-Fors, 2011). Whereas the urban landscape consists of urban, suburban, exurban and rural areas from the city centre to its periphery, the rapid expansion of exurbanization has seen several terms come under this general category, namely, sprawl, exurbia, extraurban, periurban and rural areas (Ban & Ahlqvist, 2009). However, even with these terms there is no consensus as characteristics such as population density, distance, household lot-size, human activities and land use continue to complicate meaning. A further complication is determining 'exact boundaries between types of urban landscapes, such as between rural areas and exurban areas, or between exurban areas and suburban or urban areas' (Ban & Ahlqvist, 2009, p. 233). While there are subtle distinctions between these terms, the common feature is that each refers in

Digital Participation through Social Living Labs. DOI: http://dx.doi.org/10.1016/B978-0-08-102059-3.00018-6

its own way to peripheral, edge or interstitial spaces that occur within, around, between and outside of the city.

For this chapter, I will draw on Cope and Kalantzis's (2015) interpretation of the 'extraurban' as it offers a more fluid and flexible notion of spaces and flows that is not bound by geospatial limits. In order to narrow the focus of possibility, this chapter examines how Cope and Kalantzis's propositional flows across extraurban spaces appear to shape the rhetorical appeals of digital participation through the functions of local government websites in two high-growth extraurban spaces: City of Wyndham (Victoria) and North Lakes – Mango Hill (Queensland). Before providing a close look at these websites, the following sections begin with an expanded understanding of extraurbia before introducing research on how the functions of local government websites can support or limit digital participation.

EXTRAURBIA, FLOWS AND SPACES

Extraurbia offers a range of spatial configurations that according to Cope and Kalantzis challenge 'our conceptualization of the urban/nonurban distinction and our understandings of centripetal forces and flows which historically favored urbanity' (2015, p. 221). In reconceptualizing ways of conceiving spaces that are being transformed through digital technologies and user uptake, Cope and Kalantzis contend that 'new forms of relationality evolve' (p. 221) which take into account ever expanding networks of relations through digital participation.

Within their examples of extraurban spaces – edge urban, deurban, microurban, greenfield and off-the-grid – Cope and Kalantzis propose three 'flows' or 'transformational dynamics of connection and disconnection' between the extraurban and the urban, namely, ontological flows; flows of conviviality and representational flows (p. 227). The *ontological flows* refer to the material aspects of a community – housing, transport, infrastructure, production, consumption and socioscapes. The *flows of conviviality* encompass governance, identities and communities; and *representational flows* refer to communications, innovation and learning. There is also a resemblance between these flows and Appadurai's (1996) global flows of technoscapes, financescapes, mediascapes and ideoscapes, which represent the *flows* of people, technology, money, media images and political ideas. However, whereas Cope and Kalantzis' flows can be seen as a return to place (community and location), Appadurai's *scapes* are more representative of the global and as such can be seen as a turn away from the specifics of place and location.

The three flows characterize in many ways the changing dynamics of extraurban spaces throughout Australia. With the growth in the populations of its capital cities over past decades, Regional Development Australia (RDA, 2016) was formed to work with all levels of government to enhance the development of regional Australia. An embedded element of RDA plans is the notion of citizen/resident participation in the form of consultation, feedback and information awareness.

FUNCTIONS, FLOWS AND E-GOVERNMENT

It is becoming commonplace in many Western countries for politicians at all levels of government to espouse an emancipatory rhetoric of citizen participation. One avenue for putting this rhetoric into action is through government websites. Most governments (large and small) use a website homepage or web portal as an integrated gateway for sharing information and services. In recent years, however, Web 2.0 applications and tools have enabled government websites to be less unidirectional in their sharing of information and more supportive of interactive engagement and participation by their users (Parker, Downie, & Manville, 2012; Sandoval-Almazan & Gil-Garcia, 2012). Thus e-government websites are evolving and adapting as new technologies become available.

The evolutionary and uneven provision of e-government services means that it is difficult to evaluate all government sites using a standard set of criteria as many reflect multiple stages of evolution (Sandoval-Almazan & Gil-Garcia, 2012). Sandoval-Almazan and Gil-Garcia propose a continuum of different functions of government portals, rather than a set of discrete stages of development as some functions can be occurring at the same time (see Fig. 18.1).

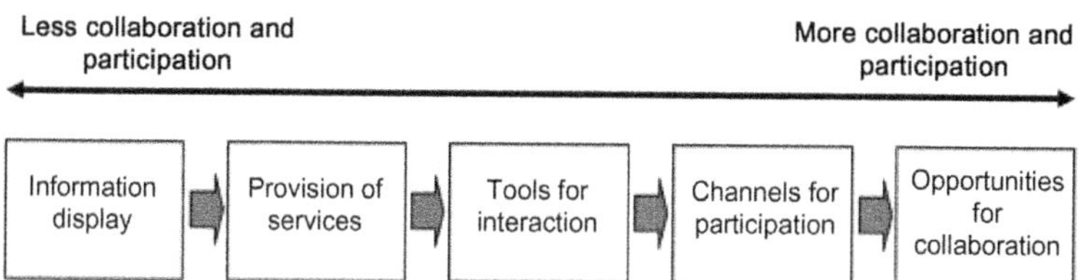

Figure 18.1 Different functions of government portals. *Sandoval-Almazan, R. & Gil-Garcia, J.R. (2012). Are government internet portals evolving towards more interaction, participation, and collaboration? Revisiting the rhetoric of e-government among municipalities.* Government Information Quarterly, 29, 574.

When considering these functions in the context of extraurban spaces and e-government websites, the three types of flows that Cope and Kalantzis propose can provide additional insights into understanding what a local government needs to do so it can respond to the changing dynamics that are shaping extraurban governance, and match the rhetoric of digital participation and digital citizenship (see Fig. 18.2). Digital citizenship is a broad term that encompasses many aspects of online participation and behaviour including digital awareness, ethical codes of conduct, political activism, personal and interest-driven activities (see Choi, 2016).

I am aware of the incongruity of bringing together what could be seen as purely functional technological tools (government websites) with complex patterns of uneven extraurban development (flows). However, my argument is that in the current context of government accountability and participatory democracy the functional systems of e-government operations cannot be quarantined from the changing social and political morphology of local governance, community and economics. Furthermore, just as Sandoval-Almazan and Gil-Garcia regard the functions as cooccurring at different stages, I also see the flows put forth by Cope and Kalantzis as contributing to one or more different functions, as the following briefly describes with respect to Fig. 18.2.

A basic function of local (and other) government websites is information provision. Generally the information tends to be about local governance and everyday life in the area. The ways of basic everyday living are what Cope and Kalantzis (2015, pp. 227–235) regard as ontological flows as they are about the realities of life with respect to housing, planning and building (propertyscapes), services such as water and waste and sustainable living (ecoscapes), and a range of local facilities and services for a

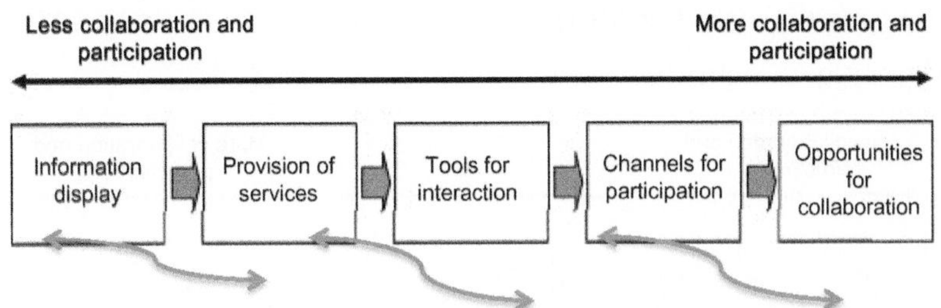

Figure 18.2 Functions and flows of extraurban government websites. *Modified from Sandoval-Almazan, R. & Gil-Garcia, J.R. (2012). Are government internet portals evolving towards more interaction, participation, and collaboration? Revisiting the rhetoric of e-government among municipalities.* Government Information Quarterly, *29, 572–581.*

culturally diverse community (socioscapes) (cf. Appadurai's scapes, as noted earlier).

How services are presented (drop down menus or directories, multimedia tools or online presentation) will influence the degree of success of the website (Sandoval-Almazan & Gil-Garcia, 2012). Many websites offer a range of services via traditional forms of communication (phone, email and postal address); others offer alternatives or supplementary functions such as mobile ICT and social media. These conglomerate functions create representational flows that connect to the local as well as disconnect or '"roam" as if location were immaterial' (Cope & Kalantzis, 2015, p. 239).

The move to include Web 2.0 tools and applications on government websites opened up further forms of communication and interaction that function to allow 'the possibility of more devolved, flexible and responsive modes of governance' (Cope & Kalantzis, 2015, p. 237). Web 2.0 tools such as blogs, Twitter, Facebook and collaborative wikis can benefit both government and citizens by promoting internal and external participation, improving relationships and enhancing decision making (Sandoval-Almazan & Gil-Garcia, 2012). Whether a government website uses Web 2.0 tools or more traditional forms (online chat and comment boxes), or both, Sandoval-Almazan and Gil-Garcia (2012, p. 574) contend that it is important that there is a key strategy and genuine commitment to fostering interaction between citizens and government and other agencies, such as other levels of government and nongovernment groups.

A communication strategy that uses multiple channels will benefit government, businesses and citizens/residents. However, government websites need to be regularly updated to be of value. In addition to government channels, the proliferation of digital technologies, personal websites, blogs, forums, wikis, social and professional networks and twitter accounts mean that citizens/residents and groups can participate locally and globally in numerous online communities, as well as retain a sense of identity that is located in a specific place. These multiple flows of identities, communities and communications contribute to a more fluid understanding of digital participation that goes beyond one that is tied to local politics, economics and civic duty.

The rhetoric of participation is visually and verbally present in government websites from the ubiquitous 'Contact Us' invitation, to often hyperlinked, social media icons such as (Fig. 18.3).

While participation is largely left to individual choice, Sandoval-Almazan and Gil-Garcia contend that 'very few [citizens] explicitly want

Figure 18.3 Sample of social media icons.

to *collaborate* with government' (2012, p. 574, my emphasis). They suggest that one of the reasons for this reluctance is that people do not trust government. If this is indeed the case, then it would seem that the rhetoric of participation, collaboration and inclusion has failed to achieve its purpose. Research, however, would suggest that it is not as cut-and-dried as this (Mandarano, Meenar, & Steins, 2010).

While the top-down rhetoric of collaboration may not be finding an appreciative citizen response, the bottom-up approach appears to be having more success as social media, wikis, digital storytelling and email are examples of citizen-initiated interaction and civic participation. Cope and Kalantzis are optimistic that the flows of governance and conviviality, whereby a mix of top and bottom interests collaborate, will 'stimulate innovations in organization, collaboration and mobilization that result in the emergence of a new kind of social capital that align specifically with extraurbia' (2015, p. 237). If this new social capital means enabling individuals and groups to build trust and work together with governments, then it could indeed stimulate creative solutions to problems that governments and communities face, stimulate collaboration with other agencies including NGOs, and extend the production and consumption flows of the extraurban (Foth, Hudson-Smith, & Gifford, 2016).

Despite the efforts of governments and communities to make change for the better, there is still some way to go before the rhetoric of participation is fully enacted. As mentioned earlier, one of the issues is the implicit assumption that participation is universally accepted and desired. With respect to digital citizenship and devolved governance there is the matter of a community's 'capacity to self-determine and govern the process' (Ferilli, Sacco, & Blessi, 2016, p. 96), especially when interest may be limited to a few, or achieving consensus is frustrated by diverse and contradictory viewpoints. These issues are part of a wider discussion that goes beyond this chapter. However, they are important considerations when examining the options that are available on government websites as a way of inviting and gaining participation.

RHETORIC AND FUNCTION OF TWO WEBSITES

As a way of illustrating how local governments, through their websites, are serving extraurban spaces and encouraging digital participation, the discussion now turns to two Australian sites – City of Wyndham and North Lakes – Mango Hill, the latter comes under the governance of Moreton Bay Regional Council. These spaces have been selected because of their rapid population growth and their fit with Cope and Kalantzis's extraurban classification of 'microurban' and 'greenfield' spaces, respectively. In treating these local government websites as rhetorical situations, I am interested in how their functions, design, visuals and language communicate to their intended audience and support digital participation.

City of Wyndham

The City of Wyndham can be described as 'microurban' because its population (218,553) is not on the same scale as larger cities (such as Melbourne) but it is a region of dynamic growth with a forecast of 359,542 by 2031 (ABS, 2012; Wyndham City, 2016a). Located on the outer southwestern fringe of Melbourne, the city features a mix of industries and services (retail, health and transport), as well as being a major horticultural area for Melbourne. Wyndham has a diverse population with 34% born overseas (mainly India, United Kingdom, New Zealand, Philippines and China). It is also home to the largest population in western metropolitan Melbourne of Aboriginal and Torres Strait Islander peoples (Wyndham City, 2016b).

Information display. The website for the Wyndham City Council provides an effective and visually appealing public information display (see Fig. 18.4). It contains traditional structures such as directories and menus as well as a search engine (What are you looking for?), which is both intuitive and comprehensive. It includes 'postcard' type displays (picture and text) of coming events (What's on), and short YouTube videos. The site also provides 'Latest news' about Council matters which is repeated across social media – Facebook and Twitter. In addition, there is a trending function that provides local information about various items

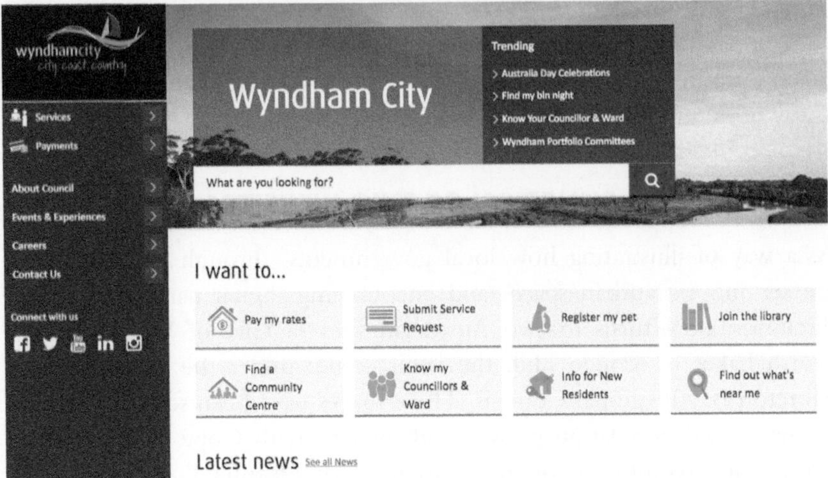

Figure 18.4 Partial screen shot of Wyndham City homepage.

from children's week picnic to garbage collection (find my bin night). This information is about the basics of living within a community (housing rates, transport, entertainment, community events, environment and sustainability). With respect to information transparency, the website contains annual financial reports (downloadable as pdf) for Council including information on public purchases.

Provision of services. The website contains links to downloadable online forms for services, numerous online service catalogues, and under 'Careers' are links to job vacancies, job application tips and year 10 work experience support. It also lists a wide range of payment options (including online) for services such as rates, business registration, town planning fees and so on.

Tools of interaction. As noted earlier, the website offers a range of tools for interaction including social media such as Twitter, Facebook, Instagram, LinkedIn and YouTube. It also includes chat (virtual assistant) as well as more traditional forms such as email, phone and an address for written correspondence. Email addresses and mobile phone numbers are given for the Mayor and all councillors. These are supplied along with a good size colour photograph of the incumbent as a way of personalizing public office.

Channels for participation. There are several channels for participation for members of Wyndham City (such as 'Get Involved', under the Advocacy subsection in the About Council menu drop). There are a number of campaigns and groups that residents are encouraged to join. While many are associated with community life, others such as 'Voice of Outer Suburbs' are an opportunity for more civic participation for individuals or groups to advocate for change or express their dissatisfaction with the current situation in Wyndham. Voices of Outer Suburbs are coordinated by the National Growth Areas Alliance (NGAA) which is a peak advocacy group for outer suburbs comprising councils from NSW, Victoria, Western Australia and South Australia. Through the Voices of Outer Suburbs, the NGAA invites residents and businesses to complete forms relating to issues that they want brought to the attention of a local government (postcodes must be supplied to aid the transfer to the correct councillor). All submissions are anonymized with sources credited as, e.g., 'From anonymous from [suburb]' or 'From Resident from [suburb]'. Residents can also send videos for the 'Our Stories' [YouTube] tab. There are numerous stories, but most are concerned with the basics of everyday life (ontological flows).

The website can be translated into languages other than English but the downloadable documents, council minutes, and so forth are available only in English.

Opportunities for collaboration. The tweets and blog comments ('Wyndham City Living' and 'Experience Wyndham') appearing on the website show a reciprocal sharing of information about forthcoming events and attractions in various suburbs. However, 'Get Wyndham Moving', a campaign comprising various local advocacy groups, community centres and businesses, actively encourages residents to submit letters to local and state government representatives, become members, receive the Advocacy eNewletter, use social media to tweet, upload pictures of traffic congestion on Instagram and to visit the Facebook for Wyndham City Living. Media releases give details of successful advocacy outcomes. The success of this transport advocacy initiative shows how collaboration and community participation can make changes that impact the residents of Wyndham (Get Wyndham Moving won the National Government Award for the best Advocacy/Public Affairs communications campaign for 2015.).

North Lakes – Mango Hill

Located in the Moreton Bay Region, North Lakes – Mango Hill is the largest and fastest growing area within the Greater Brisbane area (located approximately 26 km north of Brisbane CBD). Moreton Bay Region is also one of Australia's fastest developing places with a population of approximately 417,000, it includes diverse communities and landscapes – rural towns, mountain villages and expanding extraurban centres such as North Lakes – Mango Hill (Moreton Bay Regional Council, 2016).

North Lakes – Mango Hill is a 'greenfield' space, which boasts 'an abundance of parklands, Lake Eden, community facilities and industrial estate' and is marketed as 'the perfect place to raise your young family or simply enjoy a family day out'. This description echoes the point offered by Cope and Kalantzis that greenfield spaces are 'associated with images of nature, peace and quiet, space, family friendliness, and community belonging, often due to marketing campaigns to attract tourists and new residents' (2015, p. 226). A significant proportion of the total population was born overseas (35.5%) but Aboriginal and Torres Strait Islander people represent only 1.5% of the total population (ABS, 2011).

Information display. As the governing council for North Lakes – Mango Hill and other places under its jurisdiction, the Moreton Regional Council website provides a comprehensive range of information necessary for living, working or visiting in the region. As with the Wyndham City website, the Moreton Bay website incorporates a variety of structures to allow users to search for information, such as a row of horizontal tabs, menus, Quick Links, Online Links and so forth. The site also has an e-newsletter, which provides current information on a range of topics (cultural, business, environmental alerts and so forth). However, users need to sign up to become a Moreton Bay member in order to access these services. Information transparency is achieved in the availability of council meetings minutes, budget and operational plan, and a data portal provides extensive information and visual content on a wide range of Council data accessible through a data portal (such as Environment, Administrative, Disaster Management and Projects).

Provision of services. The site presents links to downloadable forms for services. Payments for rates and other council changes are payable online and with options for in-person or postal payments. There is also a list of current (council) employment opportunities with a job search function.

Tools for interaction. The Council provides an explicit statement about its interaction strategy outlining its steps for 'engagement' between governments, citizens and communities on policy, program and services as a way 'to inform decision making and to develop partnerships'. The Council uses a number of methods for engaging with the community – consultations forums regarding the local government infrastructure plan (to date one forum in 2016 and one in 2015); correspondence and councillor newsletters; media releases and public notices; major projects updates and eNewsletters. The site offers contact details (phone and email) and background and qualifications of the Mayor, and similar details for councillors including a signed Register of Interests which is important for openness. Specific interaction tools include social media (Facebook, Twitter, Instagram, YouTube and LinkedIn). However, these functions are not displayed on the homepage, as is the case with Wyndham City, but are accessible through a social media link (on the homepage) which takes users to the various options with further associated links to, e.g., LinkedIn and Twitter (see Fig. 18.5).

This multiple-steps approach may work against people choosing to participate via social media. While inviting people to contact the Council and have their say about projects, it is still a top-down model and unlike the Wyndham City website there is little evidence on the website of a bottom-up approach by active citizens.

Channels for participation. Through its engagement strategy (Think out Loud) the Council offers different channels for citizens to participate in the democratic process (consultations, public forums accessible by registration and moderated by the Council), to use communication channels (media releases, eNewsletters, Twitter feeds, Facebook, online services and contact details), to access services, submit claims, and gain access to public officials (via email, phone or postal address). The Council has also developed mobile apps which can display the website on a range of different screen sizes and devices, as well as specific apps for requests, reporting vandalism, road and footpath damage and so forth.

Opportunities for collaboration. The website actively provides avenues for collaboration and its community engagement strategy (Think out loud)

Figure 18.5 Partial screen capture of pathways to interactive tools on Moreton Bay Regional Council homepage © Moreton Bay Regional Council 2016.

rhetorically positions the government within the democratic process and proclaims its commitment to collaborative local governance:

> *Effective engagement is a key foundation of our representative democracy system of Government. Council currently undertakes a range of activities which aim to ensure community and stakeholder input into key decision making processes and is committed to continuing to achieve high quality, meaningful engagement between the Council and the community (www.moretonbay.qld.gov.au).*

Furthermore, the Council defines collaboration as an inclusive process: 'To partner with the public in each aspect of the decision process – including the development of alternatives and identification of a solution'. Whether this intention is matched with action on the part of both Council and citizens is not readily apparent and requires further investigation.

The procedural rhetorical style of the two websites conveys a sense that a top-down functioning of Council duties is ensuring that people are informed of their responsibilities as much as Council is responsible for providing its residents with information about its various duties and oversights.

While the websites clearly embrace the push model of getting information out to citizens, an intuitive design of the sites is essential for making this information easily accessible. The Moreton Bay Council site provides detailed access tabs for information about services, governance, news and so forth, but its multiple layering could result in frustration by users who are unable to find quickly what they are searching for. Furthermore, its generic style means that finding information about North Lakes – Mango Hill is not easy, and one needs to search alternative pathways. By contrast, The City of Wyndham website offers a much less busy homepage and icons, and clear headings provide direct access to the key service areas.

These local government websites with their attention to place and the surroundings spaces for living, working and relaxing reflect the ontological flow of the extraurbia as 'spaces of being' (Cope & Kalantzis, 2015, p. 221). However, their visual and verbal rhetorical style is similar to the websites of the capital cities in Australia, which are designed to inform, entice and 'sell' the city as a comfortable and good place to live, work and play. In this sense, it is difficult to accept Cope and Kalantzis's view that the 'newly extraurban' is distinguishable from the 'anachronistically urban' (2015, p. 227), at least with respect to the approach employed by

Australian e-government websites. While these authors argue that the ontological, convivial and representational flows that have produced the dynamics of connection and disconnection between the urban and extra-urban are largely conceived in relation to the United States and the global economic crisis that began in 2008, my interest here is the influence of these flows in shaping the rhetorical practices in local government websites for the two sample extraurban areas in Australia.

FLOWS AND RHETORICAL PRACTICES OF THE WEBSITES

The following brief discussion attends to three areas on the two local government website examples – market-driven interests, environmental sustainability and social inclusion – and considers how the rhetoric of each website contributes to an appreciation of the ontological, representational and convivial flows that are impacting these communities and their Councils' gateways to participation.

Market-driven interests combined with a desire for a lifestyle change have seen the consumption of extraurban spaces such as rural areas, coastal fringes and greenfields for 'residential, tourism, recreational and investment opportunities' (Tonts, Argent, & Plummer, 2012, p. 295). These changes are part of the ontological flows that not only shape the way people live, work, enjoy or visit the extraurban, but also change societal values regarding sustainability, land use, environmental protection, counterurbanization and 'amenity migration' (Amenity migration refers to the mobility of people to places and regions that are perceived to be more desirable than their current urban environment (Borsdorf, Hildalgo, & Zunino, 2012).) (Tonts et al., 2012). While the ABS population data are an indication of the amenity migration that sees people moving to greenfields such as North Lakes – Mango Hill, and Moreton Bay region generally, it is not clear if the main driver behind this move is the rhetoric that promotes these ecoscapes with its vision of a better lifestyle or whether it is more an economic choice. Perhaps both play a part in the decision.

The Moreton Bay Regional Council website gives clear evidence of how ontological flows are shaping its governance through the rhetorical appeal to its trustworthiness and commitment to the environment: 'maintaining and enhancing biodiversity through good urban planning, smart natural area management, and by providing knowledge and support services to residents managing habitat on privately owned property'.

However, in its promotion of North Lakes – Mango Hill, the Moreton Bay Council's rhetoric shifts from a formal, business style to a more informal, real-estate language which attempts to entice potential residents or visitors to the area by focusing on its shopping, recreational and environmental attractions with accompanying colourful photographs of (white Anglo-looking) families, wildlife, environmental areas and recreational activities. There are tabs for property sales (hot offers), a community directory and a blog of community events. This selling of the utopian promise of an environment – human communion aligns with what Cope and Kalantzis see as an extraurban understanding its ecoscape as 'a place where people's *environmental sensitivities* are shaped by being closer to nature' (2015, p. 236, my emphasis).

Moreton Bay Regional Council's website attempts to put the 'closer to nature' rhetoric into action by actively encouraging participation in a range of programs to protect native vegetation and habitats for wildlife (such as Land for Wildlife; Backyards for Wildlife and Bushcare). There are incentives and benefits to join these programs (e.g., free trees, nest box, access to small grants and free management advice). The language of these programs appeals to the 'environmental sensitivities' of private landowners and community groups by inviting them to care about the region's natural environment and to inspire others to become involved: 'You can play a role in protecting and improving your local bushland, wetlands and waterways by participating in fun and interesting activities that aim to conserve and protect the local environment'. These programs with their strong appeals for people to work for the environmental betterment of the region may promote engagement in the kind of 'innovative, green practices' that Cope and Kalantzis (2015, p. 237) propose for the future of extraurbia.

The Wyndham City Council website attempts a balance between the kind of procedural rhetoric suited to information searching regarding the necessities of living and the more persuasive rhetoric to encourage active citizenship. The ontological flows with respect to property are mainly restricted to payment of rates, and there is little enticement about real estate or the so-called 'hot offers' promoted on the Moreton Bay Regional Council website. However, the flow that defines its socioscape is encapsulated in the website's rhetorical appeal to social inclusion and support of migration.

The rhetoric of diversity in the Wyndham City website acknowledges that '34% of Wyndham's residents are from overseas, over 100 different languages are spoken in our community and we have the largest

Aboriginal and Torres Strait Islander population in the west (i.e., Western NSW)'. These statistics are complemented with a practical heuristic of community support links to a wide range of services and groups (e.g., Multicultural Support Groups & Services; Wyndham Indian Cultural Precinct and Senior Citizen Multicultural Group).

Cope and Kalantzis believe that while evidence of social integration among different groups in extraurbia is varied and dependent on many factors, there are signs that 'a social transition is taking place' (2015, p. 235). This would seem to hold some truth for Wyndham. However, readers of the website need to navigate from 'Services' in the side menu to 'Community Support' in order to find these services. Once the desired support is found, there are contact details for support services, links to other websites, forms to complete and local contacts for workshops and training sessions for start up programs for local businesses (as part of the Council's Economic Development Plan).

There is specific support for the local Indigenous population (The Wyndham Aboriginal Community Centre Committee). There is also acknowledgement of the traditional custodians of the land – the Kulin Nation. For the census period 2006–11 Wyndham's Aboriginal and Torres Strait Islander population increased by 61.7% (437 people) which was a higher rate of increase than non-Aboriginal people (44.3%). For the same period, 1654 people settled in Wyndham on a humanitarian visa (mainly from Burma and Thailand) (Wyndham, 2016b). All residents are invited to take part in the national 'Racism. It Stops with Me' campaign and the website offers ways individuals can play a part in stopping racism in Wyndham. Wyndham appears to be a space where its convivial flows of communities and identities are being recognized and supported through its rhetorical statements and actions of inclusion. It is beyond this discussion to ascertain how this translates into increased social interaction and conviviality within Wyndham's diverse community.

CONCLUDING COMMENTS

This exploratory investigation has shown that there are clear attempts on behalf of two local governments to encourage digital participation at different levels. While the main function of a local government website is to provide information about services and life in the community, there are also indicators of encouraging a more active, inclusive citizenship through avenues for responding to proposed changes, seeking input to plans, or taking a stand on human rights issues. These instances, however, are not extensive or uniform and a wider investigation beyond the two examples is needed to build a more comprehensive picture.

At a macrolevel, it is clear that the flows of ontology, conviviality and representation that Cope and Kalantzis propose are implicit in the structure and functions of the websites. At the microlevel, the government portal functions that Sandoval-Almazan and Gil-Garcia have developed provide a useful guide that can apply to the Australian context. However, the usefulness of this guide for future reference will depend on how local governments respond to ongoing social, economic, political and technological changes which may impact on the nature of the extraurban and how individuals and communities wish to participate.

While we can be swept up in the rhetoric of digital participation, we also need to be mindful of factors that limit its desired democratic potential. These factors come from the same personal, social, economic, technological and political processes that enable digital and nondigital participation to occur. Rather than argue that digital participation is a good thing, we might want to ask ourselves: Participation for what purpose? Who benefits? If we embrace notions of community, digital citizenship and other collective and individual forms of action that influence ideas of belonging and association then these questions are not simply rhetorical but prompt us to think about 'new forms of relationality', and the responsibilities these bring.

REFERENCES

Appadurai, A. (1996). *Modernity at large: Cultural dimensions of globalization*. Minneapolis: University of Minnesota Press.

Australian Bureau of Statistics (ABS). (2011). *North Lakes –Mango Hill (SA2)*. Retrieved from <http://stat.abs.gov.au/itt/r.jsp?RegionSummary®ion=314021390&dataset=ABS_REGIONAL_ASGS&geoconcept=REGION&datasetASGS=ABS_REGIONAL_ASGS&datasetLGA=ABS_REGIONAL_LGA®ionLGA=REGION®ionASGS=REGION>.

Australian Bureau of Statistics (ABS). (2012). *Melbourne revealed as 2011 Census data is released*. Retrieved from <http://www.abs.gov.au/websitedbs/censushome.nsf/home/vic-44?opendocument&navpos=620>.

Ban, H., & Ahlqvist, O. (2009). Representing and negotiating uncertain geospatial concepts – Where are the exurban areas? *Computers, Environment and Urban Systems, 33*, 233–246.

Borsdorf, A., Hildalgo, R., & Zunino, H. (2012). Amenity migration: a comparative study of the Italian Alps and the Chilean Andes. *The Journal of Sustainability Education, 3*, March (np).

Choi, M. (2016). A concept analysis of digital citizenship for democratic citizenship education in the internet age. *Theory & Research in Social Education*, *44*(4), 565–607.

Cope, B., & Kalantzis, M. (2015). ExtraUrbia, or, the Reconfiguration of spaces and flows in a time of spatial-financial crisis. In D. Araya (Ed.), *Smart cities as democratic ecologies* (pp. 219–246). New York: Palgrave Macmillan.

Ferilli, G., Sacco, P. L., & Blessi, G. T. (2016). Beyond the rhetoric of participation: New challenges and prospects for inclusive urban regeneration. *City, Culture and Society*, *7*, 95–100.

Foth, M., Hudson-Smith, A., & Gifford, D. (2016). Smart cities, social capital, and citizens at play: A critique and a way forward. In F. X. Olleros, & M. Zhegu (Eds.), *Research handbook on digital transformations* (pp. 203–221). Cheltenham: Edward Elgar.

MacGregor-Fors, I. (2011). Misconceptions or misunderstandings? On the standardization of basic terms and definitions in urban ecology. *Landscape and Urban Planning*, *100*, 347–349.

Mandarano, L., Meenar, M., & Steins, C. (2010). Building social capital in the digital age of civic engagement. *Journal of Planning Literature*, *25*(2), 123–135.

Moreton Bay Regional Council. (2016). Retrieved from 2016 <https://www.moreton-bay.qld.gov.au/>.

Parker, D. W., Downie, G. W., & Manville, G. (2012). Development of a community e-portal constellation: Queensland smart region initiative. *Electronic Journal of e-Government*, *10*(1), 1–15.

Regional Development Australia (RDA). (2016). Retrieved from <https://rda.gov.au>.

Sandoval-Almazan, R., & Gil-Garcia, J. R. (2012). Are government internet portals evolving towards more interaction, participation, and collaboration? Revisiting the rhetoric of e-government among municipalities. *Government Information Quarterly*, *29*, 572–581.

Tonts, M., Argent, N., & Plummer, P. (2012). Evolutionary perspectives on rural Australia. *Geographical Research*, *50*(3), 291–303.

Wyndham City. (2016a). *A snapshot of Wyndham*. Retrieved from <https://www.wyndham.vic.gov.au/sites/default/files/2016-10/Wyndham%20Snapshot-September%202016.pdf>.

Wyndham City. (2016b) *Aboriginal and Torres Strait Islander profile – Key statistics*. Retrieved from <http://profile.id.com.au/wyndham/indigenous-keystatistics>.

FURTHER READING

Australian Bureau of Statistics (ABS) (2016a). *3218.0-Regional population growth, Australia, 2014–15. Melbourne our fastest-growing capital*. Australia: Regional Population Growth. 2014–2015. Retrieved from <http://www.abs.gov.au/ausstats/abs@.nsf/lookup/3218.0Media%20Release12014-15>.

Australian Bureau of Statistics (ABS). (2016b). *3218.0-Regional population growth, Australia, 2014–15. Queensland. State summary*. Retrieved from <http://www.abs.gov.au/ausstats/abs@.nsf/Latestproducts/3218.0Main%20Features302014-15>.

North Lakes & Mango Hill. (2016). Retrieved from <http://www.visitmoretonbayregion.com.au/precinct/north-lakes-mango-hill/>.

INDEX

Note: Page numbers followed by "*f*" and "*t*" refer to figures and tables, respectively.

C

K

L

M

N

O

P

R

S

Printed and bound by CPI Group (UK) Ltd, Croydon, CR0 4YY

08/06/2025

01896869-0006